H. D. F. Kitto was born in 1897, educated at St. Johns College, Cambridge, and taught at the University of Glasgow from 1912 to 1944. Since 1944 he has been professor of Greek at the University of Bristol. Professor Kitto has written *In the Mountains of Greece* (1933) and the Pelican volume, *The Greeks* (1951).

Greek Tragedy was first published in 1939, and a second, revised edition appeared in 1950. For this Anchor edition, Professor Kitto has translated a large number of passages left in the original Greek in the second edition, added a short glossary of the less familiar terms, and made some small changes in the text to help the reader who knows no Greek follow the argument.

GREEK TRAGEDY: A Literary Study

By H. D. F. KITTO

Professor of Greek in the University of Bristol

Doubleday Anchor Books

Doubleday & Company, Inc.

GARDEN CITY, NEW YORK

Reprinted by arrangement with
Barnes & Noble, Inc.
Designed by Joseph P. Ascherl

Printed in the United States

PREFACE

A book on Greek Tragedy may be a work of historical scholarship or of literary criticism ; this book professes to be a work of criticism. Criticism is of two kinds : the critic may tell the reader what he so beautifully thinks about it all, or he may try to explain the form in which the literature is written. This book attempts the latter task. It is neither a history nor a handbook ; it has, I think, a continuous argument, and anything, however important, that does not bear on that argument is left out.

Longinus says, in his fine way, ' literary criticism is the last fruit of long experience.' My criticism is the fruit, if it is fruit, of an experience different from that which Longinus had in mind, the experience of putting awkward questions to a class and having to find answers to them—why did Aeschylus characterize differently from Sophocles ? why did Sophocles introduce the Third Actor ? why did Euripides not make better plots ? This book is nothing but the answers to a series of such questions ; the answers may be wrong, but the questions are right.

I make one basic assumption of which nothing that I have read in or about Greek Tragedy has caused me to doubt the soundness. It is that the Greek dramatist was first and last an artist, and must be criticized as such. Many Greeks, like many moderns, thought he was a moral teacher. No doubt he was, incidentally. Many English schoolmasters assert that cricket inculcates all sorts of moral virtues. No doubt it does, incidentally ; but the writer on cricket does well to leave this aspect of his subject to the historian of the British Empire.

Not that any dramatist, especially the Greek, who was so consciously a citizen, can be indifferent to morality. His material, the thoughts and actions of men, is essentially moral and intellectual, more obviously moral than the musician's, more obviously intellectual than the painter's, and he must be honest with his material. But the material will not explain the form of the work. There is something deeper that does this, something apprehensive, not dogmatic, something as intuitive as that, whatever it is, which moves a composer or painter to activity. Aeschylus, Sophocles and Euripides each have a different fashion of tragic thought; this it is that explains the drama.

When therefore we say that the Greek dramatist was an artist, we are not using a tired platitude meaning that he preferred pretty verses and plots to ill-made ones; we mean that he felt, thought, and worked like a painter or a musician, not like a philosopher or a teacher. Being a dramatist he must deal with moral and intellectual questions, and what he says about them is a natural subject of study; but if we are to treat the plays as plays and not as documents we must, as in criticizing painting, free ourselves from 'the tyranny of the subject'. If we can grope our way to the fundamental tragic conception of each play or group of plays, we can hope to explain their form and style. If not, we expose ourselves to the temptation of thinking that changes of form and style were sought for their own sake (which may be true of us but is not true of the Greeks), or to the temptation of treating form and content separately, or of falling back on that unreal figment 'the form of Greek Tragedy', something which evolves historically and takes the individual plays with it. For us, there is no such thing as 'the form of Greek Tragedy'. The historian, looking at Greek Tragedy from the outside, can use this conception, but our business is with individual plays, each a work of art and therefore unique, each obeying only the laws of its own being. There were limits fixed by the conditions of performance (practically the same for Euripides as for Aeschylus); within these wide limits the form of a play is determined only by its own vital idea—that is, if it is a living work of art, a *zoon*, and not an animal 'after Landseer'.

We shall therefore always begin by trying to understand the nature of the dramatic conception that underlies a play or group of plays. We shall ask what it is that the dramatist is striving to say, not what in fact he does say about this or that. The 'meaning' contained in many a dramatic speech or chorus may be as direct as the 'meaning' of a passage in

Aristotle's *Ethics*, but that 'meaning' which alone will explain the form of the play is something more akin to the 'meaning' of a Rembrandt or of a Beethoven sonata. It is of course much more intellectual, for the dramatist's apprehensions go at once into imagery closer to our intellectual life than the imagery of the painter or composer. The difference of medium, and consequently of method, is so great that direct comparison between drama and these other arts is rarely of much use except to the one who makes it. Nevertheless, we must remember where we are, and hold fast to the difference between the 'meaning' of a philosopher and the 'meaning' of an artist.

Can we go further? Can we explain, by reference to the communal life of which the poets were a part, how it came about that they 'meant' these particular things? We can certainly guess, and some of our guesses will no doubt be right; perhaps we can do more, but I have not regarded this as any business of mine, as our present concern is criticism and not biography. Criticism, it seems to me, can without discredit begin with what is in the poet's head, without inquiring how it got there.

The literary importance of Greek Tragedy has not yet been forgotten by Professors of English, who sometimes expect their pupils to have some acquaintance with it. It is because I hope that this survey may be of interest to students of literature who have no Greek that I have given translations where possible. But we Hellenists have our feelings, like other men, and I have left in Greek two recurring words : *hamartia* is the tragic flaw of Aristotle's theory, and *hybris* is hybris.

My obligations are many and difficult to count ; I hope I have been honest in acknowledging debts. I realize uncomfortably that often I quote others only to disagree with them. I am grateful to the Editor of *The Times*, who very willingly gave me permission to use copyright material valuable to me. My warmest thanks are due to my colleague Mr. A. W. Gomme, for reading my scripts and making many salutary remarks about them. For the same friendly and critical services, most generously given, I owe a debt which now I cannot pay to my late colleague W. E. Muir, whose early death has taken away a good scholar, a firm and sensitive judge of literature, and a good friend.

H. D. F. K.

THE UNIVERSITY
   GLASGOW
     March 1939

NOTE TO THE SECOND EDITION

Naturally, I should have liked to rewrite this book. Naturally, that was impossible. I have removed what was the worst mistake, the treatment of Sophocles' *Electra,* and have tried to mend other shortcomings. I hope that these changes have left no inconsistencies behind them.

I am grateful to reviewers and others who have said kind or useful things about this book; particularly to Professor Warmington, who sent me a list of misprints, false accents, and other errors.

H. D. F. K.

THE UNIVERSITY
   BRISTOL

CONTENTS

CHAPTER I

LYRICAL TRAGEDY

1. THE SUPPLICES   The great interest that the *Supplices* has for us lies not in its primitiveness but in its maturity.   It is important, and interesting, that in it we can see the new drama coming to birth, that in the halting speech and fumbling actions of Danaus we may see the origins of Oedipus the King and Macbeth, but it is more interesting that in the dealings between the Chorus and Pelasgus we have before our eyes the splendid and assured triumph of the Tragedy of Thespis, the drama of a chorus and a single actor.   We, looking back into this distance, with the *Oresteia* and Sophocles in our minds, see a drama strange to us.   There are two actors, but Aeschylus scarcely knows what to do with one of them, and the protagonist is the Chorus.   There is a certain confusion, as there must have been on that historic day at Rugby when a schoolboy picked up the ball and began to run with it. We, inevitably, are struck by the confusion, and are apt to watch the innovator running rather than the firm and beautiful outlines of the game as it was being played.

'The excitement of it [said the Dramatic Critic of *The Times* in commenting on the Delphi performance of the *Supplices* in 1930] was not in witnessing, in a few fragments, the birth of a drama to come, but in striving to recognize in its substance the form and the spirit of the ancient tradition from which it sprang. . . .   In performance at Delphi the *Supplices* is neither primitive nor obscure.   When the Chorus is felt as a living presence with collective individuality and character, the play appears not as a primitive struggling towards a new drama, but as a fully developed product of an older tradition.   In departures from this tradition Aeschylus was certainly experimenting, but the impression given by the performance is that the experiments were being made as much in reluctance as in eagerness.'

It was perhaps not exactly in reluctance that the experiment was made, although it is true that Danaus is a dull figure, that some of the dialogue is undramatic, and that the scene with the Herald, though sharply and boldly handled, is not the dramatic climax of the play. The significance of any play, if it is properly made, should lie where the dramatic effect is greatest ; and here that is certainly the 'ritualistic' part, not the new, experimental scenes. It has been said of Danaus that the new tool, the Second Actor, has been invented, but Aeschylus hardly knows yet what to do with it.[1] The real explanation of Danaus' dramatic poverty lies elsewhere ; Aeschylus was not likely to demand this new tool before he knew what he wanted it for. We however may congratulate ourselves that Danaus is so superfluous, because we can so easily think him off the stage and see in the *Supplices* an example of a drama otherwise lost to us.

It is natural, but wrong, to approach any drama with a pre-conceived idea of what it ought to do, and how ; but with a play as remote as the *Supplices*, criticism of this kind may go very far astray. The critic tries to read into the play what he expects to find, and if he cannot he is disappointed. Thus Tucker finds that the *Supplices* 'fails in dramatic effect'. 'There is no thrilling action in the piece, and, despite its admirable poetry, it would have fallen flat' but for the spec-tacular effect of the chorus.[2] Missing such effects as the evocation of Darius or the trial scene in the *Eumenides*, and assuming that Greek drama must do something like this or be 'undramatic', the critic fails to see what a magnificent dramatic thrill the *Supplices* does contain, and that it is one of passion, not action.

Or, knowing that the play presents the first part of a long story, we unconsciously assume that it must be about the Danaids, and find it in consequence rather undramatic and ill-constructed. 'Such plot as there is consists of their efforts to secure protection and the arrival of a herald from Egypt an-nouncing the presence of the rejected suitors'[3] —a summary which leaves out that on which the dramatic emotion is built.

[1] J. T. Sheppard. *Camb. Anc. Hist.*, IV, 117.

[2] *Supplices*, Introd., p. xvi.

[3] Bowra, *Ancient Greek Literature*, p. 81.

Or, starting with the doctrine that Aeschylus was a religious teacher and the educator of his people (*Erzieher seines Volkes*), we may say, with Pohlenz, that the play concerns the protectors more than the protected (which is true), and holds up to the Athenian democracy the inspiring picture of a whole people, the Argives, taking upon itself the greatest dangers because it puts religious duty before everything. But this means that it is an ill-designed play, for Aeschylus lays the emphasis on the wrong things, on the King much more than on the people, and on the dangers which Argos will incur if it rejects the Suppliants more than on the dangers which it undergoes out of religious duty.

Although Aeschylus was a young man when he wrote the *Supplices*, he was already Aeschylus, and we may suppose that he built the play as he felt it. Technical difficulties we may allow him, but we will not readily suppose that he got his proportions and his emphasis all wrong. We must find out where the dramatic emphasis is laid, remembering what we have lost. The essential drama of a Greek play, and of this very lyrical one more than most, lies not in the text only but also in the music, the dance, and the resources of the 'producer'. Purely intellectual analysis of what is said may miss the point, or some of it ; on the other hand, though we can guess at the 'producer's' effects, we are deprived of that part of the drama which lay in the music and dance, except to the small extent to which metre can help us. Nevertheless we must try to make allowance for this in looking for the drama, and must be sure that we have made allowance before we call a play undramatic. With the *Supplices* we may be quite sure that those who find it undramatic cannot, except by chance, tell us what it is about, for they have not seen the drama.

There is no prologue. The chorus enters with an extremely dramatic invocation of Zeus. The marching-song is businesslike, and gives us the chief facts easily—Zeus, Danaus, the flight from Egypt to Io's city of Argos, the *hybris* of the suitors. Why the Suppliants object to them we are not told yet ; Right forbids, and there is Impiety. We are given a clear idea of the character of these young women—full of energy, passionate in resisting wrong, firm of faith in Providence.   There is no sign of primitive stiffness here ; Aeschylus knew all there was to know about writing dramatic anapaests.

The entrance-song is followed by a long ode.   There is no suggestion of immediate action, debate, or intrigue.   The orchestra, as it were, strikes up, a slow and steady rhythm is started, and the chorus proceeds to dance and sing some 140 verses.   The *Antigone*, with music, takes about two hours and a quarter in performance ; the *Supplices* is a short play.   If we allow it an hour and a half, then this ode, one-sixth of the whole, would take ten or fifteen minutes, or the time of an ordinary symphony-movement.   This shows what wind is blowing in the theatre ; the audience clearly is in no hurry to see the actors.

The composition of the ode is striking.   It opens, with Zeus and Epaphus, in the stately ' Dorian ' rhythm.   With the more personal tone of the second pair of stanzas the rhythm changes to the quicker and more irregular choriambic, but still closes quietly with a smooth trochaic (or iambic) verse. The third pair is beautifully proportioned, opening with a slow hexameter, working up to choriambic, and once more closing quietly in trochaics—a rise and fall which admirably suits the sense of the stanzas.   In the fourth pair of stanzas we return to Zeus and a steadier rhythm, which leads most effectively to the unmistakable outburst of the fifth strophe, in which the climbing, impulsive rhythm [1] marks the climax of this part of the ode.   The next strophe introduces something quite new, tribrachs and harsh, clumsy spondees in harmony with the passionate lamentation and the foreign-sounding invocations in the stanzas and their refrain.   Strophe 8 begins with easily-moving iambics which reflect the sense of the words, and, with the same matching of rhythm and sense, it closes in heavier iambics.   Finally, there is no mistaking the solemn effect of the unbroken trochees of the last stanza, an effect which is effectively modified by the hint of barbarism in the refrain.

It is clear that the young Aeschylus had little to learn in the

---

[1] $\cup - \cup - (\cup) - (\cup) - \cup -$
       $\cup - \cup - (\cup) - \cup - (\cup) -$

technique of choral composition. This element in drama is already fully grown. It is clear also—for we must assume that this mating of rhythm to sense means that the music and the dance were similarly mated to it—that such an ode is in the highest sense dramatic. In this flood of poetry, music and dance, tremendous as even now we can faintly discern, but so supple, so perfectly under control that it can mirror the subtlest change of mood and about-face with the swiftness of a trained charger—in this lay the perfect medium for the presentation not of the thoughts of an individual but of the emotions of a group ; and the audience, during such an ode, would no more feel that the action was being delayed than we, during a swirling chorus in the Bach *Mass*, are impatient for the succeeding tenor aria.

In view of what happened to the tragic Chorus before the century was out, it is not superfluous to notice how closely the poet sticks to his dramatic theme. We are always told that Aeschylus is a great religious poet : what impresses us most in this ode is that he is a great dramatic lyrist, never making philosophical or mythological diversions. So dynamic a combination of rhythms as this is essentially of the dramatic poet. To the chorus, Zeus is to be their protector, Io is their claim on Argos. They think, naturally, of Philomela, but they do not stop to narrate her story. Then comes the appeal to the Justice of the Gods, followed by those two splendid stanzas in which, for their own assurance, they sing of the power of Zeus. Here we reach an almost Hebraic intensity of religious feeling, but it is the intensity of the poet and not of the philosopher, for it is directly inspired by and seen through the dramatic situation. The chorus speaks as it does not because it is the mouthpiece of the poet, but because suffering and danger have raised them to a plane on which it is natural that they should so speak. After this, the abrupt change described above. Greeks by descent, they are Egyptian by upbringing ; they have begun in Dorian and have spoken of Zeus in true Greek strain ; they end with the rhythms of despair, with wild, uncouth language, and with threats of hanging themselves at the altars of the Gods—threats which they are presently to apply to the King.

After all this, the first actor in European drama speaks, and it must be admitted that he is a disappointment. Danaus has little to say, and he does not say that very well. His opening lines, harping on prudence, dressed up with a frigid antithesis between his marine and his continental behaviour, may give us a moment in which to recover from the terrific ode ; but Danaus continues to be dull. We shall see that the reason for this is not incapacity on the part of Aeschylus, but an adventitious difficulty. In the second and third plays of the Trilogy Danaus is an important figure, and he cannot escape appearing in the first—but here there is simply nothing for him to do. His, in fact, is the part which was later entrusted to the leader of the chorus ; he makes the transitions between ode and episode, but dramatically he is an embarrassment.

The King enters, and at v. 250 is invited to tell us who he is. This, as Croiset points out, is dramatically necessary ; but is it necessary that he should explain at such length to these strangers exactly how large his realm is ? Yes, it is. The point is not, as some critics have supposed, that Aeschylus, for reasons of current politics, wished to be polite to Argos. Presently there is to be the question of war with Egypt, and we need to be assured that protective Argos is strong enough to protect. But when Pelasgus (it is convenient to use the name, though Aeschylus does not) goes on to explain why his country is called Apia, we can but think that Aeschylus' interest in current speculation has got the better of him. He was, as we remember from the *Prometheus*, always interested in geography and anthropology, but we may perhaps be excused if we think that the King might have ended more happily than by saying ' Be brief, for this city loves not long speeches '.

On the stichomythia that follows, H. W. Smyth remarks,[1] ' As two Homeric warriors, before they engage, introduce themselves by proclaiming each his lineage, so with Pelasgus and the Danaids. Together they indulge in a veritable genealogical orgy . . . all told in long-winded, undramatic dialogue.' This is to misunderstand the passage. What we have here is the proof of their Argive descent which the

[1] *The Drama of Aeschylus*, p. 40.

Danaids offer to Pelasgus ; their half of the story exactly fits his. It does not take much acuteness to see that the 'proof' is remarkably thin ; the chorus proves only that it knows the story. But in a play pitched on this lyrical plane it would be a blunder to demand rigid proof. What we need here is a symbolic one ; it is indeed almost enough that the forms of proof are duly gone through, for we have not yet reached that degree of naturalism which demands logical cogency, still less the degree of realism which leads the dramatist to try to beat the rhetorician at his own game. 'Dramatic' dialogue as in a Euripidean recognition-scene would be ridiculous in this play, even though it were couched in the finest Aeschylean. The important point for the critic to remember here is that we are not primarily interested in the 'proof' ; this is a minor issue. The major one, which absorbs all our attention, is whether the King will extend his protection to the Suppliants.

Though the first part of this act is rudimentary, what remains makes ample amends. From v. 324 to the end of the scene we have a presentation of a tragic situation which will hold its own with any. The power and the certainty of it are astonishing ; twenty-four verses are enough to explain the coming of the chorus and to show the King that a chasm is opening under his feet. 'I see and shudder', he cries. He is in a cleft stick ; either he must undertake a dangerous and unwanted war, or he must risk the displeasure of the Gods. This having been made perfectly clear to the unhappy King, the Danaids take advantage of their lyrical position to push home their appeal by a liberal use of dochmiacs, to whose passionate strength the King can oppose only the weaker instrument of the ordinary iambic line.

In the whole of this scene, with Danaus not indeed off the stage, but quite insignificant in the background, we can see the effect that late sixth-century tragedy might have produced in the hands of a master.[1] All is formal, as formal and as vivid as a Miltonic sonnet. The doubts, fears, considerations of prudence which pass through the King's mind are distilled into five-verse stanzas, and between the form of these and that of the chorus' utterances there is just the difference that

---

[1] See further below, pp. 31 f.

there is between intellectual reserve and emotional appeal.
The character, the speech, and the arguments of Pelasgus are
all formalized to the same degree, necessarily. There is no
pretence that we are following, with a Sophoclean subtlety,
the successive thoughts or emotions which pass across his
mind. Everything is formal, but passionate and tragic ; the
more powerful that the expression is subjected to so strict a
discipline. 'Let no quarrel, unexpected and unforeseen,
come upon the city. The city has no need of these.'—'Assist
you I cannot, without hurt ; yet it is hard too to reject these
prayers' (357 f., 377 f.). Translated, the words are plain ;
but no one familiar with the early Greek manner will miss the
significance either of the formal style or the formal scene.
Our standard must be Simonides' Epitaph, not a speech from
Oedipus.

This may put into its proper light the short speech 406–17.
To call it stiff and undramatic is easy and wrong. In it the
poet is still working in his unnaturalistic manner ; it is not that
he has not yet emancipated himself from his lyrical origins,
but that he may not do this while his tragedy remains so
abstract and his chorus so prominent in it. We must not at
one moment praise the odes for being Pindaric and at the next
censure the dialogue because it is not Sophoclean. This
speech, formally set forth, its last verse echoing its first, is a
formal close to a formal scene, a coda in which all the tragic
themes which have been brought to bear on the King are
briefly restated.

While the King stands still, contemplating the terrible alternatives, the chorus dances before him singing an ode in the
heavily-swinging Cretic rhythm. Mazon marks it 'grave et
religieux' ; it is this, but it has too something of a hypnotic
force. It presents to us the appeal of the Suppliants carried
almost beyond the reach of language ; it becomes visible, a
supernatural actor.

We are told that Pelasgus is no character, only an abstraction. That is not quite true. He is a man of intellect and
strength, for he can maintain his powers of judgment under
this assault, and that is no mean achievement. He emerges

clear-eyed : ' There is no issue free from disaster.' [1]   With no rhetoric, but with a most eloquent restraint, he leads up to his anguishing point ' But that our kinsmen's blood be not shed . . .'; the overmastering thought to which he recurs presently, ' That in a woman's quarrel men's blood should stain the ground.' [2]

It has been said that Aeschylus is a master of situation, but not of plot.[3]   His plots lack fluidity, they are apt to flounder a little from one situation to the next.   This may be true of the *Supplices*, but it is certainly true that once the situation is reached none can deal with it more surely.   If the Athenians, in the decade before Marathon, had any other dramatist who could devise a scene of pure tragedy and exploit it as the young Aeschylus does here, they were indeed a fortunate people.   The simplicity of it is worth attention.

We left the King contemplating the situation.   His un-invited guests have suddenly brought him to a pass in which he has to choose between a war whose horrors he does not gloze over and the unnamed terrors of offended Heaven. Half an hour ago he was the contented ruler of a peaceful state ; now he is in torture.   This, unless Aeschylus was not a builder but only a decorator, must be the centre of his tragic idea ; and this perhaps explains the slightly too bland tone of his opening speech—it was to prepare for the contrast.   And why has this come upon him ?   Because in Egypt certain men want to marry certain women, who have a real but hitherto unsuspected claim on Argos.   The King has tried reason.   He has argued that marriage between cousins is no bad thing—it keeps the money in the family ; a mere man's plea which is brushed aside.   He has asked, ' What about your native marriage-laws ?   What if they sanction this mar-riage ? '   This too is instantly dismissed ; the very idea of marriage is repulsive, and Justice is on their side.   Through no Aristotelean flaw of character, through no deficiency of sense, intellect or morality, has the King fallen suddenly into this awful dilemma.   A disharmony in the make-up of things,

[1] V. 442.
[2] Vv. 449, 477.
[3] But see below, p. 105.

and a perfectly innocent man is broken.   Here, in the earliest
of Greek tragedies, we find one of the most purely tragic
situations ; the Flaw in the Universe, which the philosophers
will have none of,[1] is plain enough to Aeschylus.

In this last speech the King is overwhelmed by the situation ; his mind is numb.   But the poet has not yet done with
him ; the Suppliants are equal to the crisis.   They have already applied the screw to the King ; they proceed to turn it
with a deliberation which seems almost devilish :

> ' We have one more word of supplication.
>
> I am listening.
>
> We have strings and cords for our robes.
>
> That is very proper in women.'

A commonplace verse ?—As commonplace as Duncan's ' This
castle hath a pleasant seat '—very pleasant, for Duncan.   So
here ; the chorus continues its tortuous path :

> ' New ornaments for the altars.
>
> You are giving me riddles.   Speak clearly.'

They do.   They explain that they will insult and defile the
Gods by hanging themselves at their very altars.

> ' It is a thing that scourges my heart.
>
> Now are your eyes open.'

So, we may say, are ours.   We remember the King's pathetic
attempt to bring the matter before the bar of reason ; perhaps
the marriage is no bad thing ; perhaps by Egyptian laws . . .
He little knew what manner of people he was dealing with.

Before this awful threat the King can hesitate no longer.
He is under no delusions.   The price is the blood of his subjects staining the ground, a price so high that he dare not pay
it without the full consent of those whose lives will be at
stake.   The people must decide.

It is surely false criticism to see here a naïve intrusion of
contemporary democracy, or some vague laudation of the
ways of Argos, or a desire to hold up to the audience an
example of how Leader and Led should work together.   In
such a scene Aeschylus has deeper motives than these.   We
are not to suppose that any and every Royal decision has to be
ratified by the Argive assembly ; that is to destroy the point,

[1] See W. Macneile Dixon, *Tragedy*, pp. 128 f.

and to introduce something for which our minds have at the moment no room. This decision is so serious and so unusual that the people, traditionally quick to blame (v. 485), would have every reason to disobey. Pelasgus is the Homeric King who knows how far he should go. The reference to the people is a means of emphasizing the seriousness of the dilemma.

The action has reached a pause and the stage is left empty. This is the moment for the chorus to amplify the story of Io. The narrative is a relief from the tense scene we have been through, and it impresses on us again the real claim the Suppliants have upon the protection of Argos. Moreover, as told here, the story becomes a splendid hymn to the power of Zeus, the god in whom they have put their trust. In every way it is dramatic, and its relevance is underlined when Danaus returns. He, in the shortest episode in Greek drama, tells us that with one voice the Argives have decided to support the cause of the Suppliants,[1] and ascribes this to the working of Zeus. The episode therefore is but the fulfilment of the ode.

With scarcely a pause the chorus proceeds to a prayer of gratitude for Argos, a prayer which, like nearly everything in the play, is cast in a severely formal mould. But formalism is not dullness. This is a long and splendid prayer, full of dignity, and in the Greek way very explicit. After a curiously dry little prelude it begins, ' Now is the time when we would have the Zeus-born Gods hearken to us as we pour forth our blessings over this race '. This serves for the traditional invocation ; but the chorus does not ' pour forth ' its blessings in a tumultuous flood. It blesses thoughtfully, in the accusative and infinitive construction like a law or proclamation, through four pairs of stanzas very similar in form, rounding off the whole with two majestic stanzas of a different rhythm.

The blessings called down are all concrete. Not for the Greek are vague conceptions like Plenty and Peace, Prosperity and Honour. It happens that Peace with Honor does appear

[1] The very brevity of this scene makes it difficult to suppose that Aeschylus was as interested in the Argive democracy as Pohlenz believes.

among other desirable things, but it appears in concrete form : ' May they offer to strangers before girding themselves to war, satisfaction by fair agreement.' Nothing Utopian ; they pray for what is possible. Prosperity too is concrete : ' May the ewes in their fields be fertile. May the land be rich in crops in each season.'

For the second and last time we may venture to look at the rhythms. The rhythmical figures fall into three clearly marked groups, each having its own emotional significance. Group A, which begins each of the first eight stanzas, alternating with group B, consists mainly of two figures, $- \cup \cup - \cup -$ and its kindred rhythm $\cup \cup \cup - \cup -$, with of course a few variations (final cadences and the like) which have the same significance. These, the 'Aeolian tripody'[1] and the dochmiac respectively, from their shortness and irregularity, are suited to the expression of lively emotion. Group B is composed mostly of $- \bar{\cup} - \cup \cup - -$, with a glyconic $- \bar{\cup} - \cup \cup - \cup -$: a much calmer type of movement. These alternating and contrasting rhythms obviously help the formality of the ode and give it musical and rhythmical variety, but they are also used to reinforce the sense. In the first strophe and antistrophe the prayer is set to the more emotional rhythm, while the other group is used to explain why the prayer is being made. In the second and third strophes the suffering which is deprecated is, on the whole, given to the *assez agité* rhythm and the opposite state of happiness to the other. When we reach the last two stanzas, which sum up the whole ode in a prayer for peace with men and peace with the Gods, we find a beautiful strophe written in a bigger and more swinging rhythm, admirably characterized by Mazon *large et décidé* :

$$\cup - (\cup) - (\cup) - \ \cup \ - \cup - (\cup) -$$
$$\cup - \ \cup \ - (\cup) - \ \cup \ - \cup - (\cup) -$$
$$\cup - \ \cup \ - (\cup) - \ \cup \ - \cup - (\cup) -$$
$$\cup - \ \cup \ - (\cup) - \cup -$$
$$\cup - \ \cup \ - (\cup) - \cup -$$
$$\cup - \ \cup \ - (\cup) - \ \cup \ - \cup - (\cup) -$$

It is a most subtle and beautifully constructed composition.

[1] Here the figure is certainly a dochmiac $> \acute{\cup} \cup - \cup -$. (See Aristeides Q. *apud* Westphal, *Metrik*, p. 59). The smooth ' tripody' makes no rhythmical sense here.

Up to this point the handling of the dramatic material has been firm and masterly ; what follows—the 'experimental' part—is less assured. When the hymn is ended Danaus announces that he can see the Egyptian fleet coming, and at the end of the episode he goes to Argos to raise the alarm ; but before going he first assures the Suppliants that they will be safe in their refuge, and then wastes time explaining that there is no hurry, as the mooring of ships, especially towards evening, is a slow business. Actually, Pelasgus arrives only in the nick of time ; but what is the reason for this undramatic behaviour of Danaus ? Not that Aeschylus wanted to talk of ships.[1] The episode preceding was only twenty-five verses long, and as it would hardly do to have another just as short Danaus talks to fill up time. Again, Pelasgus has not taken the elementary precaution of posting guards at the landing-place, so compelling Danaus to give the warning himself. Such unrealistic behaviour need disturb us less than it would in a more realistic play, but there is a good reason for it. Danaus has to be removed from the stage in order to come back as the Herald.[2] As the mere father of this chorus he practically immobilizes one of Aeschylus' two actors, so that Aeschylus is put to it to make his plot work. However, like a good dramatist he makes capital out of his misfortunes, for the fact that the Egyptians find the Suppliants undefended, except for the mere altars in which Danaus had put his trust, enables Aeschylus not only to contrive the perhaps rather obvious excitement of the attempted Rape, but also to give us a convincing demonstration of the brutality of these pursuers.

The last ode is short and rapid. Its purpose is to show that the resistance of the chorus remains unbroken. Their assertion that they would rather die than submit leaves nothing to argue about : it precludes hope of compromise, and it completes our picture of their character.

---

[1] Méautis, in his excellent *Eschyle et la Trilogie* (pp. 47–8), remarks that Aeschylus creates a characteristic background ('ambience') for each play. In the *Supplices* 'c'est tout l'infini de la mer'. But here the background undramatically becomes foreground.

[2] Croiset, *Eschyle*, pp. 63 f.

The first part of the Exodus is so badly mutilated that we can discern only the brutality of the Egyptians and the passionate resistance of the chorus. The scene between the King and the Herald is vigorous and the dialogue is terse and pointed. Once rid of Danaus, Aeschylus can use his two actors with some effect. The King is given one or two individualizing touches—his proud refusal to give his name, his readiness to throw the taunt of beer-drinking at his adversary ; but when the Herald goes, all the stuffing goes with him. What is the purpose of this tedious question of the lodgings of the chorus ? In any case, why cannot they decide the point for themselves, seeing that hitherto they have conducted their affairs with so much firmness ? There is inconsistent character-drawing here. These vivid young women are no conventional Athenian *jeunes filles bien élevées,* yet they must needs send for Danaus, and he arrives with a promptness almost supernatural in an old man. And when he comes he does nothing to help us. He announces, to be sure, that the citizens have been very kind, but this we could have taken for granted. He plunges into a speech full of moralizing, giving advice how to behave in a strange city, when we feel he might better have been receiving advice how to behave when you are a dramatic character. There is no mention of the lodgings ; the question is dropped entirely.

The whole difficulty is again that Danaus is wanted to lead the procession off the stage. There had to be the question of lodgings, or something like it, to give the actor time to change back again to Danaus ; but granting this, why so flat a way of doing it ? Mazon's comment is that the passage shows the new art of Tragedy continuing the tradition of the gnomic and lyric poets, with whom moral maxims were popular. True, but in lyric poetry there were more interesting traditions that Aeschylus might have summoned to his aid. If Danaus must be brought back, then the King's question about entertainment is the natural way of doing it ; and when Danaus is back, he speaks as he does less, I think, because of the gnomic tradition than out of Aeschylus' desire to justify him. After all, he is the father, and throughout the play he has been pushed into the background by his daughters. Here is his opportunity to justify his dramatic existence, and how he could do it except by talking like a father it is not easy to see. In these fumbling scenes we need not necessarily see signs of primitiveness, or even of inexperience on the part of the young dramatist. The source of the difficulty still seems to be the dramatic emptiness of Danaus, whose thunder is all stolen by the chorus. The chorus and the King are both actors and characters ; Danaus is only a nuisance in this part of the trilogy. With more experience Aeschylus might have dealt with him more boldly and successfully, but it is very characteristic of him to set himself dramatic problems to which there seems to be no answer. In the *Prometheus* he set himself an impossible task and accomplished it ; here the solution is not found. Danaus preaches not because Aeschylus wants to preach, but because when there is nothing to say preaching is inevitable.

The march-off has been delayed, but when it comes it is given an altogether unexpected significance. The chorus prays to the Gods of Argos and to the rivers of the land, paying especial honours to Artemis the Unwedded and none to Aphrodite, thus leading the way to the rest of the trilogy, as well as to the *Hippolytus*. The simple story of the protection of injured innocence is no dramatic material for such as Aeschylus, and his Suppliants are no pre-Raphaelite creation. Blind opposition to the just claims of Aphrodite is to be the ruin of the Danaids—in some degree ; and in order that they, and we, may not proceed without warning, Aeschylus liberates the tongues of the serving-maidens. The effect of choral strains suddenly coming from those whom we had taken only as stage ' supers ' must have been considerable— though not enough to have any effect on the Suppliants. They are implacable, and leave us with an uneasy feeling of ill to come.

It is possible that some of the weak or dull passages in the *Supplices* would acquire more significance if we knew the course of the whole trilogy, but we do not. Leaving for our next chapter further criticism of the play, let us here inquire how the story probably went and what it is about.

This is the first of the three plays. The assertion would not
be worth making if it had not been denied. In criticism there
is no position so untenable that some intrepid spirit will not be
found occupying it. Of the antecedent circumstances we are
told little. Legal arguments have been based, by Ridgeway
and others, on Pelasgus' well-meant but useless pleas to the
chorus (335 ff.). Croiset disposed of these. Wilamowitz [1]
thought of a battle in Egypt in which the cousins had won a
claim to the Danaids by conquest; this is the only possible
explanation why the Egyptians 'think of themselves as their
lords', and it is supported by the very general remark about
altars at v. 83—'Even to oppressed fugitives from war an
altar, seat of God's majesty, is a refuge from violence'—and
by v. 742, where Danaus is represented as knowing well how
insatiate the Egyptians are in war. This is very thin.
Everyone knew what altars were for, and why should Danaus
have to fight the Egyptians himself in order to observe what
they were like? If we have to prowl about in the outskirts of
the play like this to discover what lies 'outside the drama',
the inference is that Aeschylus never bothered his head about
it, and therefore, for us, it does not exist. Had there been a
battle, were it necessary that we should know this, he would
have told us plainly; there was room enough for so simple a
piece of information in one of the odes. The Egyptians may
have advanced some justification in a later play, but we may
notice that the Herald mentions none to Pelasgus. The
Egyptians are fierce and lustful; they wish to marry cousins
who object strongly and whose father objects too; the male
faction is the stronger and the other has to flee. The situation is plainly one which we can accept as an *arche*, a 'beginning', in Aristotle's sense, something which requires no
explanation.

It is equally natural, and right, to be impatient with juristic
arguments about the legal status of the Danaids in Argos.
Wilamowitz finds Danaus a legal inconvenience because he
becomes a *metoecus* after his daughters: 'Es ist verkehrte
Welt, wenn der Vater Annex seiner Töchter ist'; a topsy-
turvy world too when an Athenian poet cannot use the word

proxenos in a metaphor. It has been said that the Suppliants were *epicleri*, and the objection is made that this is impossible, as Danaus was still alive. But it is foolish to suppose that Aeschylus, in the throes of creating a thing like the *Supplices*, had a thought to spare for this kind of irrelevance ; that he could not, as a good citizen, have a reasonable interest in civic technicalities without being haunted by them as an artist ; that even a moderately sensitive and sensible audience could watch the King growing numb with spiritual pain and then wonder if the chorus were becoming *metoeci* or not. This kind of verisimilitude is proper to a ' crook ' play ; Aeschylus offers us something different.

It is more profitable to discuss the future of Danaus and his fifty daughters than their past, or their present legal position. The points of certainty are few. That the *Danaids* was the concluding play is beyond dispute. From it we have the fragment on the power of Aphrodite, and another fragment which appears to form part of an Epithalamium. It is a reasonable assumption that the forty-nine Danaids who took their husbands' lives were dealt with by Aeschylus much as they were by Pindar.[1] Beyond this we can hardly go. About the middle play we do not know so much. We do not even know what it was, for that it was the *Egyptians* is only a probability—having the Danaids as the chorus of the first and third plays, the poet might well look for a contrast in the second, and if the Egyptians appeared at all, not merely through their Herald, it could only be as chorus. From the *Egyptians* only one word is preserved, *Zagreus*, and this is not illuminating. It is a great pity, for it would be interesting to know what sort of thing Aeschylus had in mind. Somehow the Danaids consented to the marriage, but on the secret understanding that they should all murder their husbands that night. Their devotion to Artemis remains intact, but the impiety to Aphrodite remains to be expiated. This may have been done in the foot-race, over which Aphrodite herself apparently presided. But the important questions we should

---

[1] Pyth. IX, 111 ff. They were placed at the end of the course and raced for by suitors. Each suitor upon reaching the goal took his choice.

like to be able to answer are how the compromise was ef-
fected, and what was the meaning of the whole trilogy.
Quot lacunae, tot sententiae.

Hermann [1] maintained that Pelasgus was slain in battle.
This allows Danaus to succeed him, gives Danaus an important role in the later parts of the trilogy to balance his un-
importance in the *Supplices*, and accounts for the name Danai
for the Argives.   Ancient authorities knew of two variants.
Apollodorus makes the King cede the throne voluntarily to
Danaus ; Pausanias records that the change was made by a
decision of the people.   If Aeschylus used either of these, the
former, though improbable, is the more likely.   To be sure
the King said that ' the people is quick to blame ', but his own
behaviour was so irreproachable that one does not readily
foresee deposition.   Croiset believes in the substitution of
Danaus for Pelasgus in order that Danaus may be in a position
to treat with the Egyptians, now become the enemies of
Argos ; but if this is all, we can surely do without the substitution.   If Danaus told Pelasgus that he was now satisfied,
Pelasgus could in honour make terms with the Egyptians.
Croiset further supposes that King Danaus, perplexed in the
presence of superior enemies, and possibly urged by the Argives to make terms, did so with his stratagem in mind.   But
in the *Supplices* Aeschylus has gone out of his way to describe
the great extent and power of Argos ; is that so soon to be
overthrown ?   To say nothing of the welcome extended and
the sacrifice accepted by the Argives ?

Wilamowitz' view is that there was no war but a compromise.   He says,[2] and surely rightly, that Ovid (*Heroides,
Hypermnestra* 23) is remarkably poor evidence for Aeschylus
(' ich hätte eine so schwere Gelehrsamkeit dem Ovid auch
nimmermehr zugetraut '), and argues that certainly Aegyptus
himself did not come, or he would have been mentioned in
v. 928, and that if there is a war, a Chorus of Egyptians is
difficult to imagine.   Why so ?   If we assume that the second
Chorus was one of Egyptians, and that they are already victorious (for we need not suppose that Aeschylus condemned

[1] *De Aeschyli Danaidibus* (Opusc. II, 319 ff.).

[2] *Interpretationen*, p. 20.

himself to represent on the stage every important detail of the story), then the arranging of a compact between them, the Argive representative and Danaus, with ironical speeches from Danaus showing what his real intentions were, would give enough material for a play. But the difficulty in Wilamowitz' view is the compromise. What is the quid pro quo ? Marriage and not conquest, says Wilamowitz : ' Ehe, aber eine rechte Ehe.' But the Danaids have made it abundantly clear that they will have no marriage, *rechte* or otherwise. We cannot have them submitting to marriage in order to murder ; this would be too melodramatically bad. They must submit only because they have to, and the compulsion must be such as to cast no discredit on the honour and gallantry of the Argives.

We must, I think, find (*a*) substantial justification for Danaus' ' stratagem ' ; (*b*) reasonable ground for the Argives to look for a compromise without losing their honour ; (*c*) no easy victory for the Egyptians, which would leave the long description of the power of Argos quite unexplained. This inclines me to think that Hermann was right. I would assume a battle in which the power of Argos is equal to that of Egypt, but in which Pelasgus is killed. Now Argos, deprived of its leader, is in danger ; Danaus is offered the throne if he can come to terms. Both the pride and the honour of Argos might be considered satisfied, and Danaus could accept with some moral justification. The Danaids have necessity to extenuate their perfidy and a royal position in Argos to console them ; and the Egyptians get what they deserve. Dramatically too this seems the logical ending to the tragic dilemma which engulfs Pelasgus in the *Supplices,* and its ruthless consummation in the death of the King is what we might reasonably expect in a young dramatist.

And what is it all about ? What was Aeschylus thinking at the age of 30 ? We are not certain how the trilogy went, but at least we can hold fast to what we have.

The trilogy was not simply a stage-version of the renowned story of the Danaids. What arrests and detains the attention most in the *Supplices* is the tragic dilemma of Pelasgus ; this is where Aeschylus was most engaged—not in the running about of Danaus. Certainly the Danaids have to gain admission to Argos, but there was no need to begin here (and not for example with the clash in Egypt), nor to make so much of it, nor to set it in so tragic a light. Aeschylus in fact has almost flown in the face of providence in order to make Pelasgus and not Danaus the tragic hero of his first play, for the price he had to pay was the superfluity of Danaus. Unless we can imagine that Aeschylus contrived this terrible screw-turning by accident and can ascribe the comparative failure of the latter part of the play to incompetence, the first situation in the Danaid-legend that impressed itself on his mind was the agony of Pelasgus.

The trilogy is not concerned (except perhaps as a by-product) with demonstrating to the Athenians how a noble people puts religious duty before its own safety. They were welcome to draw this lesson, if they could get nothing better out of the play but the proof that Aeschylus was not being didactic happens this time to be easy ; he goes out of his way to make the King and the Argives yield not to a clear call of duty but to duty backed by threats of what Heaven might do to avenge altars polluted by blood. The choice is not between war and dishonour, but between war and unmentioned horrors, so that if Aeschylus intended a stirring political lesson, an *Erbauung* and an *Erhebung*, he managed it rather badly. Let us by all means take the Argives as an ideal, but let us first understand what they are in the play, not simple Heroes and repositories of all the virtues, but, like Pelasgus, tragic victims of a situation.

The trilogy is not a hymn to the glory of Zeus. We may indeed say, and truly, ' It is from Zeus that the whole trilogy derives its significance, and around his name that the composition is designed '.[1] But what is Zeus ? Aeschylus tells us more than once that he does not know. What is the significance ? ' A question of religion', this critic continues, ' is thus raised which is going to dominate the whole play, or rather the whole trilogy. Is Zeus indifferent to justice ? Will he allow brutality to triumph ? ' But this is so evidently

[1] G. Thomson, *Greek Lyric Metres*, p. 82.

a question expecting the answer No that none but a simple-
minded dramatist would put it. Aeschylus' questions were
not so easy as this.

There are two particularly interesting remarks in Pohlenz'
treatment of the *Supplices*.[1] On Zeus he says ' His mind is an
abyss which no eye can fathom' : ' Sein Sinn ist ein Abgrund,
den kein Blick ermisst '—which is true, tragic, completely
Aeschylean, and must never be forgotten. But 'Zeus verlässt
die Seinen nicht ', if true, is not tragic, but belongs to a Ger-
man chorale as much in feeling as it does in rhythm. Does
Zeus protect his own here only by treading upon Pelasgus and
the Argives ? Is he so clumsy a god ? And are the Suppliants ' die Seinen ' ? We must not hastily suppose this because they say so, and win our sympathy. Aeschylus has told
us enough about them, and if we take the Suppliants' odes as
being Aeschylus' own confession of faith and not what he
wants the Suppliants to say, that is our own fault. They believe in Zeus, but does Zeus believe in them ? They are no
conventional band of ill-used maidens, simple victims of
cruelty. Aeschylus has been careful to characterize them, and
he has been careful to illuminate them most strikingly at the
end of the play. He characterized them because their character was important to the tragic idea, not because they are
the Protagonist and in the earliest tragedy it was usual to
characterize the chorus. We must not allow our just sympathy for them to blind us to the streak of violence that runs
through them—a reflection, almost, of their cousins' violence.
Should Suppliants threaten to defile holy altars ? If they put
their trust in Zeus, let it be pure trust. But at the end
Aeschylus goes further. Like Hippolytus, they honour Artemis and dishonour Aphrodite—and what are these ? Not
sworn foes, as these one-sided, tragic creatures imagine, but
complementary powers; is not Artemis herself *Eileithuia*,
helper in child-birth ? They are parts of a whole, parts which
must receive due honour, or the whole is dishonoured, and the
Whole is Zeus. The play is not a demonstration but a tragedy ; the Suppliants may place themselves under the protection of Zeus, but Zeus does not automatically protect ; Greek

[1] *Griechische Tragödie*, pp. 35 and 33.

altars gave asylum only on terms. To win the protection of
Zeus you must surely obey his law.

In the end, when the Egyptians are dead, probably Pelasgus
and a few hundred Argives too, and the Suppliants married
off again, not very gloriously, we have much more than an
answer to the question Will Zeus allow brutality to triumph?
much more than an illustration how Zeus cleaves to his own.
Brutality is defeated, but by murder, not by Zeus, and the
Suppliants are compelled to render to Aphrodite her due.[1]
At last they are brought into harmony with Zeus.

So far we can go with the data that the play provides. We
cannot see all that was in Aeschylus' mind, as we lack the later
plays, but we can see clearly that the Suppliants are not only
pathetic, as the victims of outrage, but also tragic, as the victims of their own misconceptions. Zeus does indeed preside
over the action, but not the Zeus of the Suppliants; these do
not yet know Zeus' law—they forget Aphrodite. Nor do the
Egyptians know Zeus' law—they forget Artemis. We have
all sympathy for the one side, none for the other, but it is in
melodrama, not in tragedy, that the side we sympathize with
must be wholly right.

In the clash between these two parties the first stage that
Aeschylus chooses to present is neither a calm moral lesson nor
a comforting revelation of Zeus' universal plan. The innocent
Pelasgus is drawn into the vortex and spiritually, if not also
physically, destroyed. Antigone cries; 'What law of Heaven
have I transgressed?' Pelasgus might ask the same. 'Zeus
verlässt die Seinen nicht' will be no comfort; nor will 'Sein
Sinn ist ein Abgrund', but at least this will be true. This,
perhaps, is the profoundest tragedy—certainly the form which
has vexed the philosophers most; for the philosopher must
explain his universe, the tragic poet knows that it cannot be
explained—and Aeschylus was a tragic poet.

But what were the Suppliants to do? Where, in their hard
case, did justice lie, *to metrion*, that middle course, so hard to
steer? We have lost Aeschylus' working-out, and we can
only be tentative. They do in fact escape the Egyptians, by

[1] This is certain: it is the necessary fulfilment of the antiphony
that ends the *Supplices*.

their own violence ; but at the beginning, in Egypt, was there
no middle course which would have avoided the tragedy in
Argos ? Were they simply to submit to lust ? This is monstrous.

Perhaps so. We may notice however that one of them,
Hypermnestra, did (probably) submit in the end, and that
she came off best. The fundamental idea seems tolerably
clear. There are in Egypt two parties, of whom the one
denies Aphrodite, the other Artemis.[1] We have every sympathy with the one, none with the other, but this must not
blind us to the fact, carefully pointed out by the poet, that
both are at variance with Zeus' law, and if we suppose that
from such a situation there must be some middle way out,
one which will not involve the innocent, we deceive ourselves.
Once the moral balance of things is disturbed in this way
there is no telling how far calamity will not spread. This
tragic conception must have lain very deep in Aeschylus' mind,
for we find him presenting it again at the end of his life, in
the *Oresteia*. Agamemnon sinned against the Gods, and also
against Clytemnestra. Had Clytemnestra been a Socrates,
preferring to suffer rather than to do injustice, the evil might
have stopped there, but she was not. We can compare her to
the Suppliants only with apologies to the Suppliants, but essentially the comparison holds ; neither can accept injustice,
to metrion becomes impossible, and calamity surges on. Clytemnestra, avenging herself, involves the innocent Orestes ;
the Suppliants, unable to accept injury, involve innocent
Argos. They destroy their persecutors—and it serves *them*
right—but the disturbance is not at an end until they are made
to bring themselves into harmony with Zeus' law. It may be
hard, but Aeschylus never pretended that life was easy, or that
Zeus was simple, or that only the guilty are tortured.

2. THE SUPPLICES AND PRE-AESCHYLEAN TRAGEDY   Greek
tragedy passed through distinct forms, and unless we wish to
stultify our criticism by complaining that the *Troades* is not so
' well-constructed ' as the *I.T.* (*Iphigenia Among the Tau-
rians*), or by finding the *Septem* stiff in comparison with the
Tyrannus, it is well to make clear the main features and pe-

---

[1] ' Rival ideologies.'

culiar virtues of each. The significant forms seem to be four,
of which the first three are clearly marked. Aristotle remarks
briefly, and without a word of explanation, that Aeschylus
introduced the second actor, and Sophocles the third, with
scene-painting. The meaning of these innovations will be the
theme of much that follows ; for the moment it is enough to
observe that they give us important landmarks. Tragedy was
profoundly modified by each. We have the Thespian lyrical
tragedy with one actor, the early Aeschylean with two, the
Sophoclean with three. It will be convenient to call the early
Aeschylean Old Tragedy, the Sophoclean Middle, and the late-
Euripidean drama New ; not for the sake of using fresh terms,
but because the distinctions we have in mind are often other
than the personal differences between the three dramatists ;
Sophocles wrote New Tragedy and Euripides Middle.[1] From
Old Tragedy our surviving plays are the *Septem*, *Persae* and
Prometheus—the last in spite of its three actors, and even if
Professor G. Thomson is right in putting it later than the
Oresteia. The *Supplices* is a link between Old Tragedy and
the still older Lyrical Tragedy which is the subject of our
present inquiry.

Neither about the form nor about the essential spirit of pre-
Aeschylean drama have we any direct evidence.[2] We know
that it was enacted by one actor and chorus,[3] but this does not
take us far. Aristotle speaks of tragedy casting off the satyric
element and discarding the trochaic metre, but there is little
help here. In the first place, Pickard-Cambridge [4] gives se-

---

[1] The *Medea* and the *Hippolytus*.

[2] Kranz, *Stasimon*, is full of interesting speculation on the development of choric forms, but here we are concerned with the
dramatic form of the plays as a whole.

[3] What the size of the chorus was I resolutely refuse to discuss ;
but one question interests me. It is generally accepted that it was
a chorus of 50, and Wilamowitz, in his robust way, said that it was
ridiculous to suppose that the later chorus of 12 could possibly have
impersonated the fifty daughters of Danaus. This has great force ;
but in the last play, when Hypermnestra had presumably severed
herself from her sisters, did Aeschylus use a chorus of 49 ? The
effect of a dance with one dancer missing would be striking, and
perhaps not too bold for Aeschylus.

[4] *Dithyramb, Tragedy, and Comedy*, pp. 128 ff.

rious grounds for supposing that Aristotle was only theorizing, and in the second, even if Aristotle's account is true, we cannot imagine that tragedy was satyric and its tone *orchestikoteron,* ' more like dancing,' ten or even twenty years before the *Supplices.* Whatever theory we hold on the origin of tragedy, we must assume, considering what the *Supplices* was like in 495 c., and what difficulties Comedy encountered, ' being refused admittance to the city ', that when Tragedy was established by Peisistratus it was already a serious art-form.

However, if we limit ourselves to the period immediately preceding Aeschylus we may form a general impression by arguing backwards from the *Supplices,* an apparently hazardous enterprise which is made possible by the dramatic idleness of Danaus. The play is in all essentials single-actor drama up to the point where Danaus is able to do something useful by going into Argos.

The first and most obvious merit of the *Supplices* is the power of the lyrical passages. Aeschylus deals with the chorus as surely and confidently as Sophocles with dialogue. There is no sign of hesitancy. If we had no external evidence, we should still be certain that the lyrical was the oldest part of tragedy, for it is sufficiently obvious that Aeschylus had behind him a long tradition. But not only is the composition of the odes firm and varied ; the characterization too is mature. These people are no band of singers and dancers, but the Danaids, and they could never for a moment be confused with the Chorus of another play. Sophocles' choruses, praised though they are by Aristotle, never reach this degree of characterization.[1] We realize clearly enough in the *Ajax* that they are Salaminian sailors, in the *Antigone* Theban senators ; these all sing in character, but their character is not stamped on their songs or speech as the character of the Danaids is. They will sing ' wonders are many, but of all things is man the most wonderful,' and we think of them as pure Chorus ; a moment later they will say something to Creon, and we realize that they are Theban senators ; the Suppliants never for a moment allow us to forget that they are the Suppliants.

We can go further. Aeschylus makes this character dy-

[1] Not a complaint but a compliment, see p. 28.

namic as well as vivid.   Greek tragedy never interested itself,
except perhaps in some lost trilogies of which the *Prometheia*
is a possible example, in the development of character, but
it did gradually reveal an already developed character.   Aeschylus does this simply but very powerfully with his chorus
here.   The Danaids are partly Greek, partly barbarian ; their
reliance on Zeus emphasizes the one strain, their violence the
other.   The first long choric movement closes very dramatically with the emergence of the barbarian strain, and sets up
a contrast which Aeschylus uses repeatedly, like some powerful and unifying basic rhythm.   Sophocles never did this
either ; Aeschylus scarcely again.   We shall see later why not.

For pre-Aeschylean tragedy then we can postulate a high
level of competence in the management of the chorus and in
its dramatization.   'The Chorus was the Protagonist.'   This
is the conclusion drawn from its position in the *Supplices*,
and it is a doubtful one.[1]   We must not think of the *Supplices*
as Greek Tragedy, example no. 1.   It is the *Supplices*, a
unique and individual play ; and Aeschylus never quite
learned the art of turning out plays to a pattern.[2]   The myth
which he uses in this trilogy is obviously unusual in this respect, that the chief agent was not an individual but a crowd.
If the fifty daughters of Danaus were to appear on the stage
at all, it could only be as chorus.   The same problem cropped
up forty years later, and was solved in the same way.   In the
Eumenides one of the actors was a multiple personality, and
these Furies inevitably and effectively become the chorus and
virtually co-protagonist with Orestes.   We do not say of this
that Aeschylus is becoming primitive again, returning to the
dramatic traditions of his youth ; neither should we make too
certain that the dramatic position of the chorus in the *Supplices* is a sign of date only.   This special degree of dramatization is not necessarily in the tradition at all, but was probably a direct consequence of the lay-out of this particular
myth.   The lyric element was predominant, but we have no
reason to suppose that it was in this specific sense dramatic ;

[1] Aristotle, it should be noticed, does not say that the chorus was
the protagonist but ' the lyric element,' which is a different thing.
[2] See below, p. 100.

it probably stood to the chorus of the *Supplices* as the chorus of the *Agamemnon* does to that of the *Eumenides*.

We may now look again at the futility of Danaus. The difficulty that Aeschylus has in using him is not simply a sign of primitive technique and inexperience, but a special consequence of this legend. To the end of his life no amount of dramatic difficulty stopped Aeschylus from making a play once he had seen in its story a tragic idea; we need only look at the *Prometheus* to see that. Sheppard's comment therefore, that Aeschylus has invented the tool but cannot yet use it properly, must not pass unchallenged. The second actor is used well enough when he is the Herald, and we need not doubt that Danaus was effective enough in the later plays, when he had an independent part. The character of the daughters is one of the two important dramatic forces that make the *Supplices*, and this may not be overshadowed by any strong characteristic in the father. For Danaus, if he is to do anything dramatic here, can do it only by becoming a third dramatic force, additional to the chorus and the King. He must be the driving-force behind his daughters, or oppose them, or present their situation from another point of view; and none of these things belonged at all to Aeschylus' tragic conception of the story. He is therefore only ' an eponymous ancestor dressed up for the stage ', but because the situation allowed nothing else, not because Aeschylus knew no better.

This unusual position of the chorus in this play explains too why it is specifically dramatic in a way in which later choruses (except the Furies) are not. Had Aeschylus in the *Agamemnon* or Sophocles in the *Antigone* attempted to dramatize his chorus as fully as Aeschylus does here, he would have detracted from the dramatization of the stage-characters and done something which might have been interesting but would have obscured the tragic idea. If there is one thing which may be said without reserve of all Greek Tragedy (so long as it remained tragic), it is that it never admits anything which does not directly contribute to the tragic idea. It has to the full the austerity and logic of every other classical Greek art, and it will use neither characterization nor anything else needlessly.

We may now for the moment leave the Chorus. We have
seen that Aeschylus is already as much at home with it as he
is in the *Septem* or the *Oresteia*. His personality grew, but
in this respect his art was already mature, and we may infer
that those who had immediately preceded him were also, in
their own degree, masters of this part of drama. What of
the other parts ?

' The *Supplices* is deficient in characterization.' This is a
misconception. Certainly Danaus' few incursions into character are tedious, but Danaus is already explained. There
remain the Herald and the King. For Heralds the good and
sufficient rule is, as H. W. Smyth says, ' like master like man ',
and no quarrel will be picked with Aeschylus on this score.
But Pelasgus is said to be no character ; he is no Eteocles, no
Oedipus. And why should he be ? His tragedy turns on no
hamartia ; it is not even remotely based on his character. Be
he what he will, he is lost, and Aeschylus is too good an artist
to invest him with irrelevant character. All we need is that
he should be morally and intellectually big enough to realize
to the full what has come upon him and to see the dilemma
in which he and his people are placed ; and this we have.
Sophocles drew character so brilliantly not because he was
good at it but because his tragedy turned on it; Aeschylus
drew Pelasgus as he did, not because he was a primitive and
could do no better but because his tragic conception demanded this and nothing more.

Aeschylus' power of presenting character was fully equal to
his need, and we may find that in other respects he was not
following a tradition of puerility. The passage of the turning
of the screw is masterly : Aeschylus never did anything better.
Was this something new to the Greek stage, or was it in the
tradition ? The power of it is surely pure Aeschylus, but in
a sense—in its clarity and its directness—it is pure Greek. All
we can say is that the possibility of such dramatic effects lay
to hand if there was a poet capable of using it. It is clear too
that iambic speech of a dramatic kind was no novelty. That
there were earlier masters of this art we may perhaps infer
from such passages as 468–89, which do not read like the
poetry of a pioneer. Croiset remarks, ' The poetic style,

though it has admirable qualities of strength, grandeur and brilliance, is defective in its excessive tendency to remove itself from the level of normal speech. To avoid resemblance with prose it loads itself with an excess of images sometimes bizarre, of artificial periphrases, of turns of speech almost enigmatic.' [1] This is just, if we remember that iambic speech brought into so close a connection with lyric speech must avoid the prosaic at all costs. We think of the artificial antithesis between sea and land (77), 'Dust, the dumb messenger of an army' (180), 'This is no lamb from the flock of my thoughts' (929). These things are significant perhaps not of an early stage in the writing of iambics but of the youth of Aeschylus. Twenty years later we find one more bad shot, worse than any of these : 'the voiceless children of the undefiled', meaning fish (*Persae* 577). These strained phrases of the *Supplices* are genuine Aeschylus, like the homely vividness of 'an eye clear, not too wined-up', which reappears in the ox on the Watchman's tongue in the *Agamemnon*. We have here the real Aeschylus in his strength and weakness, and one can but feel that the weakness would have been more pronounced had he not had some earlier masters on whom to model his style.

We know then that in the dramatic lyric, and, we may feel fairly certain too, in the dramatic iambic, Aeschylus had some considerable predecessors. Can we venture to form a more definite idea what this earlier tragedy was like ?

We infer a chorus which, though not an actor like the chorus of the *Supplices*, is yet essentially dramatic, expressing in its long movements the urgency of some tragic situation, and bringing to bear on the actor some moral or spiritual force. The normal chorus then, as later, was surely a group of citizens, senators, captives or the like, representing in its passionate formalism a big collective idea or emotion—the city, the vanquished, the wronged ; a body surpassing the individual stature, but not a mere abstraction deprived of all personality. Even if less fully characterized than the Suppliants, it was probably more fully characterized than later choruses ; for of the two forces which clashed in the drama,

[1] *Eschyle*, p. 67.

one necessarily proceeded from them. There was no room for the 'idealized spectator'.

Against this chorus stands the single actor. He too must have been drawn in outline only, like Pelasgus, for a detailed character-drawing would be wrong against this background, and the exiguous dramatic personnel would not have allowed it, nor the type of tragic idea called for it. The actor must represent the complementary idea to the chorus—the King, the victor, the wrongdoer. Pelasgus is the perfect type, neither an abstraction nor very individual. His diction, like his characterization, must harmonize with that of the chorus, for any approach to naturalism would be out of drawing. In conformity with the strictly-regulated lyrical measures which form the bulk of the play he must speak regularly. A passage like *Suppl.* 347–406 obviously belongs by nature to this kind of drama, and so does stichomythia, provided that it is formal enough. Intellectual subtlety and eristic could play no part here.

It is the usual assumption that the pre-Aeschylean tragedy was only a sort of Oratorio : ' Aeschylus found Cantata and turned it into Tragedy.' If the word Cantata can be stretched to cover such essentially dramatic and tragic things as the major part of the *Supplices* (still discounting Danaus), then there is nothing to be said ; but if the word means a series of exchanges between a chorus and an actor, both playing a part but neither being specifically dramatic, then the assumption seems to be unjustified. Phrynichus was evidently more lyrical than dramatic, but we need not assume that everyone else was a Phrynichus too. The early plays about which we are best informed are his *Capture of Miletus* and *Phoenissae,* and these seem to have been pathetic narrative-drama rather than tragedy ; real cantata in fact. But it may be noticed that such chronicle-subjects were not the normal ones, and were particularly difficult to put into dramatic form. Aeschylus, most would admit, was not altogether successful with his *Persae* ; and if the *Persae* were our earliest surviving play, who would believe that a play twenty years older had displayed the purely dramatic assurance that the *Supplices* does ? The whole middle part of the *Supplices* is, from the dramatic point of

view, incomparably more mature and confident than the
Persae, and analogously it seems likely that normal pre-Aeschylean drama was more specifically dramatic than the
Phoenissae and the *Capture of Miletus*. Again, we are perhaps inclined to overestimate the importance of the second
actor and to underestimate the possibilities of the single actor
with chorus. From the *Supplices* we may gain some idea of
the kind of plot and the kind of tragic situation that early
drama could have dealt with ; and if it is shown that the possibility of real drama is there, no one who knows his Greeks
will care to deny that the possibility was realized.

The plot, like the diction and the characterization, must
have been highly conventionalized, not in the least naturalistic.
This was inevitable, for unless the actor was to spend most
of his time in the changing room, free movement of plot was
impossible. The chorus enters and expounds the situation ;
the actor enters and gives us an impression of his general position. Now all the dramatic forces are present ; something
may be kept back, as in the *Supplices* the threat of suicide
is kept back,[1] but nothing new can enter. It is more important however to notice that nothing new is wanted. The
limitation, like most limitations to the great artist, does not
mean poverty, but intensity. It means here the opportunity
to display one form of Tragedy, and that perhaps the profoundest, in its purest form, free from distracting irrelevancies ; and that is the form of Tragedy which we have in the
Supplices, the spectacle of the hero isolated before some awful
rift in the universe, looking, like Pelasgus, into the chasm that
must engulf him. The simple form of Thespian tragedy was
marvellously fitted to such a tragic idea : No issue free from
disaster, and it is hard to suppose that nobody saw the fact
before Aeschylus altered the form with his second actor. The
cantata theory does not explain the *Supplices*.

It has been assumed that the crisis is that of the actor, not
of the chorus, and that in this sense the actor really was, or
became, the protagonist. The assumption is necessary. It
may not have been true when Thespis won his famous victory

[1] Kept back, that is, from the King. Aeschylus might have given
us a cheap dramatic surprise by keeping it back from us too, but
he was an artist, and a Greek artist. (See below, p. 298.)

in 534, but it obviously was when tragedy got within hail of
Aeschylus.   The single actor necessarily attracts the eye ; he
must be the centre of our most poignant interest, as he is the
focus of the moral forces working in the play.   The chorus
is the voice of Humanity, its sufferings the common sufferings
of Humanity ; only those of the actor can be made tragically
significant.   He is bound to stand out above the crowd ; his
must be the choice at the crisis ; he, the individual, must be
seen at grips with his destiny.   Drama in which the chorus
takes first place can only be pathetic ; it is not in the strictest
sense tragic to be the population of a captured city or the
victim of cruel oppression ; and though the chorus in the
Danaid-trilogy as a whole is the protagonist, really a tragic
hero that acts tragically and suffers tragically, it is because it
is not a normal chorus, simply a representative group, but an
individual character multiplied fifty times.   They are tragically one-sided like Hippolytus, not a community like the
chorus of the *Persae* or *Agamemnon*.

We may therefore tentatively, but not without some evidence, suggest the following as a type, not the only one but
the best, of early tragedy.

First ode.

Entrance of the Actor and disclosure of the general situation.

Second ode, in which pressure is brought to bear on him.

The crisis grows.   Kommos ?

Third ode.

Actor faces the crisis and takes his decision.

Fourth ode.

The result.   Messenger ?

Fifth ode.

It is a simple form, but not infantile.   It is a form which permits the most exquisite and most powerfully dramatic lyricism,
and can express the profoundest and most moving of tragic
situations.   Its ' stiffness ' is no defect.   ' Is it not possible ',
said the critic whom we quoted at the outset, ' that the pre-
Aeschylean drama already held a key that gave it freedom
from the bonds of naturalism—a key for which modern dramatists from Strindberg to Lenormand have been desperately
striving ? '   It is, I think, not possible only, but certain.

CHAPTER II
OLD TRAGEDY

1. INTRODUCTION We come to that form of Greek drama whose outward mark is the use of two actors and the chorus.[1] Our task must be to try to gain some idea why this form was brought into existence, why Aeschylus wanted the second actor, why he did not want a third ; in other words, what the special virtue of this type of tragedy was. We have been maintaining that it is not necessary to regard Lyrical Tragedy as something immature and incomplete which was waiting anxiously for Aeschylus to give it form and significance ; so too we must be careful not to think of Old Tragedy merely as Greek drama without the third actor, another, though less, incomplete form. Regarded historically or biologically it may be a primitive form ; regarded aesthetically it is not. It is perfectly adapted to the purpose for which it was designed, and is therefore complete. Aeschylus added one actor and not two, not, fundamentally, because he was conservative and cautious (no dramatist has been bolder), nor because his technique was not yet equal to managing three actors, but because his tragic conceptions demanded this form and not the other.

Why Aeschylus introduced the second actor and invented his characteristic use of the statutory trilogy will be discussed later,[2] but it seems well to anticipate one or two points here. It is quite certain that he had no idea of using the second actor as an antagonist to the first, turning tragedy into an *agon*, a contest, between the two. This comes only upon the third actor's appearance and is quite foreign to Aeschylus' tragic thinking. The essence of Old Tragedy was the solitary hero facing his own destiny or playing out an inner drama of his own soul-like Pelasgus.[3] Pelasgus is not more solitary than

---

[1] The *Prometheus* is included in this group, in spite of its three actors, because the use of the third is quite incidental.

[2] See below, pp. 104 f.

[3] For convenience, I speak here confidently ; really Aeschylus is

Eteocles and Prometheus ; Eteocles does not grapple with Polyneices but with himself—not because Aeschylus was hampered by his small caste, but because he did not want Polyneices.

But if the second actor did not revolutionize drama in this respect he did in another ; he enabled plot to move, to move longitudinally, in action, as well as vertically, in tension. The plot of Lyrical Tragedy was, in a certain sense, static ; when chorus and actor met, the ring was closed. Now it is not ; there is a second actor who can come in with fresh news—as Darius does, or the Spy in the *Septem*—or can present different facets of the situation to the hero—as do Oceanus and Io in the *Prometheus*.

This movement of plot seems not to have been contrived merely for dramatic reasons, for the sake of making drama more life-like. It is natural for us to think like this, but the innovating artist thinks differently ; at least we may be fairly confident that Aeschylus' first reason for innovating was that the older form did not enable him to say what he wanted to say. We have a fine example of his use of static plot in the middle part of the *Supplices*, but already this is part of a much wider dramatic theme. The second actor makes it possible, dramatically, to set the hero in a position which not only seems, but also is innocent. Now the situation can change ; messengers bring news or heralds make proclamations, and what was safe becomes perilous. Of this dramatic method the *Septem* is the perfect example ; there we see no sudden pit opening beneath the hero, but a horror growing before our eyes. Technically this is no doubt a vast improvement, but it was not first thought of in this way. The tragic implications of the second actor are even more important than the dramatic ones. Since the situation moves, the hero must be of a certain kind ; he must—if we are to have tragedy—be of such a moral constitution as to oppose himself to this movement, not to conform to it. The hero of the pure tragedy of situation was Man, almost undifferentiated ; the hero of the *Septem* must be like Eteocles, one who will not, like the nor-

the critic's despair, because he would never write two plays alike, not even in the *Oresteia*.

mal man, say at v. 653, 'Circumstances alter cases ; of course
I cannot fight my own brother'. In other words, the moving
plot was designed to display and test moral character, to give
room for moral choice and for its results.

Such seems to have been the genesis of the second actor.
Once there he could naturally be put to other uses ; Darius
for example gives us our first dramatic surprise ; and we shall
see one or two approaches to realism—of which indeed we had
one example already in the *Supplices* : the King could hardly
have mentioned beer to the chorus, but he can to the Herald.

When we examine the three plays that survive from this
stage of drama we at once meet an illuminating difficulty ; in
two of the plays Aeschylus is wrestling with material which
will hardly go into drama at all. In the *Persae* he is sailing
closely into the wind of Epic ; in the *Prometheus* his imagination is seized with a subject which any other dramatist would
have rejected, in this form, as impossible. The technical interest of the *Persae* is to follow the steps whereby an essentially epic story is made ready for the stage ; of the *Prometheus* to see how Aeschylus extracts the inner dramatic
movement of a situation essentially immobile ; of the *Septem*
to see Old Tragedy at its best.

2. THE PERSAE This, the second play of Aeschylus' preserved to us, was produced in 472, at least twenty years after
the *Supplices*. What Aeschylus has been doing in the interval
as dramatist we do not know ; as citizen he has been fighting.
He has seen his country within an ace of becoming a Persian
satrapy, but repelling Darius' expedition at Marathon and
Xerxes' at Salamis and Plataea ; furthermore, in the years that
followed Plataea, driving the Persians back into Asia and
founding the League which promised to prevent any repetition of the attack ; so that six or seven years of retrospect increased rather than diminished the glory of Salamis and
Plataea, victories which seemed the more complete and miraculous the more one thought of them.

Therefore, as the dramatization of recent events was no new
thing—for Phrynichus at about 493 had staged his unfortunate
Capture of Miletus and in 476 his version of the Persian War—

it was natural for Aeschylus to be attracted to the subject. As it happens, we are fairly well supplied with facts about the war, and we know a little about Phrynichus' play, so that we are in a position to see what was Aeschylus' idea in such a dramatization—not only to see what he did but also what he refused to do—and we can to some extent compare his dramatic outlook with Phrynichus'.

About Phrynichus' play we know this ; the scene was laid in Susa, the chorus consisted of Phoenician women, and a eunuch, placing seats for the Persian nobles, speaks a prologue in which the defeat at Salamis is mentioned. We know the first verse of Phrynichus' play : Aeschylus borrowed it, giving to Phrynichus what Mazon well calls ' a courtesy-salute.' [1]

From these few facts Croiset has drawn some interesting conclusions. As the chorus is composed of women, these nobles must have been given some other part in the play, and one actor must have been their spokesman, leaving for the other the part of messenger. There could not therefore have been much dramatic complication, especially as the defeat was already known in the palace. The staple of the play must have been lyrical lamentation—at which we know Phrynichus excelled. Surprise there could not have been ; as Mazon says, it seems to have been less a tragedy than a cantata. Phrynichus used Aeschylus' second actor but remained faithful to his own conception of tragedy ; we shall presently find Aeschylus in his turn doing a similar thing.

By taking the same theme only four years later Aeschylus shows that he had something new to contribute. He too lays the scene in Susa. That was necessary. Only from the Persian point of view was the event tragic, and truly tragic not in the Persian camp but in the centre of the threatened empire. Again, there is the point roughly expressed by saying that remoteness of place compensates for nearness in time. The great danger was that the poet should be betrayed into naturalism, into situations where realistic treatment was the only possible one. The events were still fresh in men's memories, and details would be inimical to the development of a broad moral theme, such as alone would justify the dramatiza-

[1] See J. T. Sheppard, *Greek Tragedy*, pp. 45–6.

tion of a recent event. The danger could be avoided only by going to Susa. There only could the story be sufficiently simplified. Moreover Susa gave opportunities, such as Aeschylus never despised, of striking scenic effects. In this respect therefore Aeschylus had to follow Phrynichus.

The choice of Persian nobles and not women as the chorus is significant. Technically it was an improvement in that it set free an actor to play other roles and so to develop the dramatic force—in which Phrynichus had little interest. Morally it is even more important. In a play whose chorus was Phoenician women the prevailing tone must obviously have been pathetic, ' Alas for the dead ! ' With a chorus of Counsellors the tone becomes deeper. ' Alas for our fallen nation ! ' The chorus of the *Persae* can take the historical view, and can develop the tragic theme which Aeschylus sees in the story—they, and they alone, can show us that Xerxes' policy of boundless aggression is responsible for the disaster.

Nor does Aeschylus follow Phrynichus in allowing the news of the disaster to be already known when the play opens. He was composing a drama, not a threnody, and needed therefore all the dramatic movement he could get. But this raises an interesting question : if Aeschylus was concerned—as he must have been—to create dramatic situations out of this epical material, why did he not anticipate Herodotus, and begin his play with a triumphant message from Xerxes announcing the capture and sack of Athens ? What could be more obvious, or more effective ? Let the play begin with scenes of rejoicing : they will be the perfect foil for the catastrophe to come. Incidentally, this stroke would have circumvented one awkward moment, the transition from the first ode to the first episode (vv. 140 ff.). ' Come,' says the Leader of the Chorus, ' let us deliberate. How is Xerxes faring ? ' Since they have no idea how he is faring, there is no material for deliberation ; but we have to be informed who they are, and why they are there. The chorus is, in fact, in an unprofitable situation, and we are glad when the Queen arrives, to rescue them from it.

Since the *Persae* is not a play in which mundane realism is of importance we need not exaggerate this blemish ; but it is one, and one that would have been unnecessary if a first mes-

sage of triumph had been contrived, for then the chorus
would have had matter for debate. So that we ask, once
more, why Aeschylus did not begin with a message announcing victory.

It is of course possible to say—though hard to believe—that
at this date Aeschylus was incapable of so dramatic a stroke.
It is perhaps safer to assume that a dramatic idea obvious to
us was accessible to Aeschylus also, and to enquire if the true
explanation does not lie deeper. Before doing that, we may
raise other questions of the same kind, and in trying to answer
them we may become a little clearer on two matters, about the
relation between Old Tragedy and Epic, and about the meaning and purpose of the *Persae* itself. For it has been said,
wrongly, as I think, that the play represents a stage in the
development of drama at which drama had not yet emancipated itself from the epic tradition and technique ; while as
for the other point, are we to call it a religious or a patriotic
play ? Politics and religion were certainly not so clearly
separated in the fifth century as they are to-day ; nevertheless,
if one critic says ' This is a religious play about the punishment of hybris ' and another, ' This is a patriotic piece celebrating the victory,' they are not saying the same thing, and
it is perhaps possible to prove that the one is substantially
right and the other substantially wrong. For if Aeschylus
was a competent dramatist, not struggling with a form that
he had imperfectly mastered, proper appreciation of his form
should lead us directly to a proper appreciation of the content. If we ask ourselves the right questions about the form
of the play we shall be led, I think, straight to the conclusion
that he did not set out to compose, for the stage, a piece in
celebration of Salamis and Plataea—a theme which might have
made good epic—but to create drama, and nothing but drama,
on the theme of hybris and its inevitable punishment. What
patriotic celebration there is—and there is obviously some—is
incidental.

For his material, Aeschylus had the Persian invasion ; but
we find that he used it with the same freedom that the dramatists were accustomed to use in handling myth—and for the
same purpose, namely, to remove everything irrelevant to the

dramatic idea and to emphasize what is significant, in order that every detail of the plot may be dramatically efficient. In Aristotelian language, ' what happened ' is modified until it becomes ' what *would* happen ' ; drama becomes ' more philosophic than history '.

Believing that the form embodies the thought, and that Aeschylus was able to manage his form as he wished, let us look at it, asking ourselves certain questions about the plot and the manipulation of the material. One such question we have asked already : why does Aeschylus not begin with the news of a considerable success ? Other questions are : why does he represent Darius as the prudent King who never set foot out of Asia, although Darius had invaded Scythia, and had had something to do with Marathon ? Why does he so exaggerate the importance of the small action on Psyttalia ? Why does he represent Xerxes' retreat from Salamis as an incontinent flight, such that he arrives at Susa as a broken fugitive ? Why does he invent that quite impossible disaster on the Strymon ? Why, in describing the battle of Salamis, does he so notably avoid mentioning individual names and personal exploits ? Why does he represent as impious the building of the bridge and the cutting of the canal, when the ordinary Greek attitude to these contrivances seems to have been (as we should expect) one of interested admiration ?

Needless to say, answers have been given to most of these questions, and not all of them are bad answers. The difficulty is that they are all different, while the questions are the same—namely, why did Aeschylus shape his play like this ? As for the character of Darius, we are told that the Athenians, not having the *Cambridge Ancient History*, did not know very much about him ; further, that the prudent Darius makes a strong contrast with the furious Xerxes, and that dramatists like contrasts of character. They do—but was Aeschylus altering history only for a dramatic ' effect ' ? As for the autumnal freezing of the Strymon, the Strymon was a long way off, and probably the Athenians did not know much about its habits ; in any case, Aeschylus loved marvels. (This answer is a bad one—for this reason if for no other, that instead of trusting to Athenian ignorance, Aeschylus goes out

of his way to call the frost *aoros*, unseasonable.)   As for the
action on Psyttalia, it has been suggested that here Aeschylus
had in mind the need for promoting social unity in Attica : he
is showing the Athenians that every class of citizen had his
share in the glory of Salamis, the poorer classes afloat, the
hoplites on the island.   But exaggeration is poor propaganda.
Then, Xerxes' disorderly flight is honest misconception ; alternatively, Aeschylus is ridiculing the Persians—again, a poor
way of celebrating a victory.   That no Greek names are used
is a master-stroke of artistic simplification, which at the same
time avoids the invidious—though we may perhaps feel some
doubt here ; for suppose that Aeschylus had chosen to treat
his theme in epic style, with a Catalogue of Ships, in a speech
bristling with Greek names—should we not have found this
' artistic ' too, and filled our commentaries with parallels from
Milton ?   The ' artistic ', after all, is only what is necessary
and right.   Let us then show that the theme demanded precisely this treatment ; then we shall know why it is artistic.

Of the answers given here, some are plausible, some may be
even partially true.   But they are extremely various, invoking
as they do politics, ignorance, and the pursuit of certain
isolated dramatic effects.   If we found one single answer to
all the questions—including the first one, not yet answered at
all—we should feel some assurance that we were on the right
track.   And we do find such a single answer in the assumption that Aeschylus was not writing a play—epic, patriotic, or
anything else—about the victory, but was constructing a religious drama out of the Persian War, in just the same spirit
that he constructed another out of the Trojan War.   Xerxes'
hybris led him to break a divine law.   He sinned as Paris
sinned, and Agamemnon ; and like those sinners he was punished by Zeus through instruments chosen by Zeus, Paris
through the two sons of Atreus, Agamemnon through Clytemnestra, Xerxes through the Greeks and Greece.   The difference—a profound one indeed—is that in the *Agamemnon* the
' justice ' inflicted is in each case a crime, itself calling for
justice, while in the *Persae* the punishment is simple and final.
With this important reservation the parallel holds, and it
explains the play.

First, the 'mythical' treatment of recent history. Mr.
D. S. MacColl relates how a sitter complained to a Scottish
sculptor that the bust he had made of him was not like him.
'It's no every mon,' said the sculptor, 'can be like his bust.'
That was Darius' trouble. Xerxes was to be smitten by
Heaven because he had committed hybris. The poet, wanting a clear symbol of that hybris, uses the sharp distinction
between Europe and Asia ; here are bounds laid down by
Heaven. Obviously, history or no history, Darius cannot be
allowed to have passed these bounds, or the judgement of
Heaven would have fallen on him. Darius must therefore be
wise and prudent ; he must scrupulously have respected this
law. The contrast of character is indeed effective, but it is a
by-product.

What of the description of the battle, Psyttalia, the precipi-
tous flight of Xerxes ? To Aeschylus, the Greek forces are an
Avenger, an instrument in the hands of Heaven. Individual
names must therefore be suppressed at all costs. This is the
reason why the treatment of the battle is 'artistic'. One
individual exploit is, in fact, referred to plainly enough, the
stratagem of Themistocles. And what does Aeschylus say
about it ? That there came to Xerxes some Alastor, or some
evil spirit.

As for Psyttalia, that becomes a second blow from the god,
one that destroys not Persian allies, like Salamis, but the Persian nobility itself. And then Xerxes flees in terror. In fact,
he did not, in the play, he does—because his real adversary is
more than human. And as for the Strymon, let us not talk of
Athenian ignorance, or Aeschylus' love of marvels. In the
first place, the preliminary sufferings of the Persians on the
retreat are all attributed to 'natural', not human, causes ; not
harassing attacks by patriots in the mountains, but hunger and
thirst. It is the very soil of Greece opposing the invader. In
the second place, it is 'the god' who freezes the river, 'out of
season' ; and when the Persians were on the ice, thanking the
gods for their deliverance, 'the god scattered his rays', and
the Persians were drowned. There is a direct parallel to this
in the *Agamemnon*. 'Let them remember', said Clytemnestra, 'to spare the temples, for they still need a safe re-

turn.' They did not spare the temples, and they found no safe return, for 'those bitterest enemies, fire and water, conspired together' to destroy the fleet. This conspiracy of enemies is no idle decoration, but a sign that the god was at work, here as in the *Persae*.

Now the reason becomes clear why Aeschylus will have no preliminary message of victory. The God of Aeschylus does not move in the mysterious way of the God of Sophocles; he is direct, and when he hits, he hits straight and hard. He does not mock first. The news that Athens was already destroyed would suggest that he did; it would be a 'dramatic' effect ruinous to the idea. And finally, the reason why Aeschylus makes such an ominous point of the bridge and the canal is not to be found in plain fact; it is not that he thought differently about them from Herodotus, or supposed that the Persians might; it is simply that he needed his symbols of Xerxes' hybris. These two feats can be made explicit cases of Xerxes' transgression of limits fixed by Heaven; and Aeschylus' audience, not unaccustomed to poetry, can accept them as such, whatever they may have thought privately about this civil engineering.

We find, then, the same answer to every question; the form shows the content. The *Persae* is as purely dramatic, in conception, as any other play by Aeschylus. It has no real connexion with epic, and should not be used to buttress a theory that Tragedy is in some sense descended from the epic. The 'epic colouring' comes from an accident, not from essentials —the accident that much of the action must be presented through narrative; and after all, in this respect, the *Persae* is very like the *Prometheus*. In the *Prometheus* the action is partly past action, partly inner action, in the mind of the hero; in either case, necessarily conveyed in a series of speeches. Neither play has any real link with epic; indeed, one of the notable points in the account of Salamis is precisely the way in which Aeschylus has avoided epic expansiveness and detail. What we have here is pure drama; not indeed the form we are accustomed to, but one which we can readily understand once we lay aside prepossessions derived from later forms. 'Slices from Homer' was a brilliant phrase, but one that hardly does justice to the real independence and integrity of Old Tragedy.

We may now examine in detail how Aeschylus put this dramatic conception into dramatic shape. Since the days of Sophocles, especially as interpreted by Aristotle, tragic form has implied clash of character, converging lines of intrigue, surprise, and ' happiness ' passing into ' unhappiness '. Aeschylus could not work like this ; his religious philosophy could not be expressed through this form. That God will punish the sinner is certain ; the only surprise possible is the swiftness and completeness of the punishment ; the only movement possible is from foreboding to fulfilment.

It is hardly necessary to follow in detail the means by which Aeschylus imposes on his abundant material this necessary movement. The anxiety of the chorus is, at v. 115, emphasized, to the eye as well as to the ear, by the sudden change from the ionic music and dance to the trochaic rhythm that Aeschylus regularly uses in moments of anxiety, mourning or great earnestness. Atossa's dream brings something more definite. Then comes the Messenger with his four speeches, of which—significantly—the account of the battle is not the climax. First he gives his terrible list of Persians slain ; then he tells of the ruin of the navy, brought on by the Avenger ; then of the destruction of the flower of the army on the island ; finally, a real climax, the catastrophe wrought by the god himself on the Strymon.

But Aeschylus still has in reserve the powerful Dariusscene, itself a drama in miniature. Darius arises, ignorant of what has happened, and is greeted by the incredible news which the living have to give to the dead. But he can tell them the inner meaning of it all ; and then, instead of giving the comfort hoped for, he prophesies the last overthrow at Plataea. Finally, in the scene of which the modern reader can make very little, the broken Xerxes limps home to port. Xerxes is not an impressive character—hardly indeed a character at all. But, in considering this scene, we must not forget that the dramatist has other instruments than words. Aeschylus knew a great deal about the possibilities of the choral lyric, and although the words here mean little it is likely that the dance meant a lot.   One editor has suggested that in this scene Aeschylus was trying to be comic ; if we remember that Xerxes is a man who has been blindly struggling with the god, and that the accusing and menacing tone of the chorus was no doubt reinforced by accusing and menacing dances, we may perhaps judge differently.

Even after devising this general rhythm, Aeschylus still had details to think about, for the series of speeches might yet have been undramatic.   We may for a moment compare a great epic with a great dramatic narrative.   Odysseus relates his wanderings to the Phaeacians one night after dinner. The night is long, we are all comfortable ; as we listen, we identify ourselves with the Phaeacians ; we do not keep half an eye cocked on them to see how they are taking it.   But in Sophocles' *Electra,* when the Messenger reels off his false tale to Electra and Clytemnestra, we do watch the audience ; we are as much interested in them as in the story.   So in the *Persae* ; the narrative would not be fully dramatic if we felt that the stage-audience was passive—a mere excuse for having the story told to us.   Aeschylus has not been unmindful of this.   In the first place, it helps that the chorus and the Queen have already expressed uneasiness ; this wins for them our sympathy, so that we are the more ready to see things through their eyes.   Then, he is careful not to allow the Messenger to tell his tale off his own bat ; the Queen, by her questions, spoken and unspoken, directs affairs, so that our attention is continually directed to the stage-audience—exactly the point in which epic and dramatic narrative differ.

Making all necessary allowance for the last scene, largely inaccessible to us, the *Persae* is not one of Aeschylus' best plays.   Wilamowitz was troubled by its lack of continuity, finding it a short trilogy rather than a play, since the action must be assumed to take place at three successive places, the council-chamber, the tomb of Darius, and the palace.   It is safe to say that this matter of *Lokal* was not of the smallest concern either to Aeschylus or to his audience, nor could it be until drama became much more realistic than it was in 472 B.C.   Aeschylus never describes the scene, and it is fairly certain that the Athenian theatre did not have, at this time, any back-stage building that would anchor the action to one spot. And as for continuity of action, this is less important than continuity of theme, which the play undoubtedly does possess.

The weakness of the play is not a lack of continuity but the lack of a clear focal point in the action. There is a unifying theme, but there is neither a strong central character whose mind or will animates the whole, nor is there a predominating character whose existence serves as a constant point of reference—like Hecuba, for example. The subject was not an easy one. A strong character pressing forward to a fatal decision is a good dramatic situation, but Xerxes is not conceived as a strong character [1]; and there is no decision to press towards, only results. But even as a not very heroic character Xerxes might have been useful in holding the action together had Aeschylus been able to keep him on the stage throughout, constantly before our eyes, the guilty author of all these disasters, the centre and focus of the action. But Xerxes was in Greece.

Is not the chorus this centre that we are seeking? Is not the tragedy that of Persia, and the Chorus Persia? Such is the natural view, but the chorus seems not quite to live up to this part. It has shrunk considerably in importance since the days of the *Supplices*. Traces of its ancient supremacy do indeed remain; it opens the play, the Messenger and Darius both speak to them first and not to the adjacent Queen; it evokes the shade of Darius and takes up the discussion with him when the question of the future of Persia arises.[2] But for all this prominence we hardly feel that it dominates the play as it should if the downfall of Persia is the central theme. The coming of the second actor has radically altered things. Atossa is not the tragic heroine, but she is an interesting character, and the interest that we feel in her is taken from the chorus. The chorus, instead of soaring above her in lyric measures, meets her on the common ground of trochaics, and

---

[1] Aeschylus does his duty to Xerxes by calling him *thurios*, or 'impetuous' but we do not really believe it, least of all when we see him.

[2] Sheppard, *Greek Tragedy*, p. 51.

it is the Queen who wins, as the individual is bound to win in such a contest. She has a definite and interesting character as the Mother, political enough to understand what her son has done, woman enough to sympathize with the bereaved, sensible enough to ask the right questions of the Messenger, prudent enough to think of invoking the aid of Darius' ghost, mother enough to find excuses for her son's folly. She leaves upon us the impression of a wise and gracious woman, and such an impression must encroach upon the ancient prerogatives of the Chorus. The Nobles are pale in comparison, and half of their task of conveying to us the tragedy of Persia they have had to surrender to the Queen. Chorus and Queen stand on equal terms and on the same ground (though the chorus is political and the Queen personal), and there is no one centre.

But the Queen is prominent obviously because Aeschylus wishes to show two aspects of Xerxes' hybris, the purely political, and one more personal. The play in fact is not the tragedy of Persia's downfall, but the tragedy of Xerxes' sin ; the chorus fails to be the undisputed centre of the action because it is not the centre of Aeschylus' thought. A tragedy of Persia could have ended with Darius' prophecies and a choral ode, and could have dispensed with Atossa. We may then indeed say that the extension of dramatic interest which the second actor brought with him has destroyed the balance of the older drama, and that the *Persae* does not attain to a new balance, but we may not think of this as a dramatic problem which Aeschylus has not yet solved. He did not think in terms of plays, but in tragic ideas, and the *Persae* is not the last of his dramas in which the idea puts the form to a considerable strain.

3. THE SEPTEM   One-third of the fifth century had passed when Sophocles won his first victory, and in the following year, 467, Aeschylus showed what Old Tragedy could do by producing the *Septem*. When two-thirds of the century had passed and new things were again in the air, Sophocles turned to this Theban legend and crowned Middle Tragedy by producing the *Tyrannus*. Each play marks an epoch, and marks

it emphatically and worthily. The *Tyrannus* displays the virtues peculiar to Middle Tragedy with a completeness and a finality that show that something new must soon be attempted or tragedy decay ; and the *Septem* is as perfect an example of Old Tragedy. It has that complete balance of form and content which is the chief glory of the *Tyrannus*, and in our lamentably small inheritance from Old Tragedy it is the only play which places first actor, second actor and chorus in that relation which seems to have been predestined. The *Prometheus*, though it is vaster in conception and has been much more important in the world's education, lacks the beauty and the poise of the *Septem*, and the *Oresteia* is, in our definition, not Old Tragedy. It is a tribute to the Theban story, and one which the formal sense of the Greeks would have approved, that not only these two climacteric plays, the *Septem* and the *Tyrannus*, but also that last and most strangely beautiful of Greek dramas the *Coloneus* turned to it for inspiration.

We saw, or inferred, that the lyrical tragedy of the single actor was peculiarly fitted to convey one kind of tragic situation, that in which the hero, irrespective of his character, irrespective of what he may do, is engulfed as Pelasgus was engulfed. Such a drama cannot and need not move, but nothing is more foolish than to assume that on this account it is undramatic. The drama lies in the lyrical plane, and consists of an increasing tension. The second actor enables the plot to move, and now the true dramatic thrill will arise out of this movement. Instead of watching a Pelasgus caught inextricably, we shall watch the reaction between the moving situation and the hero ; and, since a tragic issue depends on this, that the hero shall not be such as to accommodate himself harmlessly to this movement, the hero will have to be characterized. Pelasgus is lost whatever kind of man he is ; Eteocles, though in peril, is not lost if he is sensible enough to listen to the chorus. The greatness of the *Septem* lies in this, that it so perfectly realizes the peculiar virtue of Old Tragedy, to be the tragedy of character, and of a single character ; that it relates this character closely and significantly to every movement in the situation ; and that it achieves the perfect balance between the actors and the chorus. This last we

could not say of the *Persae*, nor shall we be able to say it of
the *Prometheus* ; we shall, however, say something very similar of the *Tyrannus*.

Of the first two plays of the trilogy we know practically
nothing, but at least the outline of the story is well established.   As subject for his third play Aeschylus had the ac-
complishment of the curse laid upon his sons by Oedipus ; as
material, the Argive expedition to Thebes and the death of
the brothers in single combat.   With these, the only necessary, data it is clear that Aeschylus had a free hand in arranging his plot, and no formidable task in finding enough action
to fill a play.   It is interesting to see what he chose, and more
interesting to see what he rejected ; for the plot which he
made is not inferior in tragic effect to the renowned plot of
the *Tyrannus,* and is as perfectly suited to the genius of Old
Tragedy as that to Middle.   The difference is characteristic ;
Sophocles' plot is wonderful through what it can bring in,
Aeschylus' through what it can leave out.

The remarkable omission is Polyneices.   The play is all
Eteocles.   It is perhaps not surprising that Polyneices does
not appear in person—this might have been difficult to arrange
plausibly ; what is surprising is that nothing is made of the
quarrel and its effect on Eteocles' mind, that there is no par-
leying between the two, no defiance, no mention even of
Polyneices before the fatal moment.   One cannot imagine
any later dramatist taking this theme and leaving out the
central situation ; it is *Hamlet* without the Prince.

The reason for this is not that Aeschylus had some idea of
keeping back Polyneices' name for the sake of dramatic effect.
He has in fact based his plot on such a silence, but the complete concentration on the one brother is anterior to this.
Aeschylus was not interested in both brothers, only in one.
His mind and dramatic imagination were absorbed in the
questions of Man's relation to God, fate, the Universe, not in
his relation to Man.   Sophocles, it is safe to assert, would
have made of this situation a study in the fatal play of the one
brother's character on the other's ; Aeschylus sees in it the
question of one man and his destiny.   The second brother is
the dramatic but not the moral point of the play.   A scene

between Eteocles and Poylneices therefore was exactly what Aeschylus did not want ; it would have implied an interaction of characters which was not his dramatic preoccupation—if it had been, he and not Sophocles would have introduced the third actor ; and the day when scenes like this were engineered for the sake of their own excitement was still far distant. In the *Septem* we have again the hero alone with his fate.

His isolation is magnificently complete. The second actor is a colourless person, or persons, since it is a matter of perfect indifference whether the Spy and the Messenger are the same man or not. They are mere instruments in the plot. The chorus too is reduced in stature ; no longer the centre of the action, for Eteocles is that ; less sharply characterized than the Suppliants. To this chorus a single broad characteristic, Fear, is attributed—an emotion natural to a group—and this is put to important use in the plot ; but for the greater part of the play the chorus is pure Chorus, not a personal agent like the Suppliants. But although Eteocles, the actor, opens this play and leaves us in no doubt who the Protagonist is this time, the chorus is still so integral a part of the structure that artistically it shapes the whole drama.

Aeschylus then chooses one brother, and invents a situation —a particularly fine one—in which all the interest is concentrated upon him. But this is only the beginning. The plot has to be made to move, and the poet has to decide how destiny is to overtake its victim. If by pure fluke—then the ancient nonsense [1] about Fate in Greek Tragedy would all be true and there would be no tragedy ; if by his deliberately seeking out Polyneices in the open field, we might have an edifying display of wickedness, but again no tragedy, only melodrama. Dramatically it will be best if we can be shown the destined fratricide passing from an apparent improbability to a dreadful probability ; morally, if we can see that, Eteocles being what he is, no other outcome was possible ; that the inherited doom is but the projection of inherited situation and

[1] And not all of it ancient. Willems (*Melpomène*, pp. 43, 91, 93) can speak of Aeschylus' characters as ' jouets ', ' assujettis aux caprices des dieux '.

inherited character. If the plot of the *Septem* merits comparison with that of the *Tyrannus,* it will be because Aeschylus has succeeded in giving it this shape by simple and natural means, and by the use of the conventions proper to Old Tragedy. He has done this, with the minimum of means and the maximum of effect.

The opening scene is splendid in setting, poetry, and characterization. Eteocles' strength is measured against the sombre background, the imminent peril in which the city stands, and we are made to feel at once that he is assuredly a man worthy to meet the crisis. Calmly and prudently he makes his dispositions ; he is completely in command. But suddenly (v. 70), when we hear his invocation of ' a father's avenging curse ', we realize that the threatened city is no more than a background for the working-out of Eteocles' own doom. Certainly the public danger shows us what desperate men the brothers are, or Polyneices at least, but unless we are to see them only in the light of public dangers suppressed, the working-out of the doom must rise in the dramatic scale above even the threat to Thebes. Aeschylus is a confident dramatist.

In this scene there is no suggestion that the brothers are to meet that day in personal combat.[1] Eteocles is King, and as King he makes his dispositions for the city's defence, which, as the Messenger tells him, involves posting at the seven gates ' the chosen champions, the bravest of the city '. Polyneices too is the leader of an army. His name is carefully kept back, and we are not encouraged to think that the two leaders will engage. We do know what the outcome must be ; but to Eteocles, and to us if we analyse the actual situation, the possibility seems remote that this day will see the fulfilment of the curse.

But the chorus alters things. In striking contrast to the manly dignity of the opening scene there comes pouring in

[1] My debt to Verrall here will be obvious. I have never seen an answer to Bayfield's question (*C.R.,* 1904, pp. 160 f.), what can be the point of vv. 653 ff. if Eteocles has suspected that Polyneices would himself be one of the Argive Seven ?

pell-mell [1] a chorus of young women, frightened to death by the enemy without, appealing wildly to the Gods within. Against this turbulent background Eteocles stands firm. Again we are given the measure of the man—but there is more than this in the incident. So dangerous an element are the women in the besieged city that to reassure them Eteocles says that he will himself stand at one of the gates. The alteration in the natural and foreshadowed plan is made almost casually, a mere by-product, apparently, of the turbulence of the women. The chorus, we think, has already justified its existence by providing so admirable a background ; now we see something more than simple decoration in it. The improbability that the brothers will meet has become sensibly less, and that through no fault in Eteocles.[2] He has no reason to suppose that Polyneices too will fight in person ; he acts out of sheer prudence—but we know, and his unconsciousness is terrible.

Having at last coerced the chorus into decent order, Eteocles goes about his business, leaving the chorus to sing its vivid ode on the terrors that fall upon a city captured— terrors which Polyneices is prepared to inflict on his own city.

Now comes the long and crucial scene. The Spy tells the King what he has discovered. Seven champions have been chosen from the Argive host to assail the gates. Each, at each gate, is described—his character, his appearance, and the device and motto on his shield. Against each Eteocles appoints the appropriate defender, and the chorus each time sings a short stanza. If we are content to accept anything from Aeschylus provided that it is good poetry and good morality, waiting for our dramatic thrills until tragedy shall have grown up, we may find the scene long, formal and dull. Formal it is, as Pelasgus' colloquy with the chorus was formal,

---

[1] And with the excited dochmiac rhythm, not the marching-anapest which was usual. Aeschylus forgot for the moment how statuesque Greek Tragedy is.

[2] Kranz (*Stasimon*, p. 172) points out that this Chorus gradually loses character, becoming plain representatives of the city and calling Eteocles ' my son ' (686). This is what we should expect : the Chorus is vividly characterized *only while it is to affect the action* : date is irrelevant. (See p. 84.)

and for the same reason, that the chorus is still a controlling element in the play, not a background for the actors ; for the reason too that this formality is the perfect accompaniment to the volcanic fire that smoulders underneath the surface. This elaborate parade of heraldry, this antiphony of vices and virtues, are an ironical and ceremonial procession, leading Eteocles to his death.

There are seven gates, and we can guess, though Eteocles has no suspicion, that Polyneices is to take the seventh. Eteocles therefore has six chances of safety—but the whole point of the scene is that Aeschylus does not leave it to chance. He makes Eteocles not merely a prudent commander but also a man of acute moral perceptions, and ruins him this way. Against each attacker, who is prefigured equally in his physique, his device, his motto, his language, he appoints not merely an adequate fighter, but the man best fitted by his moral character to meet that particular assailant. Each time it is impossible for Eteocles to say, ' I am the man to withstand this form of wickedness '. He does not meet his natural opponent until he comes to the seventh gate.

At the first Tydeus blasphemously rages. ' Whom ', asks the Spy, ' do you oppose to him ? ' It is not, I think, without design that Aeschylus makes the answer begin : ' No man's array could daunt me. ' It sounds as if Eteocles is going to take the first gate. For ten verses we are kept in suspense ; then we hear the pronoun again : ' I, against Tydeus, will set the good son of Astacus '—and we see that it was impossible. Five chances remain, and Eteocles does not know that Polyneices is fighting.

Capaneus is worse than Tydeus. ' Who will await without flinching this man and his boasts ? ' Eteocles continues his unconscious minuet with Death ; again it is inevitable that he should think of another than himself. Four chances.

The third gate ; Eteoclus. Surely the King will accept an omen ? Eteocles against Eteoclus ? No ; Megareus, ' by a happy chance ', has been sent already—a fine stroke. At the fourth gate stands Hippomedon, another Capaneus ; and the opponent marked by nature for him is Hyperbius. This time the King does accept an omen ; Zeus on the one shield will overcome once more Typhoeus on the other. Next, the romantic figure of Parthenopaeus, whose match in character and therefore in battle too must be 'a man who boasts not'. The choice, to Eteocles, is once more obvious ; Actor is sent, and one chance of safety is left.

But alas ! At the sixth gate stands the nobly tragic figure of Amphiaraus, ' the seer, most virtuous of men and bravest in the fight', doomed himself not to return home and, by standing at this gate, doomed to cause the fulfilment of another's curse, the curse of Oedipus upon his sons ; for now more than ever it is impossible for Eteocles to think of himself. We all knew, of course, that Amphiaraus belonged to the story. He was bound to come in, and as a tragic figure, but we did not know it would be like this. It is a searing flash of tragic irony, hardly to be paralleled in Aeschylus, not approached elsewhere. This last chance, seeing that the opponent was Amphiaraus, never existed ; it remains only for Eteocles to hear who is his own opponent, to hear of the insensate rage which animates Polyneices and challenges his own.

Of the power with which this scene is brought to a close there is no need to speak. We are given, in a sudden revelation, the other side of Eteocles, his hatred of his brother, his inability and his unwillingness to control his mad and fatalistic leap upon his doom.[1] This is the consummation of the rigid control which has been exercised so long.

Throughout this scene the chorus is active, singing and dancing a stanza after each pair of speeches, and keeping to the one theme, the danger that hangs over Thebes. It is because the chorus is interwoven with the dialogue in this

[1] I can see no sign here, or anywhere else in the play, that Eteocles is devoting himself to death in order to save Thebes and Pohlenz' theory of Greek Tragedy. It is a dramatic idea that he should do this, but not, I think, Aeschylus'. This aspect of the curse, that any offspring of Laius would destroy Thebes, is kept very much in the background ; obviously Aeschylus cannot allow us to feel that if Eteocles is sensible enough to listen to the chorus Thebes is lost. Accordingly it is not mentioned until *after* the fatal choice is made (vv. 745 ff.). Méautis also (*Eschyle*, 105 ff.) makes an interesting Eteocles, but one who depends too much on the *ge* ('at least') of v. 71 and on inferences which are possible but not necessary.

way that the speeches have so antiphonic a ring ; brisk dialogue between these formal lyric utterances would be impossible. The whole is architectural in conception, a perfect balance : the plastic chorus trembling for the city, the hero, who can see so clearly and be so blind, advancing slowly upon his fate, the almost automatic Spy supplying the facts. The second actor, being only an instrument, cannot diminish the stature of the hero ; the only personal force allowed to enter, beside the hero's, is that of the chorus, and this, being the communal emotion of fear, does not compete with the hero's personality, but sets it in a frame which isolates it and makes it the more impressive.

In the ode that follows the interest widens somewhat ; we are approaching the end of the trilogy. Forgetting for the moment their own peril the chorus thinks only of the ruin of the royal house. The image of the Chalybian Stranger appears, a characteristic piece of Aeschylean imagery, this time entirely at the service of its inventor ; a strained note wonderfully expressive of strained minds. The ode rolls on in sombre magnificence, touching only for a moment the common peril, and comes to rest on the Curse, as the Messenger comes in with his news of victory sounding strangely remote.

The actors have now had their say ; we are in a region where only the chorus can live. Middle Tragedy would have ended this story with a soberly eloquent messenger-speech describing the end of the two brothers, and a brief lament from the chorus. Rightly so, for such descriptions of the actual event are the logical conclusion of its more realistic treatment. Old Tragedy omits the details, for these do not belong to its more lyrical tone. Passing judgment is a foolish pastime ; it is enough to say that this end also is logical and beautiful.[1] This last scene too is a warning that we should not be too ready to explain the last scene of the *Persae* by citing the absence of the music and dance. They are missing here too, but the nobility of the funeral hymn is none the less apparent. It is a long hymn, for it has to bear the weight of the whole trilogy, and it is carefully worked, illuminated by

[1] The scene between the Herald and Antigone which appears in our text is spurious.

an imaginative symbolism which sounds nearly non-Greek—the Pontic Stranger. We met him in the previous ode (v. 727). The Messenger corroborates, as it were, with his *Skythe sidero* (Scythian iron) (817) ; and through the simple *syn sidaro* (with iron) of v. 883 and the double *sidaroplacti* (struck by iron) of vv. 912–13, we come to the full personification, in v. 941 ff.

' Cruel resolver of strife, the Pontic stranger that leaps out of fire, the whetted sword.' [1]

The imagery is felt so vividly that the Stranger becomes almost a supernatural actor whom only the chorus can see. This ode is no stop-gap, no mere libretto, but a dramatic lyric composition thought out and felt as intensely as anything in the play, bringing the trilogy to a close on the verge of a new dimension.

We can now see the answer to some of the questions that the second actor raised. He does not in any way encroach upon the loneliness of the hero ; Eteocles is as solitary as Pelasgus. The second actor was not intended to be a foil or complement to the first ; simply to supply him with the facts to which he has somehow to accommodate himself. There is no interplay between the two. The Spy brings certain forces to bear upon Eteocles and Eteocles absorbs them all ; we do not look back to see what effect he in his turn has on the Spy, as we look back when any two Sophoclean characters come into contact. Nor is the function of the chorus very different. The chorus has indeed personality, but this is used only as one single ' moment ' in the situation. Once its panic has caused Eteocles to take his first fatal step, its personal influence is exhausted and it becomes pure Chorus. There is no real interplay of personality, and we are as far as ever from the Sophoclean cross-scene.

What the second actor does is to make the situation grow. Instead of the static situation of the *Supplices* which grows only in intensity, we have one that moves, thanks to the fresh information that the Spy can bring in.[2] This has the im-

[1] Cf. the adverb *kalos*, ' well ', in the *Electra* (p. 174), and the name Cithaeron in the *Tyrannus* (p. 175).

[2] It is one mark of the superiority of the *Septem* over the *Persae* that insofar as Eteocles is affected by anything personal, it

portant consequence that the hero has to be characterized.   It
did not matter much what sort of man Pelasgus was ; it matters vitally what Eteocles is.   If he is not the man that he is—
the bold but prudent commander, a man of profound moral
insight but combining this with the fatal recklessness that
carries him over the brink—then nothing happens.   The *Septem* is our earliest tragedy of character, Eteocles the first Man
of the European stage.

We see Eteocles in the round, not as an outline like Pelasgus
nor as a flat character like Xerxes ; but we must beware of
treating Aeschylus' characterization as a matter of chronology.
Aeschylus does not, in these essentials, ' improve,' nor is
Sophocles' characterization an ' improvement ' on his.   It is
different because the tragic idea is different.   Agamemnon is
conspicuously less in the round than Eteocles because his
tragedy is differently conceived ; and why are we told that
Oedipus is impatient with his subordinates, Creon a bully to
his, while Eteocles has simply no attitude at all to his Spy?
Not because Aeschylus is still learning the art of dramatic
characterization and is as yet unconscious that these are good
dramatic effects.   He refrains from dramatizing Eteocles'
bearing towards the Spy just as he refuses to tell us how he
behaves to his wife, or whether he has one ; because it has
no significance to Eteocles' tragedy.   The impatience of Oedipus, the harshness of Creon, are significant ; that is why the
traits are there.   The Greeks left it to the modern masters of
characterization to exhaust the possibilities of the insignificant.

That is to say, the characterization is as highly conventionalized as the style, the diction, and the plot—for it is highly
conventional that the attack and defence of Thebes should be
morally idealized like this.   The use of convention must be
thorough, or disharmony will follow.   The stiff structure of
the play, the disregard of naturalism, the restricted use of
characterization, are not the quaint archaisms of a drama
which has not yet grown up, but conventions deliberately

---

is by the chorus.   The chorus affects him by being something, the
other actor only by saying something.   The personality of the
chorus, being communal and kept in the orchestra, will obscure
that of the hero less than a personality beside him on the stage.

sought to keep at bay the intrusion of a naturalism that would destroy the illusion.

The severe lines of the play are, however, relieved in one notable respect. The plot offers no turns, twists and palpitations, but is simply one terrific crescendo ; yet a striking relief is obtained by the manipulation of the chorus. To this are allotted two main themes, the danger to the city and the danger to Eteocles. At first the former predominates ; when Eteocles has quelled the chorus into submission and begins to reject his chances one by one, it is still—naturally—the common danger that fills the mind of the chorus. Eteocles draws visibly nearer to disaster, but still Aeschylus keeps back with his chorus, ' timing ' his stroke, until at the last moment, when Eteocles rushes out, the danger to the city is forgotten and the chorus throws all its weight into the theme of the fall of Laius' house. Thus we watch the dramatic movement through two mediums, in the action and in the minds of the chorus ; and the chorus, being woven into the very fabric of the drama in this way, plays a more important part than it does in the *Persae*, even though it has had to give up to the actor the privilege of opening the play. The technical history of Greek Tragedy is largely an account of the efforts to make the Chorus an integral part of a continually changing system. Several times the balance was lost and found. It is achieved here, and the tremendous power of the play is the result. It is perfectly shaped, the theme is exactly realized in the form, the plot is sheer genius, and the characterization and poetry are as fine as anything Aeschylus ever did. ' Nothing but well and fair.'

4. THE PROMETHEUS VINCTUS The *Prometheus*, whatever its date,[1] belongs to the type of drama that we are calling Old

[1] As to the date, the judicious remarks in Sikes and Willson's edition (Introd., pp. 35 ff.) still seem to me to give what can profitably be said, that it lies between the *Septem* (467) and the *Oresteia* (458) ; though the almost apocalyptic theme might incline one to put it nearer the *Oresteia* than the *Septem*. Professor G. Thomson (in the introduction to his edition) argues for a date later than the *Oresteia*, and I would not deny the possibility, but his analysis of the doctrine of *pathos mathos* (learn by suffering)

Tragedy. Although in the prologue it uses three actors,[1] and that to some purpose, for the rest of the play the whole interest is centred on the hero and his fate, everything being subordinated to him as rigidly as in the *Septem*. We look always from the minor persons to the hero, never back again, except perhaps to a very slight degree with Oceanus ; certainly we have no juxtaposition of characters in the least like that of Agamemnon with Clytemnestra.[2] Indeed, as if to assert in their extremest form the rights of the older drama, Aeschylus gives us a hero who literally cannot move, and a plot that can be regarded as a reaction from that of the *Septem*. The new and busy drama that was coming into fashion is put firmly in its place. In the prologue Prometheus is enchained by Hephaestus, under the direction of the personified abstractions Might and Force, and from this point to the arrival of Hermes the situation remains unchanged. The chorus of Oceanids comes to sympathize, and Oceanus to urge submission ; Io passes by in her flight and provokes fresh indignation against the common persecutor ; but, in the crude sense, nothing ' happens ' until Hermes orders Prometheus to reveal his secret and Prometheus is thrust down to Tartarus for his disobedience. In the real sense we have two related dramatic movements during these scenes. The cruelty of

---

is, to me, unconvincing, and in any case too uncertain a thing to be made a basis for precise chronology ; and his stylostatistics at most only prove that the play is a late one. And let us not forget that what stylostatistics prove is not date but style—until it is further proved that the poet's style did change chronologically. Euripides' did, but not Sophocles'—not at least without very large reservations—and I should hesitate to make so simple an assumption of so bold a dramatist as Aeschylus. (On Aeschylus' style Pohlenz puts a pertinent question to those unhappy men who believe that Aeschylus did not write this play : Why *should* Prometheus talk like Cassandra ?)

[1] On the idea that in the prologue Prometheus was represented by a lay-figure and that therefore there were only two actors, Croiset is good : ' Il n'est pas donné à tout le monde de croire à ce mannequin ' (*Hist. Litt. Gr.*, III, 188, note).

[2] It is this that makes me reluctant to accept Professor Thomson's date, for the *Prometheus* seems definitely to close an epoch ; but I am far from supposing that such epochs do not overlap.

Zeus and Prometheus' determination to resist to the end are more and more clearly revealed ; and a powerful dramatic movement is drawn from the gradual disclosure of the secret which is Prometheus' weapon against Zeus.

Aeschylus was committed here to the task of turning a long series of events into drama almost without the help of action. He has to outline the relations between Zeus and Prometheus from the beginning—how Prometheus deserted the Titans and helped Zeus to victory because the Titans were too unintelligent, Zeus not, to make use of his stratagems (207 ff.) ; how he saved the human race from Zeus (231 ff.) ; how, doing this from sheer pity of man, he went further and taught man all the arts of life. The rage of Zeus, the punishment of Prometheus, his continued defiance and his long-distant hope complete this part of the story, and form the only part which can be represented on the stage. Aeschylus in fact dramatizes the emotions and not the events.

In this, there is not much obviously dramatic material. The enchainment, clearly, will make a scene, but a state of continued defiance is not the most apparent source of dramatic action. There were certain other difficulties. The dealings of omnipotent gods one with another are not easily made dramatic ; what really happens when the irresistible meets the immovable ? Homer, undoubtedly, made his gods not very godlike partly because this was the only way of using them as dramatic agents ; Aeschylus takes over the primitive conceptions, some of them, that underlay his myth, in particular the shadowy conception of a Necessity stronger even than the gods. In this we need see no more than a dramatic convenience. Aeschylus is not propounding a theological idea, but making a contest between the two gods possible ; for if nothing is superior to Zeus, Prometheus can have no hold on him. Other difficulties are simply ignored, as for example how it was that Prometheus was able to save the human race in defiance of Zeus. The two are treated vaguely as co-ordinate powers, Zeus certainly the stronger but not omnipotent.[1]

---

[1] Méautis (*Eschyle*, pp. 78) discusses this point very sensibly, and Bogner (*Philologus*, 1932, 470) points out that in spite of

The powers of Zeus being in this way limited, his adversary's continued defiance becomes dramatically significant ; but it cannot be drama except in the spirit of lyrical drama, whose essence is not movement and action but dramatic emotion and intensification. The real dramatic movement here is one which takes place in the mind of the immovable Prometheus, and Aeschylus' presentation of this is one of the greatest achievements of the Greek stage.

Aeschylus begins this apotheosis of Old Tragedy by boldly grafting on to it Sophocles' invention of the Third Actor. On Aeschylus' use of this we shall have more to say when we come to the *Agamemnon*. It has been said that he used three actors together only on the condition that all three should not speak at once, but such timidity is not in the least like Aeschylus. He rarely wanted three actors to be speaking together because his tragic conceptions did not run in this direction. Here at least the case is perfectly clear. The third actor enabled Aeschylus to represent the crucifixion scene in progress without sacrificing the great dramatic effect of Prometheus' disdainful silence ; his mind is fixed on Zeus, and he will not condescend to speak to his minions. But if Prometheus will not speak, someone else must, and a monologue from the crucifier would be less interesting and valuable than the dialogue that can now be arranged. Aeschylus might indeed have produced his chorus at once, but this would have used up too quickly the dramatic movement available, and would have sacrificed another dramatic effect, the utter solitude of the spot. The third actor solves all these difficulties. Cratos (with Bia as a supernumerary) directs Hephaestus, and Prometheus remains silent. One, two, or three persecutors—it is all the same to him. Further, now that two agents are present, it is more dramatic and interesting if they are characterized differently, and this obvious point is turned to a good use : Cratos is quite inhuman, Hephaestus reluctant, and sympathetic towards his fellow-god. Moreover the contrast, interesting in itself, gives us a powerful sense of Prometheus' stature that he so superbly ignores it,

Homer the gods are not ' fixed ' ; Zeus could be made subject to *Moira*, or destiny.

and it contains a strong criticism of Zeus. Hephaestus is a 'hostile witness' in that he belongs to the side whose privileges Prometheus has infringed; fire in particular, 'thy flower' as Cratos reminds him, he has stolen and given to man. Yet Hephaestus shows the greatest repugnance to his task. He admits that Prometheus has acted wrongly, but the punishment is of a savagery which only the newness of Zeus' sovereignty can explain. However, neither the accusation nor the sympathy draws a single word from Prometheus.

When they are gone Prometheus, we may suppose, remains silent for some time. The prologue is over and the play begins, a play of one static situation whose whole movement is an inner one, beginning with the almost interstellar silence of this remote spot [1] and ending with the thunder of splitting mountains. It is built on a series of impacts—the chorus, Oceanus, Io, Hermes, upon Prometheus—but impacts that produce light and heat rather than movement. Prometheus is shown in a series of carefully arranged relations; first alone, then with the chorus of Oceanids, then with Oceanus, then with Io. The choice of these and the order of their appearance is not arbitrary, but it is by no means inevitable; we cannot say that they come by Aristotle's law of inevitable or probable sequence. It would be possible and just as natural for Io to appear before Oceanus—but this does not involve Aristotle's censure of plays in which scenes could be transposed without making any difference. Aristotle's rule is not valid here. There is a law, but it is one of increasing tension, not of 'natural' or logical sequence. To transpose Oceanus and Io would outrage no logic—except the logic which makes Prelude precede Fugue and Scherzo follow Andante. Oceanus and Io are not there to assist in the presentation of a logical series of events, for as we have seen Aeschylus is dramatizing a state and not events; they come simply to develop the inner drama, Prometheus' defiance of Zeus.

After the crucifixion Prometheus is seen alone, uttering his indignation to earth and sky.[2] The purpose of the scene is

---

[1] The loneliness and silence are both mentioned by Hephaestus in his first speech.

[2] Schmidt-Stählin (I, 2, p. 73, note 5) state, as part of the argu-

fairly clear. It still postpones the entrance of the chorus,
which is an effect not to be used up too soon, and it brings
home to us that silence and remoteness of which Hephaestus
spoke, a powerful dramatic effect (and an essential part of
the punishment) which is not to be frittered away. The
benefactor of mankind has no one to whom he can turn but
inanimate nature. But in this short passage there is more
than dramatic economy and pathos : the solitude gives a wider
amplitude to the rhythm of the piece. As Sophocles shows
us Electra alone before he subjects her to the dramatic forces
which make his play, working as it were from the lowest possible pitch to the highest, so Aeschylus prolongs this solitude
as much as he can : it is the best possible contrast to the terrific
catastrophe in which the play is to end.

The next step is to introduce the chorus, a band of half-
imagined sea-maidens ; a splendid contrast to Prometheus, the
rock chained to a rock. These gentle interlocutors allow
Prometheus, in Aeschylus' good time, to relate his services
both to Zeus and to mankind ; but besides this obvious purpose they have another, by their sympathy to draw from
Prometheus more and more of his indignation with Zeus, to
lead up to his first allusion to the secret (189 ff.),[1] and to
reinforce the picture already suggested of the cruelty of the
new tyrant. The character of this chorus is determined
largely by the needs of the dramatic rhythm. The climax

---

ment that the *P.V.* is spurious, that Aeschylus does not know the
monody : ' Aischylos kennt diese Form nicht.' What this means,
I cannot imagine. If it means that we know for a fact that he
never wrote one, it is not true and is a *petitio principii.* If the
implication is that in a dramatic situation like this Aeschylus would
not have had the wit or the courage (if courage was wanted) to
use a monody, it is worthless. If it means that Aeschylus would
never have allowed himself to get into such a situation, it overrates
Aeschylus' dramatic caution. The monody does not appear in
Sophocles until the comparatively late *Electra* not because Sophocles did not ' know it ' until then, but because until then he had no
use for it. The reasons for the monody in the *Electra* are perfectly
plain if one looks for them, and are very similar to the reasons for
the monody here.

[1] Hephaestus has given the first hint (v. 27) ; ' Thy deliverer is
not yet born.'

in the disclosure of Zeus' cruel ways and in the resistance to him is being reserved for Io; the chorus therefore must be comparatively gentle.

As for the series of speeches which Prometheus makes to the chorus, we must observe what they are ; in the actual performance the point would be clear enough. Aeschylus is not simply explaining the situation for us, how it has arisen. What Prometheus has done for Zeus, what he has done for Man, are not only things which have led to the present situation ; they *are* the present situation, part of Prometheus' present mind—for the essential drama is precisely his present mind. Milton does the same for Samson (the *Agonistes* is pure Old Tragedy) in those opening speeches in which Samson compares what he is with what he was ; speeches which make one wonder how any critic has ever had the audacity to call Milton ' undramatic '.[1]

In order to bring a new force to bear on Prometheus and to deepen our sense of his hostility to Zeus—and incidentally to break this sequence of speeches—Aeschylus introduces Oceanus ; a friendly, politically-minded person who can give advice and offer mediation as the chorus cannot. Prometheus' reply is to urge him not to concern himself in what may bring him to ruin ; Zeus is implacable and invincible. The punishment of Atlas is described, and the might and punishment of Typhoeus, with an elaboration which might superficially seem undramatic, inasmuch as it keeps Oceanus waiting. But in this timeless play, which is not concerned with a series of events, waiting does not matter ; the description is dramatic, not decorative, because it springs directly (even the description of Etna) from the dramatic theme of the play, Prometheus' thoughts about Zeus. The sole purpose of the Oceanus-scene is to give us the measure of Zeus' power and of Prometheus' defiance of it.

When Oceanus has been firmly dismissed the chorus develops the theme by singing explicitly of Zeus' tyranny, and, ranging over the whole world, it represents all nations as

[1] Whether in the *Agonistes* or in *Paradise Lost*. Where *Paradise Lost* is undramatic it is so because Milton, unlike Aeschylus, could not set any limit to the power of his God.

mourning Prometheus' fate. This wide gathering of peoples
goes with the geographical speeches delivered to Io ; it goes
too, in feeling, with the account that follows it of Prometheus'
services to Man. Here too Milton is Aeschylean. When
Michael and Adam 'Both ascend In the visions of God', and
from the summit of Paradise survey the extent of the world
and the future course of Man,[1] Milton is (at first) very close
in spirit to Aeschylus as he surveys the extent of the world
and the past course of Man—even if, later, we may begin to
feel that in Aeschylus it was the hero, in *Paradise Lost* the
poet, who was in chains.

The silence which Prometheus maintains at the end of the
ode and the despair into which he falls at the end of his next
speech are powerful moments in the dramatic rhythm of the
whole. Here, in the middle of the play, as he contemplates
what he has done for man, he is at his lowest ebb—a contrast
with his determined rejection of Oceanus' offers of help, a
greater contrast with what is to follow Io's appearance.[2] The
scene ends with Prometheus' second allusion to the secret ;
Zeus too is subject to Necessity—but what Necessity has in
store for him it needs a more powerful personality than that
of the chorus to wring from Prometheus.

When the chorus has suggested to Prometheus that he has
honoured Man, the helpless weakling, too much and Zeus too
little, this more powerful personality appears. Io, rushing
frantically to and fro pursued by her imaginary gad-fly, is the
complete contrast to the chained Prometheus, but is equally a
victim of Zeus and his ' private law '[3] ; she is almost an im-

---

[1] *P.L.*, XI, 370 ff.

[2] Again a similarity can be seen between this play and the
Electra. (See below, p. 181.) And the two speeches here, the
first dealing with the most primitive of the arts which Prometheus
has taught man, the second with the higher arts of civilization,
must surely have been in Sophocles' mind when he was constructing the second ode of the *Antigone*.

[3] ' Private judgment ' (543) recalls ' ruling by his private law '
(403). Both adversaries are acting ' privately '; a clear suggestion
that some more universal system is to be established at the end.
—Méautis (*Eschyle*, p. 82) makes the point that Io, suffering at
the hands of Zeus, is a sort of parallel to Prometheus, so that her

personation of the God's simple-minded cruelty. Her part is still further to stimulate our indignation with Zeus, and to provoke Prometheus to disclose the secret of Zeus' final over-throw—so bringing on the catastrophe. Io's account of her fearful persecution, though it has little to do with Prometheus, is an essential part of the rhythm of the play ; and the geography, like the details of Etna, lends its weight to our sense of what the victims of Zeus have to suffer, and so carries us on towards the climax.

That is to say, the feeling of the whole scene is essentially lyrical. In spite of the geographical details, the conception and movement of the whole is nearer the drama of music than the drama of the intellect and of prose. Indeed, in presenting it through actors and not a chorus, Aeschylus puts himself into difficulties. To avoid repeating the story of Prometheus' wrongs he has to ride off on the Aeschylean ' This is enough ; I reveal to you no more' (621). The past history of Io (which cannot be spared) is brought in not unnaturally—supposing the Oceanids to be Hellenic—by the simple curiosity of the chorus, and the sequence of speeches is once more care-fully broken, this time by dialogue about the secret (757 ff.) ; but when Prometheus restricts Io to a choice between two speeches and then delivers one to her and the other as a gift to the chorus, we cannot but feel that the material is putting the form to a severe strain (780–5), especially as a few verses later Prometheus contradicts his own unexplained reluctance to talk by giving us an ' extra' for which no one has asked (823 ff.). These rather uncomfortable artifices are not signs of primitiveness or lack of skill. Aeschylus could make plays well enough, if that was all that was wanted, but he was more than a playwright. His material here, whose dramatic quality is imaginative rather than directly intellectual, would perhaps have gone gratefully into a big ode like the opening odes of the *Supplices* or *Agamemnon*, but the dramatic situa-tion did not allow this, Prometheus not being a chorus ; so that a certain artificiality is inevitable. Aeschylus, however, like Plato, would go whithersoever the argument led, and a

---

eventual release is warrant for his—as indeed it is her descendant who will release him.

mere dramatic inconvenience never deterred him (or Euripides or even Sophocles, for that matter) from making tragedy where he saw a tragic idea.

A smaller problem that arose during this play was that of bringing in and sending off the actors who are wanted not to do anything but to be something. Shakespeare, on one incomparable occasion (*The Winter's Tale*, III, 3), gets rid of a character by the simple stage-direction *Exit Antigonus, pursued by a bear* : Aeschylus finds a solution ready to hand and extremely dramatic in the gad-fly. The second victim of Zeus resumes her dreadful flight in circumstances which bring our indignation to its highest pitch.

Is not the succeeding ode a little disappointing ? It is dramatic, in the sense that it is apposite to the situation ; the chorus prays that it may never inspire a god with love but find love in its own station of life—a perfectly natural reflection on the fate of Io ; but it is dramatic in the later manner, accompanying the action, not controlling or transfiguring it. This chorus, as we saw, is necessarily a weaker figure than Io, and as lyrical force it has been superseded by her and cannot build a higher climax upon her exit.

The sufferings of Io, past and to come, have carried the dramatic rhythm to a height that only the catastrophe can crown. The secret, given more and more definition at each stage of the drama, is now blazed forth by Prometheus to an incredulous and terrified chorus. Now it moves even Zeus. He sends his ' lackey ' Hermes to extort the secret with the direst threats. Prometheus refuses, and, still enchained, is thrust down to Tartarus amid deafening convulsions of the firmament—the fulfilment of the unearthly stillness with which the play began. Yet even this majestic climax is, like the enormous church of Beauvais, only a promise ; we are only one-third of the way through the trilogy.

Such is Aeschylus' way of dealing with this part of his myth. The solitary hero is everything ; and not what he does, but what he feels and is. Of action, between the prologue and the catastrophe, there is none. Prometheus' narratives, though they may give the illusion of action, were not designed for this. It is a drama of revelation, not action ; of increasing

tension in a situation which does not move. In spite of the
second and third actor, in spite of the freedom and limpidity
of style that distinguish this play from the rest of Aeschylus,
the *Prometheus* is the last triumphant affirmation, in an extreme form, of the rights of the oldest tragedy.[1]

[1] I have discussed the interpretation of the trilogy in *J.H.S.*, 1934,
pp. 14 ff. In brief, my suggestion was, and is, that Aeschylus
presented a contest between Zeus (= Power, Order) and Prometheus (= Intelligence). Both have to concede something, and
assimilate something, before they are reconciled in the later perfect
cosmic order of Zeus. Such an evolutionary theme explains the
prominence given to the evolution of civilization in our play, and it
accords very well with the evolutionary theme which becomes
prominent in the *Oresteia*. (See below, p. 97.)
    I should like to take this opportunity of thanking Professor
L. A. Post, who has, I think, strengthened my original argument by
citing a passage I had overlooked, Plato, *Ep.*, II, 310e–311b
(*A.J.P.*, LVII, 206–7). Plato, speaking of his relation to Dio-
nysius, remarks that wisdom and great power naturally attract each
other ; and after citing stock examples from history and poetry
(Solon-Croesus, Teiresias-Creon), he adds, ' In my opinion Prometheus and Zeus too were joined in this sort of relation by the ancients.' The passage is interesting, and it is a flattering suggestion
that one may perhaps be right with Plato.
    The myth in the *Protagoras* (320c, ff.) is also worth considering
in this connexion. Practical wisdom, Man had from Prometheus :
' Political wisdom he did not have, for that was in the hands of
Zeus.' Zeus, in Plato's version of the myth, was the source of
social morality and order.

CHAPTER III

THE *ORESTEIA*

1. THE AGAMEMNON ' Oh God ! when will my toil end ? '—
' Lying on the roof ', he goes on, ' like a dog, watching the
nightly company of the stars, season after season, year after
year, waiting for the signal, keeping myself awake with a
song . . .'

This is a powerful beginning, and it is new. The man on
whom is laid the solemn duty of opening the *Oresteia* is nothing but a common soldier, but Aeschylus makes him live.
This man on the roof is no mere instrument, but a character,
the ancestor of Antigone's captor, Launcelot Gobbo, and many
another delightful person. He is incidental as well as humble,
for he appears only in this one scene, and yet he lives. In
comparison with the severity of the *Septem*, this is wild prod-
igality, and the *Prometheus*, whatever its date, can show
nothing like it. Tragedy has entered a new stage. Sophocles, for reasons which we shall examine later, had introduced the third actor perhaps ten years before. Aeschylus
now uses him not incidentally, as he did in the *Prometheus*,
but with full acceptance of its implications ; but in accepting
Sophocles' gift he did not write Sophoclean tragedy. He
used the third actor in his own way for his own purposes, and
our present task is to try to see what these were.[1]

The third actor is of course only a symptom. The obvious
and fundamental difference between the *Agamemnon* and
the earlier plays is that there the whole interest was concentrated on one person : here on two. Polyneices is no longer
a dramatic force off the stage, but appears in person and demands the same kind of treatment as his brother. Xerxes
and Agamemnon are tragic heroes of much the same kind,
but Xerxes meets ruin at the hands of the undifferentiated
Greeks and ' the god ' ; Agamemnon meets his at Clytem-

[1] In this chapter my omissions are more generous than ever, but
the student may consult Méautis with pleasure and profit.

nestra's, so that both must be characterized ; he must be such
as to give mortal offence, she such as to take it.   That is to
say, there are virtually two protagonists, and the Instrument,
the one who used to fetch and carry for the hero, is now the
third actor.

But we must be careful not to think of the *Agamemnon* as a
clash of character in the Sophoclean sense. Sophocles uses
the greater fluidity of plot which the third actor gave to show
his hero in different relations, that we may know more fully
what kind of man he was ; as we examine the *Agamemnon* we
shall see that Aeschylus had no desire to do this.   To say that
we know Agamemnon less than we know Creon or Oedipus is
perhaps misleading, for of each we know all that is essential,
but we certainly know him less extensively.   Agamemnon remains as single-minded a character as Xerxes, but our sense
of his sin is immeasurably increased.   Aeschylus' tragic idea
is still catastrophic ; his heroes are not men, like Ajax or Oedipus, who deserved a better fate, but men built for ruin from
the start.   The Curse in the house of Atreus, that moral violence which provokes further violence in like-minded men,
has him firmly in its grip from the beginning, from before
the beginning.

What is new is that the instrument of doom is presented as
fully as the hero.   Had Agamemnon returned from Troy into
Old Tragedy, he would have found Clytemnestra waiting for
him behind the scenes ; as it is we see more of this superb
creature than of Agamemnon himself, and the amplitude of
the drama is doubled.   We must see why she does this thing,
and, in order that the murder may appear as a cosmic and
not as a merely domestic incident, we must see that she is big
enough to do it ; a sinner as catastrophic as Agamemnon, not
simply a false wife who takes to the sword.   It is significant
that Aeschylus reverses this order.   We are not told why she
does it until the murder is accomplished ; Aeschylus is not
proposing to make a character-study of Clytemnestra any
more than of Agamemnon.   When Agamemnon arrives she
comes forward to make a long and clever harangue.   She is
false ; we knew that.   She is determined ; we knew that.
What we did not know is that she is a woman of intellect and

intellectual courage. She ventures on a long speech full of
elaborate lies, leading up to the affair of the purple carpet.
Plain revenge with the sword is not enough.

Yet these two are essentially different from Antigone and
Creon. Agamemnon, though he falls not through a flaw in
the Universe, and through another's character as much as
through his own, is still recognizably akin to Pelasgus and
Eteocles in that, like them, he faces one issue and is driven
irresistibly upon it by the force of his own deeds. Dramatically, the strength of Clytemnestra is as necessary as the
sin of Agamemnon ; logically her act is but the complement of
his. He pursues his way independently of her, solitary as
Eteocles ; he kills Iphigeneia, he plunges Greece into war,
he destroys temples, he walks on the carpet, and he falls. He
is not in constant touch with her. She too has her solitary
path, and the two paths cross. They collide, and her strength
matches his, as does her moral build ; but here the interplay
stops. He, like Xerxes, is the sinner who meets his doom ;
she is the sinner who continues the chain of evil ; the
characterization of each and the relations between them are
limited to what this conception requires.

If we compare the *Agamemnon* with the *Septem* we shall
find it hard to say that anyone here is more fully characterized
than Eteocles there ; but on the other hand everyone in the
Agamemnon has some distinctive traits of his own : there is
no colourless spy. The relaxation of the old concentration
means that a new level in realism is reached ; Heralds and
Watchmen take on personality in sympathy with this new-
found personality of the Queen. The Herald here is no piece
of news walking, but a man ; he takes his part into his own
hands and deals with it himself. He begins by expressing
what he himself feels on his return, and his actual news
(521–4) comes as a parenthesis in his personal remarks.
Later, speaking still as an individual, with independent rights
in the play, he proceeds quite naturally to tell us what it was
like at the war. He lives ; not so vividly indeed as the
Watchman, but there are reasons for that. The Watchman is
evidently something of a natural, and heralds were important
and dignified figures ; moreover, the Watchman, having the

stage to himself, could do what he liked, but when the Herald appears the tragic rhythm is well under way. The Herald then, within his proper limits, lives, and though a minor character he detains us for a hundred verses. It is all very natural, but why does Aeschylus do it ?

The Herald increases our expectation by ushering in the King in a kingly way, and he gives a detailed account of the war which would come less naturally from Agamemnon himself ; but this is his excuse, not his purpose. His purpose is to throw light, from an unexpected quarter, on what Agamemnon has done, and this light is the more revealing the more naturally and casually it is produced. The chorus has told us how Iphigeneia was sacrificed to her father's ambition, how urns came back to Greece in place of living men ; now we hear of the miseries that were inflicted upon the living, and of something worse. Clytemnestra aroused our apprehensions (v. 338) by her remark, ' If they reverence the Gods of the city . . .' The chorus echoed it (v. 370) ; ' The Gods do not fail to punish those who trample upon holy things.' Now comes the Herald to tell us, with an off-handedness that lends fearful point to his words, that the victors overthrew the very altars of the Gods. The count against Agamemnon is piling up.

Here we can see very clearly the difference between the Aeschylean and the Sophoclean methods. Sophocles would have used such a character to increase the complication of the plot, and either to bring a new force to play upon the hero, or to set him in a fresh light and increase our understanding of him as an individual—perhaps both at once. The Herald does none of these things. He does not complicate the issue nor throw new light on the character or motives of Agamemnon—only on what he has done. The personality that is lent him is interesting in itself, but its chief use is the dramatic effect which it adds to his words ; he is not another cross-current in the play. With all the extension in the character-drawing, the interest is still in the thing done rather than in the motives and nature of those who did it. Agamemnon is still the sinner who presses onwards to his doom ;

the Herald does not illuminate more of his character, but he does fearfully illuminate his sin.[1]

The Watchman is no less interesting a personage. Structurally he is unnecessary. It was possible for Aeschylus to leave the announcement of the beacon-signal to the chorus or to Clytemnestra ; ten years earlier he would have done so, but now the third actor is at hand, waiting to be used, and concessions can be made to naturalism ; the plot begins to move at once. But though the Watchman, like the Herald, is not strictly necessary to the plot, he contributes to it enormously, and in the same way. He too is not merely a dramatic decoration. He is of course a splendid prelude ; his ordinary figure gives the scale of those who are to follow ; he represents the plain Argive citizen whose sufferings are more than once contrasted with the misdeeds of their rulers ; he gives, perhaps more vividly than the chorus could, certainly more tersely, an impression of the weariness of the years of waiting ; but above all this his value to Aeschylus was that he could so suddenly and so penetratingly sound the note of uneasy foreboding. With his obscure remark, ' This house, if it had a voice . . .' (v. 37), he starts a rhythm of apprehension which increases through the choral odes and reaches its climax with the statements of the Herald. Again the third actor is used not for the sake of plot or characterization, but to contribute to the atmosphere.

In fact, to restrict ourselves to the *Agamemnon*, we may say that the third actor's effect on the plot is very little. This is as simple as ever ; even Cassandra brings no complication. The extra attention given to the dialogue does not mean diminution in the part played by the chorus. Lyric passages account for exactly half the play—the same proportion as in the *Persae* and the *Septem*, and considerably more than in the *Prometheus*. Nor, in spite of the Watchman, are we long left in doubt as to the nature of the play, for the chorus enters to a march-song of 60 verses—a sure sign that something big is to follow ; and in fact we have an ode long in proportion to this prelude. There is no trace of shrinkage here ; it is still the Chorus at its most majestic.

[1] This point will be discussed more fully in the next chapter.

An ode like this is not a prelude to action; it is action. The anapaests—themselves as lyrical as other poets' lyrics—do indeed outline the situation: it is ten years since the eagle-hearted brothers set out for Troy, taking with them all but the aged, and now the palace flames with sacrifice: but with the solemn rhythm of the first verse of the first strophe all thought of action vanishes. The actors will have their turn—the Watchman has guaranteed that—but for the time being the situation is rendered lyrically; the past, what Agamemnon has done and therefore what he is, is illuminated by flashes of memory and poignant emotion. The chorus does not tell a plain tale plainly; it is not interested in the telling of a tale. It allows memory to hover and to pounce on the memorable scenes and to omit the rest. Logical and chronological order are nothing to them; these are lyrics and this the lyrical method. The chorus does not narrate, putting itself at our disposal and arranging its material for presentation to us; it follows the wheeling flight of its own thought and we are to accommodate ourselves to it. So, as in Pindar, we are given a series of vivid moments, not a narrative. Pedestrian continuity is for prose. Pindar tarries where he feels most pleasure, Aeschylus' chorus where it is most deeply moved—not by the gathering of the troops, the splendid sight of the armament,[1] not even by the fortunes of the war, but by the omen, by Calchas' interpretation, by the picture of Iphigeneia at the altar. What did Calchas demand? The chorus does not tell us; it is not interested in us.[2] Its next picture is that of the King bursting into tears, smiting the earth with his sceptre. Iphigeneia stood at the altar; was she slain? The chorus does not say; it harks back, passing over the slaughter, to the ominous words of Calchas which still await fulfilment. He did it; he must suffer.

[1] To hear about this we have to wait for the *Iphigeneia in Aulis*. There the chorus, having no part in the tragic theme, can do nothing but narrate and describe in a rather tired, Bacchylidean manner.

[2] The fact that the myths used in Greek Tragedy were well known saved the dramatists from this tedious business of explaining and narrating and left them free to concentrate on what really was dramatic.

It is the old technique, the more striking here in that we might have expected the actors, now so much more prominent than they were, to appropriate this part of the story. In Sophocles' *Electra* they do. There, the slaughter of Iphigeneia becomes a matter of debate between Electra and Clytemnestra, and the murder of Agamemnon, which is to that play what the sacrifice of Iphigeneia is to this, is presented not by the chorus but almost entirely through the mind of Electra. The reason for this is not decadence in the chorus and growth in the dialogue, but a different dramatic purpose. Sophocles is interested in the tragedy of the character, motives and situation of Electra as an individual ; Aeschylus in the deeds of Agamemnon and Clytemnestra as sinners. Sophocles therefore presents what is past as the background of Electra's own life and consciousness.

In the *Agamemnon* there is no revelation of motives. The great fact in the killing of Iphigeneia is that Agamemnon did it ; motive is given only in so far as it is dramatically necessary for so fearful an act to be explained, and for us to know that it could have been avoided. There are hints of ambition, of power begetting hybris, and that is enough. Surprisingly little is made of it ; he simply submitted, ' did this mad and wicked thing ' (218 ff.). So with Clytemnestra. She may justify herself, after the murder, but there is no picture of conflicting passions in her heart. She may have had them, but they do not belong to Aeschylus' conception, and he will not decorate his play with anything inessential. This side of the action is indeed not omitted, but it is given to the chorus, not to the actors, to be made part of the general atmosphere of the play and not an irrelevant part of the presentation of the tragic heroes. Hence, in spite of the increased activity of the actors we still have odes on the old scale and pattern.

The relations between chorus and actors are so harmonious that it is difficult to see where analysis should begin. The most obvious though perhaps the least important point is the exigencies of the dramatic situation. Clytemnestra and the chorus play into each other's hands perfectly. To this chorus Clytemnestra cannot avow her purposes or her feelings before the deed is done, for no chorus sympathetic to her is possible, or if possible would be suitable. She has to keep up appearances. She can display her energy, her practical wisdom, her self-confidence ; her inner feelings she must hide. She keeps up her pose marvellously. She comes out and talks of beacons as if her mind were full of beacons—beacons and victory—but the chorus, in its first ode, has told us of something which must surely be in her mind, and the Watchman has given us another clue.

But if it was dramatically necessary or convenient that we should see Clytemnestra through the eyes of the chorus, externally, inferring her mind from her acts, it was also a necessary result of the whole Aeschylean conception of the myth. In Sophocles' *Electra* the tragic conception is such that the heroine and the circumstances in which she is living are of the first importance ; [1] therefore we are shown these circumstances through the eyes of Electra. Here, it is the situation that is predominant ; therefore character and circumstances are drawn in much less detail. The theme is not the tragic workings of a mind ; it is that men of violence do things which outrage Justice, bring retribution, and provoke further deeds of violence. All that we need to know of the characters is that they are violent enough to play up to the situation ; what passes in their minds is a minor interest. The extreme case of this predominance of situation is Orestes, who is very nearly Pelasgus over again, a man in a cleft stick, lost in either case. The drama demands only that he shall be strong enough to choose one form of ruin—the dramatic one—rather than another. We must not lose ourselves therefore in any one character, but always see the situation as a whole and see the actors standing, however vividly, against this background of violence and ruin. Such a background only the chorus can make for us.

Again (though this is only the same point put differently) we are to feel that the Past is an active factor in the Present ; not merely that the characters do what they do because of something that happened before, but that the past horror is waiting to be reincarnated as a present horror. The sacrifice of Iphigeneia is part of Agamemnon's sin as much as his

[1] This view of the *Electra* is argued below, pp. 135 ff.

destruction of the Trojan temples. That the one happened
ten years ago, the other recently, is nothing at all. The
ghastly stories that Cassandra will recall from the past history
of the house of Atreus are as much part of the theme as the
treading on the purple; they add more and more weight to
the head of water which breaks out in this play. They are
still earlier acts of hybris, part of Agamemnon's moral inheritance. The *Oresteia* is not a trilogy only in that the whole
action is continuous; it is also a unity in that all the action is
always relevant. The Past is always a menace to the Present,
'the art of Calchas is unerring'; even the Future throws its
shadow behind it. Such an effect can be brought off only
by this independent chorus—and by Cassandra. We may
compare the *Agamemnon* this time with Euripides' *Electra*.
His Electra has the past in mind vividly, she is always harping
on it; but her nursing of old affronts sounds, and is, pathological; designedly so, since it cannot occupy the whole of a
mind without raising in us such doubts. Even Sophocles'
Electra barely escapes suspicion; the chorus wonders (122 ff.,
137, 153, 177, 215, 223), and Chrysothemis urges her to
forget things. The Aeschylean conception demands that the
past shall not be forgotten for a moment; not by the actors,
for it does not matter whether they remember or not—the
more tragic indeed if they forget—but we must not forget.
Only the chorus can do this for us, and only the chorus should
do it.

From which it follows that the chorus must be of the old
type, quite superior to 'dramatic time'. To illustrate this
point we may turn to the *Tyrannus*, where also there is a past
story to be understood. The obvious difference is that there
the past story is conveyed gradually (and with some skill)
through the dialogue, and this again is not merely a matter of
different technique. In the first place, the action in the
Tyrannus lies entirely in the hands of the actors, for it is the
action of Oedipus proceeding from the character of Oedipus
and recoiling upon Oedipus which is the whole theme of the
play; therefore it is the actors who, as it were, set the tempo
of the piece. The chorus is no longer free to roam as it will
in space and time, but must follow the course taken by the

actors, augmenting their dramatic rhythm but not controlling it. Secondly, Sophocles intends us to see this tragedy as the tragedy of Oedipus ; through his eyes therefore. The background to the whole action is not a moral law outraged, but the hero's own mind and will. Oedipus therefore brings out his own past. In the third place, there is between the past of Agamemnon and of Oedipus precisely the same difference as between the lyrical and the intellectual ; in the later play the past is what has led logically to the present situation, and (as it happens there) is something to be realized and discovered, whereas in the *Agamemnon* it is a living and controlling element. We may indeed truly say that the sacrifice of Iphigeneia is dramatically an event which takes place within the trilogy.

In the *Agamemnon*, then, we see the new dramatic technique combined with the old Chorus. The Actors have a new and a greater stature, but in this play, and in this one only, they are made to move easily and harmoniously within the old framework. And what a stroke of dramatic simplification these first choruses are ! When Agamemnon appears before us, rejoicing not unreasonably in his victory, he comes to us out of this murk of evil ambition and blood-guiltiness ; he may be shining like an Apollo, but he is accompanied by the ghost of these two odes. The Watchman has done the same for Clytemnestra. This vivid personality with his obscure labours may have been washed out of our recollection by the torrential ode, but his note of uneasiness is not forgotten : Clytemnestra too has her ghost.

So, when they meet, the stage is set. The past is there as well as the present. Crude fact need not be mentioned ; the still atmosphere of tragic irony is undisturbed. There is no word of vengeance, no word of sin, no word of injury. Clytemnestra has not diminished her magnificent stature by giving hints ; she has preserved her pose marvellously. But we know. Agamemnon too : his confidence, his blindness, are not news to us, only the ironic fulfilment of what we already know of him. Other dramatists in drawing their characters begin at the bottom and work up to the top ; Aeschylus, in the *Agamemnon*, begins at the top and goes higher.

The splendidly conceived affair of the purple carpet is the perfect consummation of the lyrical, ' atmospheric ', presentation of events past. The scene is new, as we have seen, but it is new in the old way. It is not new and exciting action, nor new and exciting dialectic, for we are beyond and above both, but it is action and dialectic made lyric. We know Clytemnestra tolerably well, but nothing of her inner self. She confronts Agamemnon, and she fences with him in a way which shows her to be intellectually his superior. Then, suddenly, we see all. She will kill him, of course, but she will first demonstrate her right. She sees herself as the servant of Justice ; she will defy Agamemnon not to fall into one last, damning sin. And he ? Clytemnestra is right. He, though he has his qualms—as he had before slaughtering Iphigeneia—falls ; and the irony is that he does it as much out of regard for Clytemnestra as from sheer weakness. Here, as in the first ode, we see by the light of lightning. The scene is more than a glimpse of Clytemnestra's nature, sensitive even in butchery ; it is argument and reply made manifest.

This is then the dialectic of Clytemnestra. When the deed is done she can speak to the Chorus openly, but even here there is no dialectic. She cites Iphigeneia and Chryseis to justify herself ; she explains, but there is no examination of motive. She argues in carpets.

We now return to the third actor. The most important, and by far the most remarkable, of the roles which he had to play was that of Cassandra. Entering royally, though a slave, behind Agamemnon, she remains motionless, neither speaking nor addressed. Clytemnestra does not notice her openly ; Agamemnon does not refer to her except in that marvellously foolish and pathetic ' Take her in and well entreat her.' At the beginning of the next scene Clytemnestra calls her in, the Chorus encourages her, but she will not speak. Not until she is again left alone with the Chorus does she break silence—with her wild cry to Apollo. From this point she has, it might seem, too much to say, for her dialogue with the Chorus lasts through 250 verses.

Evidently then Aeschylus had a use for the third actor quite his own. Once more, as in the *Prometheus,* there is not the slightest suggestion of a Sophoclean cross-scene. It is not difficult to suggest a dozen topics which these three could have discussed with some effect—but Cassandra remains silent. It can indeed be said that the chief points of the scene—Cassandra's miserable fate, and the affront offered to Clytemnestra—are sufficiently obvious without speech ; Cassandra silent in her chariot is more eloquent than Cassandra speaking, even if Euripides should have written a speech for her ; but there is more than this. Clytemnestra's hatred and Agamemnon's sin go back to the killing of Iphigeneia ; on that day he doomed himself to fall by her sword. What has happened since—the slaughter of so many Greeks before Troy, the despoiling of the Trojan Gods, the bringing home of the Trojan Princess—these things are merely aggravations of the original offence, merely fresh illustrations of what Agamemnon's sin is. The original sin, which is by far the most important for the trilogy as a whole, must not be overlaid with these accretions ; Clytemnestra the insulted wife must not obscure Clytemnestra the outraged mother ; no Cassandra-scene must be allowed to blur that offence on which Clytemnestra has been brooding these ten years. Cassandra is there. Gradually, in her strange immobility, she imposes herself upon us as a symbol of all that is wrong in Agamemnon. She does not stand between us and Iphigeneia ; rather does she sum up, in her supernaturally tragic posture, the wickedness done to Iphigeneia, to Troy, to humanity, to the Gods. In how pitiless a light she places Agamemnon as he is confronted by his murderess ! Iphigeneia he has forgotten ; Clytemnestra he never knew, if he thought that her house could accommodate a Trojan Princess. His weakness and blindness in the matter of the purple carpet perfectly reflect the blindness he is showing in his dealings with Cassandra. Clytemnestra, consummate artist in crime, spreads purple for his feet ; he sees the presumption, but he falls. Cassandra is sitting there, equally a testimony to his presumption ; she, who accepted Apollo's gifts but recoiled from paying Apollo's price, she who kept the god at bay, has been appropriated without a scruple by the King of Men. He hopes that the Gods will look upon

him without anger as he treads on their purple : Cassandra,
whom Apollo desired in vain, is to him only ' The army's gift,
choicest flower of great spoils.' He even persuades himself
that she ' followed him '. So he goes in, ' treading on purple.'

Once more, the third actor is not used to complicate the
situation ; neither to present a fresh point of view, nor even
(like Chrysothemis and Ismene) to serve as a foil to the
protagonists. She is indeed a new insult to Clytemnestra, and
another dramatist might have used her as such, but to
Aeschylus this is a minor matter. She illuminates Agamemnon, but chiefly her function is to accentuate, at the moment
of crisis, the ethical and emotional undertone of the play.
She brings to our minds swiftly and immediately a whole train
of associated ideas, like a remembered scent or tune. In
fact, had Aeschylus been so ill-advised as to write this play ten
years earlier, what Cassandra does here, and what the Watchman most vividly did in his sudden and chilling presage of ill,
would have been expressed in a choral ode. These ' atmos-
pherics ' were the perquisite of the Chorus : now it is seen
that the minor actor can create them too. It is a new effect
which can exist side by side with the old one, for it is different ;
more economical of time, less overwhelming, but sharper and
possibly more disturbing. The rest of Cassandra's part will
show much more clearly how Aeschylus regarded her as a reinforcement of the lyrical resources of his art.

Of all the cries that re-echo through the Theatre of
Dionysus two stand out above all the rest ; one the frightful
' O ! O ! Man of Doom ! ' of Iocasta, the other this sudden,
unearthly ' Otototoi ! Apollo ! Apollo ! ' of Cassandra. At
one bound she is soaring above the Chorus, to say nothing of
actors. She makes the Chorus sound prosaic. ' To what
house have I come ? '—she asks, and the Chorus replies ' To
the house of the Atreidae.' Aeschylus repeats and outdoes
here the effect of his Amphiaraus in the *Septem* : we knew
from Homer that Cassandra came, the strange prophetess, and
was killed. We have perhaps been wondering what her part
in the play is to be ; we soon see. She is slain, but not before
she has spread before us a filmy screen on which we see, as
in a phantasmagoria, all the horrors of this House, past, pres-

ent, and future.   Time and action are suspended ; or rather
past and future action are made to live on the present stage.
Cassandra does again what the Chorus did in its early odes, and
does it much more powerfully.   They had vague foreboding
of the future ; she can see.   They could tell of what they remembered in the past ; she can go further back, back to
Thyestes.   In Cassandra's hands the present action becomes
not merely a middle, in Aristotle's sense, that which naturally
follows one thing and is naturally followed by another ; it is
rather a centre, the central horror of a circle of horrors ; and
the more horrors, past and future, that Cassandra brings into
the circle, the more frightful does this one become.   Cassandra is a prophetess to some purpose here.   The Chorus,
dazed, tries to sing its way in tune with her, but it cannot
reach this spirit from Heaven or Hell which can use the lyrical
method as it has never been used, before or since.   This then
is Aeschylus' real use of the Third Actor in the *Agamemnon* :
lyricism focused to a dazzling, almost unendurable point in a
single person.

2. THE CHOEPHORI   If this analysis of the *Agamemnon* suggests that the play is pure Old Tragedy, in spite of the three
actors, analysis of the two remaining plays may lead one to
think of New rather than of Middle Tragedy.   These terms
are of minor importance ; what is important is that during the
course of the *Choephori* the trilogy, and Drama itself, begins
to move in a new direction, and it ends, in the *Eumenides,*
with something unlike all that has gone before.   With some
truth one might say, if one chose to be Tory in Aristophanes'
manner, that the *Eumenides* marks the beginning of the end.

Let us first see what Aeschylus was not trying to do in the
Choephori.   It is not a play of character.   In the Theban
trilogy, when Laius and Oedipus are finished with, Eteocles
comes forward to dominate the third play in his own right ; it
is his character that makes the tragedy and fulfils the curse.
The character of Orestes has no such significance.   He is in a
situation which arouses all our interest and all our pity, and
Aeschylus, being a dramatist, has been careful to lend him
characteristics which are natural, plausible and interesting,

but what Orestes is does not belong to the essence of the play, for he is the victim of his parents and can only choose this road to ruin or that.

But is not this the tragedy of Pelasgus over again ? No ; there is an important difference. It is true that Orestes can say, in his most tragic moment, ' Let me slay her and die ', (438) ; he is in a sense between the devil and the deep sea ; but as we know that he is acting under Apollo's direction we feel that there can be no question of ' perishing ' ; that though meanwhile he suffers terribly, some way out will be found. The tragic quality of the play is quite different therefore from that of the *Supplices*.

Thirdly, Aeschylus has not chosen to make of the situation a picture of conflict in the mind of the hero.[1] Apollo's dire command is indeed reinforced by Orestes' natural desire for vengeance and for the recovery of his patrimony ; opposed to this there are signs of misgiving in plenty—one we have cited, another is firmly removed by Pylades ; but in general his course is determined before he comes to Argos, and Aeschylus is proposing to show us not a conflict between one part of his mind and another, but the resolution, firm but not unclouded, with which he pursues the path pointed out by the God, his own filial duty, and his own just ambition.

This is partly the consequence of Aeschylus' conception of the *Eumenides*. As that play is to be not so much a new stage of the story as the resolution of this one, this one must be careful not to anticipate ; since there Apollo is to appear as the *de facto* defendant, Orestes' own responsibilities must not be allowed to absorb all our attention here. The fundamental issue is being reserved, and as Orestes' own character is not ultimately essential in the tragedy, it is treated as a matter of dramatic interest rather than of tragic significance ; the play is built largely around this free character-interest and the sheer excitement of getting the awful deed done. One of the tasks that the *Choephori* has to perform is to accomplish the transition from the Old Tragedy style of the *Agamemnon* to the realistic style of the *Eumenides*, and this

[1] Though it is one of the functions of the long Commos to suggest his agony.

is a transition that we can follow. It is closely connected with the use of the chorus.

In its first ode the chorus continues the feeling of the *Agamemnon*, presenting the moral and emotional background of the present action ; the blood lies upon the ground, fear reigns, Justice tarries. But soon a difference in dramatic outlook makes itself felt, in the recognition scene which Euripides rather superficially parodied. The mechanics of the scene are perhaps elementary, and in transferring to an extremely realistic setting what Aeschylus designed for a lyrical one, Euripides was able to make some easy fun out of it, but the analysis of Electra's feelings that we have here is neither childish nor uninteresting. In offering her libations at Agamemnon's tomb, Electra, with her absent brother always in her thoughts, sees the lock of hair. Immediately she jumps to the conclusion that it is Orestes', but she cannot bring herself to pronounce his name. In her new and exciting hope she wants independent support, she wants the suggestion of Orestes to come from the chorus ; therefore she fences, until the chorus mentions this as a possibility. Now she welcomes it excitedly. There follows a conflict of suppositions in her mind : is the curl from Orestes or from one of their enemies ? The latter idea she fights down—and suddenly, in even greater excitement, she sees footsteps. It must be that Orestes is come. The footsteps fit her own ! ‘ Anguish seizes my distraught mind.’ At which moment Orestes himself steps forward, and Electra, by a natural and very dramatic transition, becomes all reserve and suspicion, convinced only when he produces his token and shows the place whence the lock was cut. As Orestes says, ‘ When you see me in person you refuse to recognize me, though when you saw my curl and footprints you were all excitement, and thought for certain that I was here ’. We must allow Euripides his gibes,[1] even though he does conveniently forget the ‘ distraught mind ’

[1] Those offended by the parody will recall with great satisfaction Polyidus' criticism of the recognition-scene in the *I.T.* (*Poetics*, 1455a, 6 ff.). From the dramatic point of view there is no doubt that Sophocles took the right line in treating this recognition as a necessary nuisance, doing it quite conventionally, and making as few bones about it as possible.

which makes a deal of difference ; the means that Aeschylus
uses here are indeed not slick, but we should not overlook
the sureness of his insight into the workings of a girl's mind
in a state of great excitement.

In this scene we have for the first time two actors face to
face, both of whom are treated purely as individuals for their
own sakes.   The important point is that this study of Electra's
emotions at a crisis has no bearing on the theme of the play.
In exchange for what he is renouncing or reserving, Aeschylus
has leisure to do other things, to develop one of the new possibilities of his art for its own sake.

The long lyrical passage which follows looks like many an
earlier one ; actually it is quite different.   This scene does not
range backwards and forwards in time like Cassandra's ; no
storm-clouds are rolled up to lend a greater and more fearful
significance to the action.   It is strictly subordinate to the
actors and action,[1] for the interest is twofold ; it creates an
atmosphere such that the murder of Clytemnestra shall be
both dramatically and psychologically probable, and it distinguishes the attitude and motives of Electra and of Orestes.
In order to do this, the chorus is made to play a different part.
It has already paid its lyrical tribute, in the ancient manner,
to the dead King ; now it begins to acquire a more definitely
dramatic character, so preparing the way for the purely
dramatic chorus of Furies in the *Eumenides*.   The non-Greek
character of these slaves, suggested by the extravagance of the
words and actions that accompany their entrance, appears
much more clearly now (v. 423 ff.) :

' I smite myself to the rhythm of the Arian lament, and Lo !,
according to the rite of the mournful Kissian dirge, thou canst
see the beating of my hand blow upon blow, up and
down . . . '

Moreover—and this is no accident—all the appeals to the
primitive law of retaliation and most of the faith in the power
of the dead are theirs.   Their part, far from enveloping the

---

[1] We might say what we said of the big ode of the *Agamemnon*,
that this Commos *is* action.   It contains the spiritual action of the
piece : the second part of the play presents the physical counterpart.

action, is to be subordinate to it, in that they are continually presenting one point of view to Orestes.

During this scene we find character and motives carefully drawn, as it were, in three depths of relief. Electra is moved throughout by personal feelings—grief for her father, pity for his hateful death, despair at his present way of life. Orestes expresses other ideas. He, the son, thinks of the dishonour to his house ; he prays for his father's help that he may expel the usurper and recover his inheritance. Meanwhile the chorus keeps up its savage *ostinato* : ' A blow for a blow '. The most that Orestes can bring himself to say about Clytemnestra is (385 ff.), ' Even must a present pay '. This thought the chorus at once puts into its own language :

' May it be mine to sing loud the sacrificial song over the man smitten and the woman destroyed.' Similar in effect is the subtle difference betwen Orestes' wish and Electra's, with the replies of the chorus (345 ff.):

OR.   Would that thou hadst been slain by a Lycian spear before Troy. Glory wouldst thou have left to thy house ; a noble tomb across the sea thou wouldst have won, no cause of grief to thy kin.

CHOR.   So, outstanding among the friendly dead, would he have ruled in the world below, for he was a King here.

EL.   Nay, not slain at Troy ! not buried with the other dead beside the Scamander ! Would that his murderers had so been slain !

All this scene is a necessary period of preparation, necessary for the audience if not also for Orestes. It might have been filled with nothing but a long invocation of Agamemnon, like the invocation of Darius ; but now, as well as the invocation, we have these lyrics which do not sweep away individual personality in something bigger, but subtly reveal the differences in the character and attitude of those concerned in the scene ; and this, again, for its own sake, for this contrast between brother and sister is nothing in the main theme of the tragedy. We have in fact a partial anticipation of the typical triangular-scene of Sophocles ; partial, because his threefold contrasts are directly related to the tragic theme. Aeschylus is beginning

to do what the greater number of actors in any case suggests,
to take a situation in a more naturalistic way and to draw from
it what it reasonably contains and not only what the theme
imperatively demands.   Throughout, Electra and Orestes are
treated as persons placed in a certain situation, saying now
this, now that, as the course of the dialogue or their inner
selves suggest ; while the Chorus, equally a ' person '—and
one strongly reminiscent of Sophocles' Paedagogus—keeps implacably to one point : ' He was mutilated, I tell thee ' (439).

The character of the chorus being in this way defined and
its utterance being made subordinate to the present situation,
we are not surprised that its next ode is, in part, of a new type.
' Many things does earth nourish' inevitably reminds us of
the greater ode of the *Antigone* ; but these first two stanzas
are dramatic comment at least as natural as the marriage-ode
in the *Prometheus*.   What makes this ode sound so new is
not so much this chance resemblance as the similarity between
the later stanzas here and such things as the Danae-ode in
the *Antigone*.   The comparison between Clytemnestra and
Althea, Scylla and the Lemnian Women is, in the later manner,
decorative rather than dramatic.   The choric temperature has
fallen somewhat ; the chorus can now permit itself to be reminded.   It became a common formula—in Sophocles' hands
no mean source of dramatic relief, in others, often little more
than an interlude.   The chorus has now ceased to preside
over the action, which, become naturalistic and not symbolic,
has passed into the hands of the actors.   The chorus follows
the tempo set by the actors, and instead of wandering free in
space and time it begins to obey the rhythm of the piece and
to say what from time to time the development of the action
suggests ; no longer the supernatural lyrico-dramatic agency
which it was still in the *Agamemnon*, but only a body of
lyrical attendants, ' ideal spectators ', already showing signs
that they may, when the temperature drops further, become
also learned spectators.

But in a moment, having shown signs of the approaching
change, this ode returns to more Aeschylean paths, and ends
with two of the weightiest stanzas that even this poet ever
wrote ; and this return is of considerable significance to the

next scene. From now onwards the play is crowded with action ; it is conspicuous for the first emergence of what we know as dramatic intrigue ; in the Nurse we have perhaps the most realistic character in the whole of Greek Tragedy ; and the Chorus is at one point so deeply involved in the action that it has literally to retire into the background. Orestes goes through the everyday formula of knocking at the door, and is answered in an extremely colloquial way by the porter. To him Orestes replies in the stateliest Aeschylean, with metaphors of the Car of Night and casting anchor in the house of a guest. Is there not a little stiffness, a little incongruity in this ? Not in the least. Those two last stanzas are still ringing in the ears of the audience : ' In the fullness of time the Erinnys, renowned for dark intent, is bringing against the house the child of ancient bloodshed, for the avenging of the impurity ' : and Orestes knocks at the door. Without the chorus it would have been realism unsuccessfully carried out ; with these stanzas it is a highly dramatic symbolism. The porter can answer colloquially—he has not heard the ode, and he can be casual ; but Aeschylus sees in that no reason why the ' child of ancient bloodshed ' should be casual too. Realism is still an effect, and not a creed. Aeschylus, like Shakespeare, has no compunctions about working in two planes, realism and symbolism, and letting the two meet, unresolved. For the moment we have returned to the atmosphere of the *Agamemnon* ; once more the chorus raises the action to a higher plane of significance.

From this moment however we leave the atmosphere of the *Agamemnon* behind us and move towards that of the *Eumenides*. The action becomes swifter, the chorus is pressed into service as a minor character, and its purely lyric functions pass into partial eclipse. When the double vengeance is accomplished it is not the chorus which brings the piece to an end with an all-embracing musical movement ; this chorus of loyal slaves is no longer in a position to take wings and soar, and the logical conclusion of the detailed action is that the chief actor comes forward to explain his motives and to face his future. That is to say, the *Choephori* ends like the *Tyrannus,* and not like the *Septem.*

The third actor[1] who appears in this play, the Nurse, is
as different from the third actor in the *Agamemnon* as the turn
of plot here is different from the carpet-scene there.   Instead
of a poetic symbolism we have a naturalistic complication ;
instead of the extreme of lyricism we have almost the extreme
of realism.   The appearance of the Nurse is totally unexpected ; for the first time in Drama something unforeseen has
happened, and we are thrown into a state of suspense which
only the actor can remove.   It used to be the dramatist's
practice, in the days when drama was chiefly lyrical and
musical, to prophesy what was going to happen ; now that the
actors have charge, it is seen that new effects can be drawn
from surprise, even disappointment.   The suspense created by
the entrance of the Nurse is renewed at v. 769 and kept up
until the Chorus carries its point.   We are treated to what we
may fairly call a battle of wits ; the chorus sets itself to defeat
Clytemnestra, and thanks to the loyalty of the Nurse it
succeeds.   This is an important point.   Not only is there no
need, in this new type of drama, for the minor character to
remain a mere agent ; we may go further here, and say that
she must not.   If the Nurse were a mere Messenger, a piece
of clockwork wound up by Clytemnestra and set walking, her
change of direction would appear mechanical and dramatically
unconvincing.   The Spy in the *Septem* may be as clockwork
as he likes, for we have no interest in *him* ; here an appropriate characterizing is necessary.   This is the essential
point ; our further interest in the passage is to see what
Aeschylus builds on this basis.

Once the need for character is there, Aeschylus proceeds to
make a vignette of extraordinary vividness, with no sort of
fumbling or hesitation.   Clearly he is as ready to make a
nurse chatter of napkins as a Chorus to sing of Zeus.   A baby
may cry from hunger, thirst, or wetness, in the middle of
high tragedy without the least self-consciousness.   Again
Aeschylus is Shakespearian and Shakespeare Aeschylean, and
no one else comes into the reckoning.   This effect is not in

[1] Whether this part was actually played by the Tritagonist is of
no importance.   The part is one which could exist only in three-
actor drama.

the least Sophoclean ; where his dramatic planes met he carefully tooled over the sharp edges to make all smooth and
harmonious.

The plot then demands some individual character here,
and the character that Aeschylus so marvellously invents we
gratefully accept on her own merits, but the poet is doing
much more than merely giving rein to his genius for character-
drawing. The Nurse is more than an amplification and a
decoration of the plot ; she is also a subtly contrived relief to
it, a relief not lyric, nor sub-comic in the Sophoclean manner,
but tragic ; tragic because of her sorrow, relief because we
know that the sorrow is ill-founded ; and this natural grief, so
naturally expressed, is welcome to us in the midst of characters
who either never had or have been denied the luxury of
natural affections, just as the homeliness of washing napkins is
a relief from the unnatural strain of doctrines like Blood calling for Blood. The Nurse in fact is the perfect foil, a scale
by which we may measure the rest of the action and the other
characters. We contrast the baby she loved with the tragic
man whom circumstances have made ; the unnatural mother
with the simple devotion of the slave. This broken-hearted
sorrow is what *she* ought to be feeling, but instead, she ' hides
laughter in her eyes ' (v. 691).

This suggests another point which surely was not absent
from Aeschylus' calculations, a small one, but worth mentioning in face of the common view that *de minimis non curat
Aeschylus*. Through this phrase Aeschylus gives us the clue
to his Clytemnestra. Had vv. 691 ff. been preserved to us as
a fragment : ' Ah me ! how thy words bring me utter ruin !
O Curse of this house, invincible one, how dost thou see everything, and from afar with thy unerring shaft hast smitten what
lay well sheltered, and dost strip me, alas, of dear ones '—we
should never have guessed that the words were insincere. In
this speech is she not perhaps expressing real grief, as does
the tense and complicated Clytemnestra whom Sophocles
imagined ? For an actor in this big theatre, working behind
a mask, to convey the necessary hint of insincerity was perhaps possible but must have been difficult—for the situation
will stand no more than the slightest hint ; but, thanks to the

invention of the Nurse, Clytemnestra need not risk hints,
and the effect is finer. She can keep up her pose as magnificently as she did in the *Agamemnon*, for the Nurse will
tell us of the laughter in her eyes. Our admiration for her
consummate acting rises even higher ; the woman is equal to
anything.

The effect of the third actor in the *Agamemnon* was stu-
pendous and remains unrivalled ; here, though the character
of the Nurse is one of the great things in dramatic literature,
the dramatic effect of the complete scene—the intrigue, the
suspense, the surprise—is inevitably dwarfed by what Sophocles was able to do later. Nevertheless, Aeschylus is scarcely
less to be admired for this scene than for that, for the insight,
freedom and boldness with which he met the demands of the
new kind of situation, and for the sureness of touch which
drew from it effects that not only were new but also remain
new. In all these qualities the *Choephori* is a worthy fore-
runner of the *Eumenides*.

3. THE EUMENIDES The *Agamemnon* was a play tragic in
tone and lyrical in method ; the *Choephori* partly lyrical,
partly dramatic with quite a new emphasis laid on action.
The *Eumenides* carries this development further ; it is a play
entirely different in spirit and purpose, therefore in technique
too, from the *Agamemnon*—a difference which is felt as soon
as we compare the calm and interesting opening speech about
the transmission of the oracle with the uneasy cry of the
Watchman or the solemn beginning of the *Choephori*. Instead of a steady tightening of a static situation, made more
and more taut until it breaks, we have an exciting series of
events and a more obviously dramatic treatment of them. No
longer does the play move inevitably along a foreseen path ;
the *Eumenides* leads us through a succession of dramatic
surprises.

The *Agamemnon* began with a realistic monologue and
continued with the longest choral movement in Greek Tragedy. The *Eumenides* begins with an explanatory speech from
the Pythia which we can hardly call realistic—for we cannot
suppose that she made such a speech every morning ; it is

what the poet wants rather than what the story demands, conventional therefore somewhat in the manner of the Euripidean prologue. Its substance, ten or twenty years earlier, would have been grateful material for a choral ode ; as a speech, though it is perfectly dramatic, it gives ever so slightly the air of theatrical contrivance, so far unknown. This impression is emphasized when we see what the purpose of the scene is. The Pythia with her short account of the history of the oracle and her preparations for the day establishes an atmosphere of holy calm, in order to shatter it a moment later as she comes stumbling out of the temple in a transport of terror. The difference between the disquieting note that the Watchman sounded and this sudden attack on our nerves is, in brief, the difference between the *Agamemnon* and the *Eumenides*—a difference for which we must try to find some explanation.

The most cursory survey will suffice to show how this kind of dramatic effectiveness is sought throughout. After the Pythia has managed to give us some idea of what has so terrified her in the temple, we are shown the interior, and see at once the radiant figure of Apollo. But the holy calm of the shrine is qualified by the pitiable figure of Orestes, red with the blood of Apollo's purifying sacrifice ; and still more by certain black-robed, inhuman shapes asleep on the floor. With words full of reassurance and comfort Apollo sends Orestes forth, with Hermes to guide him ; the Furies will indeed pursue, but the end will be peace.

The temple is left empty, but for the sleepers. We are now to imagine the Ghost of Clytemnestra appearing, and this woman dead is more terrible than when she was alive. Even to these awful beings she speaks with something like authority, reproaching them with their sleep, telling them of her dishonoured place among the dead, spurring them on in the pursuit of her son and murderer. With groans and snores they gradually awake from their sleep of exhaustion ; Clytemnestra gives them more horrible orders before disappearing, and we see these ghastly figures at last, dancing a *Danse macabre* in the temple of Apollo. Not however for long, for Apollo soon returns to drive them out. There is a sharp

contest, full of loathing on the one side and protest on the
other, and then the Furies resume their pitiless chase.

We have had four scenes of the utmost dramatic effectiveness and are yet only at v. 235 ; at v. 235 of the *Agamemnon*
we were still listening to the first long ode of the Chorus. It
is clearly a totally different conception of drama.

We must notice in the first place that if the dramatic method
here is utterly unlike anything that we have yet seen, so too
is the dramatic idea. Aeschylus makes it perfectly clear that
the theme of the play is not to be the increasing tragedy of
Orestes ; Apollo's first words, ' I will not forsake thee,' show
that. We need not underestimate Orestes' present danger
and sufferings, and his dramatic attainments are such that we
shall not think of him as a puppet in another's drama, but
when Apollo promises him deliverance and himself assumes
responsibility for what Orestes has done we feel the assurance
that the outcome will be, for him, a happy one. He may
have the Furies against him, but he has the God on his side.
Therefore, as the dramatic interest is transferred fundamentally to the conflict between Apollo and the Furies, we
cannot have a play, like the *Agamemnon*, in which the whole
movement is the gathering of the storm-clouds over the head
of the hero and his house, nor like the *Prometheus*, in which
it is the drama in the hero's own mind, nor like the *Septem*,
in which it is the inevitable ruin of the hero.

But if this drama of intensification is impossible with Orestes
as the subject, it is impossible too with Apollo and the Furies.
When Creon and Antigone come to grips, the contest can be
dramatic, because their whole personalities are engaged ; and
tragic, because they stake their all on the issue. These, as in
a kind of spiritual chess, bring up more and more of reserves,
building up an antagonism higher and higher until the position must collapse, to the ruin of one or both. Apollo and
the Furies cannot bring out forces and stake their immortal
souls like this ; they cannot be tragic. When you have said
that Apollo is a god you have said at once all there is to say
—or very nearly ; for the god here, as in the *Prometheus*, is
circumscribed in order to be dramatic. Apollo, unlike Aeschylus himself, will allow nothing that is good to the Furies ;

the onslaught he makes on them in the temple is an *ex parte* statement, and shows the god to be far from omniscient. The Furies, for the same reason, are extremely dramatic in their implacable insistence on their rights ; nevertheless they cannot be tragic, and a piling up of the account against them, as against Agamemnon, or the turning of the screw on them, as on Pelasgus, would be quite without meaning.

Aeschylus was not trying to turn his theme into drama of this kind. He did not see it through the eyes or in the mind of any of the characters in the play, and therefore abandoned the method which belonged to drama of this type. Orestes has now become the occasion of conflict between certain moral powers of the Universe ; and the resolution of this conflict, however poignant our interest in Orestes, must be the chief interest of the play—a moral and intellectual rather than a tragic interest. Although the *Eumenides* is no problem-play (for the dramatic conflict between the two moral orders is far greater than the question that provokes it), yet there is a problem at the heart of it, and problems are not best stated in music.

Having then this intellectually conceived theme, and not having any central character who can be made the subject of the older technique, Aeschylus treats his dramatic material as it were externally. There is no presentation of an inner drama of the mind, of an agony in the hero's soul, but a conscious manipulation of the material in the interests of the dramatic theme which Aeschylus wishes to present through it —a step on the road towards the deliberate manipulation of the material in the interests of dramatic entertainment. The sharp contrasts of the first four scenes are aimed directly at us, the audience, and are not forces applied to any one in the play. They are designed to present as forcibly as possible the strength of the contestants and the gulf that divides them ; to present, that is, Aeschylus' problem in the clearest possible light. The difference in tone between this strong intellectual drama and pure tragedy is felt when Clytemnestra's ghost appears. Here alone we feel that complete engagement of a tragic personality whose general absence leaves the *Eumenides* as great a play as any, but different.

After these four scenes we are to suppose the lapse of a year, and we move to Athens. The blood-guilty Orestes has received from Apollo the ceremonial purification which allows him intercourse with strangers during his year of exile ; now at Athens he demands the absolution which will enable him to return to Argos. The Furies will have nothing to do with this dispensation of Apollo's ; the blood of a mother demands blood. Still pursued, Orestes takes refuge at Athena's altar, and the succession of thrilling scenes continues—the Binding-song, Athena's appearance, the pleas, the institution of the trial, the trial itself, with accusation, defence, testimony, voting and verdict. The Furies are overwhelming ; their insistence, their threats to haunt Athens with plagues if their prerogatives are not honoured, make us tremble for Orestes, though he has Apollo for advocate. This scene must have been a remarkable spectacle—the city itself on the stage now ; and the dialogue approaches just as nearly to realism, for the alternate bribes and threats to the jury sound like a page out of Demosthenes.

Sophocles must have been exceedingly interested at this use of his third actor, for here, with judge, jury, accused, accuser and counsel for the defence, we have virtually five actors and no chorus. The whole secret of the speed and fluidity of this play is that the chorus, while remaining wonderfully lyrical, is entirely an actor, and a realistic one. In order to contend with his chorus, Pelasgus had to assume the bonds of lyricism ; here, in order to contend with Apollo the chorus descends into the actor's sphere, arguing, fighting, pursuing, and bringing its lyrics with it. There are no statutory pauses in the action for the screwing-up or musical exploitation of a tragic theme ; all is action, the Furies are always the Furies. If any one looks like the usual chorus it is the jury.

But we must note that Aeschylus does not surrender entirely to this new-found realism. We know how Euripides argued questions like this one of Orestes' guilt, even without the excuse of a trial-scene ; Aeschylus once more gives the illusion rather than the substance of debate. He is more interested in the conflict than in the debate, and invents (as before, in the temple-scene) more taunts than arguments.

Certainly had he been passionately interested in the question
of blood-guilt he would have made Apollo argue better.   To
be sure, a god is at a disadvantage in a witness-box, but
could not Apollo have put up a better case ?   He argues first
that he has never issued an oracle that Zeus did not give him.
This we are bound to accept as true ; Athena repeats it (797
ff.), and it is of fundamental importance to the play ; but we
must not fail to observe that it does not bring overwhelming
conviction to the jury.   The Furies too think little of it :
' Zeus, as thou sayest, delivered thee this oracle to proclaim
to Orestes, in exacting vengeance for his father's life, to have
no regard for a mother's due ? ' (622 ff.).   Apollo rides off
on irrelevancies—it is different when a King is slain, and that
by a woman, and so treacherously, ' as you shall hear '.
' Zeus, by thy account, hath especial regard for a father's
doom ; but he himself bound his aged father Kronos.   How
does this accord with that ?—You, Sirs, I ask to hearken to
this.'   Apollo, descending to abuse, says again that this is
quite different ; that the prisoner can be freed, but the dead
never restored to life.   ' What advocacy ! ' cry the Furies ;
' Clytemnestra is dead, yet this man thinks he should live in
Argos and join in its religious rites.'   Apollo's reply to this,
which ends the pleadings, is as weak as the rest of his case ;
he puts forward the astonishing argument that the mother is
no parent, but the father only, and backs it by the present
example of Athena, born of Zeus and no mother.   His perora-
tion is an offer to favour Athens for ever if he gets judgement,
and a promise of the perpetual friendship of Argos.   There
is no more argument.   The dialogue that accompanies the
voting is nothing but a series of most vivid bribes, threats
and insults.

How are we to interpret all this ?   As a debate it is poor ;
as conflict it is magnificent—especially if we remember, as we
always should, the scene : the radiant god, and the twelve
swirling figures in black robes.   Not a setting that would
predispose the audience to the following of a close debate, if
by ' debate ' we mean rational discussion leading to rational
decision, nor does Aeschylus devise anything of the sort.   Nobody for example asks the simple question what is to be done

with Clytemnestra (because the answer to this question is being reserved for the end of the trilogy), and on the issue whether it is worse to murder a mother than a husband there is nothing intelligent to say. We are given the form, not the substance, of debate ; as if to emphasize that, Aeschylus makes Athena give her vote on grounds that are irrelevant. Apollo uses a current medical theory—and incongruously supports it by myth—to defend his position, but the significance of it is symbolic, not literal. It is a move in the conflict—and what is the conflict about ?

We must see it in its Aeschylean setting. The first point is one that cannot have been obvious to those misguided men who have deprived Aeschylus of the *Prometheus* ; for here too Zeus is defied, and that not by fallen angels, but by deities who are defending something necessary and vital. Through-out the trilogy we have been concerned with the question of *dike*, retributive justice. In the *Agamemnon*, time after time, sin was punished, but always through further sin—and always on the command or with the consent of Zeus. Agamemnon, for example, is sent by Zeus to punish Paris, and the great net of Zeus is thrown over Troy, such that neither young nor old could escape ; yet it is one of the counts against Agamemnon —and the source of the wrath of Artemis—that he is a man of blood ; he has brought mourning into every home in Greece. The Justice of Zeus, at this stage, is clumsy and ineffective, and it provokes the hostility of another Olympian.

When we reach the *Choephori*, some sort of order has been introduced into the chaos. At last we have an avenger who is not following evil desires of his own ; we have instead one who is reluctant, driven to his awful deed by the express com-mand of the god ; we have too a better prospect than unend-ing crime, since the god himself takes the responsibility. But we also have something worse—the idea that it should be right and necessary for a son to take the life of his mother. This is something that we cannot accept.

Neither can the Furies. It is their whole function to pro-tect those instinctive sanctities which Apollo, on the authority of Zeus, is setting at naught. To protect these they revolt—those Erinnyes who, earlier in the story, were the willing servants of Zeus (*Agamemnon* 59). And their revolt is successful, for in the final reconciliation, their rights are recognized and even enlarged.

But for what purpose has Apollo infringed these rights? For the sake of the moral and social order that is growing out of the chaos.

In Greek religion it is the Olympian gods, notably Apollo Aguieus and Athena Polias, who are particularly associated with the usages of civic life and what goes with it. In both these late trilogies, the *Oresteia* and the *Prometheia*, Aeschylus is concerned with the growth of moral, social, political order out of primitive disorder, and in each trilogy Zeus the Conqueror is the symbol of authority—not yet of wisdom and mercy. In the *Prometheus* it is crude, naked authority; Zeus may have overcome the Titans, but he is not undisputed master in the universe, nor can he be, until he has learned to temper authority with wisdom and mercy. Until then, Prometheus holds out against him; Prometheus must suffer, but he will not yield—and he can look forward to the downfall of Zeus.

So in the *Oresteia*. We are reminded early (*Agamemnon* 168 ff.) that Zeus is the Conqueror, and that he is all-wise; but in spite of this, we see little sign that divine wisdom has yet manifested itself in any tolerable moral and social order on earth—or, in Heaven, that his sway is yet absolute; for when he sends against Paris his ministers of Justice, Artemis recoils in horror from 'the Eagles' lawless feast' and holds up the expedition. The *Agamemnon* offers nothing but crime upon crime, all avenging crime. But in the *Choephori*, as we have seen, something better emerges—and it is a very notable thing in this play that Agamemnon himself is a very different figure from the blind sinner of the first play. He is the King, who has been foully and lawlessly struck down by a false wife. Kings hold their sceptres from Zeus; the murder of a King is a blow struck at authority and order. The marriage-bond is the keystone of society, and the authority of the husband is the counterpart of that of the King. (In this debate, both of the Olympians are for the male.) Clytemnestra's is a double crime against the social order, and it must be punished. But how? Apollo takes the responsibility, and promises to protect his agent Orestes. But it proves to be a promise that he is barely able to keep. Once more the imperfections of the divine plan reveal themselves in strife between gods. Apollo may vindicate at all costs the father and husband, but the Furies will never consent that the sacred ties of blood should be so violated. In the conflict, each party has its strong point. The murder of a mother is intolerable; the Furies are defending something without which society cannot exist. They can say truly (*Eumenides* 508 ff.) that they are the champions of Justice. On the other hand, organized society is patriarchal, and Clytemnestra's crime is particularly heinous. Also, the Furies are crude and undiscriminating, merciless and implacable; they do not, like the Olympians, hold out the promise of a higher order. The conflict, as the poet says twice, is one between despotism and anarchy. Law and order must not be allowed to trample on our most sacred instincts, but law and order must be vindicated.

The Olympians win—but in such a way that the Furies' main point is conceded, for the solution is the new dispensation instituted by Zeus through his own daughter Athena, Santa Sophia. Henceforward Justice will be secured neither blindly, through further crime, nor by an Orestes, guiltless but guilty, but by an impartial and disinterested tribunal. The usages of the city-state become the pattern of justice on earth, and by a most imaginative stroke Aeschylus makes Athena a member of that jury which is the prototype of all Athenian councils. But Justice is established in Heaven too; the earlier victory of Zeus over his Titan rivals is consummated in peaceful and unquestioned sovereignty. The necessary sign of this is that the Furies are reconciled, in the new conditions, with Zeus, and enter his ordered system, retaining their high privilege in a higher form: for now they will ward off and punish not only strife between kin, but also strife in the state. So, in the tremendous finale of this trilogy, the Athenian people saw, in dramatic symbolism, the age-long growth of religion and society brought to its fulfilment among them-

selves, as, persuaded by the goddess of the city, the last rebels
against Zeus accept their new home in Athens, and pass out
of the theatre, no longer Furies but Kindly Ones, to be led
in imaginary procession from the southern to the northern
face of the sacred rock.

CHAPTER IV

THE DRAMATIC ART OF AESCHYLUS

Aeschylus is a difficult dramatist to criticize. Sophocles works steadily in one style (on the whole, for we must not forget the *Trachiniae*), but Aeschylus will do anything. In the *Oresteia* we have seen him move from a method which has its roots deep in the past to one which might have made Athens wonder uneasily for the future ; we have seen that in the three very different plays which we have assigned to Old Tragedy actors and chorus think nothing of exchanging functions. For the explanation of this difference between the two dramatists we must look ultimately to the difference between their tragic thinking. The Sophoclean drama is based on one wide tragic conception, which we may for the moment describe as a feeling for the imperfection of human character and its impotence before the power of circumstances ; from such a centre his drama flowed in one deep and steady stream. Aeschylus on the other hand is seized by more specific dramatic conceptions which demand a much more individual treatment.

We must nevertheless try to generalize the characteristically Aeschylean tragic idea, and try to see how this moulded his dramatic form. A convenient standard for reference will be Aristotle.

There are two preliminary points to make, in view of Wilamowitz' theory that Attic Tragedy was not specifically tragic or dramatic,[1] but Saga, and in view of the common statement, true in itself but often misapplied, that Aeschylus was a great religious thinker.

In all the variety of the Aeschylean drama one thing remains constant. The severe beauty of the *Septem*, the busy drama

---

[1] Wilamowitz puts a not uncommon misconception in its extreme form. The mild form is to misconstrue the importance of myth to the dramatist. It was very important—as material, as Holinshed and English history were to Shakespeare. The formative idea and everything that mattered most came from the poet.

of the *Eumenides*, the *tour de force* of the *Prometheus*, are
utterly unlike each other except in this, that each is built
upon a real dramatic thrill. This, naturally, is differently
felt and conveyed in the different types of play. It is natural
for us to think of dramatic excitement in terms of the *Tyrannus* or *I.T.* and if we look for thrills of this kind in Aeschylus
(except in the *Eumenides*), we shall deserve what we get—
nothing at all. Dramatic excitement exists on different levels,
or, perhaps we had better say, in different forms. As the
strictest and most air-tight fugue of Bach can be more exciting, and more dramatically exciting, than anything Wagner
ever encompassed, so an ' actionless ' plot of Old Tragedy
can be more dramatically exciting than the palpitating turns
of a Euripidean melodrama. Aristotle observed that we
should expect from tragedy not every poetic pleasure but the
appropriate one ; so too we must look in tragedy itself not
for a standard dramatic thrill but for the appropriate one.
Aeschylus gives us, in the *Eumenides* the obvious dramatic
excitement of the Furies and of the Trial ; at the other end of
the scale, in the *Supplices* or *Prometheus*, the non-realistic
sweep of lyrical drama ; somewhere between the two, the half-
hidden climaxes of the purple carpet or of Eteocles' long scene.
The Furies would frighten anybody, but an inattentive spectator of Agamemnon treading the carpet might merely wonder
what it was all about ; yet the carpet is not less dramatic than
the Furies. It is of capital importance in the criticism of
Aeschylus to realize that this dramatic element is anterior to
everything else. All our seven plays are built on a specifically
dramatic situation, and that situation is always treated in a
specifically dramatic way ; the proof is that when we approach
them from the specifically dramatic point of view they make
better dramatic, moral, intellectual sense than they do otherwise. It is perhaps not absolutely but is sufficiently true to
say that never do we find anything that does not spring from
the basic dramatic idea—no detachable sermons, no irrelevant
philosophizing, no scenes demanded by the story but not by
the drama, no factitious spectacle or action.

What was the relation between Attic tragedy and its narrative element ? The saga-theory seems to imply that tragedy

was narrative rather than dramatic in outlook, and much Aeschylean criticism seems to assume that Aeschylus was satisfied with staging a legend, provided that it contained lessons of the required Aeschylean grandeur, or gave opportunities for stage-effects.

It is obviously probable that much Attic tragedy was only saga dressed up for the stage. Athens must have had her dull mechanicals who could do no better—but what of that ? It means nothing. It would be possible to exhume hundreds of operas quite devoid of drama, but though they may be easily in the majority, they do not prove that Opera is undramatic. The best operas *are* dramatic ; the failures are no evidence at all.

What evidence we can find suggests that early drama with its development of static plot aimed at being dramatic, not at merely presenting heroic legend, not at counterfeiting narrative. It had a form which was admirably suited for the one thing and ill-suited for the other ; the chorus was built for weight and intensity, not for speed, and the earliest dramatic form was marvellously adapted to the development of a single situation, ill-adapted to the representation of a continuous action. Greek artists better than most saw what the appropriate use of their material was, and it seems rash to suppose that the earliest dramatists, on the whole, made any but the appropriate use of their dramatic form. This supposition that early drama was dramatic, though in the lyrical manner, seems to be supported by the subsequent development both of the chorus and of drama in general ; throughout the century there is a steady movement in the direction of narrative, away from the static plot ; vertical development of the play gives place to longitudinal. In Old Tragedy the plot begins to move, but is still very short, moving in the main vertically ; the actual plot of any Sophoclean play is very much longer than that of the *Agamemnon* ; while if we want to find plays in which the succession of incidents is the chief dramatic interest, it is to late plays like the *I.T.* or *Helen* that we must turn.[1] It is Euripides, not Aeschylus, who needs narrative

---

[1] This growth of the narrative element is just as clear in Comedy. Old Comedy does not attempt to tell a comic story ; it invents a comic situation and then develops it, vertically.

prologues and epilogues. Similarly, it is the early chorus that is dramatic, the later which becomes narrative or decorative.[1] At the beginning of the *Iphigeneia in Aulis* the chorus, finding itself moved from the centre to the periphery of the dramatic interest, can do nothing but give a long description of the Greek fleet. This is the opposite to the use of the chorus in the *Agamemnon*.

Our thesis that Attic drama was always dramatic in intention is not impaired by Aristotle's statement [2] that 'though the poets began by accepting any tragic story that came to hand, in these days the finest tragedies are always on the story of some few houses.' Obviously very many more stories would yield situations suitable to the lyric method than would give the type of story which the later practitioners in plot and intrigue needed.

We may draw support too from Aeschylus' treatment of his material. The poet has worried some of his commentators by not telling us clearly what happened in Egypt before the action of the *Supplices* starts ; hence the natural but untenable suggestion that the play is the second of the trilogy. It might indeed be urged that the earlier history was conveyed to the audience by the Egyptians in the second play, but what we can see of Aeschylus' methods elsewhere makes it much more likely that what the Egyptians explained was not past history but themselves, and even if they did recount history, it remains true that in the first play we manage very nicely without it. Does the *Septem* either at v. 1 or anywhere else show any anxiety to connect itself with the preceding *Oedipus* in any but a purely tragic way ? To all appearance it is a self-contained tragedy, not the climax of a story, and we must surely assume that the *Oedipus* was the same ; that no doubt it prophesied the fall of the brothers, but ended with its own climax, the fall of Oedipus. Certainly we can hardly suppose that it dealt with that which in narrative would be indispensable, the quarrel of the brothers and Polyneices' adventures in Argos.

[1] e.g. Andr. 274 ff., H. F. 348, El. 432, 698, Hel. 1304. The odes in the *Hecuba* and *Troades* describing the fall of Troy are, of course, essentially dramatic.

[2] *Poetics*, 1453a, 17 ff. Bywater's translation.

Why should it ? The facts were known, and if not known i
any great detail, the detail was irrelevant to the dramatic idea
The build and the spirit of the *Septem* suggest that in th
trilogy Aeschylus was not dramatizing the legend, but pre
senting, with the minimum of narrative, three tragic situation
taken from it, situations whose essential connexion was no
that they made one story, but that they made up one tragi
conception.[1] That is to say, far from representing saga an
being dramatic only incidentally, Aeschylus appears to be tak
ing advantage of the separate existence of saga in order t
relieve his work of everything that is not specifically dramati
and tragic.

The *Oresteia,* which does tell a connected story in a con
nected way, may seem to contradict this view, but in fac
corroborates it. The *Oresteia* is nothing like saga ; in par
ticular, the use of Cassandra is the very opposite of saga. It i
pure drama, both in inspiration and in technique. That th
sacrifice of Iphigeneia should be more important as part o
Agamemnon's sin than as part of Clytemnestra's experience
that the Herald, and Cassandra, should be used to deepen th
colours and not to tell us facts ; that so comparatively littl
time in the *Choephori* should be devoted to the business o
getting the deed done and so much to the invocation, to th
elaborate working-up of the two separate attitudes towards th
murder and the vengeance—all these points show that Aeschy
lus is not moralizing a legend for the stage but building up hi
own private tragic idea. Above all, the end of the trilog
shows this. The inevitable saga-ending would be Orestes
restoration to Argos, but for Aeschylus this is no ending at all
Orestes does indeed himself state (*Eum.* 754 ff.) that he can
now return, but the play takes very little notice of that, and
goes on to the culmination which has nothing to do with the
saga but everything to do with the dramatic idea.

If this is true, it is of importance to Aeschylean criticism.
It means that we must be even more reluctant than before to
explain a scene as ' amplification of plot ' ; that the plays must
be first understood dramatically ; above all that the ' mean-

[1] Euripides does the same, in a rather freer way, in the Trojan
trilogy. See p. 219.

ng' of a play must be seen through the drama. In this light too we may consider the Aeschylean inventions of the second actor and the trilogy. If it had always been quite clear that Attic tragedy was something distinct from saga, not narrative in feeling but purely dramatic; if Aeschylus continued to make his effects by the dramatic treatment of situation and not by presenting a story, then we must prefer the tragic to the 'dramatic' explanation of the second actor, that he was wanted to make situation more significant rather than to make drama more lifelike.[1] As for the trilogy, we say, naturally and truly, 'In the trilogy, with its wide range of time and subject, Aeschylus was able to trace the course of this hereditary evil [of the Pelopids] and to follow the crime from its original commission down to the period of its final expiation.'[2] He could; but this, it seems, should not tempt us to believe that the trilogy was invented to enable Aeschylus to trace a story or a continuous action. He still saw a tragedy as a situation, not as a course of action[3]; the trilogy was, in essence, three tragic situations suggestive of a wider conception rather than one continuous action. The Danaid-trilogy, merely as the tragic story of the Danaids, goes off the rails very early; there is not enough about what happened in Egypt and far too much about their reception in Argos, especially about Pelasgus' part in this. But as soon as we suppose that the original idea was to set in significant relation three tragic situations, that in fact Aeschylus was using but not subserving the story, everything becomes clear, well-proportioned, and therefore convincing. The beginning of this trilogy, like the end of the *Oresteia*, is what the tragic poet wanted, not what the story suggested. These three situations might, as in the *Oresteia*, cover a legend fairly continuously (though without giving or needing a common hero); they might, as perhaps in the *Oedipodeia*, be comparatively discrete; in either case the real unity comes from the dramatic idea and not from the legend. Aeschylus used saga, as he used even recent history,

[1] As on p. 34.

[2] Haigh, *The Attic Theatre* (3rd edn.), p. 14.

[3] Sophocles, because he saw it as a course of significant action, abandoned the trilogy. See below, p. 157.

as something to be manipulated, drastically refashioned
necessary, in the interests of a purely dramatic conceptior

To pursue this argument a little further, we may notice th
the saga-theory works only on the extravagant assumption th
whatever the Attic dramatists do with legend shows that tl
spirit of Saga is still alive. But when Euripides marries c
Electra to a peasant or makes fun of Helen and Menelaus I
is showing that it is dead. Something indeed is still aliv
something which lives up to the moment when Greek Tragec
disappears from our sight. While Greek poetry was st
being made within the Greek city-state, it could use Gree
mythology in a significant way. In this general sense m
thology is the same thing to Homer, Pindar and Euripide
and a different thing to Callimachus and Catullus. Exporte
to Alexandria or exploited by foreigners in Italy it died ;
became an ornament, a peg for rhetoric, an outlet for peda
try, sometimes a mere substitute for thought, and an intole
able bore. Often no doubt it was little more than sheer orn
ment in the minor Greek poets themselves ; Bacchylides use
it in the same superficial way as Catullus, simply to mak
fine verses ; but the greater Greek poets had somthing to say
and they found in their native mythology a good way of sayin
it, so that this still lives, animated by the thought poured int
it.

But it is dramatic and tragic thought that animates th
saga, not the other way about. We can see at least three di
tinct stages in the significant use of mythology : the narrativ
the lyric, and the dramatic. Of these, the first, Epic, is sag
—or near it ; the others something else. Is it saga whe
Pindar paints that incomparable picture of Apollo watchin
Cyrene straining motionless against the lion ? or when th
chorus of the *Agamemnon* illuminates in three or four flashe
the sacrifice of Iphigeneia ? or when Prometheus and Zeu
move from enmity to a reconciliation in a new world-order
It is the lyrical intensity of Pindar, the dramatic intensity o

[1] Croiset (*Hist. Litt. Gr.*, III, 203–4) : ' Loin de surcharger I
légende, Eschyle l'allégerait plutôt. Quand il compose il est sou
l'empire d'une impression unique et profonde : c'est celle-là qu'i
veut passer tout entière dans l'âme des spectateurs.'

Aeschylus, that makes these legends live in this rehandling. But when the *polis* broke up and poetry became suddenly polite and middle-class in the new Alexandrian world, it was impossible to speak above a polite murmur. Intellect and genius were there, but the surrounding pressure of a compact and homogeneous society which had raised so high the temperature of that genius was suddenly removed. The earlier intensity was dissipated, to be re-formed in new spheres—in the sciences, in the new Hellenistic philosophies. Saga dropped stone-dead—unless we make an honourable exception of Theocritus and any others who could make of it, in the epyllion, an agreeable and lively domestic pet.

But if Aeschylus was not making drama in the pure spirit of Saga, neither is he simply a great religious thinker who happens to express himself with the help of drama. He is indeed a great religious poet, but the connexion between his art and his religion is a matter of some importance, for Aeschylus suffers more than most dramatists if his thought and his art are considered separately. Too often it is assumed that an Aeschylean play is accounted for when some important doctrine, religious or philosophical, is seen in it. An extreme example of this purely external criticism is the following. ' The *Supplices* is a mirror of the ancient rights of hospitality, resting on the sacredness of the tie of kinship . . . It shows Greek humanitarianism arrayed against the cruelty of barbarism.' Apart from the fact that the play shows nothing of the sort, and would be intolerably complacent if it did, what dramatic tension could come out of such an idea ? Even to go deeper and to ask the question ' Does Zeus protect the suppliant ? ' makes drama only if the question is No, or Perhaps—which is substantially the answer that Aeschylus does give. Aeschylus did not write this trilogy triumphantly to answer a question about Zeus, but because he saw the drama and the tragedy of the wronged putting themselves in the wrong. Wherever we look in his work we find that from the beginning the religious idea is seen as a drama, and the drama seen as a religious problem. The thought and the form completely interpenetrate, so that they become one and the same thing. Aeschylus was not simply a poet ; he is a supreme master of the art of the

theatre ; and he expresses his thought in every element of thi
complex art—in speech, plot, situation, dance, imagery.

If we are not expecting this, we miss some of the though'
and then have to write apologetically about the drama.   On
of the older critics, who did not expect Aeschylus to mea
anything unless he said it, wrote of the Herald-scene in th
Agamemnon that it ushers in the King in a kingly way, and
by mentioning Menelaus, prepares the way for the conclud
ing satyric play, Proteus ; to which a recent critic adds
cautiously, ' Still, the sinister implications of this passage i
the *Agamemnon* are sufficient to justify its inclusion.'   Per
haps they are, since this conspiring together of the ancien
enemies, Fire and Water, and the widespread destruction tha
they produced, are the most terrifying glimpses we have ye
had in the play of the swiftness and completeness with whicl
the gods can punish hybris.   If we take the superficial view
of the *Persae* we may write ' The play is designed primarily a
a glorification of the victory over the Persians at the battl
of Salamis ' ; but if we do, we shall find ourselves writing the
next moment ' Strangely enough, Aeschylus gives only the
barest mention to the glorious Athenian victory over the force
of Darius at Marathon '—and other features of the plot wil
seem no less queer.   Until the drama and the thought are
integrated, both are liable to be misunderstood.   When we
see that the Strymon-incident, for example, is not decoratior
but demonstration, the play begins to disclose its significance

Aeschylus' masterly, and silent, use of dramatic situatior
is shown in the latter part of the *Agamemnon*.   After thai
long and terrifying preparation, Justice at last has found
Agamemnon ; the man whom Zeus sent to avenge crime
through crime has been met with the inevitable punishment,
and we see the triumphant avenger standing over the body
of the man she has slain.   But Aeschylus, with a few unobtrusive touches, suggests that she has only taken his place ; she
pleads the same *dike* (justice) that sent him on his errand,
she, like him, is persuaded that all is well, and hopes that the
evil may end here.   It is a most economic and therefore
powerful way of presenting one of the ideas fundamental to

the trilogy, that at this stage there is no possibility of final justice, no ' release from toil '.

That Aeschylus' magnificent imagery is at the same time dramatic and a revelation of the underlying thought needs no emphasizing. Again we can turn to the *Agamemnon*, to the net which Zeus throws over Troy, which becomes the net in which Clytemnestra enmeshes Agamemnon ; to the eagles who are robbed and are aided by the gods, who become, while we watch them, devourers of the innocent who incur the wrath of Artemis. The whole problem and the whole tragedy of the *Agamemnon* is implicit in this one image.

Finally, we should count on the possibility that Aeschylus, if everybody had his rights, was one of the finest choreographers that Europe has seen, and that his dances were as eloquent as his poetry and his stage-drama. In several cases we can see, even now, that the dance was an eloquent adjunct to the drama—for example, in the liquid anacreontic rhythms of the *P.V.* ; which betoken a liquid dance that contrasts strongly with the situation of the inflexible hero of the play, a rock bound to a rock. But in the *Agamemnon* we can go further, and observe at least the ground-plan of a dance which becomes an idea made visible. The last six strophes of the first ode, the whole of the second ode, and the last four stanzas of the third ode are all, with occasional interruptions, composed in the same slow iambic rhythm. This implies, obviously, a certain kind of music and a certain dance-form ; and when we look at the text we find that this rhythm, music and dance are used always to accompany the idea of hybris and its punishment, the hybris of Agamemnon, the punishment and the hybris of Paris, the hybris of Agamemnon once more ; an oppressive *ostinato* in the three arts at once, leading to —what ? To the stage-direction : *Enter Agamemnon, with Cassandra*, as the dance ends—on the words ' Justice leads all to the end appointed '.

In this dance, which gains in weight and meaning with every repetition, we have thought and argument made visible, in the orchestra. Here, as indeed everywhere, Aeschylus' religion and his art are completely fused, so that the one explains the other. In no real sense was Aeschylus a poet of

saga ; and he is a religious dramatist in the full sense of both
words. He is not putting saga into dramatic form, but
dramatizing an idea ; nor can we hope to understand his
thought except by absorbing and understanding his drama.
It is said ' Sophocles was an artist ' ; so was Aeschylus, in
exactly the same way ; what he wanted to say he said through
every element of his art. Therefore it is idle to criticize him
from the historical point of view, as if he were a primitive
Sophocles. He wasn't. His dramatic form is as masterly, in
all its details, as that of Sophocles. It is different because he
thought differently. This difference we must now discuss.

It is at once evident that the kernel of his drama is very
different from that of Sophocles'. To Sophocles, the tragedy
of life is not that man is wicked or foolish, but that he is
imperfect ; even at his best unequal to a sudden demand
made by circumstances. We are not automatically punished
for shortcomings. One man may be tyrannical and escape ;
Creon is tyrannical and does not escape. He gravely offended
Heaven, but he saw his error and repented—late, though still
in time ; but Antigone was not, as it happened, of the kind
to sit and weep and wait for death, and Haemon happened to
love Antigone ; so that Creon's world collapsed. It was partly
error, partly bad luck, and it is tragic because it was at least
intended honestly. Oedipus was prudent and intelligent far
above the average, but his circumstances were dangerous, far
above the average, and Oedipus was not prudent enough.
Tragedy of situation, in which the hero is lost either way, did
not (so far as we see now) appeal to Sophocles, nor did he
present the human tragedy in the shape of an infatuate who
dooms himself by his reckless folly. The pity is, always, that
man should be so fine, yet ruin all by a single glaring fault ;
so strong, yet be brought low by stronger circumstances.

Such a conception demands first and foremost that we must
be able to enter intimately into the hero's mind and soul, to
see his strength and weakness, follow his motives, watch him,
with sympathy, understanding and a growing apprehension,
as he passes from apparent security to disaster. It implies,
in fact, the Sophoclean plot and the Aristotelian theory.

Aeschylus conceived a radically different tragedy, one

which we may perhaps call more abstract. By this I mean that whereas the Sophoclean hero is, for the time being, a complete representative of tragic humanity, the Aeschylean is not Man, in his strength and weakness, but a fearful, even an extreme case of one sinful error that inevitably leads the sinner to catastrophe. It is tragic, not moral only, because the sin is so striking, the catastrophe so overwhelming, the drama so significant of the terms on which we hold our tenure of life. The tragedy is that there are on the one hand certain fundamental moral principles, on the other hand the possibility of man being so infatuate as to set these at defiance and to be utterly destroyed in consequence. This is not the tragedy of the divided [1] or vulnerable human soul ; Agamemnon's tragedy is not one of character (as the phrase is normally used). We are not shown a hero in whom hybris, called by some circumstance into activity, ruins a character otherwise admirable,[2] nor one who, intending well, works evil through mistake or mischance. Instead of looking at such a division in the hero's own soul or mind we look at the division, the chasm, between Agamemnon and Justice ; the tragedy is in his existence, not in his spiritual composition. What passes within his mind, therefore, is of no consequence, except that when he has to choose we must see him choosing wrong. Beyond this point Aeschylus does not take us. We have a glimpse of his struggle before slaying Iphigeneia, and before treading the purple carpet ; he sees the sin, but he falls, and that is all that matters. Except for this therefore he is left a tragic outline.

Such a tragic idea needs the austere Aeschylean characterization, and explains why Aeschylus used the third actor as he did. Nothing must interfere with the picture of the King doomed by blind presumptuousness. The Herald may not make things more ' tragic ' by informing us that Agamemnon was a brave and considerate general. In the *Tyrannus* it is an important part of the tragic idea that Oedipus was a wise father to the citizens, courteous and reasonable (until suspicion intervenes) to such as Creon and Teiresias ; the pity is that with all his virtues Oedipus falls. An Ajax who

[1] The *Septem* is.
[2] See p. 198, on Macbeth.

was nothing but intolerant pride would, in the Sophoclean
type of drama, be quite meaningless ; the picture of a fool or
a monster working out his own ruin leaves us, as we say, cold.
For such an internal drama to be tragic, there must be com-
pensating even if not predominating virtues ; these make the
tragedy.   But if we could keep our distance from Ajax, so that
we saw him not as an interesting individual but as the incarnation of one major human error, on which retribution inevitably
falls, then he could be pride and nothing else.   He would not
be a fool or monster, but a tragic outline.   Everyone in the
Agamemnon conspires not to give us the additional light on
Agamemnon's character and motives which they so easily
could, because this would not illuminate, but blur, the picture
of the hero at variance with the moral laws of the universe.
Conversely, we must not think of Sophocles' more intimate
and detailed character-drawing as merely the next stage in the
development of drama, or as something added because
Sophocles could do it well ; it arose inevitably from a different
conception of tragedy, and when Euripides thought of yet
another, it inevitably vanished.

We may go further, and see how the tragic idea of Aeschylus rendered impossible the Sophoclean plot as well as the
Sophoclean characterization.   The essentials of the Sophoclean
tragedy are that the various aspects of the hero's character
should so combine with events as to lead to a disastrous issue.
The character itself is not catastrophic, but, in Aristotle's
elastic use of the word, normal.   The disastrous issue must, in
retrospect, appear to have been inevitable ; but at the beginning, before the particular circumstances have begun to play
on the hero, he must be in that normal state which we conventionally call ' happy '.[1]   He must be seen passing from this

---

[1] This, of course, is not to be taken too literally.   The play involves a course of action (a *praxis*), but need not be coincident
with it.   It is not, I think, an objection to the present argument
that Ajax, for example, is not ' happy ' at the beginning of the play.
The play involves, though it does not present, Ajax' previous standing as the mighty hero, the great champion, and in this sense the
action begins in ' happiness '.   This is not true of Agamemnon ; he
is even born heir to retribution, and his part in the drama is—to
deserve it.

normal state to a disaster which is either quite unforeseen or much greater than could be possibly expected, through this working together of character and external events. We have therefore, inevitably, the Aristotelian plot—the transit (*metabainein*) from happiness to unhappiness, the steady presentation of the course of events either as produced by the hero or as acting upon him, and those dramatic crises of recognition and reversal of fortune which bring about the unforeseen disaster and heighten its significance.

The Aeschylean plot may not move in this way; it must be, in comparison, static. There is no character to be developed, for we see the hero instantaneously, complete. He is already doomed, we can see it; he must fall. There is no question of his being ' happy '; he is a marked man, though he may be the only one who does not see it. The transit cannot exist, nor that element of sheer surprise. We may be overwhelmed by the magnitude of the disaster, but not by the fact that the hero falls. His fall is relatively independent of circumstances, in the sense that it can be no part of the tragedy of a Xerxes or an Agamemnon that we should feel that he might have escaped if events had not been so untoward. There can be no stealthy concatenation of events, no elaborate interplay between these, the hero's character, and other persons in the action. Xerxes stands apart from Zeus, the infatuate against a background of Justice; Agamemnon walks blindly towards the inevitable chasm. In comparison with the Sophoclean tragedy, we may say that the hero does not work out his own fate; he is responsible, but he is smitten by Zeus or Justice, and the ways of Zeus are not devious or contingent. Once more, the Sophoclean plot (like his characterization) is not merely the next stage in Tragedy, or an improvement; it is a necessity that comes from a new tragic conception, and will disappear when yet a third arises.

The movement which is proper to this Aeschylean tragic idea—as ' dramatic ' a movement as any—is our increasing sense of the inevitability of the fall. Nothing in the first part of the *Agamemnon* brings the catastrophe nearer (except the actual arrival at Argos), as every successive line of the *Tyrannus* does, but everything darkens the colours and makes

the chasm that separates the doomed man from Justice wider
and more awful.   Aeschylus will not buy a spurious dramatic
movement by pretending at the beginning that the chasm does
not exist ; the Persians are already uneasy, not confident, and
Agamemnon enters not as the radiant conqueror, but as the
sinner.   The count against him is gradually piled up ; he
does nothing new except symbolically tread on the purple,
but we hear more and more of what he has already done ;
already at the outset the hand is uplifted to strike—Agamemnon does nothing, the play does nothing, to bring it down.
We are only made to feel more and more terribly that the
hand must strike, that it may be the hand of an adultress but
that at least Agamemnon cannot complain.   There is no complication whatever, no relief, no turning aside to another
aspect of Agamemnon's mind or personality ; such a distraction
would be ruinous.   All the time we see the blow coming ;
the hero, nearly motionless, takes on more and more clearly
the awful aspect of the doomed sinner ; and at last the blow
falls.   This is what the lyrical method of Old Tragedy could
do.

Even the *Septem* differs in this way from Sophocles.   Being
a tragedy of character it has its Aristotelian transit from happiness to unhappiness, and it is a movement of plot and not an
intensification of situation that brings this about.   During the
play itself Eteocles has to do, naturally even if not inevitably,
certain things without doing which he would escape, and
external events (mainly his brother) have to play their part.
But although this makes a plot much more Sophoclean than
the *Agamemnon,* Aeschylus yet aims at the effect of awful
stillness rather than that of a long steady movement, gathering
momentum from other sources and quickening to the climax.
The tragedy differs from Agamemnon's in that the noble side
of the hero is tragically significant and is therefore made
dramatically efficient, but it is like Agamemnon's and unlike
Oedipus' in that the fault, the insensate hatred of Polyneices,
is not venial or potentially harmless, but is catastrophic.
The cataclysm therefore must not be brought from distant and
apparently innocent sources ; it must always be at hand.   It
is marvellously right that there should be no Antigone or

Haemon to help Eteocles to bring about the crash in a complicated way, only the perfectly colourless Spy.

The terrible intensification of foreboding that we have in the *Agamemnon* is as characteristic of Aeschylus as his tragic irony is of Sophocles, and the difference between these effects is intimately connected with the difference between the two types of tragic hero. In each case, the legend being known, we know roughly what is to happen ; but the tragedy of the Aeschylean hero is virtually complete when the play opens—complete but for the falling of the blow ; of the Sophoclean it is not. That is to say, whereas in the *Agamemnon* we know that Agamemnon will be murdered, and the Chorus too suspects something of the kind, in the *Tyrannus* we know the truth but no one in the play does. The *Agamemnon* must begin in gloom ; the *Tyrannus* (as far as the position of Oedipus is concerned) in serenity. Therefore in the *Agamemnon* our private knowledge can be used to lend to the foreboding of the chorus a dreadful undertone of certainty, but in the *Tyrannus* to invest the confidence of everyone in the play with fearful irony.

We have now seen how the tragic conception of Aeschylus governs his characterization, his use of the third actor, and the nature of his plot. Before we consider the relation of all this to Aristotle's theory we may notice how it affects the use of the Chorus.

The Chorus, Aristotle said, should be a co-actor as in Sophocles, not as in Euripides ; he might have added 'nor as in the *Agamemnon*'. The Chorus is a co-actor in Sophocles because, since we begin with an apparently innocent and 'happy' man, and since the whole play is a transit from this to guilty unhappiness, and since at the beginning nobody but the audience knows that there is to be an unhappy ending, the chorus must reflect and participate in this growing action. It cannot surround it with an atmosphere of gloom and guilt, because it does not know that such is the atmosphere. The tragic feeling of the whole is concentrated in the character and action of the hero, and the chorus must in some way follow this action. The Aeschylean chorus is not always limited

to the growing action, and can be independent of the hero.[1]
For example, Troy is captured, and Paris slain; are we to
rejoice, and to congratulate the King? It would be typical
of Sophocles to make the chorus rejoice, then, later, to change
its tune; it is typical of Aeschylus that his chorus presents
the victory as the punishment of hybris, and then, by a
natural transition, tells us that Agamemnon himself has been
guilty of hybris—leaving us to draw our own conclusions.
The Sophoclean chorus normally follows the action, like a
co-actor; we have to realize, sometimes, that the Aeschylean
chorus is used differently. In a superficial sense, it is more
detached, standing back, and enveloping rather than following
the action.

We may now inquire what is the relation of Aristotle's
theory to Aeschylus. The answer is, roughly, None whatever. Aristotle's tragic hero, who must be neither good nor
bad, but average (or a little better) and 'like' us, is the
Sophoclean hero who in himself prefigures the human tragedy,
all of it. He must be a blend of good and bad, strong and
weak, or his ruin will mean nothing. The Aeschylean hero,
who is not intended to sum up and typify in his own breast
the tragic strength and weakness of man, need not be a blend
and therefore cannot be 'like us'; he must be only the sinner,
with so much characterization as to make him intelligible.
He is, notwithstanding this, far from being the completely
wicked man in whose downfall Aristotle refused to be interested; he is not a complete man at all, for we see (as of
course in Sophocles too) only that part of him that belongs
to the drama, and it is a single part; and, what is more
important, he acts not from evil motives but from moral
blindness.

Since the Aeschylean hero is so single-minded we need to
be careful with the doctrine of hamartia. In Aristotle's
theory this is the flaw, be it great or small, moral or intellectual, without which the hero would not have fallen nor

---

[1] Except when it is an actor, naturally, as in the *Supplices*,
Choephori and *Eumenides*, or a loose appendage, as in the *Prometheus*. I have already said that there is no one 'Aeschylean use'
of anything.

his character have been a tragic one.   The hybris of Xerxes
or Agamemnon is not this at all ; it is something without which
these heroes would not exist ; it is all of them that matters.
We may speak perhaps (though I for one would rather not)
of the hamartia of Eteocles, but certainly of no other Aeschylean hero.   Orestes, like Pelasgus, cannot help himself ;
hamartia means that you might have done so—not simply that
you are not perfect.   Xerxes and Agamemnon might be
called a typical hamartia of mankind writ large and made
pure, but this is not what Aristotle has in mind.   Prometheus
has often been given a hamartia.   He may indeed be accused of stubbornness and self-will, but this is not the same
thing.   Aristotelian hamartia is not *any* shortcoming which
may be found in a suffering hero ; it is the defect which makes
his character tragically imperfect and is directly responsible
for his fall.   Prometheus' stubbornness increases his suffering
but is not the cause of it.   This is that he pitied the human
race and saved it from Zeus, which may have been a mistake, but cannot be called hamartia—not at least by us.   We
are bound to accept the act as meritorious and to see the
source of the tragedy therefore in the fact that, until Zeus
has learned to be merciful, there was no room in the universe
for both him and Prometheus.   It is essentially a tragedy
of situation.   The purpose of the stubbornness is to prepare
the way for the reconciliation—a dramaturgical point.   It
lends Zeus some reason for his behaviour, so that he does not
entirely forfeit our sympathy, and it means that in the
reconciliation both parties have something to concede.   It
does not mean that Pometheus is a complicated character
who is suffering for some defect in it.   Antigone offers an
interesting parallel.   There was, at the crisis, no room in
Thebes for her and Creon too.   Her personal tragedy springs
from no hamartia ; it was no more wrong in her to bury her
brother than it was in Prometheus to be the saviour and
benefactor of humanity.   Hers too is the pure tragedy of
situation, with hamartia quite irrelevant.   If therefore there
is anything to censure in her—and commentators (may they
be forgiven !) have found it—it is there for a dramaturgical
purpose.   She is impatient with Ismene ?   A shade hard ?

Perhaps too incisive in her general manner ? Not the sort
of girl then to sit down in her cavern and wait patiently for
death ?

Wilamowitz observed that the doctrine of pity and fear
seems not to apply to Aeschylus. It does not ; but, again,
not because Aristotle misunderstood the Attic spirit, but because he entirely neglected this form of tragedy. ' Pity and
fear ' is eloquent of Sophocles' tragedy, but not necessarily
of any other ; eloquent because Sophocles brings us right into
the mind of his hero, so that knowing him intimately and seeing his fatal error ruining the whole we do pity ; and since
he is a man who, whatever his stature, is at least, like us, a
blend of good and bad, and since this particular form of
tragedy does show us how impotent the good may be in the
face of circumstance, why should we not fear for ourselves ?
It is not in the least that we identify ourselves with the hero ;
we fear because we see that Man is less than life.

But with the Aeschylean hero we are in an entirely different
relation. We may indeed pity Agamemnon, but Aeschylus
does not see to it that we must. He has not in any sense
made him ' like ' us ; we are not such single-minded sinners.
The tragic emotion here is rather one of awe ; Agamemnon so
terribly shows the fearfulness of sin. We remain always
looking at Agamemnon from the outside ; this precludes pity.
He is obviously doomed from the start ; this precludes fear.
He sharply illustrates the penalties that life, or Zeus, can
exact from those that defy his laws ; this is why he is tragic,
but a tragic figure, not a tragic character.

Then there is the ' happy ending '. Aristotle is quite positive that this is inferior to the unhappy one ; it is, he declares,
a concession to the weakness of the audience. Yet, Wilamowitz again points out, the *Eumenides* and the *Philoctetes* end
happily—so, obviously, did the *Prometheia*—and the endings
are right. They are right because they end plays which are
not Aristotelian at all, but intellectual drama. They begin
with an intellectual discord, or a tragedy of situation which
is intellectually developed, and they move to an intellectual
resolution, which is obviously the right direction and one
which hurts nobody but rather removes hurt. Far from hav-

ing in these plays a sign of the fundamental spirit of Greek Tragedy, we have probably a sign of maturity and development. All these plays, at least, were works of old age, and, as for Attic tragedy in general, it in its old age shows a marked tendency towards the intellectual, when it had passed through its great tragic period.

But however this may be, it is quite clear that when Aristotle said this about the happy ending he was not thinking of plays of this type at all. We may surely credit him with enough critical insight to have seen that in intellectual drama the happy ending is right ; we may safely assume that if he had written the book which we all wish he had written he would have said so ; and that the happy endings he objected to were in fact objectionable—illogical windings-up of tragic themes, adopted out of nervousness or debility, like those which we endure, or do not endure, in the celluloid drama of our own times.

We see then that in many important points Aeschylus' drama and Aristotle's theory do not come into contact at all. What Aristotle says about the Tragic Hero, his hamartia, characterization, the nature of the tragic emotion, the proper movement and the best type of plot—all these things have not to be merely modified when we come to Aeschylus, as if Aeschylus were an incomplete Aristotelian because relatively primitive, but they have to be entirely disregarded ; and the fundamental reason for this is that his natural way of tragic thinking was different from Sophocles'. We shall see later that it is similarly useless to try to clamp Aristotelianism on to the tragedy of Euripides, and for the same reason. Wilamowitz says that the whole trouble is that Aristotle used the wrong method, the aesthetic and not the historical. There is no harm in being historical, certainly, but why it should be wrong to use aesthetic methods on material which can be understood only aesthetically it is a little difficult to see. Aristotle was so regrettably severe in his treatment of Tragedy because his basis was neither aesthetic nor historical, but biological—as he says himself. Tragedy is an organism, a *zoon,* and like all organisms has its growth, its perfection and its decay. We may think that any given fourteenth- or fif-

teenth-century painter is not a better painter than Cimabue,
but there is no doubt that the art of painting had developed
considerably ; whatever we think of the merits of Aeschylus
and Sophocles as dramatists, there can be no question but
that the form of drama was more complete in Sophocles.
What is more, his was a form which could be imitated to some
purpose ; it was ' classical ' and made the earlier dramatic
forms ' primitive '.   Aristotle therefore, who was writing on
the Art of Literary Composition and not on the History of
Attic drama, naturally considers exclusively the dramatic form
which is the most complete, and that happens to be the
Sophoclean.   Whether he thought Aeschylus to be aesthetically inferior to Sophocles we can only guess ; he mentions
him critically only once, and then, by an odd irony, to point
out how Euripides took one of his verses and made it grander.
To suppose that he was unaware of the essential difference
between Aeschylus and Sophocles seems rash ; it is perhaps
legitimate to argue that his complete silence about Aeschylus
the dramatist shows that he was aware of it ; nothing that
Aeschylus did could serve him either as a model or as a warning.

We may indeed regret that Aristotle was so severe.   Had
he taken it upon himself to analyse every significant form of
Attic tragedy we should have been spared a deal of trouble.
He did not do this, and if we take the *Poetics* as a universal
theory of tragedy we certainly confuse ourselves and probably do an injustice to Aristotle.   It is often suggested [1] that
his theory is defective because he had only Greek tragedy
to work on.   This is quite misleading, for of the three or
four distinct types of Greek tragedy that he might have used
he rejects all but one.

[1] As, for example, by Butcher, *Aristotle's Theory of Poetry*, pp.
332 f.

CHAPTER V

MIDDLE TRAGEDY : SOPHOCLES

1. INTRODUCTION Aeschylus is a profound religious dramatist, Euripides a brilliant, uneven representative of the new
spirit which was so uncomfortable in the old forms, and
Sophocles was an artist. We all know what an artist is : he
is one who makes things which are beautiful or at least pretty,
and if he is an artist of the right kind what he makes is good
for us. Our public thinks like this, and so did the Greeks—
with more excuse. Critics of the last century never ceased
thanking Heaven that Sophocles believed in the Gods—their
profound satisfaction lives on in the writings of examinees—
and, assured that Sophocles was an artist of the right kind,
they turned to the grateful and interesting task of examining
and admiring his astonishing technique.

But an air of conventionality could be felt. Aeschylus has
his religion, Euripides his views and his very tragic single-
scenes ; what was there to say about Sophocles except that his
religion and politics were admirable and his art perfect ?
One concentrated on the art ; indeed, when the *Electra* was
mentioned one had to. The ' happy ending ' of this play and
its avoidance of moral strife were a little puzzling. The poet
who also wrote the *Antigone* has been accused of a certain
complacency, of a bluntness of moral perception, and the
Electra has been explained by the assumption that Sophocles
retired into the Homeric age to write it. It was said that
Sophocles interested himself chiefly in the persons who did
these things ; he took the events for granted and studied the
characters of the actors in them—as if one could study character in a moral vacuum.

This simple view of the artist brought other difficulties, and
in spite of the close attention which Sophocles has received
during the last twenty years some of them remain. The most
troublesome, oddly enough, are structural. When Euripides
fails to perform what is evidently the artist's first duty, to

turn out a shapely play, we are not surprised ; we may invent
a series of special explanations, a different one for each offend-
ing play, or take refuge in a general theory of incompatibility
or ineptitude, but we are not surprised. When Sophocles
does the same thing we are perturbed ; he did know better ;
yet the *Ajax* and the *Trachiniae* fall into two parts almost as
badly as the *Andromache* and the *Hecuba*, and the end of the
Antigone has been accused of throwing the play out of balance. Sophocles does not indeed descend to unrelated scenes,
nor does he combine two distinct legends into one unsatisfactory plot, but the structure of the *Ajax* and the *Trachiniae*,
since the plays were made by Sophocles, is at least as puzzling
as that of the *Suppliant Women, Hecuba* or *Andromache*,
which can plead the magic excuse ' Euripides '.

One way out of the difficulty was to say as little as possible
about the *Antigone*, to think of special excuses for the *Ajax*,
and to write off the *Trachiniae* as a total loss. Such criticism
fails in all respects ; especially does it fail to explain why the
dichotomy is so unnecessarily absolute in the *Trachiniae*. A
modern method is to call unsatisfactory plots diptychs or
triptychs (which makes them sound better at once), and to
suppose that there was a period in Sophocles' artistic career
in which he thought that this was a reasonable, apparently
the only reasonable, way of making drama. It is assumed
that the *Trachiniae* belongs to the *Ajax-Antigone* period, *circa*
440, not to *circa* 420 as used to be thought, and the new date
is supported, vainly, by stylo-statistical evidence.

The explanation that will be attempted here is that Sophocles, because he was a great artist, had something more
important to do even than to make beautiful plays, namely
to express as directly as his medium allowed certain tragic
ideas which sprang out of a certain apprehension about human
life. If he was only a technician with a bias towards beauty
some of the ' faults ' are quite inexplicable. Being a great
dramatic artist he must, like Aeschylus, have had a tragic way
of thinking ; from this his drama sprang, to express this his
plays were shaped. When a critic can improve a play of
Sophocles', he may be sure that he is only giving it a turn that
Sophocles had already rejected. If then we can penetrate,

however dimly, to this bed-rock of the dramatist's thought, we may hope to understand the plays more intimately.

We may hope for more. Aristotle says in his bald way : ' Sophocles introduced the third actor and scene-painting.' What explains the plays should explain too why Sophocles imposed on Greek Tragedy the form he did ; questions of form and technique are fully resolved only when fully related to the mind of the artist who makes and uses them. What we should like to relate is Sophocles' introduction of the third actor, his interest in character and skill in drawing it, his marked leaning to irony in language and plot, his curtailment of the part of the Chorus, his typical tragic hero and plot— every element of his homogeneous art.

Before attempting this we may remove two obstacles. The first is to Sophoclean criticism what Aeschylus' religion is to Aeschylean ; Sophocles' character-drawing is so important that it is often taken (not perhaps consciously, but in effect) to be the determinant thing. Thus one critic writes, in a blithe moment, ' He even alters and manipulates the mythic material so that he may the more readily and brilliantly practise his hobby.' [1] This does indeed fall short of blasphemy, but it overlooks the essential difference between Sophocles and Dickens. It has been argued that the three Creons are por- traits of the same character—which may be true. But it is not true that ' it is hardly conceivable that so great an artist . . . primarily interested in the study and delineation of char- acter, could have failed to see or could consciously have ignored the need for consistency in character '.[2] There is no such need : Sophocles was not creating a portrait-gallery. The only need is that each play should present as vividly as possible the tragic idea that lies behind it.

The other stumbling-block is the fact that most Greek theory of art is moral. The Greek theory of art is nothing to us, who are concerned exclusively with the Greek practice of art. There are as many possible theories of art as there are ways of regarding art ; the Greeks regarded it from the moral point of view not because the Greek artist thought in a dif-

[1] C. R. Post, *Harvard Studies*, 1912, p. 72.
[2] D. Peterkin, *Class. Philology*, 1929, p. 264.

ferent way from any other but because their thought was predominantly political, and art, like drainage, undoubtedly performs some function in the state.[1] Sophocles was no doubt aware that his plays were good for Athens (though the passage in the *Apology* suggests that he could not prove this to Socrates) ; he may have tried to make them such. But no amount of morals will make a good play, and no moral analysis will explain a play.

In this chapter we shall examine the content and structure of the *Ajax, Antigone, Electra* and *Tyrannus*. The *Philoctetes* and *Trachiniae,* for reasons which will appear later, we class as New Tragedy, and the *Coloneus* demands separate treatment.

2. THE AJAX   It seems highly probable, though it is not certain nor even universally agreed, that the *Ajax* is Sophocles' earliest extant play, but at least fifteen and very likely twenty-five years separate it from his first victory. We are not therefore dealing with the work of a novice. The critical difficulty is that though Ajax kills himself at v. 865 the play goes on for another 550 verses, verses which are full of brilliant and hard wrangling about his burial, but which are not obviously a necessary continuation of the story. For a representative opinion of the play we might quote Dalmeyda [2] : ' Avec Ajax disparait l'intérêt principal du drama, qui consistait surtout dans la peinture des émotions diverses d'une âme héroïque, confiante dans sa valeur jusqu'à l'excès, jusqu'à l'orgueil impie. Dans la seconde partie de la pièce Teucre prend la place de son frère.' Or Bowra [3] : ' When he becomes sane he knows that he has lost his honour and therefore he kills himself. Our sympathies lie with Ajax, but true to the traditional outlook Sophocles makes it clear at the outset that the hero is guilty of presumption against the gods and is punished for it.'

That is to say, it is the normal sort of tragedy of character,

[1] Mr. Belloc, in one of his prefaces, states that he wrote the book ' for gain '. This implies a financial theory of art, but it should not affect Mr. Belloc's literary critic.

[2] *Revue des Études grecques,* 1932, p. 8.

[3] *Ancient Greek Literature,* p. 93.

the tragedy of Ajax and his hybris, but for some reason a disproportionate amount of attention is devoted to the hero's burial.

But this is extremely odd, especially when one reflects that mastery of form was peculiarly Sophocles' gift. A scholiast (on v. 1123) can remark ' Wishing to extend the drama he became frigid and dissipated the tragic emotion.' The conclusion may be sound, but the reason given, ' wishing to extend the play ', is silly. Sophocles was not a dolt, and if he had only wished to extend the play he would have done it at the other end. There was no difficulty in making a play about Ajax. Sophocles could have begun with Ajax brooding over his wrongs, coming to his resolve, making his attack (messenger-speech), passing from exultation to despair, killing himself, and being allowed burial through the efforts of Teucer and the generosity of Odysseus. This would have made a unity, and would have served all the purposes which have been alleged in explanation of the plot as we have it. If this plot had been used before, exactly, five minutes reflection would produce another capable of showing Ajax as the victim of his own hybris without defying the elementary laws of construction.

We are reminded that the Greeks attached great importance to funeral rites. They did, but there was no need to spoil a play with them, and in fact the point would be better emphasized if it were an integral part of the whole. The importance of burial did but make Sophocles' ' mistake ' possible. We need spend no time on the stock fantasies that the older critics used when in difficulties—such as that Iophon composed the second part ; nor on the theory that Sophocles was interested in an Ajax-cult, for there is no suggestion of this in the play, and if it were in some sense a *pièce d'occasion*, why was it not made a better *pièce* ? It is not true to say that the second part, like the second part of Julius Caesar, shows the greatness of Ajax. Caesar's spirit lives on, a giant among pygmies ; Ajax is scorned by the Atreidae and not even defended by Odysseus. It is just as idle to talk of the ' rehabilitation ' of Ajax : Teucer is a match for the Atreidae in vituperation, not in argument. There is no attempt to palliate

the crime of attempted treason and murder ; even Odysseus'
generosity stops short of that. Ajax was a hero, and he had
done valiantly, but (as Agamemnon points out) he owes his
burial to the enlightened self-interest of Odysseus. In fact,
Sophocles is at pains to show that Ajax is buried because
he is dead.

In the excuse that Greek plays preferred to end quietly
there are points of interest. Since the difference is so wide
between ending quietly and ending with two acts quite separate from the first three, the excuse is invalid ; but how far
is the general proposition true ? The *Supplices, P.V., Agamemnon* and *Choephori* do not end quietly, but they are not
independent plays. The *Eumenides* ends in peace, but the
ending is the climax of the whole trilogy. The *Electra* ends
on a climax which is not quiet, and the *Medea, Troades,
Hecuba, Heracleidae* end with a most evident dramatic thrill,
while all the quasi-melodramatic plays carefully pile up the
excitement to the final tableau. This is not ending quietly.
It is impossible to predicate any one thing of plays that vary
so much in kind ; all that we can say is that Greek taste preferred a play to follow its own logic. The lyrical ending of
the *Septem* is not ' quiet ' ; it is simply right ; the same can
be said of the *Tyrannus* and the *Antigone*.

None of these pleas helps the *Ajax* at all. We may agree
with the Scholiast that Sophocles made a gross error, but even
then we are bound to try to find a more convincing explanation of the error than the one he thought of.

We must weigh the character of Ajax, not selecting from
Sophocles' facts, but using all of them. It is of course impossible to transcribe these with the same colour and emphasis
that Sophocles gives to them,[1] but it is fair to say that Ajax
has virtually committed an atrocious and silly crime, which,
when he emerges from his madness and despair, causes him
no shame, only regret that he was thwarted. His vanity is
extreme, and allows him to see no possible reason for Odysseus' success in the contest except dishonesty. Time after

---

[1] A fact that Verrallians might remember when, having boiled
down and foreshortened a plot, they triumphantly ask, ' Can anything be more absurd ? '

time Ajax refers to Odysseus, and he is always wrong. His sailors, although they are the chorus, are wrong too. The chorus is a dramatic one ; and we have the advantage of seeing Odysseus for ourselves. This vanity is reinforced by the description (762–77) of Ajax' astonishing insolence to Athena ; entirely consonant with it is his indifference to the danger of his men and of Tecmessa. But besides all this we have the soldierly greatness of Ajax and his spiritual daring ; this, and the poetry which Sophocles entrusts to him, convince us that in spite of all he is a great man, but one completely lacking in *phronesis,* wisdom intellectual and moral. It is a bold but hardly a subtle character.

If we have any reason for confidence in Sophocles as a dramatist we must approach his structure not with preconceived ideas and excuses, but with a completely open mind. The structure differs from the conventional plot outlined above in its beginning and its end. It does not begin with Ajax brooding, or with Tecmessa lamenting, but with Odysseus. Why Odysseus ? The play ends too with Odysseus, who, without trying to justify Ajax, does secure his burial. Why Odysseus ? And if Odysseus, the clever speaker, why is he not made to ' rehabilitate ' Ajax ? Let us look at him more closely.

In the prologue the most striking thing, even more striking than the appearance of Ajax mad, is Odysseus' attitude to him. Athena has so directed Ajax' thoughts as to bring out his especial hatred of Odysseus, but Odysseus' reply to her boasting, or tempting, shows such moral greatness and insight that it must seem to every reader the most significant thing that has yet happened :

ATHENA. Seest thou, Odysseus, the power of the gods, how great it is ? What man couldst thou have found more vigilant than he, better and more timely in action ?

ODYSSEUS. I know of none. Still, I pity him, enemy though he is, for he is yoked to an evil fate [1]—thinking of myself no less than of him : for I see that all of us mortals are nothing but shadows and insubstantial smoke.

Odysseus is represented as the preeminent enemy of Ajax ; by

[1] *Atê* : ' une fatalité mauvaise ' (Masqueray) ; ' infatuation '.

this speech too we see him to be no ordinary man ; by frequent references he is kept prominently before our notice, and nearly every reference shows that Ajax either cannot or will not understand him. At the close Odysseus appears, to win over Agamemnon. He secures burial for Ajax not because he prevails in argument but because Agamemnon is willing to grant an unusual favour to the great Odysseus (vv. 1370–4). So far as the official view goes, Ajax is still an outcast.

In this last scene Odysseus shows the same characteristics as in the first ; the same pity, the same insight. Pitying Ajax because of his evil fate he urges his burial ' thinking of my own interests as much as his, for I too shall come to this '. He admits freely that he is working for himself ; he is, as the Chorus says, ' sound in judgment '. As in the prologue he shows prudence rather than romantic courage, so here he shows no altruism, no romantic generosity, but rather the large wisdom of a philosophic mind. As in the beginning he rose superior to Athena's temptations, so at the end he rises superior to the common morality of the Atreidae and gives burial honours to a dead foe and condemned criminal.

Odysseus therefore is no mere dramatic convenience : he does not merely give the play an external symmetry by appearing at the beginning and the end ; he is, if not as prominent as the hero Ajax, at least as essential to the play, much more essential than Teucer. The unifying theme is the antagonism of Ajax and Odysseus, of physical, and, we may admit, of spiritual daring against intellectual greatness ; an antagonism the more dramatic in that Ajax never understands Odysseus whereas Odysseus always understands Ajax. Ajax, lacking ' wisdom ', brings himself to ruin : Odysseus, rich in wisdom, not only is successful (as in the matter of the Arms), but also attains moral grandeur.

' Not the thick-set or broad of back are surest, but the wise prevail, everywhere.'
So Agamemnon says, more profoundly than he suspects.

The scenes of wrangling now fall into line. There is here a complication followed by a denouement. Teucer and the Atreidae come to an *impasse*. We feel that Ajax is too great a man to be dishonoured in death ; the Atreidae are too narrow to see this, and Teucer can only defy them, not rise above them. In these men there is no resolution of the antagonism ; that comes only when the greatness of Odysseus recognizes the greatness of the defeated Ajax and above all the greatness of the fact of Death. The end is rather the triumph of Odysseus than the rehabilitation of Ajax. In the prologue he triumphs over Athena's suggestions of crude force and resentment : by the vote of the army his intellectual greatness has already overcome Ajax' soldierly greatness ; now he brings the drama to a harmonious close by overcoming the moral violence of the Atreidae.

I do not suggest that this interpretation makes of the *Ajax* a perfect play, by Sophoclean standards of perfection. In many ways, notably in subtle control of dramatic rhythm, it falls short of what Sophocles was to do later ; only in its poetry can it challenge comparison with anything. But this view does make of it a reasonable play, and the key-stone, the importance of Odysseus, would be much more obvious in performance than it is in the reading. Moreover we shall see, I think, that the philosophic background is entirely consistent with that of Sophocles' other work in his middle period.

3. THE ANTIGONE The *Antigone* is accused, though more gently, of the same fault as the *Ajax* : the heroine drops out half-way through and leaves us to do our best with Creon, Haemon, and their fortunes.[1]

We must recognize that if there is a fault it is a radical one, due to deliberate choice and not to oversight or to the inability of Sophocles to cope with a difficult situation. It is inevitable that Antigone should disappear, but it is not inevitable that so little should be said in the Exodus about her, that her lover's corpse but not hers is brought back, that Creon should at such length lament his own fate, least of all that Eurydice should be so unexpectedly introduced in order to kill herself im-

---

[1] A critic of a Glasgow production of the *Antigone* in 1922 objected to the impressive cortège which escorted Haemon's body back to the stage because, emphasizing the shift in the centre of gravity, it underlined this fault in construction.

mediately. Why Eurydice? Sophocles had no Elizabethan relish for corpses. She is relevant only to Creon. Clearly the close of the play is all Creon, deliberately so, for there is less of Antigone than might have been. Sophocles is not even making the best of a bad job.

The difficulty that we feel arises from our regarding Antigone as the chief character. If she is to this play what Oedipus and Electra are to theirs (and the *Antigone* is often criticized on this assumption), then the play is ill-balanced, but if the *Antigone* is more like the *Ajax* than the *Tyrannus*, the centre of gravity does not lie in one person, but between two. The *Ajax* is second-rate Sophocles until we feel the significance of Odysseus; the last part of the *Antigone* makes no sense until we realise that there is not one central character but two, and that of the two, the significant one to Sophocles was always Creon. It is simply a matter of looking at the dramatic facts.[1] The older criticism (for of late things have taken a turn for the better) assumed that of course the play was about Antigone, and then set about explaining away the last scenes. The most satisfactory proof is performance. Creon can dominate the play; in the Glasgow production he did, easily and naturally.[2] But even without performance, we may note that Creon's part is half as long again as Antigone's, a point which is less mechanical than it sounds, and

---

[1] Purely formal criticism of Sophocles, by rule, is an impertinence. 'All arts aspire to the condition of music'; what this means was illustrated by (I think) Schumann. He was once asked by a man who had just heard him play one of his compositions what it meant. 'I will tell you,' said Schumann, and he played it again. The form *was* the meaning; and so it is with Sophocles—until it is shown that he was incapable of expressing himself properly. Any fool could 'improve' the *Ajax*, but only by making it mean something that Sophocles thought not worth saying. The disastrous notion that the artist is one who makes pretty things has been 'the beginning of many evils to the Greeks'.

[2] This was interesting. It was produced (Harrower's translation) in a large circus; the ring became the orchestra and a narrow stage was erected at the back. Two choruses were used, one to dance, the other placed on either side of the stage, to sing. It ran for a week; on the first two nights the audience was all high-brow and paper, on the last two the populace was fighting to get in.

that it is the more dynamic part. Hers is impressive and affecting enough, but his has the wider range and is the more elaborate. Her fate is decided in the first few verses and she can but go to meet it ; most of the dramatic forces used in the play are deployed against Creon—the slight reserve with which the chorus receives his edict (211–14), the news that he has been defied, and that too by a woman, the opposition of Haemon, the disapproval of the city (691 ff.), the supernatural machinery of Teiresias, the desertion of the chorus (1098), the death of Haemon (foreshadowed), the death of Eurydice (unforeshadowed). Creon truly says

' Old sir, ye all like bowmen at a mark
  Let fly your shafts at me.' [1]

Antigone is indeed opposed, but not like this. Her tragedy is terrible, but it is foreseen and swift ; Creon's grows before our eyes.

This must have been the balance that Sophocles designed ; whether this reading saves the play from fault is not our business. Perhaps modern minds make more of Antigone than was intended (though as the argument of Sallustius explains why the play was called the *Antigone* we may perhaps infer that ancients felt the difficulty too), perhaps Antigone upset Sophocles' plans as Dido is held to have upset Vergil's ; it is most likely that Sophocles did precisely what he set out to do, and that in this play, as in the *Ajax*, he built on a double foundation.

As to this double foundation, in the change from the bipartite structure of the *Ajax*, through the much less prominent double interest of the *Antigone*, to the splendid unity of the *Tyrannus* and the *Electra*, it is natural for us to see a technical development ; but something much more important than technique is involved, and it is not in fact easy to picture a Sophocles learning the rudiments of his art at the age of forty-five. Between these two earlier plays and the next two there is a perceptible change of tragic emphasis. The *Ajax* and the *Antigone* are based on what we may call a purely ethical conception ; this way of life is right and that one is

[1] V. 1033. My verse translations from this play are taken from Harrower.

wrong : ' Not the thick-set and broad-shouldered prevail, but
the wise, everywhere ' ; ' To be stiffnecked is folly.' [1]   Such
a general idea naturally takes dramatic shape in an opposition
between one who takes the wrong view and another who takes
the right.   In the second pair of plays the tragic idea is more
philosophical, without of course ceasing to be ethical.   One
hero, more complex, more delicately poised, less catastrophic
than either Ajax or Creon, fights not a moral law but his own
nature.   The moral and dramatic issue does not lie between
him and another, but between the various facets of his own
nature, assisted by the complexities of circumstance.   Thus
the one hero stands out more clearly from the other personages and a higher degree of unity follows.[2]   It is to some such
fundamental change of outlook, not to the superficialities of
dramatic technique, that we should turn if we wish to understand the development of Sophocles' form.   Form, with him,
is the same as thought [3] ; he did not need lessons from Aristotle.

The *Antigone* has been variously interpreted.   The transcendental philosophers, who, from Plato onwards, have never
been at their ease with the tragic poets, have done their worst
with it, and have been discomfited.   It has been a problem-
play, the poet's condemnation of contemporary statecraft, his
confession of religious faith.   What are the consequences of
regarding it as primarily the tragedy of Creon ?

First, I think we can afford to be reasonable about Antigone.   Hegel had to assume that there was something
seriously wrong with her ; later critics, rejecting this preposterous view, were nevertheless careful to maintain (partly
out of deference to Aristotle) that Antigone was not spotless.
People are never spotless, especially heroes and heroines of

---

[1] *Antigone*, 1028.

[2] I believe that this represents a fundamental development in
Sophocles' thought, but let it be said here once and for all that the
difference may be accidental.   We do not possess what a statis-
tician would regard as a big enough sample of Sophocles' plays
(though what we have, being among the best, have great significance).   (See also p. 157.)

[3] We all say this, but we do not always apply it.

tragedies. Antigone's hardness to Ismene therefore was exploited to the full—but this, surely, was no very striking blemish, hardly enough to spoil a perfect figure. We saw however in dealing with Pelasgus that the hamartia doctrine must either be interpreted reasonably or amended; Pelasgus had no fault in the *Supplices* not because he was a perfect man but because his character was irrelevant; equally we need not be assiduous in looking for saving faults in Antigone, because only part of her character comes into question here, the part which impels her to defy Creon; and where the blemish is there, only Hegel can tell us. The play is not a full-length portrait of Antigone, in which, let it be granted, perfection would be a little uninteresting. Her part is to suffer, and there is no dramatic canon which demands that victims should have faults: hardness and decisiveness were given her to explain her rebellion and her suicide. The chief *agent* is Creon; his is the character, his the faults and merits, which are immediately relevant to the play. If Sophocles is really inviting us to watch Creon, Antigone becomes much more natural, relieved of the burden of Aristotelianism, no longer the standard-bearer of the Unwritten Laws. On this, the last day of her life, she can be spared faults, as she can be spared heroics. Why indeed does she defy Creon? From a sense of religious duty? To Ismene, in the prologue, she mentions religious duty once—in an attempt to shame her sister. Her real thought comes out in phrases like

'He has no right to touch what is *mine*!—
Yes, my brother and—though you deny it—yours.'

She has a passionate feeling of what is due to her brother, to her race. Face to face with Creon's legality she indeed answers legally, and nobly, inspired to her highest eloquence, but essentially she is doing much more than championing one code against another; she is giving her whole being for her brother's honour. This leads to the genuineness of vv. 911–30. The confrontation with Creon over, we hear little more of her religious faith; she protests her innocence indeed, but the burden of her defence is again that her brother is hers to honour. Her tone is noticeably more personal. As the end draws near her defences fail one by one, until, in that

marvellously moving and tragic speech which was not to the
taste of those who saw in Antigone chiefly a martyr to the
Higher Law, she abandons everything except the fact that she
did it and had to do it. Facing death, deserted by the
Chorus, she has no confidence even in the gods, and doubts
her own impulse. For a husband, she says, No ; for a son,
No ; but for a brother—

‘ Since my mother and my father have both gone to the
grave, there can be none henceforth that I can ever call my
brother.’ A frigid sophism borrowed from Herodotus? Yes,
the finest borrowing in literature. This is the final tragedy of
Antigone : *novissima hora est*—and she can cling to nothing
but a frigid sophism.

If Antigone is more interesting than a mere antithesis to
Creon, he is more than the stubborn fool who kills her.
Sophocles was interested in his fate. He is, if not cruel, at
least insensitive ; like a tyrant, he is quick to suspect, and he
does not know how to yield. But he has his own honesty,
his own justification, and his own sense of responsibility. But
what Creon is is not the whole of the story. We have this
clear-cut moral issue between him and Antigone—itself a
little too elementary to serve as the sole background for so
subtle a thinker as Sophocles. We have too the clear-cut personal clash ; it is noteworthy that from the beginning of her
confrontation Antigone shows her contempt for this court.
She wastes no time in trying to bridge what she knows to be
an impassable gap. But behind all this there is the evolving
tragedy of Creon. Creon may be what you like, but he is
neither unintelligent nor irresponsible. He has his own field
of action and his own principles ; impulse, unwritten laws, are,
he feels, not for him ; he cannot move in this ampler region,
and he sincerely feels he has no business to. In his own
field he has thought things out and is confident of himself.
We feel his confidence as soon as we hear his

‘ Citizens, for what concerns the State . . . ’

He has tradition and experience on his side, his maxims are
sensible. True, a native stubbornness is given him, that he
may defend his position to the dramatic end, but it is not
from folly or wilfulness that he originally takes up his position.

But his confident judgement was wrong; his reason betrays him. It is true that but for his obstinacy he could have escaped with a lighter penalty, but the bitterness is that his judgement was wrong, and that Antigone's instinct was right; and in the end he has less to cling to than she. She goes 'in the sure and certain hope That dear to thee will be my coming, Father'[1]; he can say only

'Everything is turned to water in my hands.'

'By far the biggest part of happiness', says the Chorus, 'is Wisdom (*to phronein*).' And what is this? Not to behave impiously towards the Gods is part of it. And what is this? Creon was honouring the Gods after his fashion, Antigone after hers. How can you tell beforehand which is the right fashion? Alas! Piety is not an automatic thing; you may learn in time—*gera to phronein*. This is the tragedy of Creon.

4. THE ELECTRA This is a play which has troubled Sophoclean criticism more than any. As in the *Oresteia*, the central problem is a problem of *diké*, 'justice': what are we to think of the matricide? Very different answers have been given. Jebb held that it is to be accepted as right and glorious, as it was commanded by the god; that from the very first scene, in which the birds are singing their morning songs, 'it is the bright radiance of Apollo that prevails'; that Sophocles is inviting his audience to put itself at the Homeric standpoint, from which Orestes' act is seen to be one of simple merit.

This is quite impossible; all the dramatic facts are against it. The play does indeed open with dawn chasing away night, and with the cheerful songs of the birds, but from this point onwards it is sombre and unrelieved beyond any other play of Sophocles. The heroine, however much we may pity her, whatever her character may have been capable of, has become a harsh, unlovely woman, a credit to her own mother, as she herself says (v. 609). There is no sub-comic character, like Antigone's Guard, or the messenger from Corinth in the *Tyrannus*, to relieve or at least vary the tension. There is no ecstatic dance, nor any other sort of ode that gives relief. The only cheerful scene, the Recognition, has for its under-

[1] Harrower's translation.

tone the passionate cry for vengeance, and is clouded by the
terrible deed to come.   The heroine's part leads logically and
implacably to her last scenes : she stands on guard outside the
palace while Orestes is killing their mother within, and when
Clytemnestra's death-cry is heard, she shouts ' Strike her
again, if you have the strength ! '   Then, when Aegisthus is
confronted with his wife's dead body, and tries to parley,
she cries ' In god's name, let him say no more.   Kill him at
once !   Throw his body to the dogs !   Nothing less can
compensate me for what I have endured.'   It is a grim and a
bloody business, and Sophocles does not try to pretend that it
is anything else.

This interpretation will not do—and those who respect
Sophocles need not regret it ; for had Sophocles, for once,
nothing of importance to say to his fellow-citizens, that he
should invite them to get into an archaic frame of mind, and
pretend that the murder of a mother was a deed of simple
merit, in order to enjoy some poetry, stage-craft, and character-
drawing ?   We would rather suppose, if we can, that
Sophocles once more had something of significance to say.

The exactly opposite view has been taken by Sheppard.[1]
He argues that Apollo did not approve of the vengeance ;
that Orestes, in asking him not whether he should do it, but
how—presuming on the god's compliance—was falling into an
elementary blunder, like Glaucus in Herodotus ; and that the
indignant god lets the impious man go ahead and take the
consequences.   But this view is obstructed by as many
obstacles as the other.   Bowra has mentioned several,[2] but
there is another which seems decisive—and just as decisive
against the interpretation that was offered in the first edition
of this book, that Sophocles carefully dissociates Apollo from
the vengeance.   Both of these interpretations disfigure what
is perhaps the most important and exciting moment of the
play.

Clytemnestra comes out of the palace to sacrifice to Apollo.
She has been frightened, as we know, by a dream, the significance of which is perfectly plain : the rightful heir will re-

[1] *Classical Review*, 1927, pp. 2 ff.
[2] *Sophoclean Tragedy*, 216 ff.

cover his throne. This already shows how Sophocles is thinking; for if it does not mean that the gods are interested in the punishment of Clytemnestra, it is a mere coincidence —leading to nothing in particular, since its effect on the plot is slight. But if the gods are interested, then the dream and its results are momentous. For Clytemnestra comes out, intending to sacrifice to Apollo; but the harsh quarrel with Electra intervenes. ' Cannot you even allow me to sacrifice in proper silence, after I have let you have your say?' Electra promises to keep the silence necessary for the rite. Clytemnestra, with her attendants, advances to the altar. The audience too must observe the reverent silence; and the holy rite begins. Clytemnestra places her offerings on the altar and puts fire to the incense. As she does so she prays —a prayer of unexampled blasphemy; for she prays that she may continue to enjoy what she won by murder and has protected by adultery, and that her son may never return to avenge his father, but may die first—though this is a prayer that she shrinks from putting into words. Such is the petition that she thinks fit to offer to the god of purity. There is a pause; we watch the incense rising to Heaven with this prayer. The silence is broken by the arrival of a man with news: Orestes is dead, killed in a chariot-race—and at Delphi. Unless we can persuade ourselves that this impressive scene and its immediate sequel were contrived by Sophocles only as a piquant turn in the plot—and that he was so pleased with it that he repeated it almost exactly in the *Tyrannus*—we must see in it, as the original audience must surely have seen, the hand of the god. Apollo has heard the terrible prayer, and swiftly sends the fitting answer, a false message, designed to lure Clytemnestra to her death.

But the messenger was coming anyhow; his coming was arranged by Orestes in the prologue. Similarly in the *Tyrannus*: the messenger's arrival at that precise moment, as if in answer to the prayer of Iocasta, the sceptic, seems to betray the agency of the god; yet Sophocles goes out of his way there to tell us that this man has come, post-haste from Corinth, entirely for his own profit. In both these plays, as elsewhere in Greek poetry,[1] the action is seen on two planes at once, human and divine.

A satisfactory interpretation of the play, then, must explain convincingly several difficult points. Besides—as always—accounting logically for the general style of the play —for the elaborate character-drawing for instance—it must explain this dual plane on which the action seems to move. It must explain why an action which is necessarily shocking, and which is presented so starkly, such that even the hero doubts the propriety of it,[2] can be countenanced by the god, and that too without any criticism or defence from the dramatist. It must also, if we are to regard the *Electra* as a first-rate play, make its religious or philosophical content something of importance, and not leave it a mere exercise in character-drawing and play-making. Finally, we would like our interpretation to explain the conspicuous detail on which Sheppard fastened, that Apollo does *not* command Orestes to kill Aegisthus and his mother.

Bowra's treatment of the play, valuable though it is in many ways, does not seem to satisfy these demands. It is, in brief, that justice must be done ; that this is sometimes a painful task to him who has to do it ; but that when it is done, in this play, and order is restored, a new force of love arises. But, in the first place, had Sophocles wished to show the re-establishment of order and of love, he could not have ended the *Electra* as he did, with these two grim scenes, with Electra crying ' Strike her again, if you have the strength,' and ' Throw his body to the dogs.' Surely somebody, at some time, must have told Sophocles that Greek tragedies end quietly, somewhere beyond the climax. Had he meant this, he must have added a quiet scene to show order and love gathering strength. A concluding tag from the chorus cannot possibly efface from our minds the grimness and horror of these final scenes. In the second place, though the punishment of crime may sometimes be painful, in no civilized society can it involve anything so hideous as matricide. With what intention then did Sophocles take this mythical situation,

[1] See Jaeger, *Paideia*, I, 52 (English edn.).

[2] Vv. 1424 f.

without either condemning it, as Euripides did, or explaining it, as Aeschylus did, as an unsatisfactory but transient phase in the struggle for justice?

Since the problem concerns a god, and Justice, we may remind ourselves that the word *theos* may have a very different complexion from the word 'god', and that 'justice' may be a very indifferent translation of the word *dikê*. Ares, to take an extreme case, was a *theos,* but he was often spoken of in terms that we reserve for the Devil. Certainly Apollo was no Ares, but for all that in thinking of 'the god Apollo' we may unconsciously assume a degree of 'godliness' which is not there, so ingrained in us is the idea of a personal, beneficent god. As Grube has pointed out,[1] *theos* always implies 'a power', and may imply no more than that. As for *dikê*, whatever the origin of the word may have been, an early meaning of it was simply 'the way' of something, hence 'the right way'. In Aeschylus it is a moral and social word, 'retributive justice' in the *Agamemnon,* mellowing into 'justice' as things improve. But the Ionian philosophers could use *dikê* and its opposite, *adikia,* in an amoral sense, as when Anaximander said that 'things are continually paying retribution (*tisis*) to each other', for their 'injustice'. Philosophers who did not make our sharp distinction between the physical and the moral could call *dikê* what we call 'the balance of forces in Nature', 'the law of averages', and the like. If there is too much wet now, there will be too much dry later on; wet will pay to dry retribution (*tisis*) for its encroachment; and so *dikê*, the proper balance, will be restored.

What if Sophocles' *dikê* has in it something of this conception? What if his *theoi,* and Apollo, their intermediary with men, are conceived as 'the powers' who protect this *dikê*? We will assume—in order to see what happens—that in the *Electra dikê* means 'the proper and natural order of things', not now in the physical universe, but in human affairs, moral and social. If the proper order is disturbed by some violence (*adikia*), it must, in the nature of things, restore itself, somehow; the restoration of the balance is an act of *dikê* because it

[1] *The Drama of Euripides,* pp. 41 ff.

re-establishes *dikê*. If so, we need not expect the act of *dikê* to be agreeable in itself ; the deluge that ends a drought may itself do harm.

Clytemnestra, in murdering Agamemnon, violently disturbed the natural order. This was an action bound, in the nature of things, to provoke an equivalent reaction—unless indeed all concerned should acquiesce in the *adikia*. As the action was hideous, so there is no reason to expect that the reaction should be lovely. Why should it be ? The *adikia* caused a wound ; *dikê* may involve an amputation. To see that *dikê* is re-established is the concern of the gods, as well as of men. In the *Electra* it is re-established—and how ? By a perfectly natural process. We have three people to consider, the three surviving children of Agamemnon. Chrysothemis is no impressive figure. She can acquiesce ; so far as she is concerned, *adikia* can continue. The hero and heroine are not like this. Orestes cannot and will not spend his life living in exile, on charity ; he is determined to recover his patrimony (as Sophocles is careful to tell us, even to the point, apparently, of showing us a view of this patrimony on his painted *periacti*). He asks Apollo how he is to set about it ; and the reason why he is not commanded by the god, as he is in Aeschylus, is precisely that Sophocles wishes to represent the act of *dikê* as the natural, even inevitable, outcome of the original crime. A disinherited son *will* do this, unless he is a coward. Action provokes its reaction ; this is *dikê*, and the act of *dikê* is conceived and carried out entirely by the human actors, from natural motives and by natural means. The third child, Electra, is like Orestes, unable to acquiesce ; and in her we see a different aspect of this reaction. Her character, in her situation, makes it inevitable that she should live for vengeance ; that is the reason why this character and situation must be described in such detail.

So, as these two are great enough to resent and resist *adikia*, the hour comes and *dikê* is achieved. We are not obliged to admire the deed—Orestes himself clearly does not —nor to see in it the institution of a new and better order of things—about which Sophocles is silent. A violent disturbance of *dikê* has been violently annulled. It is the nature of things, and Sophocles invites us to see in this the working of a natural law.

But what of Apollo, and the two planes? If the whole action is complete on the human plane, is not the god a superfluous addition? By no means. Apollo's part is of the utmost significance. He does not affect the action in the least; he neither commands nor assists Orestes; but he does, as it were, accompany the action on his own plane. When Orestes has at last decided to act, Clytemnestra has her dream —and it would be stultifying to suppose that this is mere coincidence. Orestes is an autonomous agent; but the gods are moving on a path parallel to his. Even more significant is the arrival of the Paedagogus at that particular moment. On the human plane, this is a move that we are expecting; but the fact that he comes just when he does, as if in answer to that prayer, suggests to our minds that Apollo is working here, independently of the Paedagogus and of Orestes. In other words, what Orestes and Electra are doing, though an action complete and intelligible in itself, is at the same time part of a larger design, the will of the gods, the principle of *diké*, the universal law. It is not merely a private matter, a particular case.

Now we can see why Sophocles could take this, the most questionable part of the Pelopid legend, and present it, by itself, as an action that needed neither defence nor sequel. He is as far as possible from being 'literary' and archaistic, asking us to make impossible assumptions for the sake of some trifling dramatic effects, like character-drawing and strong scenes. He is demonstrating a law in things, that violence must produce its recoil; and the fact that the *diké* here is so grim and unrelieved is a measure of the hideousness of the original offence. That the actual form of the vengeance here is one that could not occur in civilized society is immaterial; the underlying law that it illuminates is true for all time.

One point remains, the explanation given by Electra of the sacrifice of Iphigeneia.[1] It is conspicuously different from the explanation given by Aeschylus. In the *Agamemnon*[1] Artemis holds up the fleet because, for pity, she objects to the

[1] Vv. 563 ff.

expedition; she is 'angry with the winged hounds of her father'. She gives Agamemnon the choice between sacrificing his daughter and going home; if he is bent on playing the part of a devouring eagle, let him first devour an innocent child of his own, and take the consequences. In the *Electra* the position is entirely different. In the first place, Artemis is a Sophoclean, not an Aeschylean, deity; her motives are quite amoral. Agamemnon offends her by killing one of her stags and boasting about it. He was at fault, but the goddess hits back implacably and, by human standards, unreasonably. She acts as Athena does with Ajax, when he offends her; she acts as electricity does, if an incautious tinkerer makes a mistake. In the second place, Sophocles' Agamemnon had no choice at all, for we are told 'There was no escape for the army, either homeward or to Troy' (vv. 573 f.). Agamemnon therefore was to be pitied much more than blamed, and Clytemnestra has much less justification than she had in the *Oresteia*. The reason for this difference of treatment is clear. Aeschylus wanted her crime to be the direct result of the similar crime of Agamemnon, its punishment and its continuation; Sophocles wanted it to be a wanton and unjustified disturbance of *dikê*, to be avenged, once and for all, by its inevitable recoil.

5. THE OEDIPUS TYRANNUS The story of the *Tyrannus* is of a common Greek type; something unpleasant is predicted, the persons concerned try to avert it and think themselves safe, but in some natural though surprising fashion the prediction is fulfilled. Next to the *Tyrannus* itself, the most elaborate example is the story of Astyages and the infant Cyrus in Herodotus. What does Sophocles make of this ancient motif?

At the beginning of the play Oedipus is the great King who has saved Thebes in the past and is their only hope now; no one can compare with Oedipus in reading dark secrets. At the end, he is the polluted outcast, himself the cause of the city's distress, through crimes predicted by Apollo before he was born. Is this grim determinism? Is Sophocles telling us that Man is only the plaything of Fate? Or does he mean, as Bowra has recently suggested,[1] that the gods have contrived this awful fate for Oedipus in order to display their power to man and to teach him a salutary lesson? Or is Sophocles simply making exciting drama, leaving the philosophical implications unexplored? There is only one way of finding out. Whatever Sophocles meant, he put his meaning into the play, and to get it out again we must contemplate the play—all of it, in all its aspects ; not bits of it, and some of its aspects.

As in the *Electra*, the action shows a certain duality. In the foreground are autonomous human actors, drawn vividly, and complete. Oedipus himself, Tiresias, Creon, Iocasta, and the two shepherds, are all as lifelike as characters in a play can be ; and so, in their degree, are the remoter characters who do not appear—the hot-tempered Laius at the cross-road, and the unknown Corinthian who insulted Oedipus when he was half-drunk. The circumstances too are natural, even inevitable, granted these characters. Oedipus, as we see him time after time, is intelligent, determined, self-reliant, but hot-tempered and too sure of himself ; and an apparently malignant chain of circumstances combines now with the strong, now with the weak side of his character to produce the catastrophe. A man of poor spirit would have swallowed the insult and remained safe in Corinth, but Oedipus was resolute ; not content with Polybus' assurance he went to Delphi and asked the god about it, and when the god, not answering his question, repeated the warning given originally to Laius, Oedipus, being a man of determination, never went back to Corinth. It was a coincidence, but not an unnatural one, that Laius was on his way from Thebes to Delphi. They met at the cross-road, and as father and son were of similar temper the disaster occurred. Even so, he could have arrived at Thebes safely, had he not been a man of high intelligence ; for then he could not have read the riddle of the Sphinx. But again, though intelligent, he was blind enough to marry a woman old enough to be his mother, certain that his mother was in Corinth. The story is not moralized. Sophocles could have put Oedipus in the wrong

[1] *Sophoclean Tragedy*, p. 175.

at the cross-road ; he could have suggested that blind ambition made him accept the crown and Queen of Thebes. He
does neither of these things ; Oedipus is not being given his
deserts by an offended Heaven. What happens is the natural
result of the weaknesses and the virtues of his character, in
combination with other people's. It is a tragic chapter from
life, complete in itself, except for the original oracle and its
repetition. Sophocles is not trying to make us feel that an in-
exorable destiny or a malignant god is guiding the events.

But we are made to feel, as in the *Electra,* that the action is
moving, at the same time, on a parallel and higher plane.

The presence of some power or some design in the background is already suggested by the continuous dramatic
irony—which seems overdone, if it is regarded as only a
dramatic effect. In the matter of the Plague this hidden
power is definitely stated ; and its presence is most imaginatively revealed, as in the *Electra,* in the scene containing
Iocasta's sacrifice. She who has been so sceptical of oracles
surprises us by coming out with sacrificial offerings. She lays
them on Apollo's altar, puts fire to the incense, and prays for
deliverance from fear. There is a moment of reverent silence,
and this is broken by the arrival of the cheerful messenger
from Corinth : Polybus is dead ; fear is at an end ; the prayer
has been heard. But within the hour Iocasta has hanged
herself.—And what of her offerings ? Still there, on the
altar, in full view of the audience ; the incense, it may be,
still carrying to the god a petition that he has so terribly
answered.

This is no theatrical trick, but a revelation of the dramatist's
thought. It is the action of the unseen god made manifest.
But how does the god answer the pitiful prayer of Iocasta, the
impious prayer of Clytemnestra ? Not by any direct in-
terposition. The Apollo of Sophocles is nothing like the Zeus
of Aeschylus, who works his will by freezing the Strymon or
by blasting a fleet. It was not Apollo who incited the Corinthian to come, but his own eagerness to be the first with the
good news, and his own hopes (as Sophocles is careful to tell
us) of standing well with the new King ; for besides the news
of his succession to the crown he has another and a much

more exciting tale to tell—in his own good time. He, like the Paedagogus, is completely autonomous, yet in the coming of each the hand of the god is seen. The action moves on two planes at once.

Nevertheless, the whole texture of the play is so vividly naturalistic that we must be reluctant to interpret it as a bleak Determinism. These people are not puppets of higher powers ; they act in their own right. Nor, I think, does this texture encourage us to accept Bowra's explanation.

In the first place, if Sophocles meant that the gods are displaying their power because they will, that they have ordained this life for Oedipus in order to read men a lesson, it was so easy for him to say so—to write an ode on the power and the mysterious ways of the gods. He conspicuously does not do this. Indeed, in the ode that immediately follows the catastrophe the chorus says not that the fate of Oedipus is a special display of divine power, but on the contrary that it is typical of human life and fortunes.

In the second place, although Oedipus is by far the greatest sufferer in the play he is not the only one. There are others who suffer, not by any means in the same degree, but in the same way ; and we must take account of them too, not dismiss them as being parts of the dramatic economy but not of the thought. If we contemplate, as we should, the whole play and all its aspects, we see that Oedipus is not a special case, except in the degree to which he suffers ; he is, as the Chorus says, typical ; what has happened to him is part of the whole web of human life. Why for example does Sophocles introduce the children in the last act ? Not simply because it is ' natural ' ; a good play isn't ' nature', but art. One reason must be that Oedipus may say to them what he does say : ' What a life must yours be ! Who will admit you to the festivals ? Who will marry you—born as you were born ? ' Such is life, such are the gods. The innocent suffer with the guilty.

We must contemplate also two other characters who form no inconsiderable part of the play—the two shepherds. It was not merely to liven up his play, or to indulge his talents, that Sophocles drew them like this, with their motives, hopes, fears, so sharply presented. The Corinthian, like the Paedagogus, makes no bones about expecting a tip ; not for the reason that Headlam so oddly gave,[1] that it was the oriental custom to reward messengers (as if dramatists were only photographers), but because the point bears on the drama. The news that this man brings is great news indeed, but he has something much more astonishing in reserve and the moment for producing it soon comes. 'Polybus ? He was no more your father than I am. . . . Why, I gave you to him with my own hands. . . . A hired shepherd ? Yes, my son ; but that day I saved your life.' A hired shepherd—but this is a great day for him ; he began by addressing Oedipus as 'My Lord', but now he can say 'My son'. 'No, *that* I cannot tell you. . . . You must find the Theban who gave you to me. . . .' Iocasta's last despairing shriek does not disturb him, for, as Oedipus says, probably she is dismayed to find that her husband is of low birth. The chorus is happy and excited ; and when the reluctant Theban is brought in, our friend becomes even more bland and helpful, as he works up to his climax :

'Here is the man, my friend, who was that baby !'

And this is his last speech. No reward for him ; no glory in Corinth—only bewilderment and utter dismay ; for in a moment he hears, from his old companion,

'I pitied it, my lord. I thought to send
The child abroad, whence this man came. And he
Saved it, for utter doom. For if you are
The man he says, then you were born for ruin.'

He sees his new King rush into the palace ; and then—the final ode ? Not yet. These two actors have to make their exit, by the long side-passages, in full view of the audience ; some forty yards of exit. And as we watch them stumbling out we have time to reflect that this is the outcome, for them, of their merciful interest in an abandoned baby.

Is not this too the work of Apollo ? Here, as in the greater case of Oedipus, is that conjunction of well-meant action with a situation which makes it lead to disaster. An act of mercy, tinged with a perfectly honest shrewdness, leads the Corinthian to the verge of what is, for him, greatness ; as he

[1] See G. Thomson, *Oresteia*, II, 69 (note to v. 591).

stretches out his hand, eagerly and with confidence, it turns into horror.

The other shepherd too is one who refused to kill a baby. Part of his reward comes years later, when he sees the man who killed Laius ascend his victim's throne and marry his Queen—an event which sends him, for his own safety, into half-exile [1] ; the rest of his reward comes now, when a sudden command brings him back at last to the city, to learn what he learns here.

These minor tragedies, of the children and the shepherds, are all of a piece with the major one. This is Apollo ; this is life. An awful sin is committed in all innocence ; children are born to a life of shame ; virtuous intentions go awry. What are we to think of it ? Of course, moral and prudential lessons can be drawn from it—though Sophocles draws very few—but what do we think of it ? Where is the explanation ? What, in other words, is the catharsis ? That Oedipus accepts his fate ? But when you are knocked flat, you must accept it ; and if you cannot get up again, you must be resigned. There is little illumination in this.

The catharsis that we are looking for is the ultimate illumination which shall turn a painful story into a profound and moving experience. It has been suggested by Professor Ellis-Fermor [2] that the catharsis of plays like the *Tyrannus* and *Macbeth* lies in the perfection of their form, which, by implication, represents the forces of righteousness and beneficence, of which Aeschylus speaks directly, in his choric odes. This is manifestly true of the *Tyrannus*.

Let us go back to Iocasta's sacrifice, and Apollo's swift and devastating answer. In the corresponding passage of the *Electra* the point was clear. Clytemnestra prayed that injustice, *adikia*, might triumph, and she got the answer she deserved. What of Iocasta ? She has been denying the truth of oracles. Was Sophocles then so fiercely orthodox that he could equate Iocasta's scepticism with Clytemnestra's

---

[1] For he, no bought slave, but reared in the palace (v. 1123), besought Iocasta to send him into the fields, as far as possible from the city (vv. 758 ff.).

[2] *Frontiers of Drama*, p. 133.

wickedness ? Of course not ; this was not the size of Sophocles' mind.   He means much more than this.   Iocasta has
said ' Why should we fear oracles, when there is no such
thing as foresight (*pronoia*) ?   Best live at random, as one
may '—a doctrine which would deny the very basis of all
serious Greek thought ; for while Greek life was still healthy
and stable, the Greek believed, as if by instinct, that the universe was not chaotic and ' irrational ', but was based on a
logos, obeyed Law.   The Ionian philosophers did not discover, but rather postulated, this *logos.*

The tragic poets too think in this way—as Whitehead saw,
when he said that they, rather than the Ionians, were the first
scientific thinkers.   In the *Oresteia* we find moral laws which
have the same sort of validity as physical and mathematical
laws.   The doer must suffer ; hybris leads to Atê ; the problem there—a problem for gods as well as for men—is to find a
system of Justice that will fit into this framework without disastrously contravening these laws.   To the mind of Sophocles
this *logos* shows itself (as we shall see more fully in the next
chapter) as a balance, rhythm, or pattern in human affairs.
' Call no man happy until he is dead,' for the chances of life
are incalculable.   But this does not mean that they are
chaotic ; if so they seem to us, it is because we are unable to
see the whole pattern.   But sometimes, when life for a moment becomes dramatic, we can see enough pattern to give
us faith that there is a meaning in the whole.   In the *Antigone,* when Creon is overwhelmed, it is by the natural recoil
of his own acts, working themselves out through the minds
and passions of Antigone and Haemon, and we can see in this
a natural justice.   In the *Electra,* the vengeance that at last
falls on the assassins is linked to their crime by natural chains
of cause and effect.   In the *Tyrannus* we have a much more
complex picture.   The same *dikê* is at work, though this time
the *adikia* which it avenges was involuntary and indeed innocent.   Oedipus—to repeat our image—is blasted as a man
may be who inadvertently interferes with the natural flow of
electricity.   *Dikê* here works through many apparently casual
and unrelated actions—of the shepherds, of the charioteer who
tried to push Oedipus off the road, of the man at the banquet.

. . . Things fall out contrary to all expectation ; life seems cruel and chaotic. Cruel, perhaps ; chaotic, no—for if it were chaotic no god could predict, and Iocasta would be right. ' If these oracles are not manifestly fulfilled, why should I join in the sacred dance ? ' Piety and purity are not the whole of the mysterious pattern of life, as the fate of Oedipus shows, but they are an important part of it, and the doctrine of chaos would deny even this. The pattern may harshly cut across the life of the individual, but at least we know that it exists, and we may feel assured that piety and purity are a large part of it.

Every detail in the *Tyrannus* is contrived in order to enforce Sophocles' faith in this underlying *logos* ; that is the reason why it is true to say that the perfection of its form implies a world-order. Whether or not it is beneficent, Sophocles does not say.

CHAPTER VI

THE PHILOSOPHY OF SOPHOCLES

We found, in the *Electra* and the *Tyrannus*, the two related ideas of a *dikê* that is not necessarily 'Justice', and of a rhythm or pattern in human affairs. Are these ideas peculiar to these plays, or are they found elsewhere in Sophocles?

We may begin with a special case of pattern. How often in Sophocles do we find the idea that the dead are killing the living? Of the seven plays there are only two in which this idea is not found—and they are the late plays, the *Philoctetes* and the *Coloneus*. Here are the five instances. Ajax and Hector, bitter enemies, exchange gifts (vv. 817 ff.). Ajax received Hector's sword—and kills himself with it. Teucer says (vv. 1027 ff.) 'Did you see how at last, even from the grave, Hector was to destroy you?' Then Teucer goes on to tell how Hector, for his part, was killed by means of the belt which he had received from Ajax—modifying the Homeric account in order to make the parallel. He concludes 'All these things, I would say, are contrived for men by the gods'; that is to say, we have much more here than mere coincidence. From the *Ajax* we turn to the *Antigone*, and there (v. 871) we find Antigone saying, of Polyneices, 'Ah, it is your dead hand that has taken away life from me!' In the *Electra* (v. 1447), 'The dead live. Those slain long ago will drain from their slayers *haema palirrhyton*'—literally, 'blood flowing in the reverse direction'. In the *Tyrannus* (v. 1451) Oedipus beseeches Creon to drive him into Cithaeron, 'which my parents, when they lived, appointed to be my tomb; that I may die at the hands of those who tried to slay me'. And finally, in the *Trachiniae*, we have a full-scale presentation. The Centaur Nessus, in mid-stream, insults Deianeira; Heracles, from the bank, shoots him with a poisoned arrow. It is this poison, innocently administered by Deianeira as a love-philtre, that kills Heracles and avenges Nessus—and not only Nessus, for the poison was in origin the blood of the Hydra

whom Heracles had slain.   In this elaborate instance we may
observe, first, that the whole course of things was darkly fore-
told by an oracle of Zeus (vv. 1161 ff.), and second, that it is
significantly linked with what is, in this play, the weak spot in
Heracles' character, his reckless passion for women.   This
double revenge of the dead on the living is, then, no mere
coincidence ; it is a pattern woven into the very fabric of
things.

So that in all these five plays we find, more or less prominent, the idea of a rhythm or recoil.   Things are not, in the
long run, left unbalanced.   In the *Electra* it is clearly Justice ;
elsewhere it may not be Justice—for why should Heracles not
have killed the Hydra and Nessus ?—but it is *dikê*.

We may go a little further.   The speech in which Ajax
announces that he has changed his mind, and will submit to
the Atreidae, is full of parallels from Nature :

' All things doth long, innumerable Time

Bring forth to light, and then again conceal . . . '

Winter gives place to summer, night to day, storm to calm,
and the sleeper awakes.   Why then, he says, should I too not
yield ?—That is, an eternal rhythm pervades the universe, and
man is part of it.   So, in the similar speech that Oedipus
makes in the *Coloneus*,[1] nothing remains the same, either
in Nature or among men.   *Panta rhei*, everything is in flux ;
not in a straight course, but to and fro.   To-day's friend is
to-morrow's enemy, and to-day's enemy to-morrow's friend.

This idea of a universal rhythm, ruling in the physical world
and in human affairs alike, appears too in Sophocles' formal
similes, and gives them additional weight ; as for example
when Haemon reminds Creon that it is the branches which
bend that are not broken.   This is not mere illustration, but
an appeal to Law.   And it may not be too fanciful to see in
this habitual way of thought the origin of what was surely
Sophocles' favourite word, *symmetros* and its congeners.

A correlative of this, most imaginatively enforced in the
Tyrannus, is that the complexities of life are not due to chance.
None of these other plays give us this idea so strikingly, but
it is implicit in all.   Every one of them has its oracle or

[1] *O.C.*, 607 ff.

prophecy which is fulfilled, and it is surely self-evident that what can be predicted is not directed by chance. The universe—including, again, human affairs—is rational, even though we may not be able to see the *ratio*, the *logos*, except imperfectly and rarely. As in the *Tyrannus*, the gods only predict ; they do not compel.[1] As in the *Tyrannus* and the *Electra*, we have a conjunction of gods who predict and humans who are entirely autonomous. The denial of chance is implied in the prophecies ; it is implied too in the last verse of the *Trachiniae* : 'Nothing is here but Zeus' ; and it is very clear in the *Antigone*. For the Messenger, coming in with his news of the sudden overthrow of Creon's prosperity, remarks (vv. 1158 ff.), 'It is chance that exalts the lowly and overturns the prosperous' ; but we, who have been in the play from the beginning, can see that it is nothing of the sort. It is not chance, but *dikê*.

It is another of the strands that bind all these plays together that *dikê* in the *Antigone* works exactly as in the *Electra*, not by divine intervention, but by the natural course of events. In each play, *adikia* is committed ; that Creon acted out of honest motives, Clytemnestra and Aegisthus out of guilty ones, makes no difference. Each *adikia* might have continued indefinitely—perhaps—except that in each case there were those intimately concerned who were great enough to oppose it, at whatever risk ; and in each play the greatness of the heroine is indicated by the contrast with a sister, an ordinary 'nice girl', who is willing to accept the *adikia*. We have seen how impossible this was for Electra, with her temperament, and in her situation ; impossible too for Orestes, whom every motive of filial piety, personal honour, and self-interest impelled to punish the criminals and recover his rights. So it is with Antigone. Natural piety, loyalty to her kin, love of her brother, everything that is in her character impels her to defy Creon's edict. Everything that is in his character impels him to exact his pound of flesh, and the fact that his son happens to love Antigone confirms him in his obstinacy,

[1] In the *Ajax* Athena makes Ajax mad. This is the only case of direct divine intervention.

and becomes too the pivot on which the catastrophe turns. The admired logic of Sophocles' plots is not merely a dramatic merit ; it is the reflection of the logic that he sees in the universe ; this is the way in which *diké* works.

Before we continue, we should consider a question which the last paragraph suggests : what happens if there is not someone at hand who is impelled to oppose the *adikia* ? Is *diké* then not attained, the balance not restored ? The answer to this question comes from the *Tyrannus* and the *Antigone*. In the *Tyrannus* the *adikia*—the slaying of a father and marriage with a mother—was not even suspected, much less purged. Therefore it went on festering, as it were, in the body politic, undetected, until at last it issued as a physical plague. Something similar is suggested by Teiresias in the *Antigone*, when he tells Creon that those cities will rise against him in enmity whose hearths are being defiled by the birds and dogs that have fed on the flesh of Polyneices. In one way or another *diké* must assert itself ; if not by the act of man, then by the compulsion of nature. Human affairs, as we have seen already, are part of a universal *logos ;* the moral and the physical are not divided.

In the *Antigone* and the *Electra* we are concerned with that part of *diké* which coincides with moral ' justice ' ; in the *Tyrannus* and the *Trachiniae* we are in that obscurer region where *diké* is not moral ; where Time *dikazei*, exacts requital for things done in entire innocence by Oedipus, and where Heracles is destroyed by the monsters he justly destroyed, through a wife whose only desire was to bring back her husband to herself. This is the region of which we ourselves say ' Life is cruel ' ; but in Sophocles, the fact that these things come to pass in the way they do is itself an indication that design of some kind lies behind them—but what is the design ? Why must these things befall Oedipus and Heracles, for no fault of theirs, and apparently for no particular end ? We may well ask ; but Sophocles makes no attempt to answer our question. It is not one of the achievements of the *Tyrannus* that it answers the ultimate riddle. Oedipus does indeed say, in the *Coloneus*, ' Perhaps the gods were angry with my family from of old '—a long-delayed recoil of *dikê*. But in fact this hint tells us no more than we knew already, that it is part of a pattern, a *logos*.

The Aeschylean universe is one of august moral laws, infringement of which brings certain doom ; the Sophoclean is one in which wrong-doing does indeed work out its own punishment, but disaster comes too without justification ; at the most, with ' contributary negligence '. Oedipus would not have done what he did had he been a little more prudent, a little less self-confident, nor would Heracles have suffered if he had never given Deianeira cause to use the supposed love-philtre. But this does not explain why, in a given case, a comparatively small fault should have such consequences ; still less does it explain why a Deianeira should be at one moment a loving, anxious but hopeful wife, and at the next a hanging corpse.

Sophocles' philosophy, so far as we have yet discussed it, is a confession of intellectual faith—a peculiarly Greek one. It should, perhaps, defend him against the charge of being a ' pessimist '—though certainly he understood the mood of black despair, or he could never have written that bitter ode in the *Coloneus*. But what else has Sophocles to say, whether to counsel or to comfort ?

Of this pattern, which men call the Will of the Gods, a great part is piety and purity. Accordingly, no poet speaks more than Sophocles of the need for *eusebeia*, reverence. But part of it lies beyond morality, and is incalculable. Accordingly, no poet speaks so much as Sophocles of the need for *phronesis*, ' wisdom '. ' Phronesis ' implies knowing what you are, knowing your place in the world, being able to take the wide view, with a due sense of proportion—unlike Creon in the *Antigone* and Agamemnon and Menelaus in the *Ajax*, who could see only that Polyneices, or Ajax, was a dead traitor, and could not see the more important fact, that he was a dead man. This quality is almost personified in that impressive character Odysseus of the *Ajax*. Because he can see that ' All mankind is nothing but a phantom, an insubstantial shade,' he can pity his foe when he is mad, and not exult, and plead for his burial when he is dead, weighing his worth against the enmity he has shown, and remembering that 'I too shall come to this'.

But no piety and no wisdom can protect against those blows of fate of which Tecmessa speaks, twice involved in the ruin of others ; and as for consolation, what can we say to an Oedipus ? But even if we leave these sufferers, as we must, to face their sufferings with what spirit they can find in them, we can say that on the wider view Sophocles finds much to put into the other balance. No hopes indeed of a better world ; only 'Hades that receives all '—though, as Electra says

'I see that the dead are not vexed.'

But do not the grave beauty and dignity of Sophocles' own plays necessarily reflect the beauty and dignity that he found in human life ? Man may be 'an insubstantial shade ', without the 'god-given glory ', that Pindar sometimes saw playing around the head of that same shade ; but for all that, Sophocles leaves us with a great sense of the dignity of being a man. To have been great of soul is everything. Ajax faces death proudly ; he has been Ajax, and he can pray for his son nothing better than he should be like him, except in fortune ; Antigone knows that she has done her duty, and will be welcomed by her kin among the dead. As for Oedipus, surely the Sophoclean image of Man himself, as he was the Aristotelian type of the Tragic Hero, his essential greatness (like that of Heracles too) impresses itself at last on the gods themselves :

When we had gone we turned round and looked from afar. Him we saw nowhere, but Theseus we saw, his hand before his face, as if to shade his eyes from some awful sight upon which he could not look. Then, a little later, we saw him do reverence to the Earth and to Olympus of the Gods in one and the same prayer. But by what death he perished no man could tell but Theseus only ; for no blazing thunderbolt from heaven worked his end, nor any storm arising from the sea at that time, but either some escort sent by the gods, or some dark, yawning, kindly chasm of the Earth below. For not with lamentation nor pitiable with disease was that man sent forth, but wonderfully above all others.[1]

[1] *O.C.*, 1647 ff.

CHAPTER VII

THE DRAMATIC ART OF SOPHOCLES

1. THE THIRD ACTOR We have seen what Aeschylus did in the *Oresteia* with this Sophoclean invention. Sophocles must have seen it too, with some surprise, for assuredly it was not his conception that the third actor should be grafted on to Old Tragedy and used to extend the lyrical part. Why did Sophocles make this decisive innovation ? Although the first twenty years of his dramatic activity are practically a blank, we can answer the question with some confidence : he wanted the third actor in order to do what Aeschylus resolutely refuses to do with him in the *Agamemnon,* namely to illuminate the chief character from several points of view. The Aeschylean conception implies the single-minded tragic hero, one who is all hamartia—or rather one in whom the hamartia is all that concerns us. Hybris is done, and Heaven smites, through its chosen instrument. Sophocles sees not the simplicities but the complexities of life. Certain persons, because they are like this and not like that, and because their circumstances are these and not those, combine to bring about the catastrophe. Had any detail been different the disaster would not have occurred. The working of Law is seen in the way in which all these delicate complexities dovetail, to make a pattern which is suddenly seen to be inevitable.

The Sophoclean hero, because he is complex, not single-minded, must be seen from more than one point of view. We do not know our Creon or our Oedipus, we cannot therefore understand his tragedy, until we have seen how he behaves to a diversity of people and (equally important) how they behave to him. Oedipus' consideration for his people, his courtesy to Creon and Teiresias which quickly passes to suspicion and rage, Creon's attitude to Haemon—these are not decorations or improvements ; it is essential to the tragedy that we should know our heroes like this. Similarly the Watchman's reluctance to face Creon is important as a sidelight on the King's character, not only sub-comic relief. Eteocles' colourless Spy is transformed, necessarily, into this attractive character of flesh and blood. This is not 'progress'; it is plain logic. This art of 'undercutting' is used in the *Tyrannus* as it has rarely been used since, when the supreme eminence of Oedipus is shown by the collapse of Iocasta's bold scepticism.[1]

Here, we may be sure, we have the origin of the third actor, but there was an accessory cause and a development. No catastrophe can be self-contained ; others besides the sinner are involved. To Aeschylus this necessary aspect of tragedy presented itself as a linear movement, hence the trilogy ; either the tragic event is the result of inherited character, or it leaves a legacy of tragedy for the next generation.[2] To Sophocles this idea presents itself in a complexive way, as one immediate situation which involves others at once. Ajax' vanity ruins Ajax, but it endangers too his sailors, Tecmessa, Eurysaces, Teucer ; Creon's stubbornness threatens the Watchman and destroys Antigone before, through Haemon and Eurydice, it involves Creon himself. Thus again more actors are wanted.

Further, if we may trust our scanty evidence, Sophocles began to lay more weight on the tragic interworking of circumstance with character, so that situation becomes more complex. In these four plays, as we shall see in a moment, there is a distinct 'improvement' in the manipulation of the three actors. The explanation is not that Sophocles is perfecting his technique, or not only this, but that his thought is taking a new direction. It is significant that as plot becomes more complex the hero's character becomes less catastrophic. Oedipus and Electra are very different from Ajax and Creon ; we feel that these last are so ill-balanced that a slight push may upset them ; the former are of such a nobility that only a most unlucky combination of circumstances can bring them low. So, against a more balanced characterization, we have a more complex situation, and the more complex situation brings the use of the three actors to its highest degree of fluidity.

[1] See below, p. 187.

[2] This linear movement is very clear in the *Supplices*. See p. 22.

Let us now consider this use in our four plays. In the *Ajax*
the third actor plays a restricted but significant part. Between the Prologue and the last scene his only effect on the
piece is that he enables the not very dramatic Messenger [1]
to give his news to Tecmessa as well as to the chorus. The
use of the third actor is restricted in this way because the plot
is such that the two chief actors, Ajax and Odysseus, cannot
meet. This explains why Sophocles, who had for twenty
years been writing for three actors, makes little of them here.[2]

The Prologue uses the three actors well. Athena and
Odysseus give us, as it were, the common-sense atittude to
Ajax' crime ; they also give us a direct view of Odysseus which
contrasts excellently with the uncomprehending way in which
the Ajax-group always speak of him. But it gives more than
this. It is an astonishingly imaginative piece of ' theatre '. It
is assumed that Athena, who is invisible to Odysseus, is visible
to the audience. Why ? Nothing in the scene demands it,
and if she is hidden, speaking from behind, ' like the voice
of a brazen trumpet ', we have the fine spectacle of Odysseus
alone on the stage with his raving enemy—alone but for the
presence of the unseen goddess.

In the last scene too there is imaginativeness. After Menelaus comes Agamemnon ; the succession of scenes is perhaps
a little lacking in subtlety, but not in point, for it makes clear
that Teucer has against him not the whim of one leader only
but something like public opinion, and that Teucer cannot
find the grounds for overturning that opinion. Now Odys-

[1] This scene is, for Sophocles, a poor one. The previous hybris
against Athena, worse than the attack on the Greek leaders, is
wanted here, just before the catastrophe, to complete the picture of
Ajax' character, and the archaic idea that Athena's wrath will last
for one day only is designed to send the chorus in hurried search
for Ajax and to heighten the tragedy of his intemperate suicide.
But it is archaic and stiff.

[2] There is a superficial notion, which has been received with
more patience than it deserves, that this and other innovations
were used at first with a timid reserve. Criticism has discovered
places in the *Ajax* where Sophocles would have given the third
actor more to say if he had not been writing in 450 or thereabouts.
Dalmeyda (*R.E.G.*, 1933, p. 2) has disposed of this. (See also
Schlesinger, *C.P.*, 1930, p. 230.)

seus, the arch-enemy, arrives, and while he prevails over
Agamemnon with such magnanimity and good sense, Teucer
stands by silent, astonished at this support from this source.
He thanks Odysseus worthily.   Odysseus asks to be allowed
a part in the burial, but Teucer cannot rise to this height, and
has no confidence that the spirit of Ajax could.   Teucer and
Ajax remain on the same level as Menelaus and Agamemnon,
and Odysseus has to retire disappointed but acquiescent.
Nothing could more finely indicate the intellectual loneliness
of Odysseus among these men, and the point depends on this,
that Teucer was present and heard Odysseus' argument.   He
was silent not because the play was written in 450 and Sophocles had not yet learned how to make him talk, but because
Sophocles had more dramatic imagination than some of his
critics.

The Prologue of the *Antigone* does not use three actors, but
as it is a scene such as only three-actor tragedy would contrive we may consider it briefly.   Like all prologues it outlines the situation ; like all good ones it does also something
much more important.   As the prologue of the *Ajax* presented
the situation from a point of view different from that assumed
during the greater part of the play, so here the private, personal and feminine atmosphere contrasts sharply with the full
light of publicity in which the action is to be played out.   It
is an admirable preparation for the jubilant hymn of triumph
that follows it.   The prologue of the *Electra* does the same
thing : the practical and political considerations of the two
men make an excellent foil to the desolation and the personal
sorrow of Electra.[1] In all these juxtapositions there is a finely
imaginative relevance ; Sophocles makes half his effect by an
architectural disposition of mass, and this was made possible
by the fluidity which the third actor gave.

Two other scenes in the *Antigone* demand consideration.
The first, that between Creon, the Watchman and Antigone,

[1] Those who like mechanical arguments might add this to the
discussion (p. 130) on the centre of gravity in the *Antigone*.   Both
the *Ajax* and the *Electra* begin with two subordinate characters in
order to prepare the way for the Hero.   The *Antigone* begins with
Antigone and Ismene ; therefore the hero is Creon.

is extremely dramatic, a foreshadowing of the triangular
scenes in the *Tyrannus*. The dramatic power arises from
this, that each of the three characters has his private preoccupation, his own attitude to the central fact. Creon is faced
with the incredible news that the rebel is no political agent
but his own niece; Antigone, the deed now done, stands
apart, out of touch with the scene, rapt in her almost mystic
confidence; the Watchman, finding in the situation his own
vindication and escape, is completely at his ease, struck with
the wonderfully irrelevant idea that a man should deny nothing—this is the moral that he draws. How effective is his
conversational 'It happened like this' against this background.
He, a person on the outskirts of the tragedy, has escaped.
That is how it affects him. It is only by an effort of ordinary
decency that he can remember what it means to Antigone:

> '. . . partly to my joy, part to my pain.
> For to escape oneself from scathe is sweet,
> But sore it is to bring a friend to scathe.
> Yet nature bids me hold all else for cheap
> If so mine own deliverance I secure.'

Once more, this is not dramatic decoration; it is the mocking
way in which things do happen.

The second triangular scene of the *Antigone*, Creon—Antigone—Ismene, is not of such importance as the first. Both
differ from Sophocles' later scenes of the kind in that the
situation, though dramatic, does not develop; and this second
scene is less significant than the earlier one, for Ismene does
little to modify the situation or to heighten the tragedy. It
illustrates Sophocles' methods rather than his philosophy. We
saw Ismene in the prologue; it is the natural fulfilment of that
if we see her again now, and are shown the effect on her of
Antigone's deed. Her attitude in this second scene, an attitude of pure emotionalism, is indeed a foil to the clear and
almost hard lines of Antigone's resolution, and Creon's utter
bewilderment adds a dramatic point, but the significance is
really structural; it is a link with the prologue and a preparation for the next theme—since Ismene is obviously the best
person to introduce the matter of Antigone's betrothal to
Haemon.

Coming to the two later plays we find an enormous advance in technique. In the two great discovery scenes of the *Tyrannus*, the situation is not presented practically complete before our eyes; not only does it grow, but it grows in opposite directions for the two chief actors. The conversation between Oedipus and the Corinthian Messenger is itself painfully dramatic, but the addition of Iocasta more than doubles the power of the scene. The progress of Iocasta from hope, through confidence, to frozen horror, and that of Oedipus from terror to a sublime resolution and assurance, the two connected by the commonplace cheerfulness of the Corinthian (who must be extremely puzzled by the tremendous effects his simple message is creating)—this makes as fine a combination of cross-rhythms as can well be imagined. Nor is the effect of the following scene inferior to this. Here it is Oedipus who ends in horror, while the direct contrast lies between the Corinthian, even more cheerful and helpful this time, and the Theban shepherd whose life-secret is being torn from him. There is nothing in dramatic literature to match the peculiar and awful beauty of these scenes except the passage in the *Electra* between the Paedagogus, Electra and Clytemnestra. The long and harsh wrangle between mother and daughter culminates in Clytemnestra's horrible prayer to the statue of Apollo, and immediately, as if in answer to that prayer, the Paedagogus comes in with his statement of Orestes' death. Electra's answer is a cry of anguish; against this Clytemnestra's excitement, now as later, is finely drawn :

' What sayest thou, stranger ? What ? Do not listen to *her* ! ' Then comes the elaborate and vivid account of Orestes' supposed death : the most brilliant by far of Sophocles' speeches. In his *Ancient Greek Literature* Murray called it ' brilliant but undramatic ' (and the whole play ' uncharming ')—an interesting criticism, coming from so distinguished a Euripidean. The speech is harsh ; like the Crisean plain which it describes, it is strewn with wrecked chariots ; the traditional limpidity of Greek poetry is entirely missing. Exactly : the Paedagogus is not really a Messenger, he is playing at being a Messenger. We must not criticize him and the Messenger in the *Antigone* on the same principles. He is not

charming : he has something else to do than to charm, and it is
precisely because he is not charming that he is not undramatic.
Look at the sweep of the speech. A quiet beginning leads to
the ominous words 'When a god sends hurt' (696), and he
begins again to work up, through his catalogue, to the beginning of the fatal race. The next few verses obviously lead to
a climax, and we hear 'At first all stood upright' (723) . . .
and we are sure that this is the end—but not yet. Sophocles
holds back ; Orestes is still safe among the wrecked chariots.
A second and a greater climax grows as the two remaining
charioteers go round and round the course until the terrible
end comes. It is good, but behind it all we can feel the fierce
exultation of the Paedagogus in his skill, in his piling up of
falsely convincing details, leading Clytemnestra through the
divagations of his story to her death. It is a magnificent piece
of bravura, and as we listen to it, watching the grimness behind it, observing its effect on the two women, who, fresh from
their quarrel, hang upon every word, so that it comes to us
through their minds, amplified—'undramatic' is the last thing
we should call it.

This long effort ended, a masterly scene follows. First the
Chorus thinks of the royal line here ended :

> *Pheu, pheu. To pan de despotaisi tois palai*
> *prorrizon, hos eoiken, ephthartai genos.*[1]

There is limpidity this time. Then Clytemnestra thinks of
herself, her sorrow, her relief. This Clytemnestra does not
'hide laughter in her eyes' ; her grief is genuine, that she
wins safety only in the destruction of her son. But in a moment she begins to realize how great her relief is. She is at
last safe, and she gives us a terrifying glimpse into what has
been going on beneath the surface :

'Time in its course led me along always under the shadow
of death. But now . . .'

While she bares her soul like this, the Paedagogus stands by in

---

[1] Untranslatable. A rendering is :
'Alas ! the long line of our kings, rooted out, utterly destroyed ! '
It belongs to the company of :
       'He has no children.—All my pretty ones ?
       Did you say all ? '

apparent stupidity. What brings forth Clytemnestra's most intimate confession is his ill-timed and crude suggestion of his tip. Then there is Electra, aroused from her prostration only by her mother's natural and unnatural joy. Again we are recalled from a terrible passage between them by the old man's apparent nervousness about his reward. Messengers in Greek Tragedy, as he well knows, are allowed to be frank on this point. He has, perhaps, to be a shade insistent, but he has played his part well, and Clytemnestra takes him in.

These scenes from the *Electra* and the *Tyrannus* are the climax of Sophocles' manipulation of the three actors. All three have now, as it were, been disengaged from the background and stand out as free sculpture ; each has, not only his own sharply drawn character, but also his own positive contribution to make to the drama of the scene ; and they move so freely that from an isolated scene it might well be impossible to tell which was first, second or third, none being merely a makeweight or a foil to the other two. Over the play as a whole the Protagonist stands out more clearly than he did, a clear gain in construction ; but the parts of deuteragonist and tritagonist are so closely assimilated that one has to look carefully at the exits and entrances to discover which is which, and in a single scene any one of the three may have the leading part. The last traces of stiffness have been removed. Sophocles has succeeded perfectly in conveying his sense of the irony of things through every element of his drama. The elaborateness of the plot through which the destined victims move, the baleful irony of language which illuminates their ignorance, and these cross-scenes which show the same tragedy from different points of view—these all spring from the same source and are all but different expressions of the same thing. It is as if Sophocles has made the very raw material of his art eloquent.

From this perfection it follows that Sophocles must soon do something new. In these plays we have the perfect expression of a mature view of life ; if this view remains static, his art will soon become imitative ; if it changes, we shall have plays of a different sort—plays like the *Trachiniae* and the *Philoctetes*.

2. THE CHORUS The different attitude which Sophocles
brought to tragedy affected the chorus as much as the actors.
It is indeed obvious—or it would have been had not Aeschylus
written the *Agamemnon*—that more actor must mean less
chorus. Indeed we began to suspect from the *Eumenides*
that the chorus was about to disappear altogether. From this
ignominy Sophocles rescued it : the chorus in Middle Tragedy
—when Sophocles was writing it—held a position as logical
and as secure as in the most choric of Old Tragedy. Like the
Eumenides themselves, what it lost in power it gained in other
ways.

It has been argued that the chorus was the natural and
perfect frame for the Aeschylean quasi-religious tragedy.
The atmosphere of vengeance and retribution into which
Agamemnon emerges, the background of doom and battle
against which Eteocles plays out his lonely drama, are created
by the chorus. In the Sophoclean conception the background
is tragic human relationships and the complicated web of
circumstance, and these are matters for the actors to present.
Thebes is a threatened city in the *Tyrannus*, as well as in the
Septem, and a curse is there too, but neither of these is the
most important theme in Sophocles' play. In his *Electra*,
again, the primitive law of vengeance is an important motif,
as it is in the *Choephori*, but in Aeschylus' play it conditions
everything, and is kept before our minds by the enveloping
chorus ; in the *Electra* it is part of the mind of the protagonist.
When Eteocles is killed the logical close is the funeral hymn
of the chorus ; when Oedipus finds his doom the chorus sings
' Alas, you generations of men,' but this is not enough. The
actor has superseded the chorus, and the logical ending is that
we should see Oedipus in his ruin. It is not an easy task for
Oedipus to follow and complete that tragic ode, but he has
to do it, and he does.

A further important change is that the tempo of the piece
is now entirely in the hands of the actors. The logic of the
drama is no longer that of dramatico-musical emotion, but, in
some degree, that of real life. The chorus can, by convention, fill up gaps in time, but it cannot suspend time as it and

Cassandra do in the *Agamemnon*. If past events have in the drama the significance which the sacrifice of Iphigeneia has in the *Agamemnon*, they must be presented through the consciousness of the actors on whom our attention is fixed. The drama is now theirs, and the chorus has to admit it. The chorus is limited to the present action—being in this sense more dramatic, more of a co-actor, as Aristotle requires, than the chorus of Aeschylus. We shall see how Sophocles accepts this limitation, keeps the chorus within the bounds set, and, as his drama increases in complexity, finds in this limitation one of his most powerful weapons.

How did he fit his chorus to these new conditions? First and most obviously, by making it always dramatic. It can no longer surround and control the action but it is always concerned in it. In the *Ajax* it consists of Ajax' own followers —a point of little interest in itself, but one which becomes significant when we realize that they are the first victims of Ajax' fall. Their exhortations to him to arise and assert himself are no mere operatic platitude ; they feel themselves to be in danger. The themes of the *Antigone* and the *Tyrannus* are essentially public themes, and the chorus is the public—though, as we shall see, the *Tyrannus* has an advantage in this respect. In the *Electra*, where the dramatic excuse for the chorus is less strong, Sophocles has nevertheless made it entirely relevant by a very deft link. Aegisthus is made to threaten to put Electra away ; a point which, in the manner of these later plays of Sophocles' middle period, is made to serve three ends at once, one of them being that Aegisthus' reason, the subversive sympathy which Electra arouses in the city, is personified in this sympathetic chorus. In fact, while tragedy was based on these big general themes the difficulty of finding a suitable chorus and of connecting it with the action remained in the background. Sophocles' chorus was as easy to come by as Socrates' audience. It was when tragedy turned from public to private themes, like the intransigeance of Medea or the domestic difficulties of the wife of Heracles, that the chorus became a nuisance.

Then Sophocles normally succeeded in investing his

choruses with some individual character. The followers of
Ajax come to life for us in their loathing of the war and
longing for Greece, as well as in their devotion to Ajax and
fear for themselves. More than this : Sophocles allows them
always to have their own view, not the right one, of Odysseus
and his doings. They are never the mouthpiece of the poet,[1]
and in this play they are definitely not ' ideal spectators ',
holding even the balance between Ajax and the other Greeks.
They are always pro-Ajax, therefore dramatically the more
interesting. None of the later choruses show so high a degree
of characterization as this one, and the chorus of the *Antigone*
is in addition a little detached from the action ; as if the
second actor here were so prominent that little was left for
it ; but Oedipus' chorus is so far a personality that its
character helps in making the cross-rhythms of the play.[2]
It is pious, and it is devoted to Oedipus. In the second ode
it is its loyalty and its confidence in Oedipus which prevail ;
in language somewhat bold for a chorus it says ' God is
certain, but that his prophets know more than another man,
that is not proved '. When next it speaks it has had more
shocks and its tone is different ; now its instinctive piety
asserts itself and leads it to pray for the fulfilment of the
oracles. There is real reaction and movement here ; it is not
merely singing, not simply being an ideal spectator. In the
second ode itself, still less : after Teiresias' denunciation of
Oedipus, the chorus proceeds to picture the guilty man as a
homeless outcast, slinking away from men's eyes. Not until
the ode is half over does it mention the prophet. Has the
chorus not fully understood him ? Or has it understood so
clearly that it is deliberately fighting down his disturbing
suggestion ? There is perhaps room for difference of interpretation ; what is certain is that the chorus is behaving
as a person, not as a machine, as Jebb suggested. It was his
odd view that ' there was a canon that the Chorus comments,

---

[1] Kranz (*Stasimon,* p. 191) has observed that Sophocles begins
his odes with a statement of fact, Euripides with an expression of
opinion (cf. *Antig.*, 332 with *Alcest.*, 962) : an interesting reflection of the greater plasticity of Sophocles' dramatic mind.

[2] See further, pp. 173, 187.

in order, on those things of importance which have happened since it last spoke'[1]; Sophocles did not work like this.

Sophocles did not write to formulas, and the chorus of the *Electra* is the exact opposite to that of the *Antigone*. The latter makes itself felt as a dramatic force neither by taking a prominent part in the action nor by displaying any marked character, but rather by the veering of its sympathies—by the way in which, after its first slight recoil from Creon's edict, it steadily moves away from Antigone, and then suddenly deserts Creon. In the *Electra* its character is carefully assimilated to that of Electra, as its part is to be completely dominated by her, to become—after the slight reserve which they show at the beginning—practically an extension of the heroine's personality. The formal expression of this is the lack of a Parodos; the introductory anapaests are Electra's. During the following scene it is persuaded to accept Electra's view of Piety and Reverence, and so, in entire accord with her, it leads us right up to the grim end, 'crowned by this day's work.' Its complete confidence here is as dramatic as the cheerfulness of the introductory birds; a reserved or doubtful chorus would have ruined the fine reticence and irony of the close.

These points are, however, not much more than negative; Sophocles did not fail to do what obviously had to be done. Let us look more closely into his use of the chorus, first as actor, then as singers. 'The Chorus', says Aristotle, 'must be regarded as one of the actors.' So it is; but how?

It was said above (p. 31) that the acts of the individuals are bound to be more striking than those of a group. Sophocles saw that, and accordingly when his chorus takes part in the action it is normally before the more vivid dramatis personae have set to work. Its more generalized action prepares the way for, but can hardly follow, the more incisive action of the single person. So in the *Ajax*, it is the chorus which is presented as the first presumptive victim of Ajax' fall; Tecmessa is the second, because in her the pathos of the situation can be brought to a finer point.[2] Then the

[1] Note *ad loc.*

[2] For this reason too, as well as from the exigencies of staging, it is Tecmessa, not the chorus, who finds the body of Ajax.

chorus and Tecmessa together, as minor characters, are used
to prepare for the appearance of Ajax.

The *Electra* is built as a series of attacks on the resolution
of the heroine : Chrysothemis, with the threats of Aegisthus
looming behind her, Clytemnestra, the false Messenger, are
successive moves in this attack ; but before all these is placed
the first slight reserve of the chorus, with its counsels of
submission, before the more keenly edged attack of the actor
begins.   Even the *Antigone* has its suggestion of their
participation in the action (v. 215) before the real actors
enter ; and in the *Tyrannus* when we face the situation afresh
after the Parodos and Oedipus' denunciation, the chorus
makes its only direct contribution to the action (vv. 282–92)
before the others start.   The chorus never attempts to
compete with the actors : if used as actors, it is always used
before the others begin.

When it has shot this early bolt its part as actor is normally
finished, except that, as it is always present and always
relevant, it is freely used in minor ways to lend a hand when
wanted—as to receive messengers, to announce new-comers,
and in general to make transitions smooth.   But these services
to the plot are not always mechanical.   When Creon, in the
Tyrannus, enters in indignation, the chorus is there to receive
him, but the scene gains enormously in effectiveness from the
fact that it thus begins on a level of neutrality, from which it
can gradually work up to its violent close.

The chorus has a third clearly-marked function in its part
in the dialogue.   It is perpetually saying things like

' Oh king, give heed if sense be in his words ;
Heed thou thy sire too—both have spoken well.'
                                           (*Antig.*, 724–5.)

What is the point of these tedious remarks ?   Simply, I take
it, that when one speaker had made an effective speech the
beginning of the reply was likely to be missed, if not because
of a murmur of approbation and of physical readjustment,
then because the minds of the audience were still on the
speech just heard.   These commonplace couplets are merely
buffers, designed to give a moment of rest between speeches.
Often, however, such a comment is used to give an effective

cue to the reply (*Antig.*, 278, 471, 766, *Tyrannus*, 1073–5) ;
with which minor service we may compare the habit of
Sophocles' characters of addressing their reply to the Chorus
when they are too angry to answer directly (*El.*, 612, *Tyrannus,* 429, 618, *Antig.*, 726).

As Actor, therefore, the chorus has its continuous share in
the drama, and has, in one way or another, its contribution to
make, due regard being paid to its somewhat indefinite
character. Its most important function, however, is obviously
the lyrical one, and this we now consider. We shall have to
examine the plays in order, for a distinct development in this
respect is discernible.

It is, I think, fair to say that the odes of the *Ajax* provoke
neither censure nor any great admiration. There is the
Parodos, appropriately composed in the Dorian rhythm, in
which the chorus calls upon Ajax to arise in his might and
dispel the rumours that are gathering around him. The first
stasimon is entirely dramatic ; here they think of their own
homes which they are doubtful of seeing again, and of the
ill news which is coming to Ajax' parents. Next we have
the bright ' I am thrilled with joy ', of which we shall speak
later. The third stasimon is a natural and vivid expression
of their loathing of the war. These worthy sailors do not
soar, but what they say is always in keeping with the situation
and with their own characters. However, it cannot be said
that any of their odes (with the exception of ' I am thrilled
with joy ') makes any considerable contribution to the play.

The chorus of the *Antigone*, although it hovers more on the
outskirts of the action than that of the *Ajax*, takes us further.
The Parodos this time is more than suitable ; it is astonishingly
dramatic, sweeping away the almost conspiratorial atmosphere
of the prologue, substituting for the private sorrows of Antigone the joy of the City in its deliverance, making Polyneices
not the unburied brother but the defeated traitor. It has
too an ironical close, in its call for ' forgetfulness of these
woes ' and for a festival of rejoicing to Bacchus. As for the
famous second ode, it merits all the admiration which has been
lavished upon it, but as a factor in the play it is less relevant
than any we have yet seen. The traditional explanation, that

it is suggested by the surprising defiance of Creon's edict, is surely rather lame. A dozen dramatic situations could give as good an excuse. It seems more satisfactory to suppose that Sophocles deliberately preferred to insert his magnificent poem here, trusting to its own merits, rather than make the Chorus speculate on the identity and motives of the rebel. The action and the emotional rhythm of the play are virtually in suspense until the rebel is found ; accordingly, though the chorus can end by reprobating the act of disobedience, the greater part of the ode is not closely connected with it. It is less relevant than the odes in the *Ajax*, but we would rather have this one. Nevertheless Sophocles does not allow his choruses to philosophize so freely again. This ode is one of the few which are definitely a ' curtain', separating acts. Later Sophocles makes them connect acts. This indeed is the function of the next stasimon. Scarcely less notable as a poem than the previous one, it makes a bigger contribution to the unity of the play, for its opening, ' Blessed are they who have not tasted sorrow,' is the natural culmination of the emotions aroused by the previous scene, while its sombre close, ' Evil appeareth good in his eyes whom the god is leading to destruction,' a foreshadowing of Creon's fate and the underlying cause, is in Sophocles' best manner. The short ode to Eros professes to be little more than an interlude, connecting Haemon's scene with Antigone's last appearance. It has ironical point if we suppose that Haemon is the ' just man ' in question whose mind is ' drawn to injustice ' by the power of Aphrodite. But nothing very striking is required here, for there follows the most beautiful lyrical passage in Greek Tragedy, the commos between the chorus and Antigone—or rather between Antigone and the chorus, for, by a powerful stroke, it is Antigone who has the lyrics, while the reserved chorus answers in anapaests.

The Danae-ode is the only example in these four plays of the purely decorative lyric. Certainly the effect in performance of the entrance of the soft theme ' Danaë too endured . . . ' is one of marvellous relief after the tragic tension of Antigone's last moments, but one can but feel that this searching of the mythological records for parallels to Antig-

one's fate scarcely shows Sophocles at his most inspired.[1]
Certainly at the corresponding part of the *Tyrannus* ('Alas!
you generations of men. . . .') he did something far finer.

But if *Danae* falls short of Sophocles' best, the ode that follows almost surpasses that best. Here Sophocles repeats on a
much more magnificent scale an effect which he had used before, in 'I am thrilled with joy' in the *Ajax*, and was to use
again, in the Cithaeron ode of the *Tyrannus*. In each case
the plot leads to the expectation of a happy issue just before
the catastrophe; Ajax has relented, Antigone is to be released,
Oedipus is to discover the happy secret of his birth. The
action comes to a climax, and on this climax the chorus enters,
to carry it higher and higher with the eloquence of music and
dance. The long invocation of Dionysus does this marvellously. The ode, exciting in rhythm, glorious in language,
rises to an ecstasy of joy before the Messenger comes with
his news *tethnasi*.[2] Here the chorus does not do what is
merely appropriate, it does not merely contribute to the action
of the play; it transforms it. Euripides might have written
Danae; he could never have done this.

The *Antigone*, few will deny, shows a marked development
in Sophocles' powers as lyric poet. The odes in the *Ajax* are
by no means weak; but in these of the *Antigone*, there is a
depth and a power which surpasses anything in the earlier
play.[3] Nor in the *Ajax* is there anything so fine as the
rhythmical effects in the *Antigone*.[4] Nor does the *Ajax*, with

[1] Mr. Percy Gordon, who composed the music for the Glasgow
production of the *Antigone*, confessed to me that this ode was the
only one that did not immediately suggest its own musical scheme.

[2] 'Death!' In the Glasgow production this dramatic excitement
was admirably reflected in Mr. Gordon's music. He constructed it
over a strong reiterated rhythmical figure on a pedal-point which
hurried one on to the final invocation of the 'leader of the quire
of the stars whose breath is flame', and which left no doubt what
the dramatic purpose of the ode was.

[3] One would, however, hesitate to say the same of the iambics, in
spite of Antigone's speech to Creon.

[4] For instance, the long, swinging rhythms of vv. 134 f., the
monotonous dactyls of vv. 339 f., the bold hearing rhythm of vv.
590 f.

the exception of the second stasimon, show the same dramatic imagination in the use of the lyrics as part of the structure of the whole. Nevertheless the choruses of the *Antigone*, though splendid, are from this point of view not flawless. Sophocles could improve on this, and in the *Tyrannus* he does.

The prologue of the *Tyrannus* is based on three main ideas, the Plague, the obscure message of hope from Delphi, and the beginnings of the discovery in the first clues advanced by Creon. The purpose of this third part is evidently to prepare for the suspicions which Oedipus forms of a plot between Creon and Teiresias ; the chorus has heard nothing about it. Their Parodos is based on the other two themes, the Plague and the Message. It contains nothing new, for all our attention is wanted for Oedipus and what he is going to do ; nor is there any sense of repetition, as both of these themes, vividly though they were presented in the dialogue, become something much more immediate when presented through song and dance. It is not repetition, but fulfilment. But the most interesting point at the moment is not so much the substance as the arrangement of the ode. The two themes appear in the reverse order, the Message and then the Plague ; not because Sophocles is obeying some obscure canon, but because this arrangement makes smoother the transition from the Prologue to the first episode. The chorus enters on the note of hope on which the prologue ended, and closes on the note of apprehension and prayer with which the next scene starts.[1] This method, continuation and preparation we noticed once or twice in the *Antigone* ; here and in the *Electra* it is always used, greatly to the advantage of the dramatic sweep of the plays.

The second ode, the first stasimon, we have already discussed (p. 166). It is immediately relevant to the situation, and it is highly dramatic, in that the chorus postpones as long as it can expression of the perturbation which Teiresias has caused. Further, the scene which is to disturb the chorus as

---

[1] Contrast the opening dactyls and the closing iambics.—Kranz (*Stasimon*, p. 193) makes the end a ' return ' to the beginning. Certainly beginning and end are prayers—but in different moods.

much as the prophet has done is ushered in with the confident words

> ' Never will my judgement convict him of sin.'

This long scene is broken at v. 631 by the entrance of Iocasta, and here the chorus is used with admirable effect. For the sake of showing one side of Oedipus' character Sophocles has allowed him to quarrel most violently with Creon, a quarrel which has to be allayed before the drama can go on.   Iocasta's entreaties are therefore reinforced by a powerful lyrical appeal from the chorus, which begins in the heavy cretic rhythm which was applied to King Pelasgus. So is Oedipus persuaded without any strain on our belief, and before we proceed to the next stage the musical interlude effaces from our minds the harsh details of the quarrel without impairing its general effect.

The third ode begins with a stanza on the majesty of the Unwritten Laws, but if we expect a philosophic poem like the second ode of the *Antigone* we are disappointed.   From this general tone it is soon brought round into strict subservience to the drama.   We are nearer the crisis, and the chorus is uneasy.   It is caught in a dilemma.   Its loyalty to Oedipus has not deserted it ; we see that from the fourth ode ; but the horrible story which Iocasta has told, the suspicion which is gathering around Oedipus, the recollection of his bearing towards Creon, and the ' impiety ' of Iocasta, have frightened them.   Their language about hybris they keep as general as possible, and the picture of the ' tyrant ' is conventional. Phrases like ' Struggle for the good of the city,' ' Punishment for wicked insolence,' ' If he is not going to win his gains justly,' all indicate that Oedipus is not the man they are describing.   The ode is perhaps a warning ; it is certainly an expression of fear.   They cannot now sophisticate about the difference between the God and his interpreters ; if it should come to a choice between Oedipus and the God's word, they are bound to pray for the fulfilment of the oracles.

Of the next ode, preparatory to the catastrophe, we have already spoken and shall speak again.[1]   The last one should be compared with the Danae ode, for each follows the

[1] Pp. 171, 188.

moment of greatest tension and is designed to give lyrical relief. This one is incomparably finer. Instead of a rather learned parade of parallels we have a direct and simple expression of the pain and astonishment which the chorus feels ; but it is a natural and spontaneous tribute to the greatness of Oedipus and the greatness of his fall that the chorus should instinctively think of the situation not as an isolated calamity but rather as a disclosure of what the life of Man is. The ode surpasses Danae in dramatic relief and at the same time rivals ' Wonders are many ' as a philosophic poem. The order of the themes is once more important. Had the chorus reversed the order and sung ' Alas for Oedipus ! But how like human life this is ! ' the effect would have been one of conscious moralizing, a little unnecessary and certainly undramatic. As it is, the effect is perfect. ' O you generations of men ', coming immediately after the horrible discovery, is not moralizing but an immediate reaction. Dramatically, its very remoteness is a wonderful relief—provided, as always, that it is sung and not said.[1] Then, in the most natural way, to the general succeeds the particular. The personal cry ' Would that I had never seen thee ! ' by conveying so directly the dreadful revulsion that the chorus feels vividly expresses the peculiar horror of Oedipus' fate. This personal tone, drawing our minds away from the tone of philosophic reflection, is also an excellent means of transition from the catastrophe to its results, the blinded but not broken Oedipus.

In this play Sophocles has settled all his problems. The chorus is confined strictly to the limits of the play, making no excursions from the stage either in time or place. It is no ' ideal spectator ', but an actor, its part closely interwoven in the whole fabric, but it is not pedestrian. Its greater lyric sensibility, the power which it has, and the actors have not, of vivifying the general, is used to full advantage ; it can be moved to philosophic language, but only on condition that it is moved ; this must arise out of and be subordinate to the

---

[1] For nothing can be more drab and miserable than a reciting chorus.—This arrangement of themes, the remote followed by the near-by, became a common formula (Kranz, *Stasimon*, p. 250); here we best see the dramatic reason for this.

drama. Everything that it says, in fact, arises directly from its position in the play. As plain Actor it is used with discretion and effect ; its peculiar virtue, the superior expressiveness of its medium, is used here as well as in its formal odes. Finally the odes are always brought into strict connexion with the adjacent scenes, in such a way that they accentuate their significance, amplify their rhythm, and weld the two elements of dialogue and lyric into a continuous unity. Sophocles, in fact, has ceased to regard the chorus as a ' curtain '.

The treatment of the chorus in the *Electra* is entirely different—and so is the play. In each there is one commanding figure, but whereas the drama of Oedipus is a continual reaching-out, that of Electra turns inwards. It is essentially the inner drama of the mind. We are to see not a catastrophic change of fortune, but the reaction of Electra to a series of shocks. As the external drama is less, the scope of the chorus is less. Sophocles therefore, rather than invent unnecessary odes, cuts down their number from five to three, two very short. Moreover, since the progress of the drama is not towards some distant calamity but towards the final revelation of Electra's nature, there is little apposite comment for the chorus to make : the illumination must come from Electra herself. A difficult situation, but Sophocles has met it boldly and with extraordinary success. First of all there is no Parodos. Electra follows immediately upon the prologue. Nothing is to compete with her—not yet ; there is no triumphant entry-song of the chorus to make the atmosphere —Electra must make her own, and, what is more, bring the chorus into it. Accordingly, though there are the customary anapaests to accompany the entrance of the chorus, they are sung by Electra. The chorus is subordinate, both here and throughout the lyrical dialogue that follows. And this subordination continues, for when the chorus reaches its independent stasima it is, as we have suggested, only an extension of Electra's own personality. What they say in these odes is not remarkable ; what is remarkable is the moment at which they say it.

The first stasimon (v. 472 ff.) comes at the first bright

moment of the play, after Clytemnestra's dream and the sisters' decision to use her offerings against her. This is the moment which Sophocles chooses for his first independent ode. As in the *Tyrannus*, the chorus takes up the prevailing feeling of hope and carries it up to a confident prophecy of success—ending however on a gloomy note with the recollection of the constant series of calamity which has befallen the Atreid house since the murder of Myrtilus. Sophocles is not here doing what he must or what he can ; he is calling up his reserves just when he can best use them.[1]

Where we might have expected another ode, after the triumphant exit of Clytemnestra with the Paedagogus, we have a commos, for our attention may not be withdrawn from Electra. Again, she is more predominant than the chorus. The chorus does its best to console her, but Electra sinks to the depths, from which she is shortly to rise so nobly. No ode ; for what matters is not the situation nor its general implications nor its effect on anyone else, but only how it affects Electra.

The second of the three stasima is as well timed as the first. It is placed after the scene in which Electra has risen to her greatest heights. Chrysothemis has prudently declined her proposals, but the chorus is now so full of her own spirit that it acclaims her desperate plan as the highest reverence and piety. This point is the climax of Electra's resolution, and it is here that Sophocles brings in his chorus again, that we may pause awhile on the climax. It is a hammer-blow in the making of the play.

The last ode, so brief and so terrible in its swift, stealthy rhythm, is a powerful variation of the Bacchus and Cithaeron odes, introducing the climax of the play, not, this time, through unexpectedness, but as if by a sudden onrush of the inevitable.

The use of the chorus in the *Electra,* in particular the absence of a Parodos, has been regularly used as an argument in the dating of the play. It is an argument which, I think, should be used with circumspection. Since the absence of a Parodos is eminently suitable to this particular theme, we

[1] The mention of Pelop's 'ill-starred charioteering', an ironic prelude to the Messenger-speech, is an interesting detail.

cannot infer, from this alone, that the *Electra* is later than the
Tyrannus. Its theme demanded different treatment, and
Sophocles was now sufficiently master of his craft to choose
exactly the right method for each subject. There he uses it
with a greater flexibility, here with a greater boldness. His
chorus has become, as it were, merely one instrument in
his orchestration. He does not need it to carry the emotional
' supercargo ' of his drama ; that is now expressed in the unspoken eloquence of his situations—the silent women before
the Paedagogus, the disclosure of Clytemnestra's face, the
prayers of Clytemnestra, Electra, Iocasta, to the statue of
Apollo. There is no need for the chorus to comment on these
things : it can be used for other purposes.

3. STRUCTURAL PRINCIPLES   We have considered Sophocles'
outlook during this period of his activity, his use of the third
actor, his development of the Chorus. It remains to examine,
at the cost it may be of some repetition, his art as a whole.
The fascinating but difficult question of his poetic style must
be passed over as lying outside the scope of this book. One
further point however may be admitted as relevant, the
difference between the Sophoclean and the modern drama
in the matter of side-scenes and by-plot.

We may perhaps best contemplate Sophocles' methods by
examining in detail what is probably his best-constructed,
certainly his most uncompromising play, the *Electra*.

' Sophocles' interest in this story ', we are told, ' was not so
much in its moral and religious implications as in the character
of the chief actor.' But character does not make a drama ; it
is rather character as affected by situation that he studies
here ; character, if our reading of the play is right, twisted
awry by circumstances. The Greek theatre, normally confined by its Chorus to one time and place,[1] could not trace

[1] In view of the deeply rooted neo-classical misconceptions, it
may not be out of place to say again that the Unities of Time and
Place were accidental, not fundamental, in Greek drama. It was
not usually convenient to move the chorus to another place, therefore the scene did not change ; and for a long time drama was not
the presentation of action, but of thought and feeling about action,
so that it was not natural that the chorus should run about in

change or growth in character; what it could do was to reveal more and more of the depths of a character already existing. Accordingly, in the *Electra* Sophocles presents his heroine in a series of situations so contrived that they increase in intensity, not only forming a dramatic story, but also drawing more and more upon the reserves of Electra's strength and resolution. The whole play, after the prologue, may be regarded as an attack on Electra by persons and events, a cumulative attack which calls for an increasingly strong defence. This is the general plan; the interest lies in seeing how Sophocles contrives to bind these separate attacks into a consistent and beautiful whole.

The prologue is interesting and important (see pp. 136 f.). It explains the motives of Orestes, which so well contrast with and complement those of Electra, it defines the moral attitude which Sophocles adopts, it lays the groundwork of the intrigue which is to play an important part in the drama, and it out-

---

pursuit of the action. If a change of scene was necessary and possible (as in the *Eumenides* and the *Ajax*), it was made without hesitation.

As for the unity of time, it would more closely correspond to the facts to say that time does not exist unless it is mentioned. It is not even true to say that the normal chorus, composed of people who have to go to bed, limited the action to one day. Certainly Prometheus and his Oceanids, and the Furies, do not carry a watch, so that in a special sense these plays are timeless; but so, in general, are the others. The *Antigone* begins at dawn, but there is no suggestion that Teiresias enters soon after lunch or that the chorus, at the end, goes home to bed. Time may be implied when something specific, like fighting a battle, has to be done, but it is always enough that *some* interval should be allowed. The events in the *Suppliant Women*, measured by the clock, would occupy nearly a week, but we are quite indifferent. There is an odd impression that a choral ode may indicate the lapse of some time, but not too much. Thus Jebb argued (*O.C.*, Introd. xxxiii) that the scene of Oedipus' death could not be a mile and a half from the grove, because the intervening ode is so short—as if there were some rough proportion between choric and linear feet; while Verrall, despite the expedition to Thebes and back, plus a battle, which take place during one ode in the *Suppliant Women*, could not conceive that a double journey between Phthia and Delphi could be covered by one ode in the *Andromache*.

lines the situation as a whole.   As always, Sophocles gets off
the mark at once.

At the end of the prologue Electra's voice is heard.   The
Paedagogus calls attention to it ; Orestes at once thinks it must
be Electra, and would wait.   Clearly Sophocles cannot allow
this, and the Paedagogus comes to his rescue by insisting that
nothing must come before the due performance of the rites to
Agamemnon.   Why does Sophocles contrive this point ?
Sheppard sees in it a dark hint that the Paedagogus is the
villain of the piece, always standing in the way of Orestes'
happiness.   His slavish piety certainly causes Electra an
hour of anguish, and ' Apollo ' as understood by these two
men causes a vast amount of ruin and unhappiness in this
play.   So much at least seems clear.   There is however a
further point.   Sophocles contrived this, I think, partly as a
slight dramatic thrill to relieve this rather level part of the
play : Will they meet now or not ?—and partly to give an
interlock between the Prologue and the succeeding scene.
Bare juxtaposition was not good enough ; he will have no
break in the movement of his play (cf. p. 89).   Doing this
he trusted to the ruthless ' piety ' of the slave to pull it off.
We shall meet other and bigger instances of his use of such
purely theatrical calculation.   It is worth noticing that
Euripides (*El.*, 111) uses the same device—though for very
different reasons !¹

The transition from the Prologue is indeed a change.   Instead of the bright song of the birds we hear the mourning of
Electra, instead of the hopefulness of action the hopelessness
of passivity.   Electra's monody at once gives us the key to
her character and to her part in the play ; she does indeed
invoke outraged Justice, but the tone of her whole song is
unmistakably that of personal grief and suffering.   She is as
sharply distinct from Aeschylus' Electra as from the embittered
virago whom Euripides so vividly draws.   It is an important
point too that she is alone ; we see her in the situation as it is
and has been before the first moves in the attack are made.
The first move is the friendly counsel of the chorus.   Their well-
meant attempts at consolation and their advice that Electra

¹ Below, p. 357.

should make the best of a hard lot, like her sisters, do but bring out her irreconcilable nature and her abandonment to her sorrow. At the same time careful hints are dropped which will make smooth the way of the drama ; Chrysothemis and her attitude are outlined, we hear of the long waiting for Orestes, Electra is warned that she is laying up for herself trouble on top of trouble. Unless he is aiming at complete surprise Sophocles' preparation is always most careful and unobtrusive.

The gracious yielding of the chorus brings Electra to a calmer mood, and she explains her unbending attitude by describing the conditions under which she lives—a very natural way of bringing in this necessary speech.[1] It is full of character, in that Electra describes things as seen by her, not as seen by Sophocles. Sheppard, with reason, throws doubt on her interpretation of Clytemnestra's games, and she goes very far wrong in her estimation of Aegisthus' character. Her own, however, she can appreciate : both at the beginning and at the end of the speech she recognizes the unpleasant effect her situation is exerting over her. An important detail brought forth by an inquiry of the chorus serves two ends ; Aegisthus is safely out of the way, and he is evidently a tyrant who keeps a tight hand over his subjects (310–16). The scene with Chrysothemis is admirably developed in three stages. At first she is the foil to Electra : as such already foreshadowed by the chorus. The chorus itself was a foil, but this time the contrast is sharper. Not only are these two women in the same position, so that the contrast of their attitude is more marked than that between Electra and the chorus, but also Chrysothemis is less sympathetic to Electra ; with good reason, be it said : ' I am well-used to her tirades.' Then, having done her duty as foil, she gives her reason for coming ; Aegisthus is resolved at any price to put an end to Electra's opposition—a point which does double duty.[2] It is the beginning of the real ' attack ' which is to leave her entirely defenceless and entirely unafraid, and it shows us that Electra's implacable hostility to her father's murderers is not a

[1] See further, p. 358.
[2] See also p. 160.

futile self-indulgence. We might add that it strengthens our feeling that Aegisthus is the real enemy (we felt this too in the prologue) and it gives a new urgency to the desire for Orestes' return. Thus the pace of the action, hitherto leisurely, is definitely quickened.

This second point having served at least four purposes, the third is introduced, again by the easiest and most natural of transitions, the dream of Clytemnestra. So rapt is Electra in her own dream of vengeance that before she knows what Clytemnestra's was she hails it as an omen ; in her despair she will snatch at any straw. This sudden hope, a hope caught up and enlarged by the chorus, is an ironical prelude to the news which is coming of Orestes' death, doubly ironical since that news is false and that he really is coming to bring such happy results.

The second episode opens with another indirect reminder that Aegisthus is the tyrant : of Clytemnestra Electra is not afraid. Clytemnestra here is a harsh, unlovely woman. Perpetual contact and enmity with her have not improved Electra, and she knows it. The snarling onset of Clytemnestra shows us most unpleasantly what Electra has become, and what she might have been :

'I know that my conduct suits neither my age nor my nature.' (617–18.)

It has shown us too what her doctrine of Justice really amounts to—an appalling scene, fitly crowned by Clytemnestra's appalling prayer to Apollo, which leads us, without a moment's pause, into that astonishing three-cornered scene with the Paedagogus. The attack is being pressed with a vengeance, and, by a terrible twist, even Electra's grief at Orestes' death is embittered by her mother's reception of it. 'Is it well ?', (*kalôs*) she asks, using an adverb which is later to be played on with a sinister significance.

The commos gives us a slight relief from this intensity, and shows Electra at her lowest ebb, rejecting the best consolation that the chorus can offer. This passage, like the prayer to Apollo, ends in a swift change. The words '. . . nor of our lamentations' have hardly died away when Chrysothemis enters with her 'In joy, my sister, and in haste do I come', excited by the offerings she has seen at Agamemnon's tomb. These offerings, which are used by Aeschylus to inflame Electra with the hope of Orestes' arrival, by Euripides to ridicule Aeschylus, are used by Sophocles to give a new and ironical twist to his plot and to further his study of contrasting characters. But this twist is not inserted merely to entertain the audience. It heightens our sense of the disaster which has befallen Electra, being the culmination of the attack on her ; further, the bitter double-irony with which she plays with Chrysothemis gives her time to recover herself and to take stock of her position. During these few moments of comparative calm she can face in earnest what she has often faced in hypothesis, the possibility of killing Aegisthus herself. The development of her character has reached its fulfilment : we see the complete Electra, crowned with this plan which she deceives herself into thinking will cover her with glory. She has risen magnificently to her conception of her duty, even to the point of rapture. It is this moment which Sophocles chooses to prolong and reinforce with his second stasimon.

Now we come to the long-deferred recognition scene. We have followed the gradual disclosure of Electra's character from the slow beginning of the introductory monody to this last scene where she rises almost above herself. Nothing remains but to draw the threads together and to accomplish the vengeance. The scene opens quietly, on a low note of lamentation, for it is to end on a high note of rejoicing. Electra is given a speech of lamentation over the urn—a long and a very fine passage, and assuredly no easy one for the actor. But why is it there ? Why not the recognition at once ? The dramatic excuse for Orestes is patent : he is feeling his way—he has to gain admittance to the Palace, and he cannot be sure of the chorus. The dramatic purpose is to show us yet another side of Electra. Something did remain after all : Electra was not complete. Here is a striking contrast with the previous scene : we see not the Electra rapturously in love with murder, but a very womanly Electra of whom we have yet seen little—nothing since Clytemnestra appeared. All the natural affection of which she has been so long starved, all the humanity of which she divested herself in the last scene, come back in a torrent : the balance is restored and Electra is complete.

It has been pedantically imputed as a fault to this play that the rejoicings of Electra are too long-drawn-out, that they impede the action. They certainly do, and Sophocles, as well as Orestes, realized the fact. A machine-made plot would have made shorter work of the passage, but Sophocles' point is that even the long-cherished schemes of vengeance—so strong is the woman now in Electra—must give place to her joy at the unexpected recovery of her brother. When the Paedagogus comes out abruptly to recall them to the matter in hand—to emphasize to us that Electra is no cold conspirator —and naturally gives a shock to Electra, who sees in him only the author of her late suffering—even then, learning who he is, she welcomes him excitedly and at some length. Here is the brightest moment of the play, a relief from what has gone and a contrast to what is to follow. The two men enter the Palace, and Electra, now at last brought back to the realities of the situation, prays before the same image of Apollo to which Clytemnestra had prayed. Let us hope that the God appreciated the situation.

Now at least there is no delay ; the last stasimon, in two short and swift stanzas, brings the catastrophe upon us. Electra remains on the stage, nominally to stand guard, actually to interpret to us what is passing within, dramatically that we may see how she bears herself in this crisis. Not for a moment does Electra leave the stage. Two details are worth attention here ; the continuous mention of Aegisthus, and the last appearance of the adverb, *kalôs*. We had it first, in reference to the tragedy, in vv. 790–1 :

EL. . . . Is it well ?
CL. Not thou ! But he—as he is, it is well.

There is an echo of it two verses later, and at v. 815 Electra repeats her bitter ' is this well ? ' ; the next time we hear the word in this connexion it comes from the Paedagogus (1345) :

' As it stands now, for their part all is well—even what is not well.'

Now, after the killing of Clytemnestra, we hear what all this has been leading to :

EL.   Orestes, how have ye fared ?

OR.   Within the palace all is well—if Apollo commanded well.

This is no more accidental than the re-echoing of the inhospitable name of Cithaeron in the second half of the *Tyrannus*.

And last, the swift and terrible end, a scene which even Sophocles never surpassed, perhaps the most shattering *coup de théâtre* ever invented. ' Now at length ', the Chorus briefly observes, ' you have gained your freedom.' Did all live happily ever after ?

But this ending is interesting in another way. Sophocles ends on Aegisthus, Aeschylus and Euripides on Clytemnestra. In the *Oresteia* the matricide is the central incident ; had Aegisthus been killed after her, it would have been an anticlimax and an interruption. Euripides was bent on showing Electra and Orestes in the worst possible light, so that he naturally ends with the more repulsive murder, and, though the manner of Aegisthus' death is bad enough, he was able to make the circumstances of the second slaughter even more revolting. Moreover, with his prologue and epilogue he can cover the whole course of the story, and therefore can follow the most dramatic order of events. Sophocles however was taking a line of his own. He was restricting himself to one part of the story, making his play a study of Electra's situation, not of Orestes' destiny. To have finished with the death of Clytemnestra would inevitably have raised the question ' And what next ? ' The audience would have looked for Furies. He chose to treat the event as being, to Orestes, the reversal of a political usurpation ; to Electra, vengeance on personal tyrants : this in order that their motives should be entirely within their own control. They are to be driven neither by Gods nor by hallucinations. That the recovery of Argos, and the vengeance, involved matricide was the centre of the tragedy, but nevertheless the recovery of Argos was the mainspring of the action. To end with Aegisthus therefore was both necessary and logical.

But this was a perilous course for the dramatist to take.

He had to justify his selection of Aegisthus' murder as the climax, and to do this in two ways, morally and dramatically. Morally he has done it by magnifying the part of Aegisthus at the expense of Clytemnestra's. We have seen some of the deft references to his overmastering power ; it is only because Aegisthus is ' in the fields ' that the drama is possible at all. In Electra's first speech the weight of the attack falls upon him ; she hates Clytemnestra, but it is Aegisthus who is the tyrant, he who sits on Agamemnon's throne, wears the robes he wore, pours libations where he slew Agamemnon, and sleeps in his bed. References to the actual slaying of Agamemnon are relatively infrequent ; we hear much more of the wealth and power of Argos, which now Aegisthus holds. Clytemnestra, in her prayer, speaks of the riches which she enjoys in peace ' with her friends '. She indeed hates Electra, but it is he who threatens her with death. In every possible way the absent Aegisthus is made to appear as the strong man of the piece, so that the vengeance would be nothing without his death. He is a very different person, in spite of Electra's sneers, from the mere accomplice of the *Agamemnon* and the misguided fool of Euripides' play. He is the chief foe, and this is rammed home by his being driven in to die on the spot where he killed Agamemnon.

Sophocles however is still open to attack on the other flank. It is not enough that this order of events be logically right ; it must also be dramatically convincing. Anti-climax would spoil the logic, and the killing of a usurper, even though he be an uncle, is not so dramatic as the killing of a mother. This is the danger which Sophocles has met by his final situation. When the audience sees Aegisthus uncovering the face of his wife, it will feel no anti-climax ; it will feel rather that she *had* to die first. Again, this stroke is not a mere melodramatic ornament ; Sophocles had to do it. He was in a risky situation ; and from the difficulty, as usual, he drew his most telling and most imaginative effect.

So much for the composition of this play. We see how every detail in its subserves the main purpose, that the situation, as it develops, shall reveal more and more of Electra's nature. Everything has a direct bearing on this.

The plot is complex, with two reversals of fortune, the irony
is often two layers deep; there is a long and brilliant narrative, there is an extremely nervous use of the chorus, but
nothing is done illegitimately.   Every move, however spectacular, has its direct bearing on the main theme and serves
its own purpose, sometimes two or three purposes.   The
economy of means is admirable ; nothing is wasted, but there
is no sense of bareness or poverty.   Admirable too is the
management of the rhythms of the piece, both the general
rhythm of the whole, working up from a slow start by
gradually increasing momentum to Electra's resolve (which is
a climax both in the plot and in the portrayal of her character), then held up by a new phase of her character, finally
gathering force again to the tremendous finish ; and also in
the smaller rhythms of the separate scenes, as for instance in
the Messenger's speech and in Chrysothemis' first scene.

    This firm control of rhythm, both in the gross and in detail,
is even more noticeable in the *Tyrannus*.   Here we find a
spaciousness and a leisureliness in the early scenes which goes
well with their position in the play, with the assured and lofty
position of Oedipus, and with the apparent remoteness of
the catastrophe.[1]   We are given plenty of time in which to
look at our Oedipus.   As the drama progresses and suspicion
grows, so the pace quickens and the scenes shorten.   It is no
accident that the first stages of the investigation, between
Oedipus and Creon in the prologue, proceeds in leisurely
couplets, the later ones in tense line-by-line dialogue.   The
pace grows so fast that the final scene in the discovery is
packed into seventy-five amazing verses.

    Each individual scene too grows in the same way.   Teire-
sias, whose coming is so effectively prepared, is received with
high respect, and in a speech from Oedipus of some amplitude:
Creon enters, to find the neutral Chorus there.   Most remarkable, from this point of view, is the whole section from
the end of the second episode to the beginning of the fourth—

---

[1] Note that for the sake of this rhythm Sophocles admits an improbability that was not necessary : it appears from Oedipus' first
speech that he knows nothing of the plague.   The improbability is,
of course, removed at v. 58, but its temporary admission shows how
Sophocles cared more for design than for photographic plausibility.

a good example of the way in which Sophocles thinks not
in scenes but in whole plays. Iocasta has disproved one
oracle and comforts Oedipus against another. She says, with
a subtle revelation of the difference between her feminine
mind and Oedipus' masculine mind, 'The shepherd said
" Brigands ". He cannot now say " A brigand ". The
whole city heard it.' She may be confident, but he is terribly
afraid. So, it appears from the ode, is the chorus; afraid
that their King and Queen may be marked down for ruin. In
a moment it appears that Iocasta is afraid too—but of what?
As if to fulfil the spirit of the ode she appears with offerings to
Apollo.[1] A new turn, this. What has happened to explain
this *volte-face*? Has news come? No news, but something
much more disturbing; Oedipus has broken down. That intellect which has been the soul of Thebes for so long, that
splendid self-possession, ' He gives himself to any one who
speaks terrors.' This is the awful portent which has driven
Iocasta to the gods, and this is Sophocles' way of describing
it. Then the bland Messenger. Oedipus is called—he says:
   ' My dear wife, Iocasta, why hast thou called me out?'
and
   ' This man—who is he? And what has he to say to me?'[2]
He is terrified. Now follows that masterly cross-rhythm, ending in Iocasta's exit (p. 161). What now? A silence. But
the scene must come to an end, there must be no anti-climax,
and it ought to end with Oedipus in our minds rather than
Iocasta, for the coming tragedy is his. Moreover, we cannot
have Oedipus beginning the next scene too in terror or foreboding. Oedipus is equal to the occasion. An innocent
remark by the Chorus gives him his cue. All his sublime
confidence has by now returned and he is ready to confront
whatever Destiny may bring;

CHORUS. . . . a storm evil may break forth.

OEDIPUS. Break forth what will! I *will* disclose my birth.

---

[1] A good moment too in the movement of the play. Like Clytemnestra's prayer, it is an expressive pause in the action, a moment
of apparent calm, but the calm of a cyclone's centre.

[2] Note the appealing address in the one speech, and in the other
the clatter of the monosyllables.

He rises to his highest in this splendid outburst, and this is great enough to shout down the silence which Iocasta has left. On this climax the chorus enters, to carry it to the very summit of Cyllene in a marvellous flight of lyrical ecstasy—a very different utterance from their last ! Then a sudden drop to the prosaic : 'If I, who have never met him, may hazard a guess, that man yonder would be the man we have long been looking for.' And with this the seventy-five verses start.

In this passage we have three distinct but interwoven lines of dramatic emotion, Oedipus, Iocasta, and the chorus. Each has its own line of flight, each moves with the utmost energy and freedom (for nothing freer can be imagined than the difference between the Oedipus indicated in Iocasta's prayer and the Oedipus of 'Break forth what will !'), each line moves in the most natural way possible, but at every moment each makes the most dramatic contrast with the others. It is the perfect counterpoint which makes also the perfect harmony. The risk of a breakdown at Iocasta's exit is a very real one. It is a tremendous moment, but if we delay too long over it, the rhythm of the whole is ruined. Great as it is, we must take it in our stride ; it is but an accessory. It is an impressive sign of Sophocles' confidence in himself that he allows himself to place such a moment immediately before his real climax. Only the greatest player can permit himself dangerous strokes like these.

How different this method of construction is from the methods of neo-classical drama is well brought out by Jebb in his Introduction to the *Tyrannus*. He compares with the *Tyrannus* plays on the same theme by Corneille, Dryden and Voltaire, showing that all of these had more difficulty than Sophocles with the irrational element in the plot, and that all were forced to introduce by-plot. Voltaire says that the material in Sophocles' play is not sufficient for more than a couple of acts of a modern play ; by-plot therefore is necessary to eke it out. Voltaire and Dryden were both trying to make an exciting play ; to both the turn of incident was everything ; both consequently had to use up the material at too prodigal a rate, and had to pad. But Corneille was a dramatist, and when he adds to Oedipus 'the happy loves of Theseus and

Dirce' we may pay him the compliment of looking for a reason.

'The severely simple nature of Sophocles' theme, with its natural elements of pity and terror, is found too meagre by the modern dramatist. He cannot trust to that alone ; he feels that he needs some further source of variety and relief.' [1] Farther on we are told that Sophocles' power of characterization is so great that he can sustain interest in a situation long after another would have abandoned it. Of these two points, the latter is obviously true and pertinent. The creative imagination of Sophocles was such that he could make an Oedipus who was much bigger than the mere events which befell him, striking though these were. Sophocles was not specially indebted to them ; they added distinction to his play, but they did not make it. What makes it is the conception of Oedipus, and it is this conception of Oedipus which enables Sophocles to augment his plot with the long scenes of Creon and Teiresias without sacrificing unity or losing interest. The man Oedipus bestrides the play like a colossus, an apparently inexhaustible source of dramatic interest. But no one would claim that Sophocles was the unique possessor of this creative power. We must look further for an explanation of the difference between the ancient and the modern drama.

In general one gathers from the literary historians the impression that the Athenians were a people with an almost supernatural taste for the simple and the austere, and that it is a certain pettiness in the moderns which makes us demand ' some further source of variety and relief'. This is partly true and partly superstition. The Athenian audience was evidently sharp in perception ; it was not necessary for the Athenian dramatist to use broad effects in order to make his points. It is a common complaint against the English theatre that it cannot present the high comedy of, say, Viennese opera, but invariably broadens it into low comedy ; the Viennese lines and points have to be thickened when they are brought forth. The Athenians had a very subtle perception of contrasts, but the contrasts are there, and we are in danger of falling into superstition when we neglect their force, when

[1] Jebb, Introd. to *Tyrannus*.

we allow ourselves to think that we puny moderns need a relief from the tension of Tragedy and its intellectual concentration which the ancients disdained. They demanded relief, as we do, but obtained it differently.

Apollo does not always keep his bow taut, nor does Sophocles, nor the modern dramatist. Tragedy will fail of its true effect unless it is set off and as it were measured by moments when the tension is removed. To do this is one of the functions of by-plot in the modern drama, and in 'by-plot' we may include the Shakespearian comic relief—which is not always so purely comic as the name suggests. Another of its functions is to assist in the mechanics of the plot, to provide a 'curtain', a necessary interval in the evolution of the dramatic events. Obviously both these requirements are met in Greek drama by the Chorus. Of the minor one nothing more need be said, but the major one is of capital importance. Sophocles' tendency was to make his Chorus more and more relevant to the action ; how then could it be relief comparable to the 'happy loves of Theseus and Dirce'? It is because a choral ode, though it still bears on the issue of the tragedy, appeals to different parts of our minds. We are taken into a different dimension as the music rises and we follow the patterned movements of the dance. It is lyrical relief instead of comic relief, but comic relief is often only a different kind of tension. The Gravediggers are not farce. The classical French stage, being more purely two-dimensional than the Elizabethan, could call on neither lyrical nor comic relief. Theseus and Dirce were the French equivalent.

We are not attempting to deny that the one form of drama is finer than the other, but we must be careful not to magnify the difference and then to supernaturalize the Athenians in order to account for it—for if they admired Greek Tragedy as it is sometimes presented on the English stage, without music, dance, space, colour or Greek, they would indeed be supernatural. It has been the purpose of the last few pages to show that Sophocles paid particular attention to relief and variety, not merely by the use of the Chorus, but also by the continuous changing of pace, dramatic emotion, situation, and point of view. For comic relief we have

an Attic equivalent in such sharply-drawn minor characters as
the Watchman and the Corinthian, with their suggestion of
vulgar speech and vulgar preoccupations.[1]   We have too the
contrast between the closely packed thought and implication
of the dialogue and the epic swiftness and brilliance of a
messenger-speech.   We have the most carefully calculated
contrast between slowness of thought or stillness in action—as
when Creon and Haemon discuss, to the point of tedium,
duty to a parent, and Clytemnestra or Iocasta suspend movement by praying to a statue—and the extreme of swiftness.
Plainly the severity and the simplicity of the Sophoclean
drama can be exaggerated, and the modern dramatist, with
his by-plot and side-scenes, is in part at least trying to secure
for his drama the variety and contrast in which the other
was so rich.   As the Greek audience was more civilized, or at
least more percipient, the Greek dramatist could produce
his effects within a narrower range, with a corresponding gain
in artistic unity.

There is, moreover, another interesting difference.

The device of by-plot means that the general pattern tends
to be an alternation between main plot and by-plot, high and
then flat, a scene of Oedipus and then a scene of happy love.
In Greek drama this would never have been possible because
of the Chorus.   It is present as an actor in the one plot ;
it can hardly be with any probability an actor in two.   Unless
therefore it is to be reduced to the status of an obtrusive
spectator, the plot will remain one.   The ' flat ' will not alternate with the ' high ', but will be interwoven with it.   If
Shakespeare wishes to relieve and to measure his tragedy
by setting it against the stature and the attitude of the
ordinary man, he does it most naturally by taking us into the
street.   Sophocles cannot do this.   He must thrust his
ordinary man, his Watchman or his Corinthian, into the
middle of the action, working, as it were, not longitudinally

[1] Cf. the three strata of diction in *Antig.*, 385–7 : ' But where's
Creon ? ' is offhand.   The Chorus' reply, ' Here he comes, in answer to your need ' is stately and remote : Creon's verse is stately
but not remote.   See also *Tyrannus*, 924–6, where, with apparent
carelessness, three consecutive verses are made to rhyme.

but vertically—again, with a great gain in tenseness and in unity. His drama is not a series of contrasting movements, like the old Suite, but, thanks to the continuous Chorus, a continuous web of contrasting dramatic rhythms, like the older polyphony. He made of his plays one sustained, unbroken flight, like the flight of a sonnet, but a sonnet of 1,400 verses. In this long flight there is every variety of rhythm, every kind of variety, but the rhythm is never for a moment interrupted ; and to it every element of his complex stage contributed its calculated effect.

CHAPTER VIII

THE EURIPIDEAN TRAGEDY

1. INTRODUCTION The course of literary analysis does not run smooth. From the point we have now reached there are two distinct developments, one of which we may regard as natural, the other as the creation of an individual genius. (i) The natural development is that from plays like the *Tyrannus* and *Electra*, plays in which tragedy 'fulfilled its natural form', drama should turn to something a shade less strenuous ; that it should renounce the task of using at once every element of drama in the expression of a tragic idea, and should develop certain of the possibilities of drama for their own sake—an interest to which Aeschylus had already pointed the way. Poetry, creative imagination, belongs to youth and early prime ; to maturity, analysis and intellectual imagination ; while if the artist returns to poetry in his old age it is often—as in the *Coloneus*, the late Rembrandt, the late Beethoven, the late Shakespeare—in an almost apocalyptic manner that quite transcends the hardly-won perfection of an earlier period. It seems natural that Sophocles' tragic period —we may think of what followed Shakespeare's tragic period— should be followed by plays like the *Trachiniae* [1] and the *Philoctetes*, and that in the development of the art as a whole the intensity of tragedy should be followed by the more purely intellectual pleasures of character-study, tragi-comedy, melodrama, and the use of drama for what we may not unfairly call propaganda.

Our term New Tragedy is meant to indicate this later stage of Greek drama, a stage represented by plays like the *Philoctetes, Ion, Helen, I.T.* ; plays which, if they are serious, no longer embody a specifically tragic idea ; if not serious, exploit one or more of the elements of complete tragedy—plot, or

---

[1] I am unable to believe that the *Trachiniae* is an early play. The metrical arguments used to prove an early date prove nothing of the sort. See my article in *A.J.P.* 1939, pp. 178 ff.

' intellect' (*dianoia*), or scenic effect or pathos—for its own
sake. The justification for using a term like New Tragedy is
that it does represent something independent of any one poet's
development, a stage in which both Euripides and Sophocles
participated (and apparently Agathon too, whose *Antheus*
seems to have been a romantic drama) after working through
a tragic period. Further, this is a stage of drama which demanded a different technique. It implies prologues, epilogues, decorative lyrics, and half a dozen other new features ;
and it cannot be criticized by the canons which Aristotle
derived from a different stage of Tragedy without some injustice to Aristotle, a great deal to the poet, and embarrassment
to the critic.

(ii) But before we can deal with this stage of Tragedy we
must consider that development which took its origin not in a
general change coming over the art, but in the individual
outlook of Euripides. He, like Sophocles, had his great tragic
period ; it survives to us in the *Medea, Hippolytus, Heracleidae, Heracles, Andromache, Hecuba, Suppliant Women* and
Troades. These plays are all tragic, all but the *Hippolytus*
badly constructed, by Aristotelian standards ; they have certain features in common, such as the prologue and ' episodic '
plots, and in some respects, notably characterization and construction, they are as unlike the rest of Euripides' work as the
Tyrannus itself. Yet the *I.T.*, even to Aristotle, was a model
of construction, and the *Ion, Electra, Orestes, Helen* are at the
lowest estimate well-made. Why is it that in the tragic group
there is hardly a single play which has not provoked the most
serious complaints and the most desperate apologies ?

The thesis of the following pages will be that as we were
able to trace the characteristic features of the Aeschylean and
Sophoclean tragedy to the nature of the tragic idea that possessed these poets, so all the new features in these plays can
be seen to be the logical result of Euripides' tragic idea. We
shall see him moving from a drama which he made as much
like Middle Tragedy as possible to one which, however un-
Aristotelian, was at least the powerful expression of what he
wanted to say.

Our first task, once more, must be to try to catch that tragic

idea, that tragic way of thinking about life which made these
plays what they are ; for we will not suppose, if we can help
it, that a poet of Euripides' calibre made plots like those of
the *Troades* and *Heracles* by mere inadvertence, or committed
the structural sins which Aristotle censured in the *Medea* from
simple inability to do better.   In fact we shall find, time after
time, that Euripides does very much less than he might have
done if Aristotelian perfection of form had been his aim, and
intellectual loyalty to his idea of no importance to him.   In
the dramatic methods which we see developing from the
Medea onwards there is a purposefulness, or at any rate a
positiveness, which is not to be explained by a mere absence
of something, a mere lack of harmony between the poet and
his form.

We have, to mislead us, important aspects of Euripides'
thought—his scepticism, his impatience with traditional religion (as if Pindar and Aeschylus had not been impatient and
sceptical), the misogyny which ancient critics regretted in
him, the feminism of which some moderns accuse him, his
liberalism, his pacifism.   These things are important.   Politics and religion are more significant in drama than in painting, for instance, because the raw material of drama is drawn
from the sphere of social and moral ideas ; but if we want to
understand the art either of a dramatist or of a painter we
have to go deeper.   Sophocles' religious tenets and political
beliefs do little to explain his drama, and these doctrines of
Euripides' do not help us in the least ; for they colour all his
work, while we are faced with this cleavage between the
tragedies and the other plays.   The *I.T.* and *Electra* contain
more religious scepticism, more realism, more satirical handling of traditional legend than the *Hecuba* or *Troades,* yet
they are in the conventional sense infinitely better constructed
and contain much more normal characterization.   There is
some force in the common statement that there was a deep
disharmony between his thought and the traditional form of
state tragedy, though Euripides did not handle this traditional form, whatever it was, much more freely than Aeschylus
had done ; yet the *Suppliant Women,* an ' encomium of
Athens ' as it is called by criticis ancient and modern, shows

little sign that the dramatist for once felt comfortable in hi
civic bed.

Is there one general explanation of Euripides' strang
methods, or must we either resort to a kind of Secret Servic
like Verrall's or take undignified refuge in phrases like 'un
evenness', 'lack of unity', and 'carelessness'?

Let us state the problem more fully. The *Medea* is twic
censured by Aristotle : the Aegeus scene is illogical and is no
even used properly, and the end is artificial and therefor
wrong. Moreover, by implication he condemns the murder o
the children as 'revolting' (*miaron*), and the catastrophe, th
escape of Medea and the death of the innocent, is hardly wha
he approved. Both the *Hecuba* and the *Andromache* have
sharply marked duplicity of action ; the *Heracles* contain
three actions (though with a more obvious connexion) and
character, Lycus, who seems to belong more to melodram
than to tragedy ; the *Suppliant Women* offers one scene
Evadne-Iphis, about which a recent editor conjectures that i
was put in to interest those spectators who were bored with
the rest of the play ; while the *Troades* is one episode afte
another, held together, we are told, by the passive figure o
Hecuba—as if Euripides needed Aristotle to tell him that wha
befalls one person is not necessarily a unity.

In the later [1] series of plays none of these major faults are
to be found. Euripides satirizes Apollo, he argues, he ridicules or condemns heroes of legend, he uses the realism and
the modern music that Aristophanes disliked, he expresses
'advanced' views in religion, philosophy, and sociology, he
commits all sorts of anachronisms, he does a dozen other
things to which this critic or that may object, but at least he
never commits again any of those elementary blunders in construction.[2] When we add that all of the plays in the first
series are tragic and none of the second, or, if the *Electra* and
the *Orestes* are to be called tragic, they are tragic in an entirely different spirit—then we are justified in asking if these

---

[1] It is convenient so to describe them, though the two series overlap.

[2] The prologue to the *Ion* is a special case. See below, p. 299.

peculiar features in the first series are not intimately connected with the nature of the tragic idea expressed in them.[1]

2. THE MEDEA There is no need to make phrases about the terrific power of the *Medea*. In important respects it diverges from what we think normal construction, at least normal construction as understood by Aristotle, and yet it is one of the greatest of Greek tragedies.—So one writes, almost automatically, but most of the implications of that ' and yet ' are wrong ; for had Euripides managed to put the stuff of the play into a beautiful Sophoclean mould, making a ' better ' play of it, it would not have been a better play but a ridiculous one. The *Medea* diverges from the Sophoclean pattern because Euripides' way of thinking was different.

Aristotle expressly cites the appearance of Aegus and the sending of the magic chariot as being ' irrational ', not the necessary or probable result of what has gone before ; but, lest we be tempted to think that these are only casual licences taken by the poet which can, with luck, be explained away, we ought to observe how fundamental is the divergence between the poet and the philosopher here. How, for example, does Medea fit Aristotle's definition of a tragic hero ? Not at all. Aristotle's tragic hero is ' like ' us, for we should not feel pity and fear for one unlike us. He must not be a saint, or his downfall would be revolting, nor a villain, whose downfall might be edifying but would not be tragic. He must therefore be intermediate, better rather than worse, and find his ruin through some hamartia. Medea is not like this ; it would indeed be difficult to find a Euripidean hero who is, until we come to Pentheus. Medea is no character compounded of good and bad, in whom what is bad tragically brings down in ruin what is good, and we certainly cannot fear for her as for one of ourselves. In fact, treated as a genuinely tragic heroine she will not work ; she causes at least one of her admirers to fall into a grave inconsistency. Professor Bates says

[1] From the discussion that follows I have omitted all but the briefest reference to the *Heracleidae*. In the present state of the text it is a play to be argued to, not from, and to do this would contribute nothing to my theme.

(*Euripides*, p. 37), ' In the character of Medea . . . the tragic genius of Euripides reaches its highest pinnacle. In none of the other plays is there a character which can approach Medea as a tragic figure.' This is a possible view, but it is inconsistent with the judgement (p. 44), that all our sympathy is concentrated on the unfortunate children, ' for we have little sympathy with the cruel, savage Medea'. Then she is not tragic after all, only melodramatic? The poor children, the wicked mother, the heartless father—surely this will not do?

A comparison with Macbeth is interesting. He is the romantic extreme of the Sophoclean-Aristotelian hero. He is presented at first in a favourable light : ' For brave Macbeth—well he deserves the name.' ' O valiant cousin ! worthy gentleman ! ' He is better rather than worse ; but he has the hamartia of ambition, and circumstances, as is their way with tragic heroes, play upon it—first through his very virtues:

DUNCAN.   No more that thane of Cawdor shall deceive
                    Our bosom interest. Go pronounce his present
                        death,
                    And with his former title greet Macbeth.
ROSS.   I'll see it done.
DUNCAN.   What he hath lost, noble Macbeth hath won.

It may be hazardous to claim Glamis Castle for a stronghold of Aristotelianism, but this ironic touch is very like Sophocles, and certainly it is an essential part of the tragedy of Macbeth that he has been noble, loyal, and gallant.

Medea on the other hand is certainly not all villainy ; she loves her children, loved Jason (if that is a merit), and was popular in Corinth ; but it is the essential part of this tragedy that she was never really different from what we see her to be. Euripides could easily have represented her as a good but passionate woman who plunges into horrors only when stung by deadly insult and injury. There was no need for him to rake up her past as he does—except that this is his whole point. She never was different ; she has no contact with Aristotle.[1]

Neither has Jason. In him it is impossible to find anything

---

[1] Neither had Agamemnon. Both he and Medea are tragic figures rather than tragic characters.

that is not mean ; not because Euripides is satirizing anyone
through him, though he does use his Jason to mock the complacency of his countrymen, but for the same reason, whatever it is, that makes his Medea so extreme a character. We
may notice here how little the other characters count—naturally, when the chief characters are drawn in such simple
colours. The Nurse is this, the Paedagogus that, and Aegeus
the other thing, but were they different nobody would be
much the wiser. This is not characterization as Sophocles
understood it ; we have nearly returned to Eteocles' Spy.
Sophocles drew his minor characters vividly because he
needed them, not because he was good at it ; Euripides refrains because he does need it.

From characterization we may pass to the general tone of
the play. Aristotle, in a dry little analysis, examines the ways
in which *to phthartikon*, the deed of violence, can be brought
about : the worst but one is for kinsman to slay kinsman
knowing who it is that he is slaying. This is ' revolting ',
and the *Medea* is full of it. The unrelieved baseness of Jason
is revolting ; revolting in the highest degree is Medea's great
crime ; and what of the Messenger-speech ? The horrible
death of Glauce and Creon is described exhaustively in the
terrible style of which Euripides was such a master. It is
sheer Grand Guignol. We have yet seen nothing like it in
Greek Tragedy. We have had before scenes, described or
suggested, of horror—the self-blinding of Oedipus, the murder
of Clytemnestra—but always the horror has been enveloped in
the greater emotion of tragic pity. It has brought with it its
own catharsis. Where is the tragic pity here ? In the destruction of an innocent girl and her father there is no possibility of tragic relief. We pity them, as later we pity the
children, but as they have done nothing which in reason
should have involved them in this suffering, as no flaw of
character, no tragic miscalculation, no iron law of life has
brought them to this pass, but simply the rage of Medea, our
pity has no outlet ; we are impotent and angry—or would be,
if this assault on our nerves left room for such feelings. From
these things we can turn to no grim but majestic universal
principle, only back again to that terrifying murderess.

Supposing that Sophocles had given us a comparable description of Antigone's death agonies? It is unthinkable; but is this only to say that Sophocles was Attic, Euripides already Hellenistic? And supposing that Aristotle had had his way, and that Medea, having committed these crimes, had made her way under her own steam to Athens? Or if the dramatic law of the necessary or probable had asserted itself, and Medea had been stoned by an outraged populace? The play would have been no tragedy at all, but the emptiest of melodrama; after this terrific preparation the story would suddenly have relapsed into insignificance, a mere exciting tale about Medea of Corinth. In the matter of the ending Euripides is un-Aristotelian by inspiration, not by mischance, as we shall see in a moment; but before considering this fully we may complete our survey by noting how his use of the chorus and his dramatic style differ from Sophocles'.

The Chorus, Aristotle lays down, should participate in the action, as in Sophocles, not in Euripides. The chorus in the *Medea* finds itself in a famous difficulty at the murder of the children; it ought to participate in the action and may not. Fifteen women of Corinth stand by doing nothing while Medea murders her children indoors—or rather they stand by deliberating whether to do anything or not. In meeting this improbability nothing is gained by saying that the Chorus was a body of Ideal Spectators and that a Greek audience would not expect them to interfere. They have in fact always taken part in the action when circumstances suggested it—in the *Eumenides,* the *Ajax,* the *Antigone,* later in the *Philoctetes,* to mention only a few cases—and Aristotle feels that so it is best. Moreover, Euripides himself feels that they should naturally interfere now, for if no thought of the possible intervention of Ideal Spectators could have arisen in the mind of the audience, why does he go out of his way to suggest that thought?

The question of Euripides' use of the Chorus will recur several times; he did, in the later tragedies, make it a body of Ideal Spectators. Here it is the solid, flesh-and-blood chorus of Middle Tragedy, women of Corinth who come to inquire about Medea and not to sing philosophy; and such a chorus, natural enough when the theme of the play is one which involves the city, as in the *Antigone* and *Tyrannus*, becomes more difficult to manage when the theme is private and psychological, as in Sophocles' *Electra*, and becomes a nuisance when private intrigue has to be represented on the stage. In this respect the *Medea* is half-way between two conventions, and a certain uneasiness is inevitable.

This chorus is a little surprising too in the ode that it sings at one of the most poignant moments of the play, when Medea has finally resolved that her children must die, and just before we hear the horrible story of Glauce's death. If we have in mind the tremendous effects that Sophocles produced with his chorus at moments like these, it is a little chilling to find Euripides going off into his study, as it were, and writing, in anapaests too, on the advantages of being childless.

Such indifference in the orchestra to what was happening on the stage later became a powerful weapon in Euripides' armoury ; here it is a little puzzling. The subject is germane to the context, but the treatment is not ; such generalized reflection breaks the emotional rhythm of the play. When such desperate deeds are afoot, why does Euripides insert this pleasant little essay ? It may be tentatively suggested that it is Euripides' method of preparing for the messenger's narrative, that he deliberately lulls our minds with this inconspicuous piece of pavement-philosophy in order to give the messenger's onslaught a fairer field. But whether this or something else be the true explanation of the passage, we can draw one deduction from it, and that is that Euripides' attitude to his tragic heroine is quite different from Sophocles'. To Antigone or Oedipus it would have been an unthinkable dramatic impoliteness to break off like this to say something interesting ; not because Sophocles was a better poet and dramatist in this respect, but because he was writing a different tragedy. For all the sympathy and the tragic power with which Euripides draws his characters, and although he is ' the most tragic of the poets ', it seems clear that fundamentally he is detached from them. He can, as Sophocles cannot, retire for a moment and invite us to think of something else.[1]

[1] This same detachment is displayed in Euripides' characterization and in his proneness to argument : the little essay on music

Wherever we look therefore in the *Medea* we find that Euripides differs from Aristotle's theory and Sophocles' practice, and that not merely on the surface but radically ; and the more he works his tragic vein the greater does this divergence grow, until in the *Troades* we have a play in which no single incident is the ' necessary or probable ' result of the preceding one, the characterization is slight and inconsistent, the chorus, far from being a co-actor, takes no notice at all of the action —and yet the *Troades* is magnificent tragedy. The method then must be a logical one, and the logic we must now try to find, so far as it is to be seen in the *Medea*.

Medea is a tragic figure, but we have seen that she is no Aristotelian tragic heroine. She is indeed possessed of a passionate nature, quite uncontrolled in love and hate ; this makes her dramatic, but it is not hamartia : it is the whole woman. That certain virtues may plausibly be attributed to her is dramatically of little moment. As she betrayed her father and murdered her brother in her first love for Jason, as in Iolcus to serve Jason she contrived a horrible end for Pelias (exploits which are mentioned by Euripides and are therefore evidence), so in Corinth, when betrayed and insulted by Jason, she thinks first of revenge, not the comparatively honest revenge of killing Jason, but one that shall bring down in ruin Jason, his new bride, his children, his whole house. That they are her children too is unfortunate, but not enough to deter her from her plan ; she has her struggle with her maternal feelings—a theatrical struggle rather than a psychologically convincing one—but the decisive thought is that to be laughed at by enemies is not to be borne. She is tragic in that her passions are stronger than her reason (1079) ; she is drawn with such vigour and directness, everything that she says and does springs so immediately from her dominant motive that she is eminently dramatic ; nevertheless she is no tragic heroine as we have hitherto understood the term ; she is too extreme, too simple. This is not character-study as the picture of Neoptolemus in the *Philoctetes* is, for in every possible way the characterization is concentrated in the one over-

---

(*Medea*, 190 ff.) is typical. Euripides is not absorbed in his Medea and does not pretend to be.

mastering passion, and the situation is manipulated to stimulate this to the uttermost. It is not melodrama, for Medea, though extreme, is true, and her character and deeds leave us with something more than the mere excitement of a strong story. It is tragic, but we must be careful to see what we mean by tragic.

The tragedy of the Sophoclean hero is that such strength is nullified by such weakness ; of Medea, that such a character should exist at all. She is bound to be a torment to herself and to others ; that is why Euripides shows her blazing her way through life leaving wreckage behind her ; that is why the suffering of others, of Glauce and of Creon, are not to be glozed over. That she suffers herself is a great and no doubt a necessary part of the drama, but it is not the point of the tragedy, which is that passion can be stronger than reason, and so can be a most destructive agent. Destructive to whom ? Here, to the children, Glauce, Creon, Jason, and to Medea's peace—but not to her life ; in short, destructive to society at large.

It follows that Euripides had either to describe Glauce's death horribly or to enfeeble his theme ; the sufferings of Medea's victims are as much part of the tragedy as those of Medea herself, possibly a greater part. Hence the contrast with Sophocles. The logical climax of the Sophoclean tragedy is that the hero is ruined ; others may be involved, as are Haemon and Eurydice in the *Antigone,* but only as they intensify the hero's downfall or are subordinate to it. Even if Greek taste had allowed a detailed picture of Antigone's death agonies, Greek logic would have forbidden it—and Greek taste and Greek logic were the same thing. Antigone's loyalty to her duty leads to her own death ; Creon's shortsightedness and obstinacy leads through her death to his own ruin. Horror would have spoiled the first theme and misdirected the second ; we are to watch his error recoiling upon him, not to be made feel that he is a monster of cruelty. There is no contrast here between Attic and Hellenistic ; both poets are Hellenic, doing exactly what the theme demands.

The catharsis of Glauce's horror comes when we feel that she, and all the others, are the victims of an almost external

force. ' Love,' the chorus sings, ' when it comes in too great
strength, has never brought good renown or virtue to mortals.'
Medea is drawn stark as the strongest possible impersonation
of this force ; balance of character is necessarily denied her,
and this means that we cannot lose ourselves in sympathy
with her as we do with Oedipus. Euripides is not asking us
to sympathize with her in this way, but to understand her, to
understand that such things are, that Medeas, and Jasons,
exist, poetically if not actually. He asks us to feel terror
when we hear of what her passion leads her to do, pity for all
who are broken, tragic enlightenment when we see that all
are the victims of a primitive force. So we do feel pity ' for
the savage and cruel Medea ', but only when we regard her in
the same objective way as Euripides.

It is perhaps possible to bring all this into relation with
Aristotle's theory of hamartia, and it is worth while to make
the attempt for the sake of generalizing the Euripidean
method. Euripides, like most Greeks, is a rationalist in that
he believes reason, not belief or formula or magic, to be the
guide to life ; but he sees too that we have in us, besides
reason, non-rational emotions which are necessary but may
run wild,[1] thwarting our reason and bringing calamity. In
the last analysis Euripides' tragic hero is mankind. Some
natural passion breaks its bounds, and the penalty has to be
paid, either by the sinner or by those around him or by both.
Within this dramatic cosmos the hamartia is concentrated in
one or two people ; they, Medea and Jason, are hamartia and
not necessarily anything else at all ; that is why they are so
extreme and so unrelieved. The results of the hamartia fall
on the group ; perhaps on the sinners, perhaps not ; for
though Medea suffers here, Menelaus and Orestes in the
Andromache get off scot-free.

The great difference between Euripides' and Sophocles'
approach to tragedy is that Sophocles concentrates into one
hero what Euripides splits up, prismatically, among a group.
In Sophocles it is the hero himself who prefigures Man ; he is
strong and weak ; he, and no one else (except incidentally),

[1] This point has been well treated by E. R. Dodds, *Euripides the
Irrationalist, C.R.,* 1929, pp. 97 ff.

pays for his weakness. It is from this concentration of the tragic idea into the one hero that the Sophoclean drama get its Aristotelian virtues ; it is because Euripides analyses his tragedy into the tragedy of society instead of synthesizing it in the tragedy of a representative hero, ' like us ', that he does not need these virtues, and will use them less and less.

This approach to tragedy, which becomes clear later, is in the *Medea* only partly worked out. It may seem absurd to say that Medea, with her tremendous driving-force and sharply accentuated character, is essentially or theoretically a heroine of the same kind as Hecuba, a purely passive figure. It is not absurd. Hecuba and those around her are regarded as the helpless victims of villainy or cruelty, Medea and those around her as the victims of Medea's disastrous temperament. Unless we feel Medea in this way, a tragic victim rather than a tragic agent, we shall try to sympathize with her in the wrong way, and waste valuable time working up emotions about the poor children.

But even if this analysis is correct, is it necessary to our appreciation of the play ? Not in the least, the play makes its effect directly, without the help of theory. But the analysis is necessary if we are going to criticize the play. Let us begin with the Aegeus scene, which so glaringly offends against the reasonable Aristotelian law of necessary or probable sequence. How far is this law valid ?

In the Sophoclean tragedy of character its validity is absolute. The formula there is that a hero of a certain kind is placed in circumstances such that the play between character and circumstances is bound to result in disaster for the hero. Evidently the whole point of such drama depends on this, that the character shall be a convincing one and that the circumstances, though they may be exceptional, shall develop normally, and always in significant relation with the character of the hero. It would be stultification if the dramatist had to produce a railway-accident without which the hero's doom would not be achieved. But Aegeus comes out of the blue, like a railway-accident. If the *Medea* were really a tragedy of character, if, that is, we were being invited to see how she, a woman of a certain character, was placed in a situation in which her character was inevitably her ruin, and if an Aegeus had to be introduced after all in order to bring this to pass, then the play would be meaningless, as meaningless as if Eteocles had gone to the seventh gate because the champion already chosen had broken his leg on the way. But Euripides is not doing this at all. He is presenting to us his tragic conception that the passions and unreason to which humanity is subject are its greatest scourge. This implies no tragic interlock between character and situation ; the situation is nothing but the setting for the outburst of unreason, the channel along which it rushes. What matters now is not that the situation must be convincing and illuminating, not even that the heroine must be convincing as a person ; but that her passion must be, in however extreme a form, a fundamental and familiar one. If Medea is in this sense true, we shall not stay to object that she is not likely.

The situation then being only a setting, Euripides is philosophically justified in manipulating it in order to present his tragic thesis in its strongest colours. Sophocles cannot say, ' For the sake of working out my tragic clash between character and circumstances we will here assume that a quite unexpected and unrelated thing materially alters the situation, or that my hero will here do something out of character.' But Euripides can say, without destroying his whole point, ' Excuse me ; here is a partial impediment in Medea's course. Let me remove it ; you will then have far finer view of what I mean.' Medea was in any case certain to work some ruin ; Aegeus only allows her, and Euripides, to go to the logical extreme.

This, incidentally, is the reason also why Jason can be so unrelieved a villain and yet not undramatic. If he stood to Medea as Creon does to Antigone, one whose character fatally interlocks with hers, he would be impossible ; being so extreme, he would as it were prove nothing. If the dramatist simplifies his characters far enough, he can demonstrate anything. As it is, Jason is not intended to prove anything. He is a ready-made villain, easily assumed as part of the setting, and if, regarded as a dramatic character, he is a ' possible improbability ' that matters nothing.

In fact, Aristotle's law is concerned really with two separate things, philosophical cogency and artistic effect. The former is not affected in the least by the ' irrationality ' of Aegeus ; the latter undoubtedly is. In the later tragedies the artistic unity of the plot is not so obviously impaired by such intrusions (as of Evadne and Iphis in the *Suppliant Women*) because plot there has become frankly diagrammatic instead of organic. Here the plot is made to depend on Medea's will, in the manner of Middle Tragedy, and has that kind of unity and organic growth that comes from this, so that Aegeus, who is quite independent of that will and of the crisis of Medea in Corinth, is felt to be a blemish. Nevertheless, as this is not strictly a play of character, Euripides is logically justified in not making his plot depend on his characters. He may, logically, manipulate the plot himself, or, if you like, arbitrarily interfere, in order that his creations may work out his tragic idea to the end. Our analysis may have seemed farfetched, but it was correct. The difficulty with Aegeus is that Medea is so nearly an Oedipus and the play so nearly Middle Tragedy that we may reasonably take offence. We are in the middle of a transition from one kind of tragedy to another.

As to the end of the play Aristotle's words are :

' In the characters as in the composition of the plot one must always aim at an inevitable or a probable order of events, so that it will be either inevitable or probable that such a person should say or do such a thing, and inevitable or probable that this thing should happen after that. It is obvious therefore that the ending too of the plot must arise naturally out of the plot itself, and not, as in the *Medea,* by external contrivance.'

This is not an objection to the *Deus ex machina* as such, only to such employments of it as we have here. The *Philoctetes* ends with a Deus, but the appearance of Heracles there is to some extent [1] a natural result of the action of the play ; it has at least been prepared for by the importance in the play of his magic bows and arrows. In the *Medea*, there has been nothing of this magic background ; on the contrary, the background has been at times painfully prosaic. We have

[1] This is of course not the whole explanation. See p. 320.

had a scene of bitter domestic strife in a setting of ordinary social life—children, nurses, curious neighbours, old men gossiping around the spring. Medea may be the granddaughter of Helios, but for all that we are dealing with ordinary life and never feel that the gods are within call. Medea quite rationally, and to the detriment of the play, provides herself with a refuge ; why then is an unnatural means of escape provided for her at the end ?

It is of course some answer to say that Medea is a barbarian princess and a magician ; she is descended from Helios, and she is in possession of certain mysterious powers, or more strictly poisons, which ordinary women know nothing about. We are the less surprised therefore at her miraculous escape ; less than if a magic chariot should come for the Second Mrs. Tanqueray. This may be true, but at the most it is only a palliation ; it made Euripides' error possible.

But if we look carefully into the last scene we shall see more than dramatic convenience in the chariot. Medea has done things which appal even the chorus, those sympathetic neighbours who had said, earlier in the play, ' Now is honour coming to womankind.' Their prayer now is ' O Earth, O thou blazing light of the Sun, look upon this accursed woman before she slays her own children. . . . O god-given light, stay her hand, frustrate her . . .' (1251 ff.). In the same vein Jason says, when he has learnt the worst, ' After doing this, of all things most unholy, dost thou show thy face to the Sun and the Earth ? ' (1327). Sun and Earth, the most elemental things in the universe, have been outraged by these terrible crimes ; what will they do ? how will they avenge their sullied purity ? What Earth will do we shall not be told, but we are told what the Sun does : he sends a chariot to rescue the murderess.

Is this illogical ? Could anything be finer, more imaginative ? We shall soon see, in the *Hippolytus*, that although reason must be our guide, the primitive things in the universe —Aphrodite and Artemis there—are not reasonable. The servant of Hippolytus (v. 120) thinks what Jason and the chorus think, that ' Gods should be wiser than men '. Perhaps so, but these gods are not. They exist ; as well deny

the weather as deny Aphrodite ; but they are not reasonable
and can make short work of us. Zeus, 'whoever he is', is
another matter. There may be a Νοῦς, a Mind, in the universe ; but there are other powers too, and these we may
worship in vain. The magic chariot is a frightening glimpse
of something that we shall see in full force in the *Bacchae,*
the existence in the universe of forces that we can neither
understand nor control—only participate in.

The end of the *Medea* does not come out of the logic of
the action by the law of necessity and probability, but is contrived by Euripides, deliberately, as the final revelation of his
thought. When we begin to see Medea not merely as the
betrayed and vindictive wife but as the impersonation of one
of the blind and irrational forces in human nature, we begin
to find that catharsis for which we looked in vain in the messenger-speech. It is this transformation that finally explains
the 'revolting' and deepens a dramatic story into tragedy.
Had Euripides been content with a 'logical' ending, with
the play remaining on the mundane, Corinthian level, the
'revolting' would indeed have needed justification. This
makes demands on our tolerance which cannot be met if the
only profit is the news that barbarian magicians who are passionate and are villainously treated do villainous things.
There is in the *Medea* more than this, and to express that
Euripides resorts to a manipulation of the plot, an artificial
ending which, like Aegeus, would have been ruinous to Sophocles. This imaginative and necessary climax is not the logical ending to the story of Medea the ill-used wife of Corinth,
but it is the climax to Euripides' underlying tragic conception.

This is a conception which does indeed call for and receive
purely dramatic imagery ; we need not be silly and call the
Medea an illustration of a theme. Nevertheless the conception is not so immediately and completely transfused into
drama as is Sophocles' tragic conception ; Medea is not quite
to Euripides what Oedipus is to Sophocles, completely and
utterly the focus and vehicle of his tragic thinking. Euripides
remains a little detached. We can go beneath his Medea—
for criticism we must, in appreciation we do unconsciously
—to the greater conception underlying her ; and in the last

resort it is this, not the imagined character of Medea in these imagined circumstances, that moulds the play.

As Euripides develops his method, in particular as the war forced his thoughts more on the social aspects of tragedy, we shall find this gap between the stage-drama and the tragic conception, non-existent in Sophocles but perceptible in the *Medea*, growing much wider.   Already the strict logic of plot, the Aristotelian doctrines of the tragic hero, the Sophoclean tradition of characterization and the use of the chorus are receding, and they will recede much farther.   Unity of interest, that is of tragic conception, remains ; but how far that conception is to be presented through one hero and one action, how far through a diversity of heroes and a multiplicity of actions, is a matter to be decided privately between Euripides the tragic poet and Euripides the playwright.

3. THE HIPPOLYTUS   This play was produced three years after the *Medea*, and in several respects it differs widely from it.   Its structure is much more regular, for we have no Aegeus scene or magic chariot to explain away, and the characterization is more normal.   In Phaedra we have a rounded character who is by a long way the most complete and the most tragic character in any of this series of plays, and though the Nurse has parallels in Euripides' later plays, in the tragedies she stands alone.   While Phaedra is on the stage the drama is quite Sophoclean.   Her desperate struggle between her passion and her virtue, her tragic realization whence her passion comes (vv. 337–43), the complete contrast between her and the revolting but very natural old Nurse, the Nurse's well meant and cunning desire to help, the tragic but inevitable outcome of this, and Phaedra's resolve to save her honour by leaving the lying letter to Theseus, make an absorbing drama which Sophocles could never have written but which, as a dramatist, he must have admired.

But at this point a number of questions begin to arise. Why is Hippolytus so chilly a figure ?   As a recoil from Phaedra he was very dramatic, and the romantic atmosphere he brought with him from the hunt was very picturesque, but as the chief actor in the second part of the play is he not rather a disappointing character? Is he not too negative, protesting his pre-eminent purity a little too much? And why is Phaedra forgotten? The dramatic motif of the opposition between his nature and Phaedra's disappears. There is no suggestion that her personality, so prominent in the first part, remains active in the second; no suggestion that her death works at all in his mind; no pity or remorse or hatred is seen in him. In fact, Phaedra's letter seems to be no more than a mechanical link between her tragedy and his. Having in Phaedra so tragic a subject, why did not Euripides base his whole play on it? As it is, not only does the *Hippolytus* lack real unity, but its rhythm goes the wrong way, from the very dramatic Phaedra to the less dramatic Hippolytus; and even that useful body the chorus, by saying nothing about Phaedra in the second part, does nothing to conceal the division of interest. Finally, what are the goddesses for? Is Euripides taking all this trouble only to tell the Athenians that in his opinion Aphrodite and Artemis are not worth worshipping?

It is quite evident once more that this is no tragedy of character. It was never Euripides' idea to make the tragedy out of the opposition between Hippolytus' nature and Phaedra's; if it had been the play would have been closer knit, and there would have been no room for the goddesses. We have, perhaps a little rashly, attacked the dramatic character of Hippolytus. In fact he is extremely successful as a figure in the play—but because the drama is one of tragic victims rather than of tragic actors, at least as far as Hippolytus is concerned. Again Euripides shows a certain detachment from his hero. He is not for the time being lost within him, but uses him in the interests of a further tragedy, and this time that further tragedy is made explicit. We have here a play within a play. The prologue is not a confession by Euripides that he finds the task of properly conveying a dramatic situation beyond his power; it is the dramatic embodiment of his real tragic idea. In the *Medea* we had to infer this from the treatment and in particular from the ' irrational' ending; in the *Hippolytus* the two dramatic planes of thought are made formally distinct. On the one plane Aphrodite is the tragic agent. What she is we have known

perfectly well since Aeschylus wrote the Danaid-trilogy, even
if we did not know before.   She is not a mythical being whose
existence Euripides is trying to disprove, not a cult whose
observance he is trying to discredit ; she is one of the elemental powers in nature, to Euripides as to Aeschylus.   To
both poets she and Artemis are complementary forces which
have to be reverenced.   Aphrodite says here explicitly that
she has no quarrel with Hippolytus for his devotion to Artemis,
but ' I destroy those who are haughty towards me '.   Hippolytus therefore is introduced to us not as a tragic actor but
as a tragic victim ; his part is not to have in his soul a tragic
contradiction or complexity, but a tragic singleness.   Like
Aeschylus' Suppliants, he is to be one-sided, utterly denying
Aphrodite, and like them, to pay for this one-sidedness.   To
Aeschylus the law of Zeus does not tolerate partial adherence ;
Euripides puts the same idea into psychological rather than
moral terms and will show us that there are laws of nature
that demand obedience as well as laws of morality.

Aphrodite goes on to destroy all possibility of dramatic surprise in the play by telling us exactly what is to happen ; she
will inspire with a fatal passion the virtuous Phaedra.   Phaedra will die ; that, Aphrodite calmly says, cannot be helped
and is immaterial ; and in her death she will destroy Hippolytus.   Now we know exactly where we are.   The fate of
Phaedra and Hippolytus will be seen by us always in the
tragic frame that Aphrodite has made.   It will not be in their
own hands, as is the fate of the Sophoclean hero, and it will
not arise from any complexity of their own characters, but
from their singleness.   They will be drawn as extreme characters—like Medea—for in Hippolytus at least nothing matters
but the fanaticism of his virginity.   Hence the complete
contrast between Hippolytus and the Suppliants.   The Suppliants are from first to last passionate and exciting dramatic
characters—which no one would claim for Hippolytus.   This
does not mean that there were certain things in drama that
Aeschylus could do and Euripides could not ; the reason is
that the one-sidedness of the Suppliants was only part of
Aeschylus' tragedy.   He thinks first of people of a certain
kind who between them make a tragic situation ; of incom-

patible claims which result in violence and involve others
in mischief. Wrong-doing, and a resistance that goes too far,
are of the essence of his thought; the opposition between
Artemis and Aphrodite is the expression but not the substance
of his thought. Therefore, to put it crudely, in Aeschylus it
is tragic characters who grapple, in Euripides it is tragic
specimens of humanity who come to shipwreck.

But have we not said that Phaedra is a rounded character,
not a specimen or an extreme ? She is indeed, and it is interesting to see why. Phaedra is tragic because virtuous ; a
struggle takes place within her such as Hippolytus can never
know. She is made virtuous because if she is not, the theme
will inevitably become something other than what Euripides
has in mind. His theme is, obviously, that an unbalanced
mind or temperament like Hippolytus' is unsafe ; if Aphrodite
attacks, Artemis cannot defend, only promise to destroy one of
Aphrodite's darlings in return (1420–2). By implication, too
much Aphrodite is as unsafe as too little, but unless Phaedra
too is virtuous, the parallel between her and Hippolytus will
not exist, and the point will be destroyed that Aphrodite is a
natural force, quite indifferent to human morality, one with
which we have to make terms. Moreover, if Phaedra were
a follower of Aphrodite as Hippolytus is of Artemis, she would
necessarily become a passionate and a wicked woman, a
Medea, and Hippolytus we should feel to be simply her victim,
not Aphrodite's. This, apparently, had been the theme of
the first *Hippolytus*. Phaedra there was a woman who, like
Medea, Stheneboea, and Phthia in the *Phoenix*, was prepared
to do anything to gratify her passion, a direct example of the
terrible power of human unreason ; Hippolytus was simply
her victim, as Glauce and the others were Medea's. In
such a play Phaedra's passion was inevitably the dominant
motif, and Phaedra the dominent character. In such a
situation Hippolytus' own one-sidedness would have little
scope. In making Phaedra virtuous here, therefore, Euripides was not revising his first play to placate the stupid,[1]

---

[1] At least, if he was, the fact is of biographical, not critical, interest. The remark about this in the second Argument is not a
statement of fact but a critical inference—possibly a silly one.

but taking a step which the difference in outlook demanded.

There is an interesting refinement in Euripides' treatment of Phaedra. His basic drama demands, and states, only that Phaedra is to be made a victim and tool of Aphrodite, a monument to the irresponsibility of these cosmic forces ; but when the outer drama is played through, we find Phaedra herself giving a new and tragic interpretation of her passion, for she recognizes in it a hereditary taint (337–43). This in no way conflicts with that ; it is the same fact as it appears on the different plane, a pointer to what Euripides means by his Aphrodite ; not a member of the Pantheon of whom Euripides disapproves, but a potentially disastrous element in our nature.[1]

But although Phaedra is so Sophoclean a figure, we see behind her the shadow of Aphrodite. This shows very clearly the difference between the tragedians ; there are no shadows standing behind Oedipus or Electra. Sophocles puts all his thought into these ; Euripides uses his creations to bring on to the stage a tragedy that is being played behind the scenes. We said that an inner tragedy was the real controlling element in the *Medea*, in spite of Medea's tragic will ; now that inner drama is brought into the open. Even so tragic a character as Phaedra is but a figure in it, not a heroine who in her own right claims all our attention.

It is therefore no real violation of unity when Phaedra disappears and leaves us with Hippolytus. But for the prologue we should be at a loss, for we should necessarily expect her character and personality still to count for something ; as it is, we know that the real unity lies not in her fate but in what Aphrodite is doing, and in fact the last thing that we look for is to see her passion and death prolonging itself in Hippolytus' mind. The logic of the plot and the unity of the action obviously reside in the underlying conception and not in the tragic mind of either Phaedra or Hippolytus. So it was in the *Medea*, only there we had no Aphrodite and Artemis to help us. We had indeed a unity derived from Medea's own will,

[1] It is of course because Aphrodite is this, an internal not an external tyrant, that the *Hippolytus* is tragedy. She is not a 'goddess' who torments us for her sport.

but since this was not the real centre of the tragedy, the unity it gave was incomplete.

But even with the goddesses to show us how to look at the action of the *Hippolytus,* Euripides does not seem to be entirely at his ease. He has reconciled his un-Sophoclean conception of tragedy more nearly with the Sophoclean form of drama, but if we look attentively at the second part of the play we shall perhaps see signs of strain, and these may explain why Euripides did not again use this regularity of structure until he gave up writing tragedy.

First, from the purely dramatic point of view, Phaedra's tragedy has a quality which makes Hippolytus' something of an anticlimax. We should not insist on this overmuch, for the less absorbing Hippolytus is as a tragic character, the more do we feel the unseen presence of Aphrodite. Nevertheless, however much he is a tragic victim driven before the storm, we can hardly be oblivious of the fact that he addresses Theseus as if Theseus were a public meeting,[1] and can state quite objectively that he is the most virtuous man alive. This is not untragic ; on the contrary, it is the whole point ; but it is awkward that the point must be made in this way [2]—especially after the perfect drama of the first part. We have to keep our minds on the tragedy and leave the drama a little out of focus ; to weigh the tragic fact that Hippolytus, though virtuous, is being destroyed, and to overlook the dramatic inconvenience that it is Hippolytus himself who tells us of his virtue. Above all do we have to refrain from asking why the chorus, despite its oath, allows Hippolytus to be destroyed when a hint of the truth would at least make Theseus pause awhile.

[1] Putting into Greek verse the formula ' Unaccustomed as I am to public speaking '.

[2] In suggesting here and elsewhere that there were logical reasons for Euripides' handling of the tragic form I am not suggesting that their existence automatically turns bad drama into good. Every art has formal principles which cannot be successfully defied, and sometimes no doubt Euripides went too far. But we can understand his methods without having to approve of all their results, and the critic's mere approval or disapproval is not a matter of public interest.

Secondly, the messenger-speech is not really dramatic, as Greek Tragedy understands the word. Hitherto the great messenger-speeches have noticeably quickened the pace of the drama by introducing some new factor of tragic importance: if the messenger has not had this function to perform he has been brief. We recall the Herald in the *Agamemnon*, how his announcements increase our sense of forboding; the terrible irony of the Corinthian's news in the *Tyrannus*; the swift reversal of our hopes and the unexpected blow of Haemon's death in the *Antigone*; the poignant situation in the *Electra* (with which we may compare the illumination of what Orestes is that we get from the brilliant messenger-speech in Euripides' *Electra*); the horror of the *Medea*. The two messenger-scenes in the *Septem* are interesting. In the long scene, in which the messenger has a lot to say, his part goes with the movement of the whole play, and is very dramatic; when he returns to announce the death of Eteocles and Polyneices he is reporting a single fact, which has been half-foreseen; accordingly he is brief, for long description of the manner of the event (highly impressive in the *Antigone*, where it shows the hatred with which Creon has inspired his own son) would have been irrelevant.

The death of Hippolytus is even more inevitable than that of Eteocles and Polyneices. We doubt neither the efficacy of Theseus' curse nor the power of Poseidon to destroy. All that the drama demands is this destruction, and the speech adds nothing to this simple demand. Sheer horror, effective in the *Medea*, where it illuminates Medea, is not wanted here, where it can only advertise the power of a god; a long and complicated narrative, effective in the *Electra*, where it serves half a dozen dramatic ends, would here be false. As pure narrative the speech is very good, but as drama it is something less than the best. It really marks time.

Thirdly, is there not a slightly artificial ring in the ending? Artemis is necessary and very dramatic, but the treatment of Theseus is perhaps in one respect what the play needs rather than what the tragic idea demands. Artemis balances Aphrodite, structurally and morally, and she was also the only plausible way of informing Theseus of the truth. She completes the revelation of the inner tragedy—in a rather obvious way, one would think, had it not been so often misunderstood.[1] She points out to the unhappy Theseus that he has fallen, a supplementary victim, into Aphrodite's trap, and she paints Olympus as a place of moral chaos—which can indicate only that what these deities represent, instinctive passions, is independent of reason and morality. She says, ' We gods destroy the wicked, with their children and all ', but Theseus is not ruined because he is wicked, and Hippolytus is presently borne in protesting his complete innocence. Artemis is powerless to help ; she cannot even shed a tear. She can, however, promise to destroy someone else, to annoy Aphrodite, and she can promise Hippolytus that honour of perpetual worship which he enjoys in common with several other of Euripides' broken heroes. Hippolytus has his *Aufklärung* : ' Would that mortals could bring mischief on the gods ! ' (v. 1415), and we breathe a little more freely when this sub-human goddess has taken herself off, leaving the stage to the reconciliation between father and son.

All this is fine ; but how genuine is the hamartia on which Artemis insists ? She blames Theseus bitterly for his haste in calling down the curse on Hippolytus, and this has to bear the weight of the ending. Is this fair ? It is not a mere matter of dramatic realism, whether Theseus was not in fact bound to believe the lying letter in face of Hippolytus' not very convincing defence and the general conspiracy of silence ; though certainly we ourselves should not have raised the question of Theseus' guilt if Artemis had not. Beyond this there is the question of tragic relevance. Theseus' part in the tragedy is quite clear, and is indeed described accurately by Artemis. He is one of those tragic figures who stand at the cross-roads of disaster and get overwhelmed with the rest. That is the essence of his position, and any hamartia he may show is purely instrumental. When we see him confronting and cursing Hippolytus we do not feel him as a man who is doing something foolishly or wickedly wrong, but as one who can do no other ; when we see him being railed at by Artemis

[1] As surely by M. Méridier, when he speaks of ' un rayonnement de transfiguration ', ' une sérénité céleste '.

and brokenly confessing error we are surely justified in assuming that this is being done to tighten the construction of
the last scene and to give a weightier tone to the reconciliation.   For this is an ending that needs some contrivance
The end of the tragedy is the destruction, by Aphrodite, of
Hippolytus, the tragedy demands nothing more.   But the
play within the play does not end there very easily : Theseus
has been involved, a third victim.   To end simply with the
second and third victims looking at each other and talking it
over would have been weak ; to have made Hippolytus die
' off ', the prosaically logical course, and to end with the third
victim alone, was a sacrifice of form to logic which Euripides
was not yet (or at any rate not here) prepared to make.
Hippolytus (unlike Andromache later) is brought back, and
the hamartia, which even if justifiable is not logical, is introduced in order to stiffen the scene between the two.

The *Hippolytus* is justly renowned for its tragic beauty and
power, and it is not suggested that the inconveniences just
discussed are as prominent in reading or performance as they
are in analysis.   There is, however, the question why this
play is strict in form while the later tragedies are not, and in
these few discrepancies between the logic of the tragic idea
and the demands of plot and symmetry of form we may see
the answer to the question.   A consideration of the *Troades*
and *Hecuba* will suggest that later Euripides might have been
content with presenting to us his three victims in bare juxtaposition with the minimum of logical connexion and formal
unity.   At all events, from now on, until he turned from
tragedy to melodrama and tragi-comedy, Euripides sacrifices
this external tidiness to directness of expression, being in this
truly Greek ; for surely the greatness of all Greek art lies not
in its ability to achieve beauty of form (never the first aim
of the great artist), but in its absolute sincerity to the underlying idea.   We have to wait a century or more to see the rise
of ' classicism '.

4. THE TROADES   When the plays of Euripides are considered
one by one, without distinction of kind or purpose, it is impossible not to be baffled by the vagaries of form and style in

the tragedies which we now approach. Plot becomes chaotic, characterization uncertain, the use of the chorus unsteady, and undramatic speech-making endemic. When we find Euripides flouting our conception of dramatic form and yet being 'the most tragic of the poets', we tend to take refuge in general ideas about the clash, the *Spannung*, between Euripides' intellectualism and the religious background of his art, or we cleverly discover an *ad hoc* explanation of each problem. But as soon as we do distinguish kind and purpose the problem becomes simpler—or at least very different.

Euripides wrote tragedy, and he wrote several kinds of non-tragic drama. They must be kept distinct. In this chapter and the next we will consider the remaining tragedies (all but the *Bacchae*), first enquiring what kind of dramatic idea underlies them and how that moulds the dramatic form, then trying to see the logical connexion between the dramatic idea and the dramatic style of the plays. If we were making a critical study of Euripides himself, of his poetic and dramatic personality and the development of his views, we should have to take the plays in chronological order; but as we are considering his structural methods, and as these are the same in the whole group of war-tragedies but clearest in the last, we may begin with the last.

There is no need to assert that the *Troades* is a tragic unity; we feel it or we do not, and no analysis will make us feel it more; but in order to criticize we must see where the unity is. To appreciate this, we have first to remember that the play is unique in the later drama in being part of a genuine trilogy. The first play, the *Alexandros*, dealt with Paris. His parents, warned that the child would be the ruin of his country if he reached manhood, shrank from killing him, as did Laius and Iocasta, and Paris did reach manhood. We know the plot; what Euripides put into it we do not know. The point of the second play, the *Palamedes*, is clear. It dealt with the judicial murder of Palamedes by his own Greek leaders before Troy—the act of treachery which Nauplius his father was to avenge by lighting beacons to wreck the Greek ships on Euboea as they sailed home. In these two plays the tragedy of two nations is started; in the third it is consummated.

In the prologue, shared by Athena and Poseidon, the capture of Troy is announced, and Athena asks Poseidon to destroy the Greek fleet on its way home ; she had been their champion, but their hybris, both to Cassandra and to the temples of Troy, has made her their enemy.   A reference to the coasts of Euboea reminds us of the *Palamedes,* and the gods retire, leaving the stage to the prostrate Hecuba, to whom is presently added a chorus of captive Trojan women awaiting their captors' pleasure.

The action that follows consists of four scenes.   Talthybius the Herald comes for Cassandra, the virgin-priestess, whom Agamemnon is taking ; as Andromache with her infant son Astyanax is being borne away to the Greek ships Talthybius comes again to announce the decree of death against the child ; Menelaus comes to carry off Helen to execution, and there is a set debate between Helen and Hecuba, Menelaus, as umpire, condemning Helen ; lastly Talthybius returns with the body of Astyanax to give it to Hecuba for burial, to announce the burning of Troy, and to lead the captives to the ships.   There is added incidentally to this list of miseries the fate of Polyxena, the slavery in Ithaca decreed for Hecuba, the snatching away of Andromache before she can even attend to the burial of her child, and the terrible plight of the Chorus. Everything, except the Helen-scene, is contrived to be as unhappy as possible, and not one of the incidents (the Helen-scene apart) is considered except in its effect on the Trojans. No contrast is aimed at, no explanation of the Greek point of view.   As if deliberately to make the actions of the Greeks simply impersonal decrees and to discourage us from interesting ourselves in their motives, the Herald is used throughout— not for example Odysseus, as in the *Hecuba*—coming in like a series of telegrams.

Considered superficially the play lacks both unity and a tragic idea.   As for the unity, little is gained by pointing to the continuous presence of Hecuba ; what happens to one person is not necessarily a unity, and in fact the centre of interest is successively Hecuba, Cassandra, Andromache and Helen.   Certainly the presence of Hecuba helps ; without her the play would seem more episodic.   We may fairly call her a symbol, but if she is that, and if the unity of the piece is seen in her, it must really lie in that which she symbolizes, the sufferings of the defeated.

And what of the tragedy? The spectacle of the strong trampling on the impotent, though it may be salutary propaganda, is not tragedy; but we remember the general course of the trilogy, and there is the illuminating prologue. The Greeks are under sentence of death for hybris, but before retribution descends on them they make it clear, by their further outrages, how much they deserve it. There is a moral structure not unlike that of the *Agamemnon*. The first ode there reminds us of Agamemnon's great sin, and starts the play in an atmosphere of doom; then we have the ominous aggravations of his guilt—the sufferings inflicted on Greece, the sacrilege committed in Troy, the purple carpet, Cassandra. It is an oppressive series, made the more oppressive by Agamemnon's blindness; only the carpet makes him feel uneasy. In our play the function of the great ode is discharged by the prologue. The Greeks are doomed from the start, and proceed to pile up the count before our eyes, the more awfully because it is done so impersonally. This series of outrages, episodic and merely pathetic if we look only at the Trojans, is cumulative and tragic if we look at the Greeks, and it is to ensure that we shall take this point of view that Euripides writes his otherwise unnecessary and unusually impressive prologue. The Greeks are the collective tragic hero or tragic agent, the Trojans the collective victim.

The comparison with the *Agamemnon* can be carried a stage further. There is no Aristotelian connexion between the killing of Iphigenia and the defilement of the Trojan temples except that the same man did both, and out of the same moral blindness. So in the *Troades*: the connexion between the rape of Cassandra and the murder of Astyanax is simply that both proceed from the same hybris in the Greeks. Aeschylus might have chosen other instances of Agamemnon's blindness; Euripides might have chosen other incidents to illustrate the cruelty of the Greeks—or have put these in the reverse order. Aristotelian cause and effect do not apply. The *Troades* completes a movement whose beginnings we saw in the *Medea*. It is now apparent that we have the tragedy not of the individual hero but of the group. In the *Medea* Euripides could logically interfere in his plot to make his tragic idea clearer ; now the whole plot is constructed, as it were, by Euripides and not by the will and actions of a hero ; it has become quite inorganic. We ventured to suggest that Medea, in spite of her dramatic qualities, was not a character in the Sophoclean sense, and that Euripides is slightly but definitely detached from his creation ; in the *Troades* this schematic rather than naturalistic treatment of character is carried to its natural limit. Since the character that is tragically significant is the collective one of the Greeks, Hecuba's is left an outline only. Her part in the tragedy needs, and receives, no more detailed characterization than Pelasgus' in the *Supplices* ; she shows such character as the play demands, nobility in suffering, and that is all.

The Helen-scene shows us how far Euripides was from regarding this as a play about Hecuba ; it shows too on what principles he is now making his plots. Helen pleads *force majeure* ; it was Aphrodite who caused the whole affair ; she herself is innocent. This plea Hecuba easily demolishes : ' It was not Aphrodite but Aphrosyne—your own wantonness.' Euripides will not abate his doctrine of personal responsibility. Menelaus, as judge, agrees with Hecuba ; Helen deserves death and shall be put to death—only not just now, but in Sparta, without fail. In a play about Hecuba's sufferings the point of this scene would not be very clear, but such as it is it would surely have been more effective had Menelaus given Hecuba another insult by acquitting Helen there and then. But Euripides is not thinking first and foremost of the stricken Queen ; she may be the symbol of his tragedy but she is not its incarnation—if she were, this scene would have been more of a dramatic contest and less of a debate ; for Euripides does not use the forensic style simply because he cannot help it.

The scene is there not for Hecuba's sake but because, like the last scene of the *Medea*, it embodies part of Euripides' thought. When he has given up tragedy we shall find him saying (*Helen* 38 ff.) that the gods caused the war to relieve over-population ; the essence of this social tragedy is that mankind, or some men, are directly responsible for these miseries. In the *Suppliant Women* a Socratic elenchus makes Adrastus admit that the basis of the war of the Seven was reckless folly ; here Menelaus decides that Helen is guilty. This means—whatever the man may or may not do later—that this war too was misconceived, its basis the worthlessness of a woman. The scene interrupts the plot but it illuminates Euripides' thought—and the play itself does no other.

If we consider how Euripides treats the episode of Polyxena we shall understand clearly the principles on which he constructs these plots. At v. 260 Hecuba asks Talthybius what is to be Polyxena's fate. The reply is so evasive that it ought only to have provoked a further question, but Hecuba accepts the evasion and passes on. The Scholiast expresses surprise : Why does not Hecuba either lament or ask how ' she is released from sorrow ' ? If she knows, she should lament for her ; if she does not know, she should ask and find out.[1] A recent editor, M. Parmentier, remarks, ' Euripide évite de revenir sur le sujet de l'*Hécube*.' But why should Euripides be so self-conscious about a play ten years old ? If he was, why did he mention Polyxena at all ? And in fact, far from avoiding the subject, he raises it here, only to drop it rather awkwardly and then to treat it at some length later (622 ff.). If we assume that Euripides is simply following a course of dramatic events at Troy, making of them the best plot that he can, we can offer no explanation of this procedure—unless some Verrallian comes to the rescue with a theory of private performance, *contaminatio*, or something else just as convincing. When we see that Euripides is not putting together a play but presenting a tragic idea, the explanation is obvious. The incident is used not logically, like an incident in Sophocles, but suggestively. Polyxena's fate is even more terrible than Cassandra's, therefore must come after it ; moreover the effect of its announcement is more poignant coming from Andromache than from Talthybius. Yet the pathos of the Cassandra scene is greatly strengthened if we, the audience, know that Polyxena lies behind it ; therefore the veiled reference is introduced to assure us that Polyxena will not be

[1] As emended by Schwartz.

forgotten. It is once more a deliberate manipulation of the action, now independent of the characters, contrived (at the cost of a momentary awkwardness) to increase the tension; and for such a solid advantage Euripides was well content to puzzle a scholiast.

For even if the logic of a steadily evolving action is now abandoned, the dramatist is not without his principles of plot-construction. The principle to which he now owes allegiance is that the successive scenes must bear upon his central tragic idea with an ever-increasing power; in fact we are back again, by a roundabout way, at the law of increasing tension which we noticed in the *Prometheus*. Here, as there, scenes could be transposed without any violence to the logic of fact, but we cannot say, in Aristotle's phrase,[1] that there would be no difference; the logic of fact might be as good, but the logic of the inner tragedy would not.

The law of increasing tension we saw to be essentially lyrical in conception, even if not in origin too; and its re-appearance here coincides with a remarkable revival of the lyrical part of Greek tragedy. We shall have to discuss the Euripidean chorus in detail later, but something must be said here, as without the chorus neither the *Troades* nor Euripides' methods are fully intelligible.

The Chorus had been threatened with extinction more than once—notably by Euripides himself when he found it such a nuisance at certain points in the *Medea* and the *Hippolytus*; but its inherent vitality (that is, the fact that the Greek poets were not conservative) found a new use for it again and again. If this Trojan chorus had been taught to behave ' as in Sophocles ', to follow and comment, either directly or philosophically, on the action, it would necessarily have sung a series of odes on the rape of Cassandra, the captivity of Andromache, the murder of Astyanax, and the wickedness of Helen. But this, though beautifully Sophoclean, would have been ruination to the play; it would have unnecessarily emphasized the schematic nature of the plot, and it would have given to the events that kind of dramatic significance which they are not meant to have. This chorus does not obey dramatic canons;

[1] Which perhaps was not aimed at these plays in particular.

it recognizes facts. Whatever may happen on the stage, the chorus takes no notice of it. Polyxena may be sacrificed, or Astyanax' bleeding body brought back, but the chorus says not a word about it. It has one theme only, Troy—why it fell, how it fell, and what is to happen to them, the survivors. Nothing can move it from this mournful *ostinato*.

In this Euripides was not being merely negative, avoiding what would have underlined the hazardous features of his dramatic method. The chorus sticks to the fall of Troy positively. Its lyrical nature enables it to penetrate more nearly to the inner tragedy than the actors. The actors can sharply present certain facets of the human tragedy which is Euripides' real theme ; Hecuba, no real heroine, can be an impressive individual symbol of this on the stage. The chorus sings of ruin and death—not the ruin of Hecuba, which is but a shadow, but of Troy ; thus in its own way, as Hecuba in hers, prefiguring the inner tragedy. This symbolic use of plot and action has in fact broken down the recently won supremacy of the actors, but we do not return to the earlier drama in which the Chorus enfolded the action ; rather are Chorus and actors now co-ordinate forces, each in its own way presenting the inner drama of the poet's own conception.

5. THE HECUBA   The material of the *Hecuba* is taken from two legends which have no connexion except that both come from the Trojan cycle and both intimately concern Hecuba. A purely formal unity is given by the continuous presence on the stage of Hecuba and the chorus of Trojan captives, but there is no casual unity that links the sacrifice of one of Hecuba's children with the murder of another. Like the incidents that make up the plot of the *Troades*, they remain separate ; in the *Troades* indeed there is the nexus that all the action proceeds from one side, the Greeks, but in the *Hecuba* even this mechanical help is missing. The Greeks have sacked Troy and enslaved those that they have not killed ; they now sacrifice Hecuba's daughter Polyxena to the shade of Achilles ; then the Thracian Polymestor is discovered to have murdered Hecuba's remaining son Polydorus, to get his treasure ; finally Hecuba takes a terrible revenge on Poly-

mestor. Such is the scattered material that makes up the
plot. That kind of unity that we find in the *Troades* is wanting, but in compensation we have here more character-interest ; in the *Troades* Hecuba is only a helpless victim, while
here she does retaliate on one of her oppressors. It is indeed
commonly maintained that the aim and purpose of the play
is to study the character of Hecuba. Is the view tenable ?

We may first note the chief features in the play for which
we must try to account. There is the prologue spoken by
Polydorus' Ghost, the obvious purpose of which is to hold
together the two separate actions of the play [1] ; no hint here,
as in the prologues to the *Troades* and *Hippolytus,* of what
the underlying idea is. There follows an interesting inversion
of an ancient practice when Hecuba is lyrical and the chorus
acts as Messenger. They announce to her the impending
sacrifice of Polyxena, and presently announce it to Polyxena
herself. This occupies 150 verses of lyrical dialogue, and is
a scene clearly designed for its misery-value, since in it action,
characterization and *dianoia* [2] are reduced to a minimum.

Next the demand for Polyxena is sent to Hecuba, through
Odysseus. Why Odysseus and not the regular herald Talthybius ? Obviously because Odysseus is under a peculiarly
deep obligation to Hecuba [3] ; Hecuba consented not to denounce him when Helen recognized him as a spy inside the
walls of Troy. Out of this obligation Odysseus tries to
wriggle by saying that he is indeed bound to Hecuba, but not
to Hecuba's daughter. This point, of which much is made,
is (compared with the loss of Polyxena) negligible in its effect
on Hecuba's sufferings, still more so in its effect on her mind
and character, which in any case have hardly begun to interest
us. If Odysseus is preferred to Talthybius merely for the
sake of this extra dramatic piquancy, it is a second-rate device ; legitimate enough in quasi-melodrama where piquancy
in the turns of the plot is one of the chief elements of the

---

[1] It is in fact rather more subtle than this ; see p. 297.

[2] What is the English for this ? Bywater translates it ' thought '.
In this context perhaps ' intellectual interest ', though clumsy,
would sound more natural.

[3] Euripides seems to have invented this.

play, powerful in tragedy if the added point deepens the tragedy (cf. the Watchman in the *Antigone*). Here it makes a strong impression, and if the misfortunes of Hecuba and her reaction to them are our chief interest, that impression is beside the point.

When Hecuba's plea to Odysseus fails, Polyxena is asked to plead for herself. She refuses, and accepts death—that is, murder—willingly, her reason being that she has nothing to live for. The interest we have in her therefore is purely pathetic ; Euripides has not made her an Antigone, who has everything to live for. Hecuba nobly offers to die in her stead, but the nobility is conventional rather than dramatic, as she too has nothing to live for. Euripides in fact is not seriously trying to interest us in these two women as characters ; rather in the Greeks who do these things. This feeling is reinforced when we come to the next choral ode. The chorus says not a word about Hecuba and Polyxena ; their theme is ' What will be *our* fate ? ' Is this only selfishness on their part and the waste of an opportunity by Euripides ? If we are to watch Hecuba with all our dramatic imagination, it is odd that our attention should now be directed away from her agony.

Then we have to consider Odysseus' argument, that a state in order to flourish must honour its benefactors. Odysseus is in grave danger of appearing dishonourable ; is this plea a mere excuse, rhetorical *inventio*, or is it sincere, containing some tragic point ? There was no need to send Odysseus ; if he is sent only in order that, being sent, he may extricate himself by a piece of sophistry and so enable Euripides to make a hit at politicians, we may properly accuse the poet of debasing his art—for this is tragedy, not melodrama, like the *I.T.* But Odysseus' reasoning—granting the premises—has force. We must remember too that the decision to sacrifice Polyxena was not made unanimously or easily. Agamemnon was against it—for the sake of Cassandra ; the two sons of Theseus were in favour ; so was Odysseus—who received from the chorus hard names not accorded to the two Athenians (vv. 123–33). We must, I think, be prepared to find the tragic point of the sacrifice as much among the Greeks as

among the Trojans ; the more so when Talthybius arrives, first
to start back in horror at the misery he sees, then, in describing the sacrifice, to give us the impression that the
Greeks are, after all, very decent people.

This scene ends with a remarkable bit of philosophizing
from Hecuba,[1] and is followed by an ode which, dealing with
the origin of the war and the misery it has brought to Trojan
and Greek alike, has again no reference to the action on the
stage.

Now, by an obvious link, we pass from Polyxena to Polydorus ; the servant sent to fetch water to purify the one body
finds the other on the shore, as the prologue predicted. We
wait to see what Euripides is going to do with this artificial
addition. There is the necessary interval for lamentation, and
Agamemnon is brought in. Hecuba, in a series of conventional asides, brings herself to ask his favour—not for the freedom which he, ironically, is so ready to offer, but for his
acquiescence in a proposed retribution upon Polymestor.
There is movement of character and mind here ; Hecuba is
prepared to go to any lengths to win over Agamemnon. He
has his purely political difficulties, but matters are at last arranged. Hecuba assures us, by citing the Lemnian Women,
that she and her helpers between them will be able to en-
compass revenge, and the messenger is sent to Polymestor.[2]

Still this obstinate chorus refuses to take any notice of the
action. It is as far as possible from being an Ideal Spectator.
It sings a marvellously vivid ode, not about the Lemnian
Women or just retribution or anything else connected with
the present action, but about the night on which Troy fell ;
‘ My husband lay on his bed . . . I was arranging my hair
before the mirror . . .’ Sometimes the Euripidean chorus
finds itself in a position where it can hardly say anything both
relevant and lyrical ; here it could and will not.

In the last scene there is no lack of dramatic movement.
Hecuba easily traps the barbarian into convincing himself of
treachery and murder, and, by playing on his cupidity, entices

[1] 592–602. See p. 285.

[2] Incidentally, it appears from v. 898 that the sacrifice has not
availed to raise the favouring wind.

him into the tent. But if we expect to hear of his death, we are disappointed. Hecuba, a second Medea, does something far more revolting, blinding him and killing his two sons ; and to ensure that we shall be revolted and not edified Euripides causes the wretched Polymestor to come out of the tent on all fours. He does not, in his tragedies, use such ' realism ' merely for the sake of being lively.

In most of these tragedies there comes a point at which the critic may profitably ask himself how he would have finished the play. This seems to be one. We should naturally try to contrive an account of the actual revenge, and, whether or not we were taking the line that Hecuba was justified, we should make our Hecuba dominate the last scene beyond any question ; heroine or fury, she should at last stand before us fully revealed. Or, remembering our Oedipus,[1] we might have allowed Polymestor to prophesy the approaching end of Hecuba, as Euripides has done here ; but only in order that she might rise magnificently over even this. What we should never have thought of is what Euripides does. Polymestor, practically, steals the thunder, and the secondary figure of Agamemnon is made as prominent as Hecuba, if not more prominent. We have a trial-scene, with Agamemnon acting as judge, the inevitable and horrifying account of the actual revenge, the evident revulsion of Agamemnon, but his judgement that Polymestor has got his deserts. Then the barbarian turns vicarious prophet, and prophesies not only Hecuba's end, but also the murder of Agamemnon, so that we finish not with a final revelation of Hecuba, but with the seizure and banishment of Polymestor.

It is perfectly true that in Hecuba we see first an unresisting victim, then a victim who gathers all her strength to hit back. This change gives a great impetus to the second part of the play, but to call the play on that account a study of character or psychology is a mistake. We need not underrate the character-interest, but we cannot suppose that what drove Euripides to construct this rather odd plot was the desire to portray a tragic Hecuba. This does not, to begin with, account for the ending. Then, as a character-study, it would

[1] See above, p. 188.

be altogether too simple and too violent. To put this play and the *Philoctetes* in the same category is to do an injustice to both. When Polydorus' body is found, our conception of Hecuba's character is so vague that she might do anything without surprising us. We can hardly say that in Hecuba we have a woman driven mad by suffering, because we have not seen what she was like in normal circumstances. Further, Euripides cannot have contrived all this misery and this awful barbarian merely to play on Hecuba's character, to illustrate her reactions ; it would be too uneconomical and too shocking for a Greek. The *Philoctetes* will show us how such a study should be set—in a situation which may be serious, but in which a satisfactory outcome is assured. If it is objected that the *Tyrannus* is a study of character which, however, is tragic through and through, the answer is that the tragedy of Oedipus was his character, whereas the tragedy here is first what is done to Hecuba, in which her character has no part, then in what she does to others, not in what she suffers. Fourthly, this view leaves unexplained the prominence given to Polyxena's sacrifice and to the Greeks, it also fails to explain Odysseus and the behaviour of Agamemnon, and finally it would make of the chorus a sustained irrelevance.

We have noticed that the chorus here is not the background of the action. It most remarkably keeps aloof from the action, as if it were playing out a tragedy of its own—which in fact it is doing. It keeps to its theme, the fall of Troy ; and this has nothing to do with Hecuba's character or with her revenge on Polymestor or with Odysseus or with the later dilemma of Agamemnon. The only way in which we can bring into one focus all the strands of the play and find a theme which is worthy of the magnitude of the events related is to suppose that here, as in the *Troades*, the separate actions are meant to point to one overriding idea, the suffering which the human race inflicts upon itself through its follies and wickednesses. We start, as it were, with a central heap of desolation in the ruin of Troy and the misery of the Trojans. This is continually kept before our minds in the series of choral odes. To it the action of the play makes one addition after another, each proceeding from a different source. The Greeks are

ot cruel, but their superstition and the political wisdom of
heir leaders throws the body of Polyxena on to the central
eap. Political necessity is one of the three sources of evil
sed during the play. Odysseus was honest in his plea of
onouring benefactors; it is a political necessity—and here it
nvolves murder.[1] Odysseus was chosen as the messenger,
hat political necessity may be shown to involve him in private
dishonour. This theme reappears with Agamemnon. He,
personally, is a well-meaning man, willing to give freedom to
Hecuba, sympathetic to her on all counts, anxious too that she
should be avenged on the barbarian—but unfortunately the
barbarian is an ally, and Hecuba is not exactly popular in
amp. The poor man hedges, with the result that the punishment which the King admits is deserved becomes a frightful
revenge.

But war and political necessity are not the only causes of
the misery of this play. After Polyxena comes Polydorus,
victim of the comparatively simple crime of greed, and after
Polydorus, more additions to the central heap, perhaps the
most pathetic, the two boys. The pitiful victim of oppression
herself turns oppressor, giving way not to blind rage but to
calculating cruelty. Agamemnon did not blame her; perhaps
we need not; nevertheless, when the bereaved mother
slaughters the two sons of Polymestor we shall not applaud
her, nor merely congratulate Euripides on a powerful stroke
of psychological development or a fine dramatic climax.

When all is done, when superstition, politics, lust for gold,
and blind cruelty have done their worst, there remains as a
grim finale the death that awaits both the well-meaning Agamemnon and the ill-used Hecuba. This finale, like the
chorus, is a pointer to the meaning of the whole. It is not,
as we have seen, a reasonable ending for an orthodox play on
Hecuba as a tragic heroine, for Agamemnon is too prominent
in it; it is a most imaginative ending for a play whose tragic
idea is one that embraces both the Greeks and Hecuba as
wrongdoers, and both the Greeks and Hecuba as the victims of
wrongdoing. During all these scenes of increasing misery the

[1] A theme used with Lycus (*H.F.*, 165 ff.) and with the murder
of Astyanax (*Tro.*, 1159 ff.).

chorus pursues its monotone, not because the fall of Troy had
an essential connexion with the events on the stage, but because it is made the symbol of that whole—the sufferings of
humanity—of which the events on the stage are parts and vivid
illustrations. The chorus is not indeed the hero of the action,
for Euripides does not now give us heroes, either morally or
dramatically speaking, but it it is the focus of the tragic thought.

It might be possible to devise a formula which would express the essence of the *Hecuba* more accurately and fully
than this. I do not insist on the formula. The play, taken
quite simply, makes its own impression, and that is its ' meaning ' ; only when we begin to criticize does it become necessary
to put that meaning into words—a task certainly much easier
and more natural, but sometimes hardly less grateful, than
trying to put into words the ' meaning ' of a piece of music.
What must be emphasized is that this ' meaning ' is not
the character, action, and fate of Hecuba herself, but something deeper and more general. She is a symbol in a way in
which Eteocles and Oedipus are not, and the play derives its
unity and power not from the symbol, but from the thing
symbolized.

6. THE SUPPLIANT WOMEN   With the exception of the
Heracles no play of Euripides is more baffling and ' unsatisfactory ' than this one, yet into few has Euripides put
more of himself.

' Le style en est particulièrement soigné. Les *Suppliantes*
abondent en formules saisissantes, en maximes, en vers bien
frappés ; les morceaux brillants sont nombreux, et ce n'est
point par hasard que la tradition indirecte nous en a conservé
tant de citations, souvent altérées, comme il convient à des
gnomai qui étaient dans toutes les bouches.' [1]

These are perhaps superficial merits, but they are merits,
and we can go further. Few plays, even in this group, sur-
pass this one in tragic feeling and imagination—one has only
to think of the conception of the mourning chorus, of the half-
demented Evadne, of the whole scene at the pyre. Yet,
dramatically, the play seems helpless ; the action seems to

[1] M. Grégoire, ed. Budé, p. 99.

reach its proper conclusion at v. 975 at the latest—even so we could willingly spare the Funeral Speech of Adrastus—and, besides being scattered, it is very inconsistent in tone, for the Socratic confutation of Adrastus by Theseus, not to mention the set debate on democracy, do not, at first sight, consort well with the tragic features we have mentioned. No Euripidean play atones for more numerous irritations by more evident excellences.

The usual estimate of the *Suppliant Women* seems to be that of the Argument, 'an encomium of Athens'. It is a patriotic play, in which the disinterested nobility and the sagacity of Theseus are contrasted with the folly of Adrastus and the boorish presumption of the Boeotian Creon ; just as the democratic constitution of Athens, though criticized, is favourably compared with autocratic constitutions. The play too gives to Athens a glorious part in one of the great actions of the mythic past ; it reflects recent events to the credit and comfort of the Athenian people, and it tells the enemies of Athens what Athens thinks of their behaviour.

It is indeed obvious that much of what is said in the play would gratify the Athenians, but this does not mean that 'eulogy of Athens', 'patriotic piece', are satisfactory descriptions of it ; they do not explain enough. They certainly do not explain the tone of the play, for in spite of Theseus' optimist philosophy—and Theseus here, we must remember, is a young man—the general tone of the play is surely one of almost unrelieved pessimism. In eulogies, pessimism is best omitted. Nor is it easy to cast the tragic dramatist who wrote the *Hecuba* and the *Troades* in the role of patriotic poet. In these plays we see Euripides as the poet of humanity, loving Athens without a doubt, but not finding even Athens big enough for him. In these plays he is what we should call to-day a good European, and the *Suppliant Women* only confirms this impression. Further, if this is a eulogy in purpose, what are Evadne and Iphis doing in it ? Are they really introduced only to interest spectators bored by the rest of the play ? [1]

In a play in which the characters say so much about so

[1] M. Grégoire, ed. Budé, pp. 100–1.

many things it is unusually dangerous to base an interpretation on quotations, but in this play three things are said [1] which at once arrest the attention. ' If Death were visible in the casting of the vote, Greece would not be destroying herself by her war-lust ' (484–5). ' Empty-headed mortals . . . you yield not to the persuasion of friends but only to facts. . . . You cities, who could remedy your troubles by reasoning, prefer to settle matters by slaughter ' (745 ff.). ' Unhappy mortals, why get spears and make slaughter among yourselves ? . . . Life is a short thing ; we should pass through it easily, with as little trouble as we can.'

That this pacifism (which has been often noticed) does not lie on the surface, like the debate on democracy for example, is indicated by the fact that it touches the form of the play at several points. In the first place, it explains Evadne and Iphis. Iphis we have met before, as Theseus in the *Hippolytus,* and we shall meet him again, as Peleus in the *Andromache.* Evadne is a recognizable descendant of Cassandra in the *Agamemnon.* These two characters are not melodramatic ornaments, but more examples of Euripides' abstract or suggestive use of plot. The theme is the same as that of the *Hecuba* and *Troades,* the communal suffering that comes from communal wrong-doing and folly. The wrong-doing and folly here are the remarkably stupid behaviour of Adrastus and the impious arrogance of Creon ; the suffering is typified in the mourning of the mothers and sons, and is brought suddenly to a sharp point in the frenzied grief of Evadne—just as Cassandra suddenly brings into a focus all the horrors of the house of Atreus. Of Iphis M. Grégoire remarks (p. 145 of his edition) that he goes home to die in despair, being in this no Heracles. But why is he not a Heracles —or a wild blasphemer, or something else really interesting ? Why, if Euripides was at his wits' end to stimulate his audience, did he make Iphis simply an inconspicuous old man ? Because that was precisely what he wanted. Iphis is the type of ordinary humanity that suffers because of the follies that

[1] Characteristically of Euripides, it is immaterial who says them. The first is said by the Theban Herald, the other two by Adrastus.

his play exposes, suffering not greatly and romantically,
ke Evadne, but dumbly and uncomprehendingly.

This 'pacifism' explains too Adrastus. 'Adraste visible-
nent agace Thésée.' Why? Theseus so pitilessly lays bare
he foolish behaviour of Adrastus not because he wants some
ind of stick with which to beat contemporary Argos—that we
nay believe when we are convinced that Euripides was not
 great tragic poet—but for strictly dramatic reasons, to make
t quite clear that this expedition of the Seven against Thebes
vas not something vaguely inevitable, not some misty but
;lorious emprise. The real purpose of the elenchus we do
1ot see at first, naturally; we see only what it does. There
vas the strange oracle, that Adrastus should marry his
daughters to a boar and a lion; two exiles turn up, the one a
homicide, the other a man cursed by his father, ruffians both,
for they start fighting at once. Confident in his brilliant
identification of these two with the boar and lion, Adrastus
passes over the natural circle of suitors,[1] Argives, and thrusts
his daughters upon these two fortunate men, and they (aided
by 'the clamour of the young men' which overbore him) at
once involve the silly man in the war. He began by reading
an oracle; he asked for no confirmation, and sought no more
mantic aid. Indeed, such as came unasked he rejected.
This extremely foolish, not to say impious, behaviour he
describes later (734), after the manner of his kind, as 'the
will of Zeus'.

Plainly the motive of this passage is not a simple-minded
desire to draw an Adrastus who should be different from
Aeschylus' (Euripides must have spent very few of his
working hours in trying to be different from Aeschylus),
nor to ridicule ancient stories in the easy manner of 'A
Yankee at the Court of King Arthur', but to establish the
terrifying fact that the misery which fills this play has an
origin so tragically foolish. So, when Theseus says, 'What of
that Argos of yours? Big words, and nothing else?' (135),
he is not covertly expressing Athens' irritation at the profitable
neutrality of Argos during the Archidamian War. It may be

[1] 133 f.

true that Euripides would have avoided such an expression at
a time when Athens was trying to get Argive help; it is
possible that, in spite of the poetry and the music and the
remoteness of the Athenian stage, the Athenian dramatist
could not use ' Argos ' poetically without being understood
politically. That is another thing. His point here—and he
returns to it at v. 737—is a purely dramatic one, that military
strength is no safe substitute for ordinary prudence. In fact,
if there is a direct contemporary allusion in this part of the
play we should see it in vv. 738 ff. Here we find a detail
which Euripides seems to have invented : ' When Eteocles
offered a composition, making demands which were moderate,
we rejected it . . . and when we were destroyed . . . O
empty-headed mortals . . . you settle it by slaughter.' The
Spartans offered terms to Athens in 425 B.C.

The expedition then was an act of criminal stupidity.
Adrastus' hamartia is brought out clearly—and we may again
notice that the hamartia is of importance in the life of the
community rather than in the life of the wrong-doer. Here it
is not its first function to illuminate Adrastus, nor is it of the
first importance that it recoils upon him. In fact, it does—
Menelaus in the *Andromache* is luckier—but the dramatic
results are those which affect the mothers and sons, Evadne
and Iphis.

To Adrastus Theseus behaves as a man of pure intelligence :
' Since it is your own doing, mend it yourself.' He uses that
synesis, intelligence, which is the first gift of God to man
(203). But Aethra points out that there is something else,
the claims of humanity, religion and honour ; these cannot
be laid aside. To Adrastus Theseus will not yield, to Aethra
he must. His expedition is one undertaken in defence of
law and humanity—that is why he will allow Adrastus no part
in it. It is of the nature of a sacrifice freely offered by the
city, with no hope of gain—not even of mandates—and when
he is victorious Theseus refuses to enter Thebes. The theme
demanded that Creon should turn the potential sacrifice into a
real one, a point to remember when one is considering
whether the play reflects the refusal of the Thebans to
restore the Athenian dead after Delium. In Aeschylus' play

on the same myth, the *Eleusinians*, the Thebans yield to persuasion. If there were no dramatic reason for their refusal to yield here, the inference that Euripides was thinking of Delium would be irresistible ; as there is such a reason Delium may be coincidence.[1] Here Creon must refuse Theseus' reasonable request in order that Euripides may make clear his contrast between a just and a stupid war. The horrors of the new battle are not passed over, but from it no new misery is drawn. We return to the original theme, the waste caused by the expedition of the Argives, without the addition of new Athenian mourners whose dead did not die in the cause of stupidity.

So far as Aristotelian unity goes, the play obviously might end with the return of the dead. Logically, Evadne and Iphis are an entirely fresh development ; if they come in, why not uncles of Parthenopaeus, or cousins of Hippomedon ? Evadne and Iphis are introduced in order to develop the tragic idea. Euripides in fact is not merely dramatizing the legend of the Suppliant Women and filling it out with maxims, discourses, and debates on democracy ; he is expressing a tragic vision and using the legend for that purpose. If conflict arises between the development of the idea and the smooth conduct of the action, it is the action that has to give way. The development of the idea demands that after the generalized suffering and grief of the Mothers and Sons we should see an intenser expression of grief in a single person ; that the ruin which has already come about through Adrastus' folly should be brought to a focus in the ruin of Evadne's life, and, through her, of Iphis'. There is provided, naturally, a formal link—the prominence in the first part of Capaneus ; the real link is in the idea.

When these two have sounded their very personal note and have gone, Euripides introduces, with the Sons, a new and, to my thinking, an even more tragic development. It is not that orphaned children are more pathetic than bereaved mothers ; the Sons raise the question, ' What of the future ? ' Here, unless I have entirely mistaken my play, Euripides has

[1] See Parmentier's judicious remarks about the *Troades* and the Sicilian expedition. (Ed. Budé, pp. 13 ff.)

small comfort to offer. The Sons do all that is accounted virtuous—they dedicate themselves to vengeance, but the Mothers sing, 'The evil sleeps not yet.'

This hint of vengeance to come is either a perfunctory way of preparing the wind-up of the play, or it is an intensification of the tragedy. Perfunctory because if the theme is simply and solely that of the Suppliant Women it is already finished ; the addition of the Sons can be only a stage-effect, and statements about a happy revenge were best left to the conventional *Deus ex machina*—who indeed does arrive to make them. If this is all, there is no point in the intervention of the Sons, except a certain pathos ; still less is there real development. If on the other hand the play is what we take it to be, there is both. The boys will avenge fathers who died in a war which should never have been begun, one from whose results the prudent Theseus—until won over by Aethra —held strictly aloof. The Sons, unquestionably, are showing nobility—but 'Lust for war is ruining Greece' : the destruction goes on. The more noble their aspiration, the more awful the tragedy. This is development, logical and powerful, the last turn of the screw.

Here is the end of the tragedy ; it remains only to append a formal conclusion, a perfectly artificial scene in which —seeing that it has no tragic tension whatever—we may find allusions to our heart's content. This time it is, naturally, Athena who arrives, and she arrives with a remark which is surely intended to jar : 'Hearken, O Theseus, to the words of Athena . . . Give not these bones for the Sons to convey to Argos, letting them pass so lightly from thy hands. In return for thy labours, and the City's, first exact an oath . . .' What ? A goddess less generous than Theseus ? A mandate after all ? We can find reasons in plenty for ending the play with oaths of friendship, but why is Athena so very blunt about it ? There is Euripidean precedent for deities who are morally inferior to men ; what is the reason here ? Athena winds up the *Ion* because, as she hints, Apollo is ashamed to show his face. The Dioscuri end the *Electra* partly because it is so ridiculous for a woman like Electra to have uncles in the sky, partly because it is so damaging for

the newest of divinities to say what these say about Apollo.
Athena ends the *I.T.* because Apollo, who is responsible for
Orestes, does not exist. Apollo ends the *Orestes* because
nothing could establish his non-existence better than the
impossible solution he gravely propounds. Euripides liked
to produce gods, especially Apollo, at the end less to cut
the knot than to cut their own throats. Athena here is
certainly not spoof ; for one thing the play has not been
melodrama but serious tragedy. We may however be prepared to see a certain tinge of irony in the treatment she
receives—unless indeed the play is simply an encomium of
Athens. She is less generous than Theseus, as Artemis was
less noble than Hippolytus, Aphrodite than Phaedra. How
are we to interpret this touch of acidity ? That the romantic
expedition of Theseus against Thebes is not practical politics ?
That Theseus does not after all represent the political wisdom
of Athens ? It is difficult to say.

That the *Suppliant Women* has as much tautness and
austerity as the other tragedies of Euripides we cannot
maintain. It is discursive—and Euripides is aware of the
fact (cf. the apologies in 427-8, 461-2, 567, 584). But apart
from the loosely appended passages like the debate on
democracy, the funeral-speech, the criticism of the conventional messenger-speech (846 ff.), it is a coherent and
well-designed presentation of a single theme. It obviously is
a eulogy of Athens in that it contains a great deal that would
appeal to Athenian sentiment, but, like the *Persae*, it is as
much a national warning as a national eulogy. Theseus is the
great man of the piece and Theseus was an Athenian. Excellent. But Theseus' ordinary prudence was against the
war ; he yielded only to Aethra's plea of religion and honour,
and when he defeated Creon he refused to enter Thebes—
more disinterested than Athena. Let the Athenians congratulate themselves on their Theseus when they are sure
that they are equally disinterested in their war-making.
Meanwhile the new detail of Eteocles' offer of peace remains
in the memory—and certain warnings about politicians and
the ruin of Greece.

That the play is a *pièce d'occasion* in the ordinary sense, a work inspired by one particular event or situation, it seems quite impossible to believe. The war dominated Euripides' thought for years, completely filling this group of plays. Except for the *Heracles*, we have no tragedy of his, after the *Hippolytus*, on any other theme. He could escape into melodrama, and he could escape into Macedonia and write the *Bacchae*; in Athens he could write only about the war, and as a tragic poet, not as an interested onlooker. The behaviour of Sparta could rouse him to the specifically bitter outburst of the *Andromache*, but he did not attack the Spartans as enemies, hardly even war as war. In his mind these things were linked with the central tragedy of man, his capacity for intelligence and self-control, his domination by unreason and folly. The events of Delium may have suggested to him the theme of this play, or may have decided him to use it now and not later, but this is not to say that he was still thinking of Delium in the play; for with Euripides, as with any other creative artist, the original incident would grow into something entirely different and peculiarly his own.[1] Adrastus and Creon are no longer Argos and Thebes of 424 B.C., nor Theseus Athens of 424 B.C. These belong not to current politics, but to poetry, morality and tragedy.

7. THE ANDROMACHE The *Andromache* illustrates very clearly Euripides' present method, and as the play shapes itself as a straightforward play of intrigue the very nearly complete break which occurs half-way through the plot is the more surprising. This hard and brilliant tragedy is, not incidentally but fundamentally, a violent attack on the Spartan mind, on *Machtpolitik*; in particular on three Spartan qualities, arrogance, treachery and criminal ruthlessness. These are portrayed in three separate characters, Hermione, Menelaus, and Orestes, and in two separate actions; for in the first half of the play Andromache and her child, attacked by Hermione and Menelaus, are saved by Peleus, and in the second half Orestes appears, out of a different legend, to carry Hermione off to Sparta and to murder Neoptolemus on the way. We are then left to manage as well as we can with Peleus, Thetis

[1] See Henry James' prefaces *passim*.

and the body of Neoptolemus. Andromache does not appear again.

Nowhere is it more evident that the unity of the play lies in its idea and not in the story. If we will not integrate these separate actions, and the epilogue, into one general impression we shall find no explanation of Euripides' behaviour, only a ' lack of unity ' which, as Verrall truly declared, is a euphemism for downright insanity. It is useless to say that ' the second action grows out of the first ', for it does not ' grow ', and it remains a ' second action '. This is a method of making trilogies, not single plays. Méridier points out to us an equilibrium, and in this way tries to impose a formal unity on the work ; Hermione, humiliated in the first part, is victorious and takes her revenge in the second ; Peleus, successful in the first, is overwhelmed in the second. But in the second part Hermione does not take a revenge, unless it is revenge to clutch at the first man who presents himself, and triumph to elope with an Orestes ; nor can we congratulate Euripides if the gallant Peleus is overwhelmed not for some sin but for the sake of an equilibrium. The chiasmus does not work, and if it did it would be no explanation, for the principles of dramatic construction are not those of landscape-gardening.

The orthodox defenders labour under a grave disability : Euripides refuses to give evidence on his own behalf. He might easily have tempered this ' lack of unity ', but he does nothing. There is a prologue ; why is it not used, as the meaningless phrase goes, ' to bind the play together ' ? There is an epilogue ; was it impossible to make room in it for Andromache ? Why is Orestes' name not once mentioned before his surprising arrival ? There was opportunity enough and need enough. Had Euripides made efforts to disguise the ' lack of unity ' we could perhaps believe in theories of ineptitude, but there are no signs of uneasiness.

The answer to the questions we have just asked is that Euripides never concerned himself with them. He was not merely telling a story and making a play, and had no interest in concocting an artificial unity ; as always, he is trying to embody an idea. Why does he not display Andromache in

the epilogue? The impression that the epilogue is designed
to make is that of the ruin and misery which Spartan *Machtpolitik* creates. To symbolize this the dramatist needs a
figure central to all the events of the play—Peleus; one who
has lost his son, now loses his grandson, and nearly loses
his great-grandson. Andromache might have been introduced, but though she would have secured for the play a
superficial symmetry she would have blurred this impression.
Peleus represents the stricken house; she would have been
only the ill-used captive.

Similarly no preparation is made for Orestes' coming. The
deliberate avoidance of his name suggests that Euripides
meant to challenge our minds by the shock of his arrival. The
dramatist was willing that his play should stand or fall by its
intrinsic effect; it is, we might say, a severely functional work
of art which disdains pretences. Certainly we must not think
of the *Andromache* as if in it Euripides were deftly combining
legends and throwing in some anti-Spartan venom as a makeweight. Drama can be made in this way, but such drama
must above all be neat and workmanlike. The *Andromache*
is animated and explained by one burning idea which, with its
separate aspects, incorporates itself in a plot better suited to a
trilogy than to a play; and because the play means so much to
Euripides, so much more than the *Ion* or *I.T.* meant, he
cannot find the time or inclination to tinker with it and give
it a false unity which would in no way assist the idea.

In these important respects the *Andromache* resembles the
Hecuba and *Troades*; in others it is very different. It has
a vigour of action, a sharpness in characterization, which
those plays conspicuously lack; on the other hand its chorus
is less effective. These differences are not accidental.

The theme and feeling of the *Andromache* are not universal,
as are those of the *Hecuba* and *Troades*. The play is a
denunciation of Sparta, not a tragedy of mankind. The
dramatic results of this are important. Since Euripides
wishes to arraign specific aspects of Spartan morality he presents Spartans in action rather than their victims in misery;
the plot therefore is much less passive than those of the other
plays. To swiftness and decisiveness in action is added,

from the same cause, a much more detailed characterization; obviously the Spartans, if not also their victims, must be drawn in the hardest of outlines. Moreover, we need not expect the light and shade of tragedy; in fact, both in action and in characterization the *Andromache* has the hardness and the glaring colours of melodrama. Euripides has not to keep within Aristotelian limits of the probable, the broadly human; his special and limited aim compels him to make his action and characters as extreme as he can. He must be definite, for vagueness in denunciation will not do, and he can be as extreme as he likes.

In these respects therefore the *Andromache,* though it verges on melodrama, is more normal than the *Hecuba* and *Troades,* but because it is so particular and brings everything to so sharp a point its chorus is not so happy. The lyrical background which the Trojan chorus holds up to a more poetically conceived action would here be incongruous; this time what Euripides wants to say he says in the action. These harsh and violent deeds do not permit themselves to be enfolded by music and the dance, and because the plot is schematic the chorus cannot be consecutive in the Sophoclean manner.

These points will be developed in the next chapter; meanwhile we may notice how clearly the style of the play is dictated by its indignant purpose.

In the early scenes the revolting cruelty and treachery of Menelaus are displayed with all possible emphasis in the plot against Andromache. Her child is used as a bait, and then, with an indecent show of formality, Menelaus proposes to murder both. These events produce a scene between Neoptolemus' unpleasant wife and his tragic concubine; also one of Euripides' statutory scenes of self-sacrifice. The former is often called a psychological study; but what does the term mean? If it is one that can be properly applied to the *Philoctetes,* or even to Euripides' own *Ion,* then we can hardly use it here, nor are we complimenting Euripides if we do. It is a good and effective scene, but for a study it is altogether too easy. There is a dramatic clash between opposed characters, but there is no movement of mind, no

action and reaction beyond that of blank opposition. Even
their relations to Neoptolemus are touched on only in the
most objective way ; there is no sign that either of them has
any affection for him, or he for them, except that he finds
Hermione intolerable, Andromache not. Euripides, we may
be quite sure, would learn with dismay that such a scene was
being held up as an example of his ' psychology '. It has
the ' psychology ' of melodrama, nothing but white and black ;
and rightly so, for Hermione is nothing but Spartan arrogance
and narrow-minded cruelty, and Euripides draws her pure
and strong not to make a domestic study but to denounce
Sparta. As the stage-complement of such a figure, Andromache herself can hardly be subtly drawn, nor is she. She is
middle-aged, and is a very tragic, or more accurately a very
pathetic figure, but the incessant complaint that she is un-
sympathetic and argues like a barrister misses the point.
Euripides drew his Phaedra, and his Helen, and he could
have drawn a subtle Andromache—but the play did not need
it and would not tolerate it. Her part is to be as unlike
Hermione as possible and, by talking sense, to show what
nonsense Hermione has delivered.

To Andromache's character we shall return ; we may now
consider the sacrifice-scene, the pathos of which, according to
Hyslop's remarkable Introduction, is one of the qualities which
save the play from worthlessness. There is pathos, and the
scene is very moving—but how did Euripides intend us to be
moved ? Antigone's self-sacrifice is tragic ; Andromache's
is not tragic but monstrous, designed not to display Andromache in the quality of tragic heroine but to make our
blood boil. Andromache of course puts her child before herself ; she is heroic and noble—but our blood is boiling. The
villainy of Menelaus, not the nobility of Andromache, has the
first claim on our emotions. This is what Euripides intended
and this is what he has done. When Andromache begins her
speech with ' O Reputation, Reputation . . .' is she marring
the situation, chilling its dramatic warmth, giving way to
Euripides' love of rhetoric and sophistry ? If we suppose
that Euripides thought he was writing another *Antigone*, such
must be our verdict ; but in fact Euripides thought the matter

of this speech before he thought of Andromache. She is there not to be herself but to say what she was invented for. The whole incident is conceived melodramatically, as the theme demanded. Andromache is simply caught in a trap ; she can be noble or ignoble, that is all. There is no room for any but the most elementary character-drawing, and that is all Euripides offers.

After the arrogance, cruelty and treachery of Sparta comes Spartan stupidity. Menelaus has come to defend his daughter's conjugal dignity and happiness ; he so acts that he must infallibly destroy both. What he cannot see for himself Andromache points out with clarity and force (hence her cleverness), that when Neoptolemus returns he must drive her out of his house, and who will take her then ? The answer to this question is Orestes, but we do not know that yet. Menelaus is stupid and overreaches himself ; he crumples up before Peleus, and Hermione, left unprotected, tries to commit suicide. ' I am tired out ', says the Nurse, with Euripidean humour, ' trying to keep her from hanging herself ' (815).

' Avec le vers 765 on s'attendrait à voir finir le drame ', remarks Méridier ; but the real drama is the Spartan mind, not the exciting story of Andromache and her son, and Euripides has more revelations to make. There was another legend about Neoptolemus which made it possible (with enough invention and determination) to bring in Orestes as a mean schemer and murderer. His name has been carefully kept back ; suddenly he enters, telling lies. First he pretends that he is on his way to Dodona and is only paying a friendly call on the cousin who was once betrothed to him, but quite soon (911 ff.) his questions begin to run with a surprising aptness in the direction of a possible murder. Hermione clutches at him like a drowning person at a straw ; now he blandly informs her that he knew about it all the time ; he has been waiting about, with a bodyguard, to see whether she would remain in Phthia or, ' terrified with the murder of the captive woman ', would prefer to run away, in which case ' I will take and deliver you to your father. Kinship is a strangely powerful thing ; when one is in trouble there is nothing better than a friend in the family.' Menelaus' stupidity has given Orestes a chance to blackmail him, and Hermione's hysterical jibe (170 ff.) that Andromache lives with the man who slew her husband is savagely turned against herself.

So Orestes disappears into the murk from which he came, and the completion of the picture of Spartan ways is left to the Messenger. The recital of the murder is a masterly piece of work, fit to be compared with the description of the gallant slaughter of Aegisthus by the same hand in the *Electra*. No element of the sinister and hateful is wanting ; it is a fine climax to a deadly play.[1]

A play however cannot end with a messenger-speech, and the time has passed when it can end with a funeral hymn. Moreover, that would sound very incongruous after this exceedingly unlyrical drama. To bring back Andromache would be no true solution of the problem ; she is not the heroine and centre of interest of the play, only the first victim of the Spartan machinations. We are left, when Orestes hurries after Menelaus, to contemplate the wreckage they have created, and the symbol of this wreckage must be Peleus. The war fought for Menelaus' wife robbed him of his son ; now Orestes has murdered his grandson, and Menelaus very nearly his great-grandson.

But by this time our blood has boiled sufficiently. There is indeed no catharsis, but there may be a quietly conventional ending ; there is no justice, but—in a play—there may be consolation prizes. So, as there is no catharsis, that is finality, in the emotions evoked by the action, finality is secured externally. Thetis is brought down to comfort Peleus with hopes of golden immortality and to make permanent arrangements for Andromache and the child.

In some respects this is one of the most interesting of Euripides' plays, composite in plot like the other tragedies, but vigorous in action and definite in characterization like the later melodramas : a tragedy in essence but a melodrama in execution. Unity of action is always an artistic virtue, but

---

[1] I cannot understand how Mr. D. L. Page (*Greek Poetry and Life*, p. 227) can be moderately friendly to Orestes and excuse this slow and intelligent murder as a *crime passionnel*. In Mediterranean latitudes passion, surely, is expected to work more swiftly.

it is a philosophical necessity only when the springs of the tragic action are concentrated in a single tragic hero, whose action is to be the tragedy. Here we have composite wickedness and composite suffering which allow, logically, a composite plot. They do not, however, compel us to admire that plot, and as the *Andromache* does rely on its action much more than the other tragedies of this group, the 'lack of unity' is correspondingly more obtrusive. It falls between two stools, and there is force in the ancient criticism 'The play is of the second rank '.[1]

It has however its own logic. Mahaffy called it a tragedy which ' has the air of a political pamphlet '; we might more correctly call it a political pamphlet which has the air of a tragedy. It would be an exaggeration, but it would save us from the error of labelling as ' faults '—and most inexplicable ones—features that were essential to Euripides' purpose. He did not set out to write ' a Greek Tragedy ' and then spoil it by crude characterization and untimely political references.

But although in this play Euripides' indignation burns so fiercely against Sparta, he does not become a propagandist nor cease entirely to be a tragic poet. We shall deal with the chorus later, but we may note here that the first stasimon, on the Trojan War, and the fourth, on the miseries which that war brought to each side impartially, are much more general in their tone than the play as a whole. They establish contact with the poet of the *Troades*.[2]

---

[1] Second Argument.

[2] On the date of the *Andromache* I have not thought it necessary to say anything here. The political references in the play are too vague to produce anything but discussion, but it is perhaps permissible to advance two general considerations. (1) If we assume (as we well may) that it was some particular act of inhumanity, villainy or bad faith in Sparta that produced this explosion, the treatment of the Plataean prisoners (cf. Menelaus' treatment of Andromache) is antecedently far more probable an occasion than the campaign of Brasidas. The bad faith of Brasidas was of the kind that irritates politicians ; Plataea of the kind to rouse poets. (2) The Scholiast, whom Méridier still prefers to follow, put the play ' at about the beginning of the War '. That Euripides should first have written this anti-Spartan play, and then, with deeper experience of the war should have written the deeper anti-war

8. THE HERACLES   This is certainly the most puzzling of the
plays of Euripides which have reached us undamaged, so
puzzling that it is surprising that it has reached us at all.   We
owe its preservation, probably, to the astonishing force of the
madness scene.   There can be no question that this is the
most powerful thing of the kind that Euripides ever wrote,
and that the last part of the play is, in a very different way,
equally impressive ; but what is the meaning of the play
as a whole ?   Is it a whole ?

The plot is more orthodox than that of the *Hecuba,* in that
it is based on one story, not two, but (like the plots of the
Troades and *Suppliant Women*) it is not a dramatic unity.
Between the peril of Heracles' dependants, with which we
start, and the madness that descends on Heracles, there is no
connexion but juxtaposition, and the last scene, introduced by
the opportune arrival of Theseus, has no strict causal connexion with the previous one.

Since the play falls into three distinct parts, it is not surprising that attempts have been made to find, in the play itself, a dramatic theme which will make it both a unity and
a logically developed action.   It has been put forward that
the play is a study of a genius that is close to madness ; that
Heracles is subject to delusions which turn great but not
superhuman achievements into miraculous ' Labours ', and
that the madness scene presents us with the tragic results of
the last of these storms.   Abnormality indeed had a fascination
for Euripides.   We find it already in the *Medea,* and the
thread can be continued through the *Electra* to the *Orestes.*
There is then nothing inherently improbable in some form of
the delusional theory here, especially as Heracles himself
recognizes (vv. 1258 ff.) a taint in his blood which might

---

tragedies, is a development as convincing as such things can be.
Pohlenz, in an interesting passage (p. 304), argues for the campaign of Brasidas (though the evidence from Tharyps is a little
exiguous) and suggests that Euripides refrained from putting the
play on the stage.   If we were certain that the play was published
but not produced, it would be a tempting guess that the name
Democrates which Callimachus found inscribed as the author's
name was a *nom de guerre* chosen by Euripides.   It would not be
unsuitable to the occasion.

point to an unbalanced mind. Nevertheless such an explanation of the play involves real difficulties. Lycus, who alone expresses doubt of the genuineness of the labours, is presented as so preposterous a character that it is difficult to think that Euripides intended him to represent the normal sane man. The natural interpretation of what Theseus says and does is that Heracles did rescue him from Hades. Heracles' outburst of rage against Lycus might be accepted as an indication of frenzy in one known to be insane, but I agree with M. Parmentier that it cannot of itself prove insanity; it proves only that Heracles was not the man to remain calm and reasonable under extreme provocation.

If, provisionally, we look for another explanation what can we find? Of the straightforward view M. Parmentier makes an excellent exposition in his introduction (ed. Budé). Euripides' idea was to purify the crude popular pictures of Heracles, to give a Heracles who ' n'est pas seulement le bienfaiteur qui met sa force au service de l'humanité ; il est bon fils, époux fidèle, père tendre, ami devoué, et enfin capable de supporter noblement une souffrance morale plus cruelle que toute douleur physique'. The madness comes—not from Hera, for that is a ' poets' lie '—but from fate. After his life of labours Heracles finds himself at a cross-road where he has to choose between a life of torture and salvation through suicide ; he has the greatness to choose life. The sense of the tragedy is given in Amphitryon's words (106)—' ne point persévérer est d'un lache '. The last victory of Heracles is the most heroic of all, a fitting climax to the play.

This interpretation accepts the labours as real, and it gives to a play which makes a purely tragic impression a purely tragic meaning, but it hardly goes deep enough, and it does not seem to account for the whole play. This conception of Heracles is, I think, the right one, but is the play then substantially only a portrait, its catastrophe only a means of heightening its colours, and its theme that a great hero is a great hero? This is perhaps to put it crudely ; it may be urged that the *Tyrannus* is only a portrait. Perhaps so, but it is one whose frame is nothing less than Sophocles' conception of human life and human destiny ; what conception un-

derlies this picture of Heracles ?   Secondly, it is a little difficult, on this view, to see the bearing of the first part of the
play on the whole.   M. Parmentier calls it ' the first panel of
a kind of triptych ', which is just enough, if one remembers
that it is restating, not explaining, the difficulty ; for a play
has no business to be a triptych.

If we accept the reality of the Labours and all that goes
with them, we shall have to look for an interpretation that will
explain the connexion between the first part and the rest, and
will give a reasonable account of the ' Hera ' whom Heracles
himself appears to rationalize out of the play.   If there is no
logical connexion between the first part and the rest—and
certainly none is obvious—if, that is, the play really is a kind
of triptych, we must look for some tragic and dramatic idea
which makes it a unity in thought and not merely by juxtaposition—such an idea as makes a unity of the Hecuba-
diptych.

We may begin by asking what can be made of the first
panel.   It is indeed a strange affair, the stranger in that it is
practically all free invention.   Lycus and his usurpation were
created for the occasion, but to what end ?   Euripides has
rarely invented so freely, yet is there in the whole of Greek
drama a set of scenes that can rival these in debility ?   For
consider what they contain—remembering that aphorisms like
that of v. 106 [1] may adorn but cannot create drama.   Once
more the play begins with suppliants at an altar, a situation
that is explained in an elaborate prologue.   The prologue we
easily accept as a convention, and after recent experiences we
do not perhaps expect much movement in the first scene.
Megara follows Amphitryon.   Her first twenty verses are
moving—the description of the excitement when some one
knocks at the door is one of the best things of its kind in
Euripides—but the rest of the scene is flat.   If we hope that
the chorus will introduce some decisive motive, as it does for
instance in the *Hecuba*, we are disappointed.   Amphitryon
has called himself a ' useless old man ', hardly to be counted
among men, and the incoming chorus is no better ; indeed
their two strophes are nothing but a description of their physi-

[1] ' Ne point persévérer est d'un lache.'

cal feebleness. Was Euripides really so obsessed with old
age as this ?

At last a man appears—but he is only Lycus, a melodramatic
swashbuckler, in whose mind and character we can take no
very prolonged interest, whatever may be the case with his
actions. But even as a strong man Lycus is disappointing.[1]
He begins rather weakly by assuring the suppliants that their
hopes in Heracles are ill-placed ; Heracles was only a boaster
and a liar, and now he is dead ; no hero—only a coward with
a bow. Such an imputation from such a man might well be
disdained as not a thing to take seriously, and Amphitryon
does in fact take a high line with Lycus. A great speech on
the Labours would be beyond Lycus' deserts, and in any case
the substance of it is being reserved for the chorus. Amphitryon has therefore little to contribute to the drama. The
debate on bowmen and spearmen keeps us going for a time ;
the subject is just relevant, and it was topical, so that if
dramatic movement had to be manufactured, it was good
enough raw material, but obviously it is manufactured. We
have (165 ff.) a tragic idea characteristic of this group of
plays, that political necessity is held to excuse murder : ' Not
cruelty but caution ' is very like Thucydides on the Corcyrean
affair ; but still the scene as a whole seems to be groping after
something dramatic.

At first it seems to be Lycus' part to be the *contemptor
divom*, to trample on the rights of suppliants and the sanctity
of altars, but though he may be Menelaus' equal in wickedness, he falls far short in resourcefulness. Once more, if we
are looking forward to a strong scene of treachery or violence,
even of bluster, we are disappointed. Lycus summons his
men, he is very angry and very wicked ; he will burn the suppliants out of their refuge to show them who is King now—
and to do this he sends some of the men to Helicon, some to
Parnassus, to find firewood. Even so, instead of making an
effective exit on this not very high note, he remains on the
stage looking fierce, until seventy verses later, it occurs to
Amphitryon to address him again. After the forceful-feeble

[1] Compare his entry with the impressive first appearance of Creon
in the *Antigone*.

gesture of Lycus the chorus is defiant but quite impotent ; it has lost the strength of its good right hand.   Still, it can boast of one achievement—it puts in 22 verses instead of the usual couplet between the one actor's speech and the next.   After the chorus, Megara holds the breach for 35 verses.   She despairs of Heracles' return, and Verrall made much of this, but we need see in it nothing more than the barest minimum of dramatic movement.   If both she and Amphitryon were optimistic, how could dialogue go on ?   There is no sign of firewood yet, and none of a new dramatic motif, such as the comparable scene in the *Andromache* enjoys in plenty.   After Megara, the chorus is feeble again, and turns to the feeble Amphitryon.   He asks that he and Megara may at least be slain first, to be spared the sight of the children's death, but Megara is more helpful to a dramatist in difficulties :   may they be allowed to enter their own house to put on funeral garb ?   Lycus, who has been standing feebly by for nearly a hundred verses, gives permission, Amphitryon makes a bitter attack on Zeus, the stage is cleared, and the chorus comes to our rescue with an ode on the Labours—and surely, when a Euripidean chorus goes on for a hundred verses, it is a portent.   After the ode Lycus' victims reappear, dressed for the grave—a grisly effect which would remain long in the mind ; a dramatic thrill at last.   Against this horrible background Megara makes a long and not ineffective speech of farewell, Amphitryon a supreme appeal to Zeus—and at length Heracles appears, putting an end to five hundred verses of drama which few, I imagine, have re-read for pleasure.

Surely dramatic feebleness like this is a remarkable thing in the poet of the *Medea* and the *Andromache* ?   It is quite clear that had Euripides merely wanted a dramatic scene or two to make a first panel he could have done much better with the same material.   Amphitryon is conspicuously impotent among all Euripides' old men, and he is joined with a chorus of other old men whose chief part seems to be to explain that they would like to have one but are too weak. Why, for example, could Amphitryon not have borrowed some of Teiresias' impressiveness ?   Why need Megara remain so shadowy a creation ?   Lycus too is made not only completely wicked, so that he can have no moral struggles with himself, but also completely secure, so that he can find no opposition except from those unable to oppose. How easy it would have been, if a dramatic scene had been the object of Euripides' lavish invention here, to threaten Lycus with heaven's wrath, to make him uneasy but defiant, Amphitryon powerless but impressive.

This absence of the dramatic is clearly the result of deliberate choice ; it contrasts with ordinary dramatic incapacity as the contrived ugliness of many an ' architect-built ' house does with the result of a mere builder's inspiration. If Euripides has made Lycus much less interesting than he might have done and the action much less arresting, the only explanation can be that he did not want our minds to be intent on Lycus and his doings. Verrall (a sound destructive critic) was impressed with the dramatic emptiness of much of these scenes, and held that Amphitryon talked merely to gain time. This is not enough ; everybody does, and Lycus connives at it by sending his men to the confines of Boeotia for wood. It looks as if it was Euripides who wanted to gain time, or rather as if he were writing to a programme, as it were, one which (as happens with programmes) does not at the moment suit his medium.

We are bound to look for some explanation of this ' panel ' which will make it a real though possibly a discrete part of the whole play—using in fact the assumption that the play is a triptych, but only as the old trilogy was, or the *Troades*, each part contributing clearly and decisively to one unifying idea. If our general theory of Euripides' present method of construction is true, it will not dismay us to find no organic, Aristotelian connexion between this part and what follows, but it will dismay us if we cannot see in this part a contribution to the whole comparable in importance to the madness scene itself. Moreover, as we are going on the assumption that Euripides was both a sincere artist and a competent dramatist, our explanation must explain too not only what he does here, but also what he conspicuously refrains from doing. It must show us (as simply calling it a ' first panel ' does not) why

Euripides is found fighting with one hand tied behind his back.

I cannot see that a delusional theory helps us. This would demand that the believers in Heracles, themselves deluded, should be offset by someone else who is clear-sighted, a Lycus who may be as cruel as you please but who is at least shrewd and worthy of credence—a Creon in fact. If too we had a chorus sympathetic but capable of independent judgement which was not deluded either, we should have a group natural to the idea and capable of a dramatic development far different from what we have. If the true explanation is one which should demonstrate that Euripides had to do what he did, and nothing else, it does not seem to lie here.

Is it not plain that Euripides is, in some sense, doing here what he did with his Adrastus, namely making his point as absolute as he can, pushing it to the logical extreme? The villainy of Lycus, the impotence of both Amphitryon and the chorus—to say nothing of Megara and the children—are made as extreme as possible ; obviously in order that the danger they stand in may be unqualified. Lycus is nothing to Euripides but imminent danger ; that is why he is so baldly characterized. The others are nothing but persons dear to the hero—his tenderness to them is mentioned more than once, and soon will be strikingly displayed ; that is why they are no more than sketched in. The impotence of the chorus, the sheer physical difficulty they find in reaching the place of the action, the indifference of the rest of the city, the inaccessibility of Lycus to all scruples or fear, the fact that these weapons are barely used against him—all these things, each a nuisance to the mere making of drama, are designed to underline this danger. The scenes are flat because, we may say, Euripides is really dramatizing a negative, the absence of the great man. During his absence Thebes has fallen to a buccaneer ; for lack of his strong arm his father-in-law the King has perished, and soon too will his father, wife, and children. They are entirely defenceless and their danger is absolute.

What is the point? That Heracles is in fact no hero? That he has been neglectful towards his dependants in leav-

ing them so unprotected ? But he left them in Creon's care ;
why should he foresee his overthrow ? Besides, he trusted
to Theban gratitude (558–69) ; he is surprised to find his
house so unbefriended. Are we then to blame not Heracles
but Thebes ? Perhaps the continuation will help us to decide.[1]

In a short series of questions Heracles learns the meaning
of the horrible sight that confronts him. The extremity of
the danger is emphasized, the barbarity of Lycus and the
indifference of the city—all leading to that passage (562 ff.)
which has been taken to be the beginning of a frenzy.[2] The
threats are violent, but are they more violent than the extreme
provocation would warrant, if we take Heracles to be a man
of ' temperament ' whose genius ran to heroic, not to intellectual achievement ? ' Farewell, my Labours ! I was wrong
then to give myself to you rather than to these.' Heracles
may, in the past, have been subject to delusions, but at this
moment he must be clear-sighted ; he sees, tragically, that if
the safety of those he loves is to be his concern, his whole
course has been a disastrous error.

This critical passage continues with Amphitryon's account
of the revolution that has taken place in Thebes ; Lycus came
in with the help of a faction of ruined aristocrats whose object
was to plunder those who were still wealthy. The brevity of
this—it is dismissed in five verses—warns us that it is only
explanatory, of no significance to the play as a whole. It
explains Amphitryon's caution ; Lycus has many supporters,

---

[1] Admittedly, the audience—if the play is a good one—should not
have been as puzzled as we are at this point, but the audience
would have had the advantage of seeing this part of the play presented by one who did know what was to come and had interpreted the first part accordingly.

[2] In v. 575 Heracles refers to Amphitryon as *gerouta* (' old man'
instead of the expected ' father '). Murray, rightly defending the
text, remarks, ' Videtur iam delirans mortalem abnuere patrem,
tum monitu Chori se comprimere.' But then, since in v. 1365 he
more explicitly refers to Zeus as his father, he must be still mad ;
which is absurd. The *monitus* of the chorus is only a general remark that a son should protect ' his aged father ' (*patera presbyn*),
and ' se comprimere ' is obtained from the simple verse, ' In what
way am I being too hasty, father ? '

so that it is not merely a question of cutting off Lycus' head and delivering Thebes from an oppressor. Heracles' first instinctive threat (565 ff.) would really embroil him with the dominant faction in the city, and this neither Amphitryon nor Heracles is prepared to face. Heracles is willing to take the cautious line ; indeed he has already done so, in entering the city privily. Not the act of a fairy-story hero, one who, we are told, with his own hand routed the forces of the Minyans ? We need perhaps take no offence at the contrast between this caution and the threat which he uttered at the height of his rage, that he would kill Lycus and all the Thebans who had proved themselves ungrateful to him, but the contrast with the Minyan story (220–1) is more serious. Is the latter therefore untrue, or is it enough to say that Heracles was a hero who would not run a greater risk than he need, or is there some further meaning in this detail ? We must bear it in mind.

Amphitryon's advice is followed by ten lines of dialogue which hold up the action somewhat. In them we are told (*a*) that Heracles did go to Hades and did find Cerberus ; (*b*) that Cerberus is left at Hermione (a natural place, as it was the seat of a chthonian cult, and of an entrance to Hades) ; (*c*) that Eurystheus, far from possessing Cerberus, does not yet know of Heracles' return from Hades ; and (*d*) that Heracles was so long in Hades because he added to his original mission the rescue of Theseus. Theseus is not indeed still with him, having gone home to Athens.

If we accept the story at all, these details, and the interruption of the action that they entail, are easily explicable ; (*d*) is wanted to prepare for Theseus' arrival at the end of the play, (*b*) is wanted to explain (*c*), which is itself necessary for the madness-scene, where Heracles imagines himself to be at Argos attacking Eurystheus. This visit to Argos is very much on his mind.

The following fifteen verses, with which Heracles leads his family into the house, are not easy to reconcile with the *iam delirans* theory. ' Do not grasp my robe so ; I shall not fly away ! ' ' Come—like little boats towed by a big one.' [1] Here surely we have the very accents of gentle and under-

[1] Tragically echoed at v. 1424.

standing comfort, homely pleasantries designed to banish
acute terror. If this is not enough, 'Were you then *so* near to
death ?' A moment surely of utter clarity and peace.[1]

The ode that follows this scene is a disjointed composition,
and the most irrelevant to be found in this group of plays.[2]
It closes however successfully on Heracles, and the tone is
important. 'He is Zeus' son, but his worth[3] surpasses his
birth ; his labours have freed men's lives from danger, for he
has destroyed the monsters that terrified them.' We may
choose between this, supported as it is by the second ode, and
Lycus' vulgar insinuations. If Lycus is meant to be right,
Euripides has made it difficult to choose correctly.

The slaying of Lycus need not detain us. It is straightforward and effective, particularly in the rasping irony of Amphitryon's exit. The fourth ode expresses the unrestrained
joy of the loyal chorus in the triumph of Heracles ; 'The new
King is gone, the old King reigns.'[4]

Now comes the second part of the play, and the second
puzzle. With a kind of second prologue Iris appears, a
female counterpart of Hermes, leading Lyssa, Frenzy, to attack Heracles. Lyssa herself is reluctant to do so horrible a
thing ; she goes so far as to say that she would like to turn
Iris from this wicked path, but she must obey.[5] Heracles is
driven mad, and, imagining himself in the house of Eurystheus, he slays Megara, his children, and very nearly his
father. The fit passes ; Heracles sane contemplates with horror what he did mad, and would have killed himself forthwith
but for the sudden arrival of Theseus. In the end however
he takes the finer course ; he will endure to live, and, Theseus
offering him a refuge and honour, he goes with him to Athens.

What view are we to take of these extremely unusual and

[1] We must no doubt be prepared to hear medical testimony that
madness does come and go like this, but medicine is not drama.

[2] See below, p. 277.

[3] *Arete*—conjectural but sound enough.

[4] This, coming immediately before the catastrophe, reminds one
of the hyporchemata of Sophocles.

[5] This inevitably recalls the merciless deities, more cruel than
man, in the *Hippolytus*.

moving scenes? If we knew Euripides to have been a simpleton, we might perhaps say that he was giving a dramatic version of a current legend and leave it at that; but Euripides was not a simpleton. If he were a minor dramatist, we might say that he was concerned to rehabilitate the character of a national hero, who had been badly used, especially in vase-painting; but the motive is too small for Euripides, especially for the *Heracles*. To call attention to the nobility of the characterization and to the sublimity of the Heracles who emerges from these fires is just, but it does not explain the connexion with the first part of the play. Moreover, Sophocles gives us a hardly inferior picture of moral grandeur in the close of the *Tyrannus*—but how much more than this there is in it!

Fortunately the poet himself has taken care that we should not adopt here the most simple of the possible interpretations. The last scene in which Theseus wins Heracles from his first thoughts of suicide, is more than a conventional epilogue. Theseus is a highly intelligent as well as a generous man; the ordinary taboos that surround homicide mean nothing to him, he knows that a mortal cannot pollute the gods, that human threats cannot affect them. His chief concern is that his hero, Heracles, should not admit defeat like an ordinary man, that the benefactor and mighty friend of Greece should not die *amathia*, from blind folly (vv. 1248–54). Heracles' reply to this is to give an outline of his life-story, showing how it has been one long persecution by Hera,[1] culminating in the present disaster; he may no longer live in Thebes, and no other city will receive him. It is a speech which, like this whole part of the play, implicitly, and in several passages explicitly,[2] assumes the truth of the Hera-story. Theseus accepts it too (1311–12)—indeed, his first words were 'This is Hera's work' (1191); but he comforts and tries to strengthen Heracles by saying, in his character of intelligent

---

[1] A contrast to what he says and implies at vv. 575 ff. ('Farewell, my Labours,' &c.), but there is no real contradiction. Events have now taught him to think bitterly and angrily about those imposed tasks whose performance had in fact interested him.

[2] E.g. 1127 f., 1243, 1253, and of course the Iris-Lyssa scene.

man, that it is *tyche*, Fortune, a power to which even the
gods are subject ; the gods commit crimes of all sorts—so it is
said ; why then should you, a mortal, think too much of
this ?[1] And as for the hopelessness of the future, Theseus is
willing to repay the debt he owes Heracles by giving him a
home, honour, wealth. ' When the gods favour a man he has
no need of friends, for the god's help is enough, when he
gives it.' To which Heracles remarkably answers, ' That,
alas ! does not touch my fate ; but I do not believe, nor ever
shall, that the gods commit crime, for if God is really God he
needs nothing. These are poets' miserable tales.' But Heracles is a very imperfect Platonist, for he does not draw the
obvious conclusion—nor does Theseus, less acute here than he
is in the *Suppliant Women*—for the speech ends, ' We are all,
by a cruel fate, victims of one blow of Hera's '.

This is magnificent. For once, at least, Euripides' intellectualism is put entirely at the service of his dramatic invention.
His point, instead of being made in an uncharacteristic
speech, is made the basis of a most lifelike contrast of characters. The fine and intelligent Theseus is intelligent only to
a certain point, instinctively intelligent rather than intellectual
—for example, he has never thought clearly about the gods.
Heracles on the other hand is right where Theseus is wrong,
but again by instinct, a moral instinct ; he has never tested his
instinct by his intelligence, for although his moral instinct
makes him disbelieve the crude legends that Theseus refers
to, he goes on believing in his ' Hera '. The contrast between
the two great men is absorbing.

But what does the passage mean to the play ? It forces us
to the conclusion—which in any case is obvious to any one
who knows his Euripides—that to call such a Hera a Deity is a
contradiction. But this conclusion is kept out of the play.
In the *Heracles* Hera is as real an agent as Aphrodite and
Artemis are in the *Hippolytus* ; in that play the goddesses
appear in person, therefore, dramatically, they must unquestionably exist. No one supposes that Euripides believed in a
' Goddess ' Aphrodite who adorned the sky with her ravishing

[1] This is essentially the same argument, though couched in a
different tone, as that urged by the Nurse to Phaedra.

beauty and visited Cyprus, yet Aphrodite is terribly real, both
in the play and in Euripides' thought. Zeus and Hera too
are dramatically real. The co-paternity of Zeus is accepted
by Heracles sane (1263) as by Heracles under suspicion of
madness (575), and the chorus also believes in it (805).[1]
But if the co-paternity of Zeus is dramatically real, the hatred
of Hera is mythologically inevitable. Heracles is of more
than mortal birth, as also he is of more than ordinary genius
and achievement. The genius derives, dramatically, from
Zeus ; it follows almost automatically that Hera must wish to
destroy it. While Heracles, driven by his flaming genius, is
performing his god-given task of taming the earth for mankind ' Fate protected him, nor would Zeus allow Hera or me
(Lyssa) to do him injury '. But genius of this order is, it
seems, more than Nature can long endure ; the gift from
Zeus carries with it the inevitable hatred of Hera, and destruction comes. He who was to the chorus the benefactor of
humanity, to Lyssa the one who subdued land and sea and
upheld the religion of the gods, to Theseus his rescuer and
' the mighty friend of man '[2]—such a one, deserving a twofold
honour, one from men and one from the gods, meets a two-

---

[1] See Masqueray's note *ad loc.*—The double paternity, naturally,
involves slight confusion, and rationalists who read Euripides as if
he were Bradshaw will not fail to point out that the story is improbable, that Euripides could not have believed it, and that
Heracles contradicts himself about his fathers. If Euripides had
invented a second comic character, like Lycus, to point out lucidly
that a man is unlikely to have two fathers, we should have to take
the rationalism seriously. But Euripides does nothing of the kind ;
he means something by his Zeus, and the literal difficulties he
simply ignores.

[2] Vv. 698 ff., 849 ff., 1221 f.—It is this aspect of Heracles that is
emphasized in the long ode (348 ff.). The Labours are held up
not as feats of strength and endurance but as a purification of the
earth from noxious monsters. Heracles freed the precinct of Zeus
from the lion, slew the Centaurs that ravaged the fields of Thessaly,
slew the horses of Diomed ' that devoured men ', Cycnus ' who
killed strangers ', the Lernean Hydra that ' slew many ', and he
' entered the recesses of the sea, assuring calm for men '. There is
no word spared for the intensity of the struggles, the heroic
strength displayed, the miraculous nature of the achievements.
This is not the highly personal Heracles who interested Sophocles.

fold betrayal. While he is absent from his labours those dearest to him are thrown into the extremity of danger ; when the Labours are finished, his ' destiny ' ceases to protect him, and Nature destroys what she has produced and used—or would have destroyed him had he not met, in Theseus, a man nearly as great as himself, one who successfully challenges him to show that the greatness of a great man can triumph even over the blind hostility of ' the gods '.

In so tragic a conception lies the unity of the action, and from this point of view we may find relatively insignificant certain details which, if the play is wrongly treated as realistic, are certainly obtrusive and difficult. We should observe that a play, even one of Euripides', does not become realistic merely because it may mention spades or wheelbarrows. Orestes' Nurse does not make the *Choephori* a realistic play, nor do we find it difficult to believe in the Furies because she has just been talking of babies' napkins. The political reference in this play similarly does not mean that the whole play is to be considered politically, and the very decrepit arrival of the chorus is not a piece of amusing but quite meaningless realism ; on the contrary, it is a most non-realistic abstraction, defencelessness made manifest. Euripides removes himself from the realism of Sophocles not by lyrical intensity (like Aeschylus) but by his abstract and schematic handling. The method may not be so good or harmonious—that is another question ; it is his method. It is, I think, in this light that we must consider the Minyan exploit (see above, p. 255). Take the play literally and it is almost an impossible contradiction —but then, if we take the play literally it makes very little sense at all ; it is surely a figurative statement of Heracles' unqualified claim to Theban gratitude, conventionalized as the character of Lycus and the whole opening situation is conventionalized. So too with Heracles' secret return ; it does not mean that Heracles is to be taken as the discredited leader of the Liberal party in Thebes, but it is the expression of one half of his tragedy. Instead of returning from his last Labour in triumph to an enthusiastic city, he slinks home privily, already, so far as Thebes is concerned, the outcast which soon, by Hera's vindictiveness, he does become.

CHAPTER IX

THE TECHNIQUE OF THE EURIPIDEAN TRAGEDY

1. INTRODUCTION   In the last chapter we tried to show that
the structure of the Euripidean tragedy differs radically from
that of the Sophoclean because Euripides saw the tragic in a
totally different way.   He saw tragic hamartia and tragic action not as part of the character of the individual, leading to
the downfall of the individual, but, in a more abstract way, as
a disastrous element in our common human nature which
leads to suffering, in which the guilty person may share or not.
The tragedies fall into two groups, the *Medea* and *Hippolytus*,
and the war-plays or social tragedies.   Even in the *Medea*, a
play which seems to depend entirely on Medea's own will and
tragic personality, we saw that there is, at least in analysis, a
perceptible distinction between Medea's personal tragedy and
Euripides' tragic conception ; we saw that if the wider tragic
reference is not apprehended, the heroine and the play become rather difficult—not far from melodrama, the making of
drama for the sake only of dramatic excitement.   In general,
the characters are regarded as tragic figures in the grip of
something greater than themselves, even when, as in the first
group, this something is an instinctive passion in the highest
degree personal.   Medea's jealousy and vindictiveness are not
made objective in a goddess, but for all that Euripides is
thinking of them as he thinks of the love of Phaedra and the
fanatical anti-love of Hippolytus, as psychological forces
which take entire possession of their victims and drive them
where they will.   There is not, except by dramatic accident,
any struggle in the soul of the victim between this passion and
another, no suggestion that the passion is the one thing that
ruins a nature otherwise excellent ; to Euripides it is a universal force which shows its disastrous power through this victim,
something which the end of the *Medea* suggests and the prologue to the *Hippolytus* declares to be an external dramatic

agent. This, and not the character, begins to direct the action. In other words, the poet, no longer working out the inevitable action of a tragic character from the first conjuncture of situation with character to the catastrophe, can himself step in to manipulate the plot in the interests of his real tragedy. Hence the ' irrational ' in the *Medea*, and in the *Hippolytus* the complete supersession of Phaedra by Hippolytus.

We saw that in the second group this distinction between the outer and the inner tragedy becomes greater and more explicit. The tragic beings of Euripides' stage are now victims in a more literal sense, victims of cruelty and oppression ; and as cruelty and oppression may be exercised in one play by several people—as by Odysseus, Agamemnon and Menelaus indifferently—and endured by several persons indifferently, the plot becomes more schematic than it was when the victimizing force at least was one that proceeded through only one person, a Medea, or was made objective in an Aphrodite. Now the poet may manipulate his plot still more freely ; still greater is the necessity, if we wish to explain the tragic unity that we feel, to look through the action to the underlying idea.

On such a basis not Euripides' structure only, but also the whole of his tragic technique becomes intelligible. He can never be explained on Aristotelian grounds because he was writing an un-Aristotelian tragedy, and unless we see what his real approach to tragedy was, we shall have to call him incompetent, with Schlegel, or suppose that he was so busy dropping warm tears that he could not stay to make decent plays.[1] The discovery of a logical method in Euripides will make no difference to the appreciation of his plays ; those who cannot feel the essential unity of the *Troades* will continue not to feel it. The business of criticism is not to help us to feel, but to explain how the artist contrives to make us feel. It can show us, for example, that the unity of the *Troades* does not depend on the constant presence of Hecuba, but on something much more important.

[1] A recent writer on Euripides has found it possible to attribute the Euripidean prologue to nothing more profound, or convincing, than carelessness.

On Euripides' use of plot enough was said in the last chapter. In this one we shall resume and expand what we have seen of his characterization, and then consider his use of the Chorus, his rhetoric and dialectic, his dramatic style, and those famous prologues and epilogues.

2. CHARACTERIZATION   As with plot, so with characterization ; the second group of tragedies develops tendencies already noticeable in the first. We have argued that the extreme character of Medea or Hippolytus, which we should have to call overdrawn in any other type of drama except Old Comedy, is in these plays logical, because the character is wanted by Euripides only as a vehicle for the passion of which it consists ; and convincing, because the whole trend of the play forces us to contemplate these people as victims in a tragedy greater than their own. Sophocles could not have used Medea, for she would have simplified his tragedy to vanishing point ; Euripides can, because he is projecting one tragic element of human nature into Medea and making it the hamartia which ruins not her only but the social group.

In the second series of tragedies his analytical or schematic treatment of character is given wider scope. The tragic theme is, if we may so generalize it, the social suffering which follows social wrong-doing—the dramatic antithesis to Sophocles' method, an individual fault which leads to individual suffering. Accordingly we have on the one hand the wrongdoers, on the other the wronged, and as the tragic point lies in the suffering rather than in the oppression, the drama concentrates on the victims. This is the reason why we have so many suppliants at altars, defenceless women, children ; many of them but slightly characterized, since their situation is not usually the outcome of their character and is not to be developed or affected by their character. This too explains the high proportion of old men, extremely old and decrepit old men, not as Teiresias or Oedipus of the *Coloneus* are old— Peleus, Amphitryon, Iolaus, Iphis, and the chorus in the *Heracles*. To account for this feature of these plays it has been supposed that Euripides had at his disposal a certain actor peculiarly potent in representing impotence. Did he then have other actors who were very good at being children, others good in women's parts, and none who could play the normal vigorous man—these being all commandeered by Sophocles? No; Euripides, at least in these tragedies, was more than a theatre-man, and we must look for other than mechanical explanations.

Opposed to the victims are the oppressors. As with Jason, so with these; the tragedy, normally, demands only that they be wicked. Their wickedness is not one significant element in their characters, as it is in Creon's, but, so far as we are concerned, it is the whole man. Hence men like Menelaus and Orestes, Lycus, Polymestor, the incredibly silly Adrastus. Certainly we have vivid sketches when the drama demands it —of Agamemnon, the leader who cannot lead for fear of what the army will say, of Odysseus, the politician in difficulties; but then, nobody can read the *Ion* and suppose that Euripides could not make a situation or character when he wanted to. In these plays he did not want to; nothing else can explain the contrast between the vivid full-length portraits of Electra, Orestes, Ion, Creusa, and the shadowy, floating population of the tragedies. Except for Heracles, and for Theseus in the *Suppliant Women*, there is no character who fills a play, and no character who is a normal man, even as normality is understood in drama.

But we can go further: Euripides not only simplifies his characters to a melodramatic degree, all black or all white, but also he can show a disconcerting aloofness from them. This, of course, because he is in fact not writing melodrama. Lycus as the very wicked man, Polyxena as the unspotted victim, do not really fill his mind; he has a vision beyond these, and he is liable to forget them—a fact which perhaps leaves him just as disconcerting as before, but if we are to censure, it is as well to understand first.

Of this aloofness we saw signs already in the anapaestic choral interlude of the *Medea*; in the second group it becomes common. Euripides, to our great surprise, will round upon a sympathetic character in the last act: Hecuba turns fiend, and the vague but intensely sympathetic Alcmena turns oppressor while the dreadful Eurystheus very nearly becomes

sympathetic. Elsewhere characters who ought to be sympathetic are treated with an undercurrent of irony which is a
little upsetting. Iolaus in the *Heracleidae* is to all appearance
a noble and devoted champion of the oppressed ; he is entitled
to a dignified position in any play. Yet Euripides is not
above suggesting that he is a prosy old man (unless, which
God forbid, we suppose that the stream of platitudes with
which he begins was intended by Euripides to be a contribution to moral philosophy) ; Iolaus makes us smile by climbing
into armour which he can hardly support, and finally rides
gallantly, a Greek Quixote, clean out of the play into fairy-
land. So much for Iolaus. Peleus is treated, though not so
thoroughly, in the same spirit. He totters notably, yet makes
stout work with his staff ; he, with all philosophy, morality
and tradition at his call, condescends to obscure abuse against
Menelaus (590 ff.), and elsewhere (693) to demagogic clap-
trap—unless again, with some commentators, we suppose that
Euripides really believed this nonsense about generals and
common soldiers, and did not see that v. 702, 'If only they
had courage and ability together', gave away the whole case.

Such treatment of respectable dramatic personages we can
of course call realism. We can make it characteristic either
of a sour unromantic strain in Euripides, or of a readiness
(which he shared with the rest of Athens) to make fun of
legend. The interesting point however is not that he does
these things, but that he does them here ; and unless we are
prepared to think that he simply could not help himself, like
the inveterate ' humorist', we are bound to look for some
specific justification or dramatic purpose. For the moment
we are suggesting only that the irony must be seen as part of
Euripides' attitude towards his characterization ; it is an off-
shoot of his aloofness. The aloofness goes with the simplification of character, and shows itself in one or two other ways.

We may consider the remarkable series of scenes of sacrifice or self-sacrifice or attempted self-sacrifice that these plays
offer ; there are Polyxena and Hecuba, Macaria, Andromache,
Iolaus. All are treated with dignity and sympathy, but a certain air of conventionality is felt. An entirely unmerited sentence of death is passed, or the heroine is placed in a situation

in which she must act either nobly or ignobly ; she acts nobly, and that, virtually, is the end of it. We admire her motives, but we look in vain (if we insist on looking for the wrong thing) for an intensity of feeling which we can compare with the dramatic thrill of Eteocles' leap to death, or of Antigone's tragic choice, or of Electra's self-dedication to her task. Antigone and Antigone's audience can contemplate her imminent death only tragically ; Polyxena and Macaria make fine speeches about it. Here in fact Euripides is careful to do what he was careful not to do in the *Medea,* namely to avoid ' the revolting '. The sacrifice of Polyxena—like Macaria's—is in Polyxena's own life nothing but a blind blow of fate ; it is, to speak strictly, pathetic and not tragic. Only in the inner tragedy is it tragic, when we see the incident as part of the price which humanity exacts and pays for its superstitions. Hecuba must lament, but nothing would be gained by sending Polyxena to her death screaming ; we should think of the Greeks as bloodthirsty monsters, when the whole point is that they are quite ordinary people who are persuaded to do a dreadful thing by the supposed demands of the political situation. They therefore are presented in a rather favourable light, and their victim is made to go to death willingly, preferring death to life. These all declare—all but Andromache, whose persecutors we *are* to regard as monsters—that they have comparatively nothing to live for ; Antigone has everything to live for, nothing to die for—except her sense of duty. For the same reason Macaria comes forward to offer her life as someone quite unknown to us. Again the tragic value of the incident lies elsewhere—in the disturbing fact, apparently, that Demeter, whoever she is, should have made Demophon's difficult duty harder by demanding such a sacrifice. It is to prevent our taking an interest exclusively in her personal fate that Euripides keeps her in the dark before he needs her.[1]

---

[1] It is this consideration which makes me doubt if we have lost a scene from the *Heracleidae* in which the sacrifice was described. With this method it is perhaps not altogether out of place to compare the practice of detective-story writers. They like to open their tales with a ready-made corpse because a murder is simply

As for Andromache, she is the victim of Spartan treachery, and in this lies the dramatic value of the scene. In giving her life for her child she is acting nobly. In morality, her nobility is the same as Antigone's ; in drama it is entirely different. We must look past her to the villainous Spartan, so that again the scene has a slight air of conventionality ; or, if this is too strong, it has at least a dramatic value quite different from that of Sophocles' scene. Andromache must be simply noble or simply ignoble, and the characterization is limited to this.

This logical refusal of Euripides to engage himself without reserve in the personality of these tragic victims shows itself sometimes, even more strikingly, in downright inconsistency of portraiture. Of this the clearest example is Cassandra. Within the compass of a hundred verses, Euripides gives us two distinct characters. First, we see through the wall of the tent the waving light of her torch—a most imaginative and quite unexpected scene. In a moment the crazed prophetess is before us, singing a wild song through which madness peers as terribly as it does through Ophelia's. Here is a Cassandra who will easily bear comparison either with Ophelia or with Aeschylus' Cassandra ; yet Euripides does not in the least lose himself in his remarkable creation, for presently she is arguing as closely as an Odysseus or an Andromache. If only the speech had been preserved, without its proem, we should not have the slightest idea what sort of a character was making it, still less be able to attribute it to a crazed prophetess.

But we must notice that Euripides is not doing this out of habit or mere inadvertence. He does not treat his Ion like this, nor his Electra ; to their characterization he remains faithful, and if he is unfaithful to his Cassandra it is because he has something more important to do than to be consistent with his characters. It is part of his tragic idea that the lot of the victors is no happier and much less glorious than that of the conquered ; that Troy not only has more honour than Greece, but also less suffering. Someone must sustain this theme ; not the chorus here (although the chorus was given

---

their datum and the detection of the murderer their sole interest. The tragic implications of murder they must avoid.

something similar to say in the *Andromache*) [1] because this chorus is dedicated to a special purpose and cannot make the point clearly enough. Cassandra is chosen. It might possibly have been Andromache or Talthybius, but in fact it is Cassandra. This may be illogical like the irrationality in the *Medea*, but to maintain this tragic paradox was to Euripides vastly more important than to obey the rules of someone else's drama. If we can share in the tragic vision we shall not object to the inconsistency ; if we cannot accept the inconsistency at any price, we had better not read Euripides.

It is idle to cite the Athenian love of disputation to explain such a scene. To the Athenians it would obviously have been interesting to listen to Cassandra arguing through this speech like Socrates defending a paradox against a Callicles ; but we can hardly doubt that it would have been even more exciting had Cassandra continued as she began, mad, torch-waving, and disturbing. Equally idle to attribute the inconsistency to mere force of habit in Euripides. He is conscious of it, so conscious that (as often) he slips in an apology, here a singularly awkward one (365 f.) : ' I am indeed possessed, but to this extent I can control my frenzy.' [2]

The same can be seen in the *Andromache*. Is the heroine drawn as a hard, forensic woman, so unlike Homer's noble Queen, merely because Euripides took a morose pleasure in not being romantic ? Not in the least. It is indeed obvious that it was no part of his plan to make her a vision of loveliness ; her hardness towards her serving-woman (v. 87) might have been avoided ; but in general she is what she is for Euripides' dramatic convenience. He did not begin thinking out his play with a certain conception of Andromache as the kernel of the tragedy ; not, that is, as Sophocles obviously started thinking out the *Ajax* with a conception of a certain Ajax and a certain Odysseus. Why indeed should he ? An-

[1] Vv. 1028–46.

[2] For similar dramatic apologies cf. *Med.*, 473–4, 522–3 ; *Andr.*, 91 ff. (for the elegiacs), 333 ; *Hec.*, 603 ; *Suppl. Women*, 427–9 ; *Tro.*, 634–6, 898–913. How different these are from the self-revealing apology of his *Electra* (900 ff).

dromache is only to a small extent an agent in the play ; she
is in the main a victim, and, as such, her character is irrelevant.   She becomes barrister-like by accident, as by accident
Cassandra becomes philosophical.   Someone has to analyse
the situation for the benefit of Menelaus, and that someone
can be only Andromache.   She must make her points with
the utmost clarity and force ; it is not necessary to the tragic
idea that she should be like this, but it is necessary that the
points should so be made.[1]   Again as wife she has to be the
antithesis of Hermione ; we cannot see her as the devoted wife
in action, as we do in the *Iliad* ; therefore we have to be told
about it, and that forcibly.   Hence that passage about her
improbable tenderness to Hector's bastards, a rhetorical point
rather than a convincing piece of character-drawing.   Does all
this make a consistent portrait ?   Does the elegiac lament fall
inevitably into place ?   We may prefer consistency ; we may
even find it here, with enough determination ; but if we are
unconvinced, the play is not ruined.   It will mean only that
Euripides thought it better to be vital than academic.

   From the later, non-tragic plays we see that Euripides had
no difficulty whatever in creating both good plots and consistent characters.   If in the tragedies we find neither regular
plots, nor a normal assemblage of characters, nor a normal
treatment of these characters, it seems reasonable to look for
one general explanation ; not to explain the extreme lunacy of
Adrastus by referring to contemporary politics, the prevalence
of old men by assuming the existence of a certain actor, the
prevalence of argument by invoking current taste, the intrusion of Evadne by accusing Euripides of a desire to
brighten up his play, and the treatment of Cassandra by
nothing at all.   There is a fundamental difference between
the two sets of plays ; the later ones are self-contained, the
tragedies are not.   The story of Ion, Creusa and Xuthus is,
quite apart from any light it may throw on the habits or
existence of the god of Delphi, a complete and a coherent
whole ; the mere story of the *Troades* is not the whole, and
the plot does not cohere, without reference to the tragic idea
that inspires it.   In the later plays therefore, whether they

[1] See also on Hippolytus, p. 215.

present, to the discredit of Delphi, the exciting adventures of Ion or Iphigeneia, or the savage stories of Electra and Orestes (with a politico-social background), Euripides crystallizes the dramatic idea in the characters and actions of his *dramatis personae*. We have again actors and not victims ; again actors who are regarded purely as individuals, not in any degree as types, or tragic and exemplary embodiments of some universal passion ; again the action is self-contained ; no longer are we expected to integrate separate part-actions in the light of one enfolding tragic idea. The dramatic idea, of whatever nature it may be, is completely realized in the action, limited to the play and filling the play. Therefore these plays are constructed according to the normal ' logic '. The tragedies, which do not in this way distil all their meaning into one consecutive action and one significant character or group of characters, use a different logic, deriving their unity not from some point within themselves, but from something that under- lies them. They are meant to suggest something of which the people in them and what they do are only part. They do suggest this ; that is why they are read. ' The best in this kind are but shadows ', but the shadows differ greatly in ap- parent solidity.

We may now return to a question raised but not answered just now. Even if, to serve his inner tragedy, Euripides in- terfered with the natural behaviour of Cassandra, as he inter- fered with the natural flow of the plot in the *Medea,* why does he treat Peleus and Iolaus as he does ? The plays are trage- dies, not tragi-comedies : how can he place the guying of Iolaus side by side with the self-sacrifice of Macaria ? How treat Peleus so that we can hardly disagree with Menelaus when he says ' You are altogether too fond of abuse ' ?

A thoroughgoing melodramatist would have made great play with Peleus. The gallant old man, chivalrous, wise, generous, utterly regardless of self, unhesitatingly fronts the villain in defence of an ill-used woman, who is little better than a slave, though a Queen, if everybody had had his rights. The noble mother and her poor orphaned son are snatched out of the wicked man's very grasp . . . The *Andromache*, on the surface, is perilously close to this kind of nonsense. It would not do for Peleus to raise a lump in our throats in this way, and Euripides sees to it that he shall not. The unromantic treatment seems really to be a form of stylization; we must actually be prevented from taking too literal and exclusive an interest in the stage-action. This necessity we shall meet again in another connexion [1]; meanwhile may we ask what the melodramatist would have done with the chorus of the *Andromache*? The question is no sooner asked than answered; he would have used it, as the serialist of to-day uses his weekly silences, to intensify the excitement of the plot. Nothing would be easier than to write the choral ode which ought to be sung upon Orestes' exit; it is so easy that only the end is worth recording: ' Soon, soon shall we see our lord returning in peace to these halls, having set right his previous affair with Apollo, who, saving him from the wicked preparations of the Argive, will make it plain to all that God pardons those who repent, and keeps safe the pious against the guiles of the wicked.' *Enter the Messenger.*

But neither here nor at any other crisis in the play does the chorus do anything so sensible and dramatic. The reason is not this time that it has a drama of its own to play out; it is at liberty to give all its attention to the play. It avoids doing this because to attend on and accentuate the turns of the plot in this manner would give the plot a degree of importance and, as it were, of reality which Euripides does not wish it to have; it would turn into melodrama what is to be felt as tragedy, but not as the tragedy only of Andromache and Peleus.

3. THE CHORUS The tragic Chorus passed through some awkward vicissitudes before it emerged in the *Hecuba* and *Troades* as the key-stone of the mature tragic style of Euripides. In the *Medea* and *Hippolytus* it is used, as we should expect, in the manner of Middle Tragedy, with necessary modifications, and these, like the other modifications which the theme of the *Medea* entailed, are from the formal point of view no improvements.

We must first mention again that the change from the pub-

[1] Below, p. 298.

lic themes with which Sophocles had been dealing to private, psychological subjects inevitably made the chorus more difficult to manage.[1] Creon's edict in the *Antigone*, the plague in Thebes of the *Tyrannus*, Ajax' crime, were matters that concerned the community, and the Chorus was that community ; the story of Medea (as distinct from the tragic conception) is one that concerns Medea, Jason, their family circle and no one else. From the start the chorus here is an intrusion, dramatically as much out of place as in the private stories on which New Comedy was built ; later in the play it becomes a dramatic nuisance. It has to apologize for its arrival (131 ff.), just as Medea has to apologize (214) for coming out of the house instead of nursing her grief within ; and presently, much more awkwardly, it has to apologize for not helping the children. So in the *Hippolytus* ; the Parodos, a charming ode, is in essence an explanation, and the improbable presence of fifteen women at what is a very delicate and private death-bed scene puts Phaedra to the conventional necessity of binding them by an oath of secrecy, and then to the conventional necessity of keeping it.

But these inconveniences are not serious. We would readily accept the Chorus as a dramatic convention and think no more about it, if Euripides had not, by his self-consciousness, directed our attention to the inconveniences.[2] As we have suggested already, these were plays of transition, which more than once betray a clash of styles, and no doubt Euripides was debarred from making the chorus a pure convention by its dramatic, realistic character in the contemporary drama of Sophocles.

What is much more interesting is the positive use of the Chorus. Apart from the slight awkwardnesses, and the chilling anapaestic interlude, the chorus of the *Medea* behaves like that of the *Antigone* and *Electra*. Like Electra's chorus,

---

[1] We have already seen something of this in Sophocles' *Electra* ; see above, p. 174.

[2] As Roman Comedy sometimes does with the conventions of the Greek stage. The use of these by Menander, Plautus, and Terence is discussed with very interesting results by A. W. Gomme, *Essays in Greek Hist. and Lit.*, pp. 252 ff.

it is filled with the spirit of the heroine : ' Men are treacherous, but now is honour coming to womankind.' Like the chorus of the *Antigone*, it increases the dramatic momentum by changing sides. As it begins to realize what it is that Medea is proposing to do, it veers from sympathy to protest until, in its last ode, it sees in Medea a defiler of Heaven and Earth.

The chorus can attend on Medea in this way because, although she is perhaps in theory a victim as much as Andromache, she is the victim of a very personal passion which is so concentrated in her that she becomes dramatic as the later victims are not. Her will animates the play and her actions become the tragic issue of the play. The chorus, therefore, in following her closely is sticking close to the tragic theme, and when at the end it shrinks from her in horror it does much to illuminate this theme for us. A chorus which defended Medea's actions throughout would have left us completely at a loss.

Few of the later choruses resemble this one, but this principle remains fast, whether in Sophocles or in Euripides, that the chorus sticks closely to the tragic theme. For we must remember that the mature Sophoclean chorus, which this one resembles, was not a clever device for strengthening the unity of the play ; it, like Sophocles' characterization, takes its origin from much further back. The Chorus attends closely on the hero, his actions and their outcome, without philosophical or decorative excursions, because all the poet's tragic thought is expressed through the hero, his character, and his situation : nothing is left over for the Chorus to play with. In Euripides there is always something left over ; the tragedy is always perceptibly wider than the sum of the persons in the play. In the *Medea*, since the tragedy is to a very large extent, though not completely, distilled into the heroine, the chorus, attending to the inner tragic idea, does in fact remain close to her ; this is the one extreme. In the *Hecuba* and *Troades* we find the other. The tragedy here is infinitely wider than the particular events of the play ; and by waiting upon them, by commenting on the successive blows that fall upon Hecuba, the chorus would be deserting its station. Here it stands closer to the heart of the tragic conception by remaining aloof

from the actors and pursuing its own monotone of mourning
for Troy.   Hecuba, Cassandra and the rest are but part heroes
in a tragedy of nations or of humanity ; the successive scenes,
each an ' action ' in itself, do not form a whole but are suggestive aspects of a whole.   The Chorus, by neglecting these,
not dedicating itself to the part-heroes and the part-actions
as if they were complete and self-sufficient, performs in fact
exactly the same function as it did in Sophocles, but in the
exactly opposite way.   And not only does it perform this, its
truest, function of conveying lyrically the tragic idea, but also,
necessarily, it serves the more superficial purpose of making
the play a unity.   If Euripides, instead of being logical, had
allowed his chorus to run about in pursuit of the action, the
integration which he asks our apprehension to make would be
impossible and the plays would be chaos.

Between the extremes are gradations.   The chorus of the
Hippolytus is further from orthodoxy than that of the *Medea*,
and this for the obvious reasons that the play has not one hero
but two, and that the tragedy, as we are told in the prologue,
is somewhat wider than the unhappy history of Phaedra and
Hippolytus.   There is more left over, and we can see the consequence if we compare the ode to Eros (525 ff.) with any
mature Sophoclean ode.   That it should start, not with the
unhappy Phaedra, but with an invocation of the mighty love-
god is natural enough.   Sophocles, however, would have
worked back from Eros to the tragic hero who was prefiguring
his thought, the general only a preparation for the particular.
The ode in the *Hippolytus* does not work back to Phaedra ; it
remains general because Euripides' thought is general, illustrated by Phaedra but not totally transmuted into her.

One of the difficulties peculiar to this type of drama shows
its head in the next ode.   Phaedra, betrayed by her Nurse,
goes in with the express intention of ending her life and
so bringing ruin to Hippolytus.   What is the chorus to say ?
Our minds are entirely taken up with the sudden fulfilment of
Aphrodite's threat ; she is going to strike, as she said, but only
in order to be able to strike at another.   We, having heard
the prologue, know more about the real meaning of it all than
the chorus ; what can they say that will tighten this inner

tragedy for us ? The tragic transit enabled the chorus always to augment the dramatic rhythm ; it passed from triumph to fear, or from sympathy to opposition. Now, with foreseen catastrophes and external agencies, this effect is impossible. Here the real agent and the real tragedy is invisible to the chorus, and the theme of the power of Eros has already been used. What the chorus does here is to use, not for the last time, the formula *eithe genoiman*, Would I were somewhere else. In their first two stanzas, which are largely decorative, they wish themselves elsewhere, and in the last two they reflect, quite simply, on Phaedra's coming to Greece and the fate that awaits her now. The ode is, without being undramatic (for we may read anguish in their desire to be elsewhere), as far as possible from attempting what Sophocles did ; as if Euripides were purposely making the chorus stand a little on one side, not to obscure our vision of the inner drama.

In the *Andromache* and *Heracles*, necessarily, we move still further from the classical treatment of the Chorus. Each of these plays involves difficulties which make Euripides use the Chorus in a rather indeterminate way. To use it as in Middle Tragedy was impossible, for in neither play has he a hero whose will or actions are the driving-force of the drama. In the *Andromache*, as we argued above, Euripides deliberately keeps his chorus slightly detached from the action,[1] while in the *Heracles* the ostensible action is so disjunct, and the first part of the play so schematic, that any attempt to bind the play through the chorus, besides being false, would only call attention to the absence of formal unity. And once more the unifying idea is such that the chorus cannot stand nearer to it than the actors do, as it can in the *Troades*. This idea, in the *Andromache*, resides in the action, in the ruin of the house of Peleus, of which the chorus is only a spectator ; in the *Heracles* it resides in Heracles himself. These choruses have no drama of their own to play out, one that should underlie and reinforce the drama on the stage.

Accordingly in both plays there are odes in which the chorus says what it can. The *Andromache* has four odes. The first, which deals with the origin of the Trojan War, is

[1] P. 259.

entirely relevant to Andromache's position. The second stands apart from the action, considered as tragic action; it treats the situation between Andromache and Hermione intellectually, as an example of the truth that polygamy and divided royalty are both bad things. The third also begins reflectively, praising high birth, with Pindaric reminiscences in thought and language and rhythm, and it ends with a solemn affirmation of belief in the legendary history of Peleus. There is surely irony here; not the tragic irony of Sophocles which would have bidden us rejoice in the victory of Peleus just before we see that the victory is a hollow one, but the slightly mocking irony which we have already noticed in Euripides' drawing of Peleus. The Phthian maidens are sincere enough, but how are we to take seriously this Pindaric tone and this solemn Credo after the scene which has passed? In both the second and third odes therefore there is a certain feeling of detachment which we do not find, except in the anapaests, in the chorus of the *Medea*; but the last ode, the one which we ventured partially to rewrite above, is most remarkably detached. Why does the chorus, at the most dramatic turn of the plot, abandon the House of Peleus and return to Troy? Desire for symmetry, balancing the first Trojan ode? So mechanical an explanation we will not easily accept. ' Troy ', sings the chorus, ' was abandoned by the gods and destroyed. Agamemnon was slain, and his wife. Greece mourned many dead, slain in the war; not on Troy alone did the scourge fall.' What can this be but an indication where we are to look for the tragic bearing of the play? Beneath this story of Spartan intrigue is the further idea that such wickedness destroys victims and perpetrators alike. The Gods hold themselves aloof; Trojans and Greeks alike were slain, and Agamemnon was murdered. Here then we have the same use of the Chorus as in the *Troades*; in the second and third odes little more than a conventional curtain.

The chorus of the *Heracles* is again a band of sympathetic spectators. It has two important lyrical contributions to make, namely to present the picture of Heracles the Benefactor, a picture essential to the comprehension of the whole, and the expression of its joy at his return. Its elaborate pa-

rade of weakness in the parodos and its disjointed second
stasimon (637 ff.) reflect its indeterminate position. It is
made physically weak to reinforce the idea that Heracles' de-
pendents are entirely defenceless ; it takes part in the action,
but the action is inaction. In the second stasimon it is difficult to see anything but an undisguised intrusion of the poet's
own personality, such as we have not yet encountered.[1]   It
combines a complaint against old age, rather artificially
worked out with regret that the virtuous cannot live twice,
with a truly Pindaric stanza in praise of Song, from which it
returns, not very convincingly, to Heracles. Neither is the
ode itself a unity nor has it any connexion with the action or
the thought. We may perhaps conclude that Lycus and his
inevitable destruction did not merit the attention of the chorus
twice, and that since an attempt to read the action of this play
as a logical unity could only be confusing, and since the
chorus is in no position to point to the underlying tragedy,
Euripides preferred something quite neutral, something to
remove our attention, at least for the moment, from the action.
There has to be a pause, and he fills it.

   In these plays the chorus is not completely in the action, as
it was in Middle Tragedy, nor close to the heart of the tragedy, as in the *Hecuba, Suppliant Women* and *Troades.* In
the *Suppliant Women* it virtually becomes protagonist once
more.[2]   Its suffering sums up the tragic bearing of the play,
and its appeal begins and controls the action, overruling the
worldly prudence of Theseus and succeeding where the guilty
Adrastus failed. Here is no uncertainty, no turning to moral
or social disquisitions for the sake of a curtain. In these three

---

[1] For although the essay on childlessness in the *Medea* may state
Euripides' own opinion, and the remarks in the *Andromache* on
monarchy and democracy no doubt do, they have just so much
dramatic relevance that we need not suppose these not very remarkable sentiments to have been brought into the play for their
own sake. The artificiality of the old age passage here suggests
that we should not take it too seriously as Euripides' own lament,
but as material plausible enough in this chorus ; the noble stanza
to Song is, however, altogether different ; undoubtedly personal
and not dramatic.

[2] And Aeschylean in form, as Kranz points out (*Stasimon,* 176,
208).

plays the Chorus takes as natural and apparently inevitable a place as it had in the oldest of Greek Tragedy, the representative or the symbol of suffering humanity.

4. RHETORIC AND DIALECTIC   It is clear that if Euripides' attitude to tragedy implied a restricted use of characterization, this in its turn must affect the manner in which the dramatic action is presented, what we may call the dramatic style.   In Middle Tragedy we are interested in action as the outcome of character as much as for its own sake ; the person behind the action always gives it its particular dramatic value. Creon's decree is both something that will affect Antigone and something that reveals Creon and will affect him in turn ; Electra's long struggle is more than a series of events ; it is a continually developing revelation of a will and a mind. Events are qualitative.   In the mature Euripidean tragedy they are often only quantitative.   When a Menelaus or a Lycus does something, what is done does not interest us as a reflection of the spiritual or mental balance of the doer ; he was invented to do this and for no other purpose ; having done it he is exhausted.   It is not now the case that the person behind colours the action ; in fact it is the action that creates the person behind it.   When Creon acts as he does to Teiresias, or Oedipus to Creon, we say ' Ah ! Creon and Oedipus *would* behave like that '.   When Lycus explains why he proposes to put to death the children of Heracles we do not think ' How entirely characteristic of Lycus ', but we do think of Thucydides and politics.   Tragedy in fact is being presented through Lycus but not in him ; he has no independent existence and meaning which can lend further colour and significance to what he does.

Nor are these events regarded as critical in the characters of the victims.   These are presented only as victims, and even when Hecuba hits back, this, although an ironic point, is not regarded as the result of suffering upon character.   Injuries in fact are inflicted by ready-made characters whose motive is nothing more complex than one of the general follies of mankind, and are received by victims whose part is only to exemplify what mankind suffers at its own hands.

The pathetic therefore predominates, and gives to the action its characteristic flavour. Instead of that strenuousness of thought and action which makes so powerful a rhythm in the Sophoclean drama, we find, on the whole, a series of violent actions, not essentially connected ; and these, actions which cannot provoke counter-actions. Therefore, not only does the play as a whole lack that organic growth which we find everywhere in Sophocles, and to a large extent in the *Medea* and *Hippolytus,* but the individual scenes, too, tend to be static. What can Hecuba do but cry to Heaven and lament her wrongs ? She must mourn, and when the pathetic force of her mourning is spent, nothing remains but to wait for the next blow. Even resistance is ruled out ; Euripides cannot have Polyxena dragged struggling to the altar.

This is, as we have said before, a tragedy lyrical in conception, and it cannot be set upon an actors' stage without considerable adjustment. Since Euripides has a dramatic rhythm which is not a steady growth, but one which (so far as the action is concerned) consists of periods of slackness slung between moments of violence, like the rhythm of telegraph-wires seen from the train, he is committed to what Aristotle vividly called *arga merê*, passages, quite literally, in which there is nothing doing—nothing, that is, so far as the action is concerned. Of this we had an extreme example in the opening scenes of the *Heracles* ; other scenes of dramatic emptiness could be cited if the ungrateful task were necessary. Aristotle's practical advice was ' In slack passages elaborate your style '. Euripides was not reduced to this (though the messenger-speech in the *Hippolytus* comes close to it) because he was not play-making but presenting tragedy, and there is always tragedy and tragic thought to be followed in his mind even if the actors, for the time being, have nothing in particular to do ; still, something had to take the place of Sophocles' steady development of character and situation, and this was very largely rhetoric, dialectic, and sheer theatrical contrivance.

It is a commonplace that argument, dialectic, rhetoric, were Euripides' most frequent resources, and they are often spoken of as if they were deliberately or consciously adopted. This does not seem to be true, if it is taken to mean that Euripides, having settled on his theme, put in often, or fairly often, speeches that are rhetorical and argumentative rather than 'ethical', because he or his audience or both found them stimulating. If our general theory of Euripides is sound, he was committed to this intellectualism in dialogue and speech from the start, just as he was to his restricted characterization and non-organic use of plot. Consider Medea, for example. Jason comes (v. 446) to inform her blandly that it is all her own fault ; she replies, most convincingly, by blazing at him : 'What ? You dare to come to me ? This is not courage or boldness, but utter lack of decency.' But does she continue by loading the miserable man with reproaches and contempt ? Not in the least. With the standard dramatic apology she begins to state a case : 'You have done well to come, for I shall both unburden my own heart and wound yours by speaking ill of you. Now, I will begin from the beginning. I saved you . . .' The chilling thing here is not the rehearsal of history ; that is relevant and dramatic. It is the formality of the procedure. These claims of hers ought not to be so calmly arranged in chronological order. There is a lyrical method, which disdains logic ; there is a dramatic method, which follows the course of thought and emotion ; there is a prose method, which is objective and follows the facts. This is the prose method.[1]

It is no answer to say that Euripides intended to present Medea as a woman of such self-mastery and clarity as would naturally lead her so to control her rage. This defence may be attempted with Andromache, but here the rest of Medea's behaviour contradicts it ; and since most Euripidean heroines speak like this, it would imply that this was the only type of woman in whom he was interested. Still less just is it to invoke mere habit or a personal idiosyncrasy in Euripides, unless we are prepared to say that Medea speaks intellectually because the whole play is conceived intellectually. That indeed seems to be near the truth. Euripides did not follow and reflect dramatically the natural rush of Medea's emotions as Sophocles would have done because the course of Medea's

[1] Contrast Oedipus' speech to Creon, *O.C.*, 960 ff. (p. 389).

emotions at this point does not matter. What matters is that we should clearly see the utter baseness of Jason; this is one of the chief ingredients of the tragedy. We have to see Jason as he is; not as he momentarily appears to a desperate Medea but as Euripides wants him to be. Conversely, Jason's reply might have been a torrent of abuse, a shifting of the blame upon the convenient gods, possibly something else. It is, in the main, a calm analysis of Medea's record; cynical, revolting, but not false. That Jason should state his case so clearly is not undramatic, but this is accidental. He is doing exactly what Medea did, for exactly the same reasons; not first and foremost being Jason, but giving us Euripides' picture of the essential Medea, the woman who has always been at the mercy of her passions. Certainly Jason is dramatically fortunate that in doing this he does give a picture of himself. He is dramatic while Medea, Cassandra, Andromache are in the same circumstances nondramatic or even inconsistent. Rhetorical dialectic happens to suit Jason, but all are like this because it is more important to Euripides' theme that they should say what they say as clearly and forcibly as possible than that they should say it in this way or that.

Hippolytus is in the same case. Are we tempted to think him somewhat of a prig when he expounds his virtue ? If we do, we are thinking of him as a tragic character instead of what he really is, a tragic figure. His purity is the whole point of his tragedy, consequently of his character too. Euripides must insist on it; nothing else in him counts. As Hippolytus speaks we must see him as the tragic victim of Aphrodite, going to his death because of her wrath. He speaks, like the others, out of the inner tragedy and not out of his own personality, and if we cannot take him simply as a tragic figure whose personality, except in this one respect, never comes into consideration ; if, that is, we feel him to be priggish, that must be written off as one of the inevitable inconveniences of the whole method.

Examples of this dramatic rhetoric or dialectic can be found in all these tragedies. Neither in substance nor in form is the examination of Adrastus by Theseus an amusement; it is the exposition of the basis of the tragic situation and of its underlying idea—exactly comparable, therefore, to Creon's first speech in the *Antigone*. It is not that Euripides' style has been affected by influences which Sophocles escaped ; in the difference between Creon's speech and the cross-examination of Adrastus we have nothing less than the difference between two antithetic minds ; both dramatic, both tragic, both, at the moment, working with similar material—character and politics—but the one synthetic, the other analytic. The basis of the tragedy of the *Antigone* is the character of Creon as it issues in his statecraft, and that is what fills this speech. The basis—or an important part—of the tragedy of the *Suppliant Women* is the sheer folly which leads to the bereavement of the Suppliants, and the examination establishes that. To move on to the *Troades* and its formal debate between Helen and Hecuba before Menelaus ; is this merely a brisk imitation of the law-courts ? Realism of this kind has nothing to do with it except maybe in a few quite superficial details ; the logical refutation of Helen belongs to the inner tragedy as much as the self-confidence of Oedipus to his or the practical incapacity of Deianeira to hers. It must be shown that the Greeks cannot plead the will of Heaven ; this is a tragic, not a decorative point. How more simply and directly could it be made than by the set debate, with Menelaus accepting Hecuba's argument ? This part of the tragedy cannot be shown in action, only in dialectic.

But debate and dialectic in these plays are not always as necessary and dramatic as this. The two extremes can be illustrated from the *Heracles*—the discussion on the nature of God, which is so dramatic, and the discussion on bowmen, which is only a fill-up. Between these there are many grada-tions. In most of the plays can be found moments when, be-cause the actors in the drama are passive victims unable to do anything important and not endowed with the character that would make action significant, an intellectual movement is created, or, failing that, a rhetorical one. When Creon, or Oedipus, comes to grips with Teiresias there is a clash of opinion indeed, but that is incidental to the impact of the prophet's attitude on the King ; when Theseus meets the Theban Herald there is no such impact ; that Theseus should

behave as Creon or Oedipus did, bringing up all the reserves
of his personality is impossible and would be meaningless.
He must demand the return of the bodies ; the Theban must
say No.   There would be no point in making these argue as
do Creon and Antigone, in flashes that reveal the soul of each.
The souls of Theseus and the Herald do not count.   Therefore, insofar as the issue is argued it must be argued on its
own merits, dialectically that is and not passionately.   On
these terms there is not a vast deal to say about it, and in
any case it is incidental to the chief theme of the play, the
suffering of the Mothers.   The discussion on forms of govern-
ment is not very much more remote, and can be brought in to
extend a scene which the first question is not enough to fill.
There is a lack of tragic tension on the stage ; the stage accordingly embroiders the tragedy which broods in the orchestra.

Debate then may be a direct expression of some aspect of
the tragic idea or it may be a substitute for action and the
revelation of ethos.   We may now turn to reflective, ' so-
phistic ' passages, some of which seem otiose, perhaps distinctly
out of character.   Here too we have to distinguish.   Not to
waste time I take four instances only, Theseus on *synesis*, Intelligence (*S.W.*, 195 ff.), and on Life (*ibid.*, 550 ff.), Hecuba
on heredity and education (*Hec.*, 592 ff.), and the fragment
of dramatic criticism in the *Suppliant Women* (846 ff.).   Of
such passages it is not always enough to say that Euripides
was given to thought and did not mind interrupting his play
to say something interesting ; some of them, notably the first
two cited above, have a deeper origin.   That intelligence is
God's greatest gift to man is not simply a stray thought that
occurs to Theseus (or to Euripides), which Theseus develops
regardless of his context ; it is part of the tragic thinking from
which these plays arise—our intelligence overborne by our
folly.   So is the second idea, that we should show circumspection in our conduct.   Comments like these—and not comments
only, but full statements of a philosophical view—illustrate
again the difference between Euripides' mind and Sophocles' ; they are, as it were, parts of the original thought or

emotion that do not find themselves transmuted into dramatic imagery.

But though this is true of some of these passages it is not true of all. Hecuba's inquiry and the dramatic criticism of Messenger-speeches do not belong to the original stuff of the drama ; they are another indication of the external way in which Euripides approached his characters and situations. If the *Hecuba* were really a character-study the former passage would be impossible : the mind that it implies is inconsistent with the Hecuba who revenges herself on Polymestor. This is not to say that Hecuba has no character, only that her characterization is intermittent. Not being conceived—why should she be ?—as a person whose precise blend of character is significant, she becomes, between whiles, a neutral personage who can be used rhetorically. Further (to anticipate our next point), what is Hecuba to say here ? Lamentation, invective against the Greeks, or a sheer breakdown in grief— any of which would be a natural result of the sacrifice of Polyxena—would be comparatively uninteresting : lamentation we have had in plenty ; invective or a 'natural' outburst of grief would force us to take the incident as tragedy, which would underline the 'shocking' element. Therefore what we have in this speech, the serious treatment of a serious and appropriate theme is, as it were, an intellectual stiffening to a situation which is in danger of running to melodrama or still more lyricism.

This brings us to a third noticeable result of this kind of dramatic action, the specifically rhetorical nature of the typical Euripidean speech. We may say in general that his preoccupation with an inner drama and his detachment from the persons on his stage make these speak in a standard accent. Euripides is as far as possible from creating an Oedipodean or a Creontic style for a single character ; he could have done it, but it would have meant nothing. It is easy to see that such a standard accent, in Athens and at this period, might easily become rhetorical, yet it does not seem inevitable. But perhaps we can go further. We may recall the position of Hecuba in the scene just quoted, or we may consider Andromache's position in the *Troades* when the decree of the Greeks

is announced. What is Andromache to say ? It is in some
ways a comparable moment when the Paedagogus announces
the death of Orestes in Sophocles' play. Euripides gives
us nothing like the utter limpidity of the Chorus there, the
revealing directness of Clytemnestra, the noble simplicity of
Electra's speech ; not because Sophocles was better at doing
these things than Euripides,[1] but because his situation was
tragic (though feigned) while this is *miaron* ; tragic—like
Medea's murders—only when we can relate it to the underlying
idea. As the situation is, tragically speaking, unreal, so must
Andromache's speech be to some extent unreal, rhetorical
like Medea's murders. Simple, moving and tragic accents
belong to simple and tragic situations, to Antigone facing
death ; not, for instance, to Polyxena. The character of
Polyxena we hardly know, nor does it affect her situation ;
Euripides does right to intellectualize her speech and let her
set out with a *proton men.*

Or we may take a rather different moment. Hecuba
makes a speech in the *Troades* (466 ff.) when the situation
is that Cassandra has just been led off captive and that
nothing else (except a choral ode) is destined to happen until
the next blow falls, the appearance of Andromache, captive.
The whole interval cannot be filled with lyrics ; Hecuba has
been lyrical for nearly two hundred verses already. She
therefore is given a speech (cf. Soph., *El.*, 254 ff.), but since
nothing matters, dramatically, but the next blow—not Hecuba's
'reactions', her character, possibility of counter-action—the
moment is quite static ; there is no forward movement and
Euripides does not pretend to make any. This time there is
no debate or philosophical reflection to replace dramatic by
intellectual activity. Hecuba is given a reminiscent speech,
and this consequently must be interesting as a speech, that is,
rhetorical.

5. DRAMATIC SURPRISE AND ORNAMENT We have tried to
show that debate, ' sophistry ' and rhetoric were natural results
of this schematic treatment of plot and character, whether

[1] No doubt he was, but the comparison is meaningless without
the reason.

springing directly from the theme, or introduced because other interest was not easy to come by. We will now briefly consider two further consequences, ' theatre ' and decoration.

Euripides' dramatic style is noticeably thin in texture. Not only is his poetic style simple and limpid, as strong a contrast to the weight of Aeschylus' style as to the infinite subtlety and richness of Sophocles', but every other part of his drama is in keeping. As his characterization is schematic, his speeches lack ethos ; as his plots are schematic, they lack the incessant change of rhythm which Sophocles offers. Action that reveals the depths of a complex personality, those triangular scenes, cross-rhythms and tragic irony that are an illumination of the mechanics of life, play no part in Euripides. Pathos and lamentation replace energy and tragic action, static scenes illuminated by intellectual analysis take the place of the ever-changing drama of Sophocles. And even intellectually Euripides does not make greater demands than Aeschylus or Sophocles ; it would be a bold man who would assert that his stichomythia was more difficult to follow than Sophocles', or his speeches more packed with thought than Aeschylus'. Even here Euripides' texture is relatively thin.

This not because he was addressing a different or less in-tellectual audience. The thinness is desirable as well as necessary ; it is not for nothing, or from accident, that Euripides hands out his drama in large pieces, easily to be grasped, while Sophocles demands every moment all the percipience we can muster to penetrate his subtleties. We can do one thing or the other. Sophocles does not expect us to integrate his *Tyrannus* ; all that he means is there. That is the reason why it is so rich and so difficult, with some-thing significant happening every moment. Euripides does demand that we shall make some effort of the imagination (not necessarily of the intellect ; that is the critic's business) to integrate his *Troades,* even that we shall feel the tragedy of the *Medea* to be something more than the ruinous conduct of a slightly improbable woman. Therefore the simplicity which is the logical result of his dramatic method becomes an ad-vantage. It allows us, as Sophocles never does, to lean back and ask ourselves what it is all about. If Euripides were

really as simple as he appears from the pavilion in which sit
those who edit him for schoolboys, it would indeed be difficult
to account for his greatness. He is the most tragic of poets,
not for the Hecuba and the Medea whom he made, but for
the tragedy that lies behind these.

Still, the texture of the actual drama is thin, and Euripides,
having sacrificed so much to the logic of his social tragedy,
is prepared to find compensations elsewhere, in bold theatrical
strokes and in sheer decoration. Of the compensations,
some arise as it were automatically out of his method ; others
are by no means so inevitable.

Looseness of plot and emancipation from the law of the
necessary or probable, though it deprived Euripides of the
effects which Sophocles drew from his impressive ordering
of events, made possible, and legitimate, certain effects which
Sophocles could never use. Euripides was always ready to
take advantage of his schematic construction by contriving
turns of plot which were theatrically effective as well as
contributory to his tragic idea. The chariot of Medea, whose
tragic significance we have seen already, makes a splendid
finale which Sophocles might have applauded though never
imitated ; the transformations which come over Hecuba, and
over Alcmena and Eurystheus in the *Heracleidae*, transformations which are possible because the characterization has
been slight and the plots not rigidly logical, legitimate because they underline the tragic idea of the plays, are at the
same time very good theatre. The *Troades* similarly exploits
its legitimate possibilities. Its singularly impressive ending
Aristotle would no doubt have accepted as logical, but
the scene between Helen, Hecuba and Menelaus comes from
Euripides' logic, not Aristotle's. It is strictly a part of the
theme, but what good theatre it is too ! After the scenes
of misery, and the impersonal Talthybius, we suddenly see
face to face the ruined Queen (with the desolate Trojan
women in the orchestra), Helen the lovely paramour and
faithless wife, and Menelaus the betrayed husband and
victorious general—a striking scene and a marvellous setting
for Euripides' tragic argument. To these effective turns we
might add the horrible but necessary effect of Glauce's death,

the mysterious arrival and ominous departure of Orestes in the *Andromache*, the wild and romantic Evadne. None of these would be possible in Sophocles, but all belong as strictly to Euripides' theme as do Sophocles' complications of plot to his.

The conventionalized character-drawing too, though it has its inconveniences, brings its compensations. It makes possible sharply accentuated contrasts like those between Medea and Jason, Andromache and Hermione. Because he is pushing his characterization to extremes Euripides gets an almost melodramatic strength of effect impossible to Aeschylus and Sophocles, because their contrasts, though they may be complete, are more complex. Again, since Euripides is interested in these persons as figures in a drama rather than as rounded characters to be studied from the inside, he can make a sudden and effective stroke out of what, to a different dramatist, would have been a slow process, or at least a complex one. Hermione will illustrate this. In the first part of the play she is arrogant, sure and successful ; when next we hear of her it is to be told that she has been trying to hang herself all over the palace. Euripides can short-circuit all her mental processes and present us with the startling result because she is a figure rather than a character ; it is necessary that she should now see clearly, but how she comes to see clearly is no concern of ours. Or we may compare Hecuba before Agamemnon with Antigone's Watchman before Creon. The Watchman's hesitations are naturally and dramatically reflected in a speech, for the whole nature of the drama demands that he shall be a real person and that the action shall look like life ; Euripides is giving us something that is more like a diagram than a picture of life ; there is much less need for Hecuba to speak like a Queen than there was for the Watchman to speak and think like a common soldier ; therefore he renders the hesitations in a stagey manner (to use the word in a neutral sense). Hecuba is given a series of 'asides'; her doubts are not conveyed ethically, but made the opportunity for an effective bit of 'theatre'. Sophocles, not Euripides, is the realist here. Euripides, in his tragedies, has a degree of abstraction reminiscent of those mathematical

personages A, B, and C who used to plough fields for us at
such convenient rates.   It is theatrical that the work they did
should be so neatly mensurable ; Sophocles gives us the real
ploughman.

The slight but definite degree of detachment which we
have observed Euripides showing towards his creatures opens
the door to interesting effects.   We have suggested that his
sub-ironical treatment of Peleus may have been a defence,
deliberately adopted, against a thoroughgoing melodramatic
acceptance of the *Andromache*.   Whether this is true or not,
it is certainly a legitimate consequence of the general method,
and quite an effective one.   Euripides is not wholly wrapped
up in his Peleus, and a conflict between a villain and one
who is not quite a sage is certainly more interesting than one
between pure black and pure white.   Much more obvious is
the effect in that puzzling play the *Heracleidae*, where
Euripides allows the gallant Iolaus gradually to dissolve into
fantasy.

All these effects, major and minor, are logical, and the best
of them assist the theme, not the play only, as rigorously as
Sophocles' very different effects always do.   Some contrivances, however, do not seem so successful.

Hecuba (*Tro.*, 701 ff.) is consoling Andromache, and ends
by telling her that at least she has Astyanax ; Talthybius enters
to announce the sentence of death on him.   Why is the tragic
irony rasping, not impressive and frightening like Sophocles' ?
Because it is not really tragic.   Sophocles makes Oedipus welcome circumstances which in fact are big with disaster
because he sees life, when it is tragic, as a stage on which
character is at the mercy of circumstance, one on which even
just calculation can lead to ruin.   Because this is an essential
part of his thought, even touches of irony which individually
we could hardly justify in logic become transcendentally
relevant.   In the Euripidean tragedy circumstance plays no
essential part ; the whole foundation is rationalistic—' Not
Aphrodite, but unchastity ', which, in the Greek, sounds like a
grim pun.   (*Ouk Aphroditê alla aphrosynê.*)   Such a view
of life, though it might be rich in irony as we understand the
word—something nearer to comedy than to tragedy—is not

obviously a source of Aeschylean or Sophoclean irony, which indeed Euripides seldom imitates. In the Astyanax-incident he does ; and what does it reveal ? Not that life, or indeed the Greeks, were particularly cruel in choosing this moment for the announcement ; not that some mysterious and malevolent Power lies behind human action.[1] It intensifies but does not enlarge our sense of Hecuba's and Andromache's suffering. It is a stroke very like the ending of the *Hecuba,* a kind of rhetoric of action, not indeed to be reprehended, but not to be compared with the Sophoclean irony.[2]

This looser dramatic structure is naturally more tolerant of pure decoration. Certain rhetorical ornaments have been already noticed, and the additions which we can make to the list are not many. The Chorus of Huntsmen which attends on Hippolytus may be regarded as a decoration, by no means an illegitimate one, as it reinforces the Artemidian element in the play. When it reappears, the antiphony which it sings with the real chorus is effective, but it hardly adds to the tragedy—not as the Sons do in the *Suppliant Women.*

A much clearer case of pure decoration is Andromache's Lament. This is a pure show-piece, whose undercurrent of self-pity, lack of suggestion of energy, independence and hardness, is set in striking contrast with the Andromache of the scenes that follow. If the Prologue had seriously engaged our interest in Andromache as a tragic heroine, as we are interested in Antigone, or if the action to come were felt to depend on her character as does the action of the *Antigone,* this interruption or suspension of interest would be quite intolerable. Sophocles' *Electra* begins with a monody, but

---

[1] We can imagine Hardy revelling in this incident.

[2] Only in one case (and that a curiously unimportant one) does it seem fair to accuse Euripides' contrivance of being artificial. It is the slight preparation for the Helen-scene. Andromache (766 ff.) speaks—naturally enough—of Helen, and the succeeding ode devotes a stanza (841 ff.) to Eros. At 850 the chorus mentions the ' Baleful sunlight ' which now looks upon Troy and at 860 Menelaus enters greeting the ' Glorious sunlight ' which will witness his revenge on Helen. As the Helen scene is really disjunct it is perhaps permissible to criticize this preparation as artificial ; at all events its value is less than that of similar preparations in Sophocles.

this is not decorative; on the contrary, it gives us the key
to Electra's character and situation—things which are the
basis of the whole play. It is because Andromache is important to Euripides' theme as a significant victim and not
as a significant agent that he can stand back for a moment
and pity her, objectively, in elegiacs.

In general, then, the most conspicuous strokes of Euripides'
stage, his strong contrasts and his imaginative or at least
effective juxtapositions, are the logical outcome of his method.
The method has certain weaknesses in its slight or even inconsistent characterization, its disjointed plots, its uniform
style : but it has its compensations, even if we limit ourselves
to the purely theatrical. Unable for the most part to use the
powerful dramatic rhythms which Sophocles mastered, he
could not always prevent single scenes from sagging except by
the extra-dramatic means of rhetoric, but to the play as a
whole he could give a great impetus by calling upon one of
these major effects. Because in these diagrammatic plots
Sophocles' crescendos and cross-rhythms were impossible, the
sudden stroke becomes characteristic—as of Heracles' children
dressed for the grave ; strokes which, like Glauce's death,
have a perceptible tendency to address themselves to our
nerves rather than to our poetic imagination. In fact,
we see growing here the dramatic technique which made
Euripides such a master of melodrama and tragi-comedy—his
sure instinct for a piquant turn or telling juxtaposition, his
fertility of invention, his command of the rhetoric of action,
the macabre, and the ironic. When he became content to
make plays that were self-contained and complete in their immediate appeal, he is at once placed by Aristotle on the level
of Sophocles.

When this happens, and both poets abandon tragedy, it
is interesting—and seems inevitable—that it is Euripides, the
tragedian of the sudden stroke, the manipulated plot, the
slight characterization but sharp contrasts, who begins to
write exciting melodrama ; Sophocles, the tragedian of the
close texture and complex rhythm, who produces the close
and complex study of the *Philoctetes* ; a play which, even if

we consider it only as a dramatic intrigue, has a subtlety of movement as characteristic of Sophocles as the breathless sweep of the *I.T.* is of Euripides. But while Euripides is still writing tragedy, he makes these strokes of his so subordinate to his tragic theme that it is in the highest degree unjust to think of him as a mere theatre-man. If he had been, his plays would have been better made and himself not the most tragic of the poets. Yet so tellingly are these strokes made that it is equally unjust to think of him as a great tragic poet indeed but hardly of equal rank as a dramatist.

It is, I suppose, a common experience for a reader to pass from Sophocles to Euripides with the feeling that he has gone from a cathedral into a dynamo-house, but if we find Euripides' thinness disappointing and some of his inconveniences irksome, we should probably do well to reflect that in his tragedies he has come down to us stripped of more of his essentials than Sophocles. Each has lost the stage-spectacle and the music, the movement and colour of the Chorus, but while in Sophocles these were important indeed but accessory to a tragic idea primarily realized in the characters, the plot, and the drama, in Euripides they were much more. In the *Hecuba* and *Troades* the chorus, with its communal tragedy, embodies more of the essential meaning of the play than ever it does in Sophocles, and that meaning is gravely attenuated to us, who have only a bare text. We have in fact most prominently before us those elements in which this Tragedy is not particularly strong—the stage-action and the discussion—and have lost the greater part of what was designed more immediately to present the tragic idea. The mere physical presence of one of these choruses—for example, of the Mothers with their grandchildren during some of the debates in the *Suppliant Women*—must have given to the scene an atmosphere which we cannot now recover, except by proper performance. The dialectic, so prominent to us, would be less prominent if the chorus had its true stature, and would no doubt take on a tragic hue now invisible. In fact, in so far as this Tragedy is a communal one, it lives most in the orchestra ; the stage gives a sharper but an incomplete and diagrammatic picture of it. The reader has lost much of the total impression of what proceeded from the stage, but very much more of what proceeded from the orchestra.

6. PROLOGUES AND EPILOGUES We come finally to these most characteristic and most puzzling features of the Euripidean drama. The formal narrative prologue has very little wherewith to recommend itself to a reader whose ears are full of the great choral odes with which early Tragedy opened, or whose dramatic sense has been excited by the way in which the *Agamemnon,* the *Antigone,* or even the later *Philoctetes* began. No wonder that Aristophanes laughed at such stiff and undramatic first scenes. Why did Euripides, and apparently no one else, write them ?

It is no answer at all to call the prologue a playbill. Perhaps it is that, but why is playbill confused with play ? Euripides, we are told, innovated so freely in myth that it was necessary to warn the audience beforehand that the story was to be not quite what it might be expecting. Did then Aeschylus and Sophocles not innovate ? Was Aeschylus' Prometheus the Prometheus of Hesiod, or Sophocles' Philoctetes the same as Euripides' or Aeschylus' ? Even if the myth was being severely rehandled, was the audience now so lacking in wit that it could not follow a new story in the play itself, and was the dramatist so helpless that he could not make his story intelligible as he went along ? Had Sophocles written the *Tyrannus* in vain ?

We must remember what the Euripidean plot is, and consider what were the alternatives to the not very exciting prologue. The plot is never in essence and rarely in fact a logical story in which certain characters inevitably work out their ruin, but a series of incidents, necessarily related but not necessarily a logical whole, chosen to illustrate or point to some overriding tragic idea. The plot of the *Troades* is nothing but a selection of incidents from many which followed the capture of Troy, one section of our line of telegraph-poles, one which does in fact end at an obvious terminus (unlike the series in the *Hecuba*), but is not itself a unity. Clearly the logical way of introducing this is to begin at some satisfactory *terminus a quo* and to summarize rapidly until the section under review is reached. Plot in fact has taken a decisive step towards narrative. Aristotle objected to Aegeus on the grounds that strict construction cannot allow such incursions from outside. We have defended Aegeus as being allowable in theory, though certainly not free from fault in practice. But if Euripides' tragedy had been cast in narrative form, a form which can afford to be looser in construction, Aegeus would hardly provoke any objection. So too the plot of the *Hecuba* is perfectly good as a section of narrative ; only as drama does it raise questions. To such narrative plots a narrative introduction is the obvious beginning.

Further, these plots are not regarded as being within the control of the chief characters (the *Medea* excepted). The Trojan victims can do nothing ; Euripides' Suppliants are far from being the determined Suppliants of Aeschylus ; even Phaedra and Hippolytus are presented as victims of a power greater than themselves. Therefore, when we begin to consider alternatives to the prologue we meet a difficulty at once. The typical opening scene of Sophocles is not a mere purveying of information. If this were a legitimate excuse for such a beginning, Euripides need never have done anything different. Sophocles begins decisively, showing the action as already started, producing one of the significant characters at once, because such action and such characters are the essence of the drama. This is the ideal beginning for a play in which the character and the separate interests and motives of everyone in it are significant, one in which we are to see the outcome of the joint actions. But the Euripidean drama is nothing like this. Never is the dramatic point an interlocking of character and interests, nor, in this second group, is the real interest of the play the action of the chief characters, but rather their passion. To illustrate the first point it is sufficient to ask how Euripides was to begin the *Medea*. Had the play been conceived as a tragedy of character, like the *Antigone*, a study of the disastrous opposition between Jason's self-seeking and Medea's passionate jealousy, then nothing would have been simpler to contrive than a strong opening scene between the two, or between Jason and Creon, or between Medea and Glauce ; no need to begin with the Argo cleaving the dark Symplegades—all this could have been taken for granted, or slipped in later. But as the play is not this at all, as the motives and character of Jason are accessory and those of Creon and Glauce immaterial, such a scene would in fact be mere pretence. What matters is not the quality of Jason's acts, nor the action and reaction that pass between him and Medea, but simply what a woman like Medea will do in this now complete situation. The logical beginning therefore is a plain narrative statement of this complete situation, not dialogue between two persons whose characters are a matter of indifference.[1] If this is true of a play so near to Middle Tragedy as the *Medea*, how much the more true of the later Euripidean tragedy?

But if a dialogue-opening is false, why not begin with the Chorus? The plays are lyrical in feeling, and to say that choral openings had gone out of use is only to say that Euripides did not use them. To this question there is a decisive answer. The problem we are really considering is how to bring in events past. To Sophocles, the past was significant chiefly as it affected the actions or motives of the actors in the present; to his Electra the murder of Agamemnon was a past event which coloured the thought and conduct of the present Electra, therefore it is given to her, and to Orestes, to tell us of it. So, more strikingly, with the complicated past history of Laius and Oedipus. We are told nothing about it at the beginning in order that Oedipus may appear before us without a shadow, and the story is, as it were, dragged out of the past by Oedipus himself for the sake of the tragic effect and the light it throws on his character. That this is also a neat way of disposing the material is a bagatelle. On the other hand, the past in the *Agamemnon*, notably the sacrifice of Iphigeneia, is no part of Agamemnon's present mind, nor, though it is part of Clytemnestra's, is this of importance to us at the beginning of the play. First we

---

[1] That the prologue is in fact spoken not by an indifferent person, like a god, but by the Nurse, who puts something of her own inconspicuous personality into her narrative, is a sign that in this play of transition Euripides has not gone to this logical conclusion.

are to see this past as a living element in the present, as a debt Agamemnon has to pay ; that is the reason why it is dealt with first, and by the chorus. But in these Euripidean tragedies, most of them, the past is nothing at all. It works neither as a controlling element in the conduct of the actors nor as part of the tragic atmosphere of the whole.[1] Neither actors nor chorus therefore can work it in without a considerable amount of pretence.[2] Its only significance is that it has in fact produced the present ; it is quite formal, and is formally dealt with. Nothing prevents either chorus or actors from harking back to the past when it is relevant to the present theme, but they may not recapitulate it as a way of starting the action, or talk merely to give us facts ; yet the play, not being an organic growth, can hardly begin without a summary, so that the 'playbill' prologue becomes inevitable.

Once established, the prologue could be put to some remarkable uses. We see how in the *Hippolytus* it gives the cosmic framework to what would otherwise be an exciting but not particularly significant story. Similar, but much more powerful, is the double prologue to the *Troades*. It might have been possible to open this play with the chorus ; the play is, however, not merely a pathetic picture of cruelty to the conquered, but also a tragic picture of the results of wickedness and folly both to conquered and conquerors, and it is the prologue that directs our attention to the tragic blindness of the conquerors ; serving, as we have suggested, the same end as the first ode of the *Agamemnon*.

The prologue to the *Hecuba*, spoken by the ghost of Polydorus, is put to a different but equally significant use. This prologue, in conventional narrative, tells us the antecedent circumstances, and then proceeds to 'bind together' the two unrelated themes which are to make up the play, the sacrifice of Polyxena and the discovery of Polydorus' own body : per-

[1] The *Troades* is a manifest exception to this, but obviously the tragic quality with which the past is invested in this prologue could not be entrusted to the chorus, still less to the actors.

[2] There is a reminiscent ode on the capture of Troy in the *Hecuba* (905 ff.), but this is no exception. In this terrible ode the past is brought in not for our information—we could do without it—but as part of the tragedy of the chorus.

haps a necessary, but hardly a brilliant device. Yet we may suspect, when the Ghost goes on to tell us when, where, and by whom the body will be found, telling us in fact what we must in any case learn from the play itself—we may suspect that in this prologue Euripides has a deeper motive than merely starting the play, and a more respectable one than tying together a shaky structure. Why does he virtually make Polydorus say ' At verse 657 my death will be announced by Hecuba's servant ' ? The detailed foreshadowing reminds us of the way in which Aeschylus' Suppliants foreshadow their threat of suicide, and of their reason for doing so—to discount the purely theatrical thrill of the incident (p. 31). Here we are so precisely told what is going to happen in order that, being set free of all excitement over the facts, we may have minds at leisure to take in the real tragedy. The inner drama here, unlike that of the *Hippolytus* and *Troades,* is hardly such as can be put into dramatic shape in the prologue ; still, the way can be prepared for it.[1] Such foreshadowing is quite inconceivable in a Sophoclean play ; not because these are ' better constructed ' and do not need underpinning before they are built, but because the meaning and the function of action in Sophocles are radically different ; they are so intimately connected with character and thought that they may be regarded as character and thought made manifest. If Sophocles told us what Oedipus was going to do, it would be equivalent to telling us what sort of a man he was.

Nothing could more clearly indicate the illustrative nature of these plots. We are not to concern ourselves dramatically and emotionally in the actual events, as we do with the events of the Sophoclean stage ; these do not reveal the character and thought which is the essence of the tragedy ; they are chosen as a convenient means of conveying an inner tragic idea. These characters are the dramatic counterpart of the mathematical personages A, B and C ; we were never ex-

---

[1] Note that the climax, the revenge taken by Hecuba, is not foreshadowed. This is intended as a shock. A further point in this prologue, a separate and secondary advantage, is that our fore-knowledge of Polydorus' death increases for us the pathos of Polyxena's.

pected to follow them homeward plodding their weary way when the field was ploughed, nor here are we expected or desired to enter passionately and exclusively into the heart of Hecuba and to follow these events only through the tear-stained eyes of the tragic Queen. The prologue, with its foreshadowing, slightly but definitely detaches us, as Euripides himself is detached.

In complete contrast stands the prologue to the *Andromache*. It has been felt that the connexion between the two separate stories here is somewhat slight. Had then Euripides not yet thought of the masterly device of using the prologue as string? It would have been perfectly simple to start with a prologue spoken by the god of Delphi, or his apologist Hermes, or the Dioscuri, to pull the play together and to state the connexion between the first part and the second. This, however, is exactly what Euripides does not want. This time his tragic idea does depend on the element of surprise and shock in the narrative. He wants Orestes to take us by surprise; his Hermione and his Menelaus have not, as we innocently supposed, exhausted Sparta's genius for doing evil. To tell us even the barest outline of the plot beforehand would leave us only the secondary interests of the play—the discussions and debates, the ' psychology ', the realism and the rest.

Later parallels to the *Andromache* enable us to say that when Euripides is writing any kind of drama in which the movement of the plot is an important source of interest, he is careful not to foreshadow; indeed, if anything is foreshadowed, it is something that is destined not to be fulfilled. Thus Dionysus in the *Bacchae* threatens a salutary lesson to Thebes—this in the tragic manner. As in the *Hecuba*, we are told roughly what is to happen in order that we may receive it, when it comes, tragically and not melodramatically ; we are not told the full extent and nature of the lesson, because the shock of that surprise is necessary to the poet's theme. The *Helen, Electra, Phoenissae*, on the other hand, being melodramatic rather than tragic, have prologues which confine themselves strictly to past events ; the course of future events is one of the main interests of the play and is therefore kept dark. The prologues of the *Orestes* and the *I.T.*, plays of a similar kind, look forward to the future—but incorrectly, for the sake of enhancing the surprise [1] ; while in the *Ion*, for the sake of making the plot still more piquant, Euripides makes Hermes prophesy events which Apollo fails to bring off properly.

The Euripidean prologue was then in origin a convention adopted out of artistic honesty. His tragic plots were never the self-contained interactions of a group of people, like the Sophoclean. They consisted rather of a series of typical events, bound together not by any strict law of causality, sometimes indeed by none at all, but by the fact that the poet could use them to convey a single tragic vision. It was logical therefore to start from some satisfactory *archê* (which in three of these plays was the Trojan War) and by simple narrative to continue until the section was reached which contained the events of the play. This was the origin of the prologue ; its use became something much more subtle. It could be used as in the *Hippolytus,* to close the gap between the ostensible and the inner drama ; or it could be used, as in the opposite examples of the *Hecuba* and the *Ion,* as a powerful means of controlling the story-element of the play, either by removing our interest from the crude events, all or some of them, or by directing our attention to them more closely.

It seems evident that the same circumstances which led to the prologue must lead also to the epilogue, that we shall both enter and leave the chosen section of the story by narrative. In fact, the narrative epilogue becomes standard only in the next group of plays ; the *Andromache* may end in a narrative summary, but the *Troades* can be brought to a full close by the crash of falling walls. Still, we can see in this group the difficulty of finding a convincing way of finishing a diagrammatic plot.

Here, as in the matter of continuity, the old trilogy had had

[1] In the *I.T.* Iphigeneia infers from a dream that Orestes is dead, and in the *Orestes* Electra places her hopes of safety in the arrival of the useless Menelaus.

little trouble. Its third play, like the first and second, dealt with a self-contained, though related, situation ; its plot was a logical story and a logical story has a logical end. Plays like the *Hecuba* have no end of this kind, no inevitable pause ; for if three symbolically related scenes, why not four or five ? There is no reason why the *Hecuba* should end with the vengeance on Polymestor except that nothing else is wanted and nothing could well be grimmer. The real end of the story of the *Andromache* is the death of Neoptolemus, but this neither makes a satisfactory dramatic close nor completes the poet's idea. The chorus can no longer end the play of its own authority with a funeral hymn (as it does in the *Septem*) nor, so far as concerns the idea, can it be the symbol of the community. For this, someone nearer the heart of the story must be chosen ; Euripides chooses Peleus, but nothing in the play makes this inevitable. So too the *Suppliant Women* ; the story would find its natural close in the recovery of the dead, or their cremation or removal to Argos. Iphis and Evadne are not what the story demands but what the poet wants ; the natural point of ending the story would not have given Euripides the material he wanted. Therefore, in the absence of a logical climax, there must be more or less of deliberate contrivance in the ending ; a feeling of finality has to be created.

To meet this difficulty was the function of the *Deus ex machina*. The simplest case of the Deus is Thetis in the *Andromache*. There, the action leads to a situation in which nothing more can happen, but which is not a satisfactory close. We can only watch Peleus mourning, and reviling the Spartans ; and to this there is no obvious term ; moreover there are loose ends lying about—Andromache for example, and, if the play is not to leave the wrong impression, a purely melodramatic one, Peleus must receive his consolation-prize for the sake of avoiding ' the shocking '. When the futures of Peleus, Andromache and Molossus are arranged for, when in fact the victims of this human accident are made comfortable, then the play can end.[1]

[1] This kind of ending goes naturally with any form of story in which all our sympathies and all our attention are not absorbed by

But as with the prologue, so with the epilogue ; a simple necessity is turned to powerful uses. The *Hecuba*, like the *Andromache*, leads to no inevitable end ; a god, this time at second hand, is introduced to prolong the story until finality is reached in the transformation of Hecuba and the murder of Agamemnon. But how much more than this there is in Polymestor's prophecies ! This epilogue, like the prologue of the *Troades*, suggests in dramatic form the tragic thought which underlies the whole play ; not a mere ending but an illumination of the whole action. Later we shall find the epilogue put to a markedly satrical use ; not in the tragedies, unless indeed we see satire, or perhaps irony, in the treatment of Athena at the end of the *Suppliant Women*.

Two more devices may be noticed, the first a point we have already discussed, the transformation of the Heroine. To see Eurystheus and even Polymestor on our own side of the fence as it were, to find them not exactly in the right, but at least persons to be considered with interest and some sympathy, is not in itself a climax, but it does help to produce a sense of finality. ' He was after all . . .' we say to ourselves ; it is clearly the end.

Finally, there is the *aition*, the linking of the story to some actual rite, monument or natural feature. Medea refers to an existing ritual at her children's supposed grave. Hippolytus has his worship, Hecuba becomes a rocky promontory, and so on. These serve the same end as the Deus and were usually associated with him.

Now aitia are universally popular, but especially with story-

---

the hero or heroes. At the end of the *Tyrannus* Sophocles does not have to pension off the two shepherds or tell us what happened to Teiresias ; he does not even have to arrange for Oedipus' daughters, although they are deliberately introduced, to show us more of Oedipus' character. With Thetis we may properly compare Jane Austen's charmingly conventional endings, in which minor characters are married off or otherwise provided for ; this because her comedy of manners is wider than her heroes and their fortunes. Thus the Euripidean Deus, already, it is admitted, a ' faded ' version of the Epiphany in which the earliest Tragedy ended, fades further into a mere last chapter, the god at length identified with the author—a confused situation which cannot be investigated here.

tellers and anthropologists. Why the story-teller likes them is perhaps a question for the psychologist rather than the critic. It may be that they lend an air of veracity to the story, for the audience will argue, by Aristotle's παραλογισμός, that since the thing explained does exist the story must be true ; or it may be that the aition forms a convenient half-way house between the fictive world of the story and the real world that will resume its sway when the story ends—a half-way house which has obvious advantages when the story does not end in a blaze of transfiguration. But whatever may be the psychological explanation, it is clear that when an aition turns up the play is over. It reinforces our feeling of finality, and is used when a play does not reach an Aristotelian end but merely stops.

To the anthropologist on the other hand the aition has been a matter not of stopping a drama but of beginning it. He has argued that since the aition comes in strongly at the end of Greek Tragedy it must have been there at the beginning : the Euripidean play ends with a reference to a rite because it originally *was* the rite ; the *Deus ex machina* represents an original Apotheosis. It may be so ; it is possible that we have before our eyes the awful spectacle of Euripides destroying himself, like the suicidal lemming, in blind obedience to an ancient instinct. Nevertheless as his aitia, like his gods, are so useful in his structure and so consonant with the diminished stature of his characters and the different significance of his plots, it seems safer to ascribe them to literary judgement, not to historical survival or antiquarianism. The one surviving play of Aeschylus we have that ends with anything like an aition, namely the *Eumenides,* is also the one which is intellectualist in tone. To his other plays, as to Sophocles always, they are quite foreign, simply because the quality of the dramatic thought in these plays could not endure them. Sophocles has one *Deus ex machina*—and it is in the *Philoctetes.*

CHAPTER X

NEW TRAGEDY : SOPHOCLES

1. THE TRACHINIAE We carried the classical Tragedy down to its culmination in the *Tyrannus* and *Electra* ; we have seen what radical changes Euripides made and why he made them —changes due to his personal genius rather than to anything that we can regard as an inevitable development. We now return to the main stream and begin to consider the last of our four stages of Greek Tragedy, one marked off by no such formal change as the introduction of another actor, but by a change in spirit—a change from the poetic to the intellectual or from the tragic to the theatrical or from the earnest to the gay—which does in fact affect form profoundly.

Frontiers are real, in nature and in art, but they are rarely precise. We might have included the *Electra* in New Tragedy or the *Trachiniae* in Middle, but as this frontier at least is not one to die for, we may perhaps accept this lack of precision. When we reach the *Philoctetes* it is clear that we are in a new country. This is a play that issues from no universal apprehension about life ; it is not, in the modern sense of the word, tragic, but is a study of character and situation made for the sake of its own very considerable interest. We have had character-study before, in abundance, but always in subordination to a universal and tragic conception ; now its function is not illumination but *diagogê*, serious recreation. To watch the transit of Neoptolemus from the side of Odysseus to the side of Philoctetes is absorbing, but it is no part of a universal human tragedy.

The *Trachiniae*, in a smaller degree, has this same quality ; it is the study of a particular situation. Every dramatic situation is indeed unique—if it were not it could not be dramatic—but yet the distinction between a particular and a universal situation is a clear one. The situation of the *Trachiniae*, the relations between Heracles and Deianeira and what they bring upon Heracles, is of a radically different kind from the situation in plays like the *Antigone* or *Tyrannus,* if only because Heracles is a particular, untypical character. We may not say that he is more of an individual than Oedipus ; that would be impossible. He is, however, less of a type. Oedipus, in spite of his eminence, is in a true sense 'like us' and he becomes a symbol of humanity ; Heracles is not 'like us' at all and he remains Heracles. No chorus could sing 'Alas ! ye generations of men' over his fall ; he is profoundly interesting precisely because he is so unusual. It is because the *Trachiniae* is to this extent a special study that we have put the frontier where we have.

Nevertheless, the *Trachiniae* is tragic as the *Philoctetes* and even the *Coloneus,* are not. Not only does the special tragedy of Deianeira, that is the whole middle section, display that same kind of conjuncture between character and circumstance as the *Tyrannus,* but, more important, at the end the chorus can declare 'All this is Zeus' : a recognition that in the destruction of the mighty, though amorous, Heracles by the poison of a dead enemy at the hands of a loving wife there can be descried the outlines of a Necessity, or a Justice, which we may well call Zeus.

In this combination of the particular and the universal the *Trachiniae* is not unlike the *Electra,* and we may be sure that both plays come from the same stratum of Sophocles' mind. The *Electra,* as we saw,[1] is new in style ; it is a study of a given character in a given situation—a fact reflected in its employment of the chorus. We can hardly call the play an imaginative working-up of the common stuff of life, and it may seem arbitrary to separate it from the *Trachiniae.* Nevertheless, Electra, though twisted by circumstances into something 'unlike' us, is much more nearly universal than Heracles, and the feeling which the play gives us that we are still in the older tradition, that in the warping of a noble character we have something of universal import, justifies us in calling it Middle Tragedy. Both plays show signs of transition to a more intellectualist drama, but the *Trachiniae* shows more of them.[2]

[1] P. 165.

[2] From this we may not conclude that the *Trachiniae* is neces-

About the *Trachiniae*, naturally, everything has been said,
that Sophocles wrote it young, before he had learned his
trade, that he wrote it old, when he had forgotten it,[1] and
that he did not write it at all.   These are the guesses of bankruptcy.   The influence of Euripides is commonly cited, but
what does this mean ?   If it means that plays like the *Medea*
and the *Hippolytus* suggested to Sophocles the use of the
love-theme, or that the *Heracles* suggested a different treatment of Heracles, the theory is plausible, though only biographical, for it remains to show how such a theme involves
such a structure.   If it means only that Sophocles thought that
he too would make a play with a dull prologue and a ' bad '
plot, we may safely dismiss it from our minds.   The play is
an unsatisfactory puzzle until we realize that it is a study
of a complex situation based upon the character of Heracles,
and including the married life of Deianeira and Heracles'
treatment of her and of others (notably Hyllus).   It is a
matter almost of exact demonstration that the form of the
play, so unusual in Sophocles,[2] arose directly out of this special
interest in a particular situation.

The important points that demand explanation are two, the
undramatic narrative prologue, and the lack of organic connexion between the Heracles-scenes and what has gone before.
We may take the more important first.

For what purpose is Heracles—rather inconveniently—
brought in ?   We have simply to notice what Sophocles does
with him and what he does not do—for we may assume that
he did what he intended.   The purpose, obviously, is not that
Heracles may be the conventional tragic hero, that he may
recognize, like Creon, that he has done wrong and that his
wrongdoing has brought ruin to others and to himself.
Neither in his mind nor in Sophocles' is there any suggestion
that he is one who has departed tragically from the norm.
Tragic hamartia, in the proper sense of the term, does not

---

sarily later than the *Electra*, because the periods of an artist's work
are not so sharply defined, but we can say that it is difficult to put
it back to the *Ajax-Antigone* period.

[1] On the *Trachiniae* and Sophocles' old age, see p. 323.

[2] Though cf. the *Coloneus*.   See below, pp. 405 f.

come into question. We look at Heracles for the sake of
seeing Heracles, and that is the end of it. Nor is he brought
in to wind up the play by consummating the tragedy of Deianeira. She disappears. We may indeed say that Heracles'
complete lack of interest in her death and innocence is the
culmination of her tragic life, but it is much more immediately
an illustration of what Heracles is, and we must note that Iole
is treated with almost as much disregard. Nothing could
have been simpler, if binding the play was what Sophocles
wanted, than to display Deianeira's body, or to make Hyllus
ask an indifferent Heracles for instructions about her burial.
Instead of this these concluding scenes introduce a new, or
at least a complementary dramatic interest, that of Heracles
himself ; and that most of all in his dealings with Hyllus. It
is this that makes the old explanations from juvenile or senile
incompetence so silly. Merely to have failed to tie the play
together by neglecting Deianeira is surely beyond the incompetence not only of a tired Sophocles, but also of a dramatist
who was not Sophocles at all.[1]

The end is essentially the presentation of Heracles, without
particular reference to Deianeira or Iole, and with no regard
to the formal unity of the play. Heracles is given a speech
(1046–1111) in which he laments his plight : the crafty
daughter of Oeneus has done to him what even Hera and
Eurystheus have failed to do (1048–50) ; no man was it, no
monster, but a woman, a female, who has destroyed him.
Such is his tone ; and in harmony with it he contemplates
himself as the mighty hero of many exploits, now brought so
low : ' See how I weep, like a girl ! . . . Come, look at my
poor body ! ' He remembers the Nemean lion, the hydra, the
Erymanthian boar ; no one has overcome him but this
woman : ' Only bring her to me, and even as I am I will crush
her.' Poor Deianeira is not even the treacherous wife ; only
a woman who has destroyed his body and outraged his spirit.
He is told the truth, but he has no thought for Deianeira,

[1] In fact, if the plot is bad, the author is certainly Sophocles. A
second-rate dramatist could not have failed to make a ' neat ' job
of the final scenes, and a third-rate one could not have written
the rest of the play.

only that if it is Nessus' poison that is working in him this is
the end indeed. Deianeira is dismissed, and not only does
Heracles continue to be entirely self-centred, but also Sophocles concentrates on him, to show us what he is. The
weight of what follows is thrown upon two points, two commands given to Hyllus, both utterly repugnant to him. He is
to burn his father alive, and—' a slight boon ' (1217)—he is to
marry Iole. Hyllus' horror persuades his father to modify the
first command ; as to the other, he is adamant—and his reason
for giving it is simply that none but his son must possess a
woman whom he has possessed. It is not tenderness towards
Iole, but a tribute to himself.

This complete disregard by Heracles of Hyllus' feelings is
the important motif of the scene, and reinforces our position,
that his silence about Deianeira is part of his character and
not in the first place part of her tragedy. Heracles enters the
play not to end that, but to build a new edifice,[1] though one
that rests on earlier foundations ; for we have heard already
how he has treated his wife (31 ff.), Iphitus, Lichas, Eurytus
and Iole, and we remember what he said to Hyllus (797 f.)
when the poison was beginning to work : ' Raise me, my son,
even if you must die with me.' Heracles is one who can do
heroic things partly because he can sacrifice everything to
himself. He has never a thought for another ; he is entirely
self-centred, ruthless to enemies, acquisitive, possibly affectionate (1147) but entirely selfish towards his family, unfeel-
ing to his wife, transient with other women, and a very great
man. Such a Heracles was the foundation of the interesting
and tragic situation that Sophocles imagined, and as such he
has to be displayed to us.

[1] Pohlenz (*Gr. Trag.*, p. 202) argues that the *Trachiniae* must be
roughly contemporary with the *Ajax* and *Antigone* because it is
zweispaltig like them and not a marked unity like the *Tyrannus*
and *Electra*. This is to be deceived by a word. Even if the
arguments we have given for the essential unity of the *Ajax* and
Antigone are not accepted, the fact remains that the second part
of the *Ajax* is concerned mainly with Ajax and that the first part
of the *Antigone* is not silent about Creon. Here we have two
parts deliberately kept separate, the second not the continuation of
the first but collateral. The similarity between this and the earlier
plays is quite superficial, the differences fundamental.

This deliberate disjunction can be traced also in the prologue, which is as unlike Sophocles' normal style as the middle
part of the play is like it. To the careful, dramatic and detailed development of situation that we find in the body of
the play is prefixed, awkwardly, a story that has nothing to do
with it except that it concerns the same people ; and the
interesting thing is that here, in the most Euripidean part of
the play, Sophocles is trying to be as unlike Euripides as possible. We can hardly assign the play to a date earlier than
420, by which time the conventional Euripidean prologue
was well established. Sophocles must have seen several of
them and he will not imitate them. Instead, he uses the
unsatisfactory compromise which Euripides tried in the *Medea*
and then discarded, namely the artificial dialogue. He will
not begin ' My name is Deianeira and I am living in Trachis
. . .' but prefers ' There is an old saying . . .'—so old that
we wonder what has happened to the dramatic openings to
which Sophocles has accustomed us. Then the story of the
wooing is recounted to the old Nurse, who must be familiar
with it ; nor is it told allusively, as if Deianeira were half-
musing to herself, but altogether informatively. She even
tells the Nurse where they are living now.

The scene goes on, using theatrical conventions that have
since become hoary with age. The Nurse, carefully speaking
in character as a slave to her mistress, suggests that of all her
sons Deianeira might send one—preferably Hyllus—to look for
news. At this moment Hyllus arrives with the rumour that
Heracles is at Oechalia in Euboea. Now, for the first time,
Deianeira tells him that she has a clear prophecy about
Heracles and Oechalia, oracles which indicate that Heracles
has reached a turning-point in his life. Hyllus must go there
with all speed.

Surely all this is a little limp and not really worthy of Sophocles ? To say nothing of the introductory narrative, the
artificial interlocutor is a piece of inertness unparalleled in
Sophocles, and the singular inability of Deianeira to do anything, even to tell her eldest son that there are important
oracles, is neither demanded by her character nor probable.
A certain innocence in affairs and a readiness to consult the

inexperienced chorus are necessary in her, but this complet
passivity is surprising in a woman who has such fineness o
mind, later on, and such understanding of life. In the mat
ter of the oracles Sophocles has covered up his tracks a little
the oracle mentioned an absence of fifteen months, so tha
now is the decisive time ; but we are not told this until th
next scene. It seems therefore that we should attribut
Deianeira's remarkable reticence, as well as the fact that th
first constructive suggestion comes from the Nurse, to th
need of giving the prologue dramatic shape rather than t
deliberate characterization.

The first act then is, by Sophoclean standards, no great suc
cess, and for this we must not blame the influence, still les
the example, of Euripides. He, by the year 420, would hav
made no bones about it. He would have found somebody
Zeus himself if necessary, to tell us all that this scene contains
and would have avoided this dramatic flabbiness. He ha
given up the pseudo-dramatic prologue ; why then did Soph
ocles revive it ? If he disliked Euripides' new, perfectly con
ventional prologue, why did he write one of any kind ? Why
did he not start off in his accustomed manner ? The reason
is not imitation of nor desire to improve on Euripides, bu
the same necessity that produced the Euripidean prologue
itself. The wooing of Deianeira by the un-Sophoclean mon
ster (so ill at ease in this setting), the fight, and the winning
of Deianeira by Heracles, are, like Heracles' bearing to Hyllus
at the end, part of the tragic situation in which Sophocles is
interested but not part of the main action of the play. Had
the play been designed as the tragedy of a loving wife who
makes a fatal error and destroys her husband, this previous
story would not have been wanted at all, except perhaps as a
choral decoration. But the theme is much more than this ;
it embraces Heracles, his character, and the whole of his dealings with Deianeira and even Iole. It is part of the tragic
situation that she was his victim then as Iole is now, that in
the beginning she was a prize of battle as Iole is now, that her
married life has been only the natural and unhappy fulfilment
of such a beginning. In fact, the manner of the wooing and
the nature of the marriage belong to and colour the action of

the *Trachiniae* as in a trilogy the first play colours the second. These things must come in, and it is not now enough that they should be given to the chorus ; they are important as events, and, whatever Aeschylus may have done in the *Agamemnon*, things which are important as events now belong to the actors.

Even so, most plays have a past, and the *Tyrannus* shows the proper way of bringing in past events, gradually and one at a time. Had then Sophocles not yet written or had he forgotten the *Tyrannus* ? It is not a question of technique at all, but of being true to the idea. In the *Tyrannus*, and elsewhere, Sophocles could bring in past events neatly because he could connect them with some part or other of the present action ; in fact, it was only because they bore on the present action that he mentioned them at all. So here ; the Nessus-incident can be made relevant to something in the play itself ; it is not therefore rehearsed in the prologue. What is in the prologue (apart from those few details which are manifestly due to the difficulty of starting a private theme on the public Greek stage) is both important in itself and as detached as if it were a separate story ; it must therefore, in order to make its effect, be treated as such ; not brought in piecemeal by an artificial cleverness, but narrated, and narrated as soon as possible. Sophocles could no doubt have imitated his normal openings—starting for example with the arrival of Hyllus ; but then, in order that we might see that the present crisis was only a part of a wider tragic situation, he would have had to insert elsewhere a speech of explanatory narrative. Euripides can put in speeches of pathetic reminiscence like this, but in the more closely-knit Sophoclean action such interruption would be intolerable.[1] Direct imitation of Euripides therefore plays no part here. A prologue is inevitable, to deal with matter which is collateral and not subordinate, and the only question is which form of prologue to choose. Sophocles does not choose the Euripidean form.

[1] It is interesting to see what Deianeira does say in the speech that might have been reminiscent (vv. 149 ff.). She permits herself a short comment on life, which, no less profound than most of Euripides', also illuminates both herself and the chorus ; then she passes directly to the matter in hand.

We see then that the ' foreign matter ' at the beginning and end of the play, which Sophocles has not attempted inconspicuously to incorporate in the main structure, becomes explicable when we assume what in any case the general tone of the play suggests, namely that it has the nature of a dramatic study rather than of a universal tragedy like the earlier plays. Sophocles is not working out the tragedy of the hamartia of Deianeira, but is interested in several facets of the situation created by so unusual a character as Heracles. There is no one overriding tragic conception of which the action is the dramatic embodiment ; if there had been it would of itself have provided the unity that we miss. Further, since it would have been so easy to give the play a superficial unity, we have direct evidence that at least on this occasion Sophocles approached his art with the intention of saying what he had to say, not merely of making an elegant piece for the stage.

It is hardly necessary to consider in detail the Deianeira scenes : it would be only to repeat what was said in an earlier chapter on Sophocles' technique. We have once more a tragedy which depends neither on nemesis overtaking its victim nor on some flaw in the Universe, but simply on a group of people being what they are and nothing else. Once more we have the tragic and perfectly presented combination of character and circumstance ; for had Deianeira been less profoundly understanding of Heracles' weakness and of the nature of mankind, she would long since have ceased to love him and would not have wanted to recapture his love ; had she been more acute in affairs she would have suspected the philtre from the beginning ; had her chorus been men and not maidens of Trachis she might have been warned ; had the Messenger not seen his chance of getting a good tip by anticipating Lichas, or if, having come, he had had the sense to take his lead from him, the situation might have cleared itself naturally. We have the irony which wounds Heracles, and which Sophocles underlines with an oracle, that it should have been a woman, and that an innocent one, who destroyed the great hero ; that Nessus, whose poison it was, should have been justly slain by Heracles (and then so surprisingly re-

venged) for committing the sort of sin to which Heracles himself is so prone—the one in fact which leads to his downfall.
Always we have the fatal conjuncture of people and events,
both elaborated to the significant point and no more. The
irony, the dramatic control, the vividness and the poetry will
bear comparison with anything that Sophocles ever wrote.[1]
Every feature of the mature tragic style is there, except one,
namely that continuity and amplitude of rhythm which it was
especially the function of the Chorus to assist. This chorus,
which is dramatically little more than the conventional Confidante, does not impose itself on us and can do very little
towards binding the successive scenes into one dramatic
movement. This is an inevitable result of the private nature
of the theme. The difficulty began in the *Electra,* but there
the personality of Electra enabled Sophocles to make capital
out of it [2]; Deianeira lacks this personality and cannot impose
herself on the chorus, while the chorus cannot convince us
that the action is really one which its odes can heighten or
illuminate. It is made, ironically, to welcome a happy event,
but the stroke suffers by comparison with the Bacchus ode of
the *Antigone* and its counterpart in the *Tyrannus,* and it is no
advantage that it is here used twice (205–24, 633–62). The
other odes are on the whole decorative rather than dramatic,[3]
and the chorus itself as much a spectator as it is in the *Medea.*
This is inevitable. The drama is intimate and domestic, its
tragic implications limited to itself. There are no far-reach-
ing generalizations—‘ Alas ! You generations of men. . . . ’
—which the action forces the chorus to make. From this
Heracles one cannot generalize.

[1] For irony, see especially 491–6 ; for vividness and realism,
195–9.

[2] See above, p. 175.

[3] The Parodos, for example, is made up, not tense with thought
and emotion like the typical Sophoclean ode. Compare the conscious repetition of ‘ starry night ’ (vv. 94 and 132) with the repetitions of ‘ disaster ’ and ‘ comes ’ in the *Antigone* ode. The
repetition here means nothing. Nor is the description of the fight
(507 ff.) dramatic—not as we use the word of Sophocles ; it is not
out of place, but it does nothing in particular for us. These are
charming compositions but not great lyrics.

It is difficult to leave the *Trachiniae* without a word on the comparisons which it suggests with Euripides. The poisoned robe, to say nothing of the frequent references to Eros (352, 441, 460, 489, 543, with the beginning of the ode at 497 ff.), remind one of the *Medea*, and there is Euripides' treatment of Heracles. The comparison brings out the fundamental difference in mind between the poets; Euripides' intellectual, rather abstract approach to drama, and the concrete, plastic nature of Sophocles' imagination. Love, in the *Medea*, is a natural force, and, however real we may feel Medea to be, the thought is never lacking that we are watching the workings of this natural force, beneficent when moderate, terrible when strong. Heracles is no more a typical character than Medea, but he convinces us as she does not; and though she disappears in a magic chariot and he to be heroically burned on Oeta, there is no comparison between the endings. Heracles remains solid fact, Medea is transmuted. Nor have we anywhere in the *Trachiniae*, as we have in the *Medea* and still more in the *Hippolytus*, the feeling that Love is almost a separate actor in the drama. It is always Heracles in whom we are interested; he does not exemplify anything but is simply himself. The Messenger says (354) that Heracles is overcome by Eros only, but this conception is used not to suggest the might of Eros but to illuminate the behaviour of Heracles; and when the chorus begins ' Mighty is the power of the Cyprian ', this leads not to a hymn in honour of the goddess, but to a description of the fight for Deianeira. In the *Antigone* we meet a reference (781 ff.) to Love as a universal power, but in the *Trachiniae*, where we might expect an ampler treatment of the idea, it never appears except as a part of Heracles' character.

As to the two pictures of Heracles, if the conspicuous difference between the poets was that Sophocles was orthodox, Euripides sceptical, it is remarkable that it is Euripides who glorifies the Labours as Labours, while Sophocles treats them only as individual achievements. It is the intellectualist, non-athletic, anti-Spartan Euripides who gives the most exalted picture of the athletic hero. This perhaps we may take as a warning that a poet's opinions are a much less important part of his work than they are often taken to be. The difference between the two pictures of Heracles has nothing at all to do with orthodoxy or an attitude to a hero. They proceed straight from dramatic bias. To Sophocles, the Heracles of the Labours would have been of no dramatic interest; the psychology would have been too elementary. Stripped of the supernatural and institutional, however, regarded as a man who does quite exceptional things, he becomes dramatically interesting, an unusual and an uncomfortable character. Euripides, on the other hand, did not have this interest in the tragic complexities of the individual; his tragedy, like Aeschylus', was much more likely to take a cosmic, or at least a social, flight. Heracles the unusual character did not attract him, but Heracles the supreme type of unhappy genius did, the benefactor of man and tamer of Nature whose end should have been honour and peace but was torture.[1]

2. The Philoctetes   When we reach the year 409, and the *Philoctetes*, the English word Tragedy becomes a little unsuitable, for although the play contains scenes of pathos, neither the treatment nor the issue is what we normally mean by 'tragic'. It is tragedy only on Aristotle's definition of tragedy as the representation of serious action. The interest of the play is first that of following an intrigue, and secondly that of watching the effect on Neoptolemus' mind of the helplessness of Philoctetes, and the effect on his of years of suffering. The whole basis of the play is ethical,[2] but the presentation of the ethical action is now an end in itself; the ' serious

[1] It is a disaster that we have lost Aeschylus' conception of Heracles in the *Prometheia*. We cannot suppose that he played a merely mechanical role in the drama, and in the suggestive collocation of Prometheus who taught Man the arts of life, Heracles who made the world habitable for him, and Zeus the supreme God, we can dimly descry the dimensions of what we have lost.

[2] But attempts to read the play as a moral or political lesson to the Athenians are no more successful than they deserve to be. If Sophocles wished to demonstrate that the extreme doctrine of utility is wrong and must fail (as Pohlenz argues), why did he weaken his case by loading the scales so improbably against the doctrine of utility—making the Greeks treat Philoctetes in such a way that he was most unlikely to help them later?

action ' of two interesting men in an interesting situation is enough to absorb our attention, with no reference to the larger issues of Man's place in the universe and his destiny.

We must notice too that the attack of Euripidean influence has spent its force, or very nearly. This time there is no question of the unity of the action or of the certainty with which every detail in the complex plot is controlled. We may notice further that a similar skill in managing his plots was shown by Euripides in those plays of his in which pure tragedy has given place to something lighter. Sophocles' return to the straight path and the conversion of Euripides to orthodox methods, accompanied as both are by a marked change of tone, are not likely to be accidental.

Let us consider the plot first. The play begins with no conventional prologue but in the true Sophoclean manner. We maintained that the prologue to the *Trachiniae* was to be explained by nothing mechanical, like imitation or debility, but by the logic of the play : we ought therefore to be able to show that the logic of the *Philoctetes* allows, even if it does not demand, the more dramatic start. We may point out then that the past story here is relevant to the present action, not something of independent weight ; it is only as it explains the present situation and the behaviour of the persons in the play that it is wanted. We may perhaps imagine a tragedy on this theme whose point was that Philoctetes had been cruelly betrayed by the Greeks in the past, has suffered torments since, and in the present is even more cruelly robbed of his bow that the Greeks may take Troy ; while in an epilogue, certain of the Greek leaders, Troy being successfully taken, are doomed themselves to perish by treachery. This would not be a very good play (though it might admirably illustrate the thesis that the extreme doctrine of utility is wrong and must fail), but the outline illustrates our point, that the past story would have independent weight as being the first of a series of crimes culminating in retribution, and therefore it would have to be told independently and entire, in a formal prologue. As it is, the great point of the past story is that it keeps Odysseus in the background, that it makes Philoctetes implacable, that it produces an increasing

strain on Neoptolemus' better feelings ; it is a reserve which
is drawn on as it becomes necessary.

This then being the logical method here, we may notice
how skilfully it is used. Odysseus tells his part of the story
first to Neoptolemus, putting the fairest possible front on it in
order not to make Philoctetes an object of pity. The implication that Neoptolemus has not heard the story before is not
awkward, but quite dramatic ; the spirited and generous
young man has been got safely to Lemnos before he is told
anything of the shady side of the business. There is another
point. The deeper interest of the play, underlying the dramatic intrigue but going closely with it, is the moral adventure
of Neoptolemus, who first surrenders himself to Odysseus,
then goes over completely to the other side. This assumption
that Neoptolemus knows nothing at the start not only avoids
a tedious prologue and neatly suggests Odysseus' wary pre-
liminaries, but also it allows us to watch Neoptolemus, as it
were, from scratch.

With equal skill and economy Philoctetes' side of the story
is told to a Neoptolemus who has to pretend to know nothing
about it ; so that we, the audience, learn necessary facts while
the recital of these facts is illuminating Philoctetes for us and
is also working powerfully on the mind of Neoptolemus.
Never did Sophocles more notably exploit his ability to do
three things at once.

It is no new thing that Sophocles controls the whole of his
complicated plot with this high degree of dexterity ; what is
new in the *Philoctetes* is the pellucid and unforced naturalism
which penetrates every part of the play, even the use of
tribrachs. When Neoptolemus leaves the wary Odysseus
somewhere below and climbs up alone to look for the cave
that Odysseus vaguely remembers, when Philoctetes twice interrupts Neoptolemus to ask how his old companions-in-arms
have fared, when the Merchant asks in a pretended stage-
whisper who the old man is, when Philoctetes desperately
tries to control his pain, when Neoptolemus, having changed
his mind, comes back with Odysseus at his heels, protesting—
in these and in many other places we are strongly reminded
of the delicate naturalism of early fourth-century sculpture.

The figures and the action stand before us with an easy vivid
ness unlike anything we have yet seen.

Lest we should think of this, or of any part of it, such a
the metrical details, as an independent development of Sophocles' style, we may note that it is all a logical part of the new
dramatic interest. The action of the drama *is* invested with
a new reality; it is being made for its own sake: there is no
tragic background of Unwritten Law or the frailty of Man to
colour the scene. The *Philoctetes* is not precipitated out of
some universal tragic conception. Sophocles now is interested, not possessed; his creations now are not symbols (using
the word with all reserve), but figures whose importance is
strictly limited to the play in which they appear. In this play
we are expected to take a more purely intellectual interest;
it is being worked up for its own sake. In this cooler, more
realistic, more limited sphere elaboration of detail is natural
and indeed necessary; it is, in a sense, what the play is for.
In the earlier drama with its intenser spirit it would have been
trivial and offensive.

It is, however, important to see within what sharp limits
this naturalism operates, for the setting of the *Philoctetes* is
very arbitrary, and, were it considered realistically, impossible. We have to accept a magic bow, a thing which we
should rightly reject if it attempted to play so important a part
in a tragedy. More seriously, we have to assume that there
was a spot on Lemnos from which it was impossible to make
contact with the Lemnians (or alternatively that there were
no Lemnians), a spot at which nevertheless sailors have called
by inadvertence, but sailors too indifferent both to suffering
and to money to carry a sick man to Greece, a few hours
distant; too indifferent even to take a message to his princely
father. When we remember the Hellenic desire to interfere
shown by the messengers in the *Tyrannus* and the *Trachiniae*,
to say nothing of the reward which the Greek dramatists regularly allowed their Messengers to collect, this indifference is
indeed unlikely.

But obviously it does not matter in the least. We exercise
ourselves over the 'irrational' in the *Tyrannus* without noticing the 'irrational' in the *Philoctetes* because it is important

that the *Tyrannus* should appear rational in all its parts. That play is 'a criticism of Life', and as such it must not allow us to suspect that it is a made-up case. It is important that the whole story of Oedipus should be something which *would* happen; with the *Philoctetes* that does not matter a scrap. Here we are interested in the problem only; the setting can be as artificial as it likes. Some of the best of chess-problems start with a situation that could not possibly arise out of a rational game. Our interest in the *Philoctetes* is not directly in the sufferings of the outcast and in his tragic case; if it were these large assumptions would be inadmissible; it is in watching Neoptolemus moving between two fixed points, and if certain assumptions are necessary to fix one of the points, we make them easily; they are not in the picture. In chess it is the play of mind against mind that catches our attention, and if we are wise we accept without question the unproven assumption that bishops can move only diagonally. We have therefore more realism within the now restricted ambit of the drama, and considerable room for sheer artificiality on its confines.

This realism, which comes from concentrating on the scene itself for its own interest, is essentially different, and feels different, from the realism of the tragedies, where it is always contributory to the tragic conception, never an effect; it is the complete antithesis to the method used by Euripides in his tragedies. There the action, far from being an end in itself, was only a pointer to an underlying conception; it could therefore be discontinuous and almost dispense with characterization. Now that there is no underlying conception (for we need not suppose the idea that honest men are better than rogues, or that ten years of incredible suffering make a man hard, so worked in Sophocles' mind that he had to write a play about it) strict unity of action must be restored or the play would be meaningless as well as 'ill-constructed'.

Nevertheless, it is restored on somewhat different terms. The fact that the plot, the *mythos*, has now no transcendental significance opens the door to a preliminary artificiality, as we have just seen; it has too an effect on the ending which

we discussed in connexion with Euripides.[1] A tragedy like
the *Tyrannus*, however real and self-contained it is, does pre-
figure a tragic idea such that the end of the action is also the
climax of the idea ; the two are one, and if the end of the play
is not as it were apocalyptic it is an offence. This is no
longer true. The mental and moral journey that Neoptolemus makes we are to follow for its own sake, not, as we follow
Oedipus', for its own sake and also with the feeling that we
are apprehending something about Man himself. When the
journey is finished we are satisfied ; no catharsis is wanted
and we do not wait with bated breath for some larger consummation. If it happens that part of the story is left over,
that is a minor matter ; a god can put that right, it being, in a
real sense, ' outside the play '—like the improbabilities of the
setting.

But it is not quite enough to say that Heracles, by magically
altering Philoctetes' unalterable resolution, allows Troy to
have been taken after all, as history says it was. Besides
rescuing the dramatist from a trivial difficulty, he does something positive. When Philoctetes remains unpersuaded and
Neoptolemus makes his great renunciation, our interest in the
situation is exhausted. We do not, for example, wish to know
if Odysseus was punished for his chicanery, nor would it add
any point at all to the play if the potential renunciation became a real one—rather the reverse, for it would compel us
suddenly to regard in an almost tragic light characters in
whom we have been interested simply for the sake of their
mental processes. The ' happy ending ' brings the story to a
close in the region to which it belongs, that of pleasant fiction.

But with all the harmonious unity of action, penetration in
character-drawing, limpidity of style and ingenuity of plot,
the *Philoctetes* would not have been a masterpiece of the later
Greek stage without one final stroke, eminently characteristic
of Sophocles—the welding of the Chorus into the new drama
of intrigue. This presented difficulties. A play in which the
pure story-element is so prominent does not lend itself easily
to music and dancing ; intrigue ought to go along at a pace,
uninterrupted, and Euripides has already shown how incon-

[1] See above, pp. 300 ff.

venient, or at best how superfluous, the chorus might be in drama of this order. Sophocles, however, succeeds in making the chorus fit in perfectly, making it what it was in the *Eumenides,* an Actor whose special gift of lyricism could be turned to natural dramatic use.

It was indeed something that he avoided the difficulties inherent in a Chorus of Lemnians, namely that if it apologizes for its ten-year neglect of Philoctetes the improbability is underlined, if it does not, it runs the risk of being censured, as was Aeschylus' chorus, by the impeccable Euripides. The real problem, however, was to avoid holding up the action by decorative odes, and to make the fifteenfold Presence contribute to it instead of being at best a company that one could overlook. First of all Sophocles has made it an assistant to Neoptolemus in the treachery that is to be improvised (vv. 148–9), so that we await its remarks with interest instead of resigning ourselves to the inevitable. Then, that the chorus may not only be called a fellow-conspirator but may also act like one, he has rehandled the traditional form even more drastically than in the *Electra.* There is only one set ode (676 ff.), sung at a natural pause in the action when the stage is empty, and it is extremely dramatic, for if this is the impression that Philoctetes has made on the chorus, how great a one must he have made on the more sensitive Neoptolemus ? [1] Its other utterances are all made into conversations with one of the actors, with the exception of the pair of stanzas embedded in the Parodos, and the two separate ones which relieve the long scene. These use the real lyrical note very cleverly. The former pair (169 ff.) conveys the natural reaction of the honest sailors to the story which they have heard, suggesting to us the feelings with which Neoptolemus will have to reckon. Of the second pair, cunningly placed, the first with its invocation solemnly reinforces Neoptolemus' lie ; the other, expressing pity at Philoctetes' plight, is a contribu-

---

[1] Masqueray points out (ed. Budé, p. 106) that while the stage is quite empty the chorus speaks very freely of its pity for Philoctetes, but when he and Neoptolemus are seen returning from the cave the gallant conspirators become circumspect again. The neat point is characteristic of this play.

tion (so the conspirators hope) to the abduction of Philoctetes. There is not a trace of mere lyrical decoration—no
kingfishers or nightingales.

In the third place, the chorus is given a certain interest as
a character, a foil to their master. From the beginning it
expresses lively sympathy with Philoctetes, and this theme—
the only available one both lyrical and dramatic—Sophocles
uses well. The chorus is sympathetic at the beginning and
sympathetic at the end, but it does nothing ; naturally, it has
to obey orders—it is Neoptolemus' part to take decisions ; still,
left alone with Philoctetes towards the end it does not give
way, but with dogged persistence asserts that it is his own
fault ; it can even say, ' Come with him who has shown you
such good-will.' This, lightly perhaps but perceptibly, draws
through the play a level line that shows off more clearly the
movement in Neoptolemus' part.

Finally, it is perhaps just worth pointing out that the fact
that the chorus can be left behind by Neoptolemus does more
than turn the screw on Philoctetes and still further display his
obduracy. It enables Sophocles to avoid the attempt of
showing Neoptolemus' *volte-face* on the stage. This would
have been awkward. A soliloquy, like Medea's, would have
marred the exquisite naturalness of the play, and stichomythia
would have been false, because Neoptolemus is not convinced
by arguments or by appeals, but by his own instincts. It is
far finer and truer that his change of front should be left to
our imaginations and not traced in speech.

It was a remarkable achievement for the ancient goat-song
to develop into so supple a dramatic instrument as this, and
for his success Sophocles was very largely indebted to his
management of the chorus. The absence of any deep tragic
theme took from it its most natural material, while the new
prominence of the action made this more than ever an Actors'
play. Yet the chorus must be there, and it must sing ; it must
provide the curtains without impeding the action. The skilful but unobtrusive way in which Sophocles has made this
potential nuisance one of his most delicate instruments makes
one wish that there had survived a second-rate play of his in

this manner whereby we might measure more clearly the success of the *Philoctetes*.

If then we are to look in Sophocles' work for signs of old age, it must be through the *Trachiniae* to this play, with the *Coloneus* to follow. The *Trachiniae* will now be seen as a sign of vigour, not weakness ; not the first-fruits of decay but a work of transition and experiment, leading from triumphs like the *Tyrannus* to triumphs like the *Philoctetes*. It is indeed risky work, talking of the old age of poets of this calibre, as Mark Pattison so disastrously showed in speaking of Milton.[1] Maintaining that *Samson* was the tired work of an old man whose ' power over language was failing ', he actually clinched his argument by saying ' I could almost fancy that the consciousness of decay utters itself in the lines:

> ' So much I feel my genial spirits droop,
> My hopes all flat, nature within me seems
> In all her functions weary of herself ;
> My race of glory run, and race of shame,
> And I shall shortly be with them that rest.'

Sophocles too decayed like this ; at least he began a new dramatic career at the age of 75 or thereabouts, in which the visible signs of age are the assurance of this technique and this turning away from the strenuousness of tragedy to the neater pleasures of intrigue and character-study for its own sake. To the *Philoctetes* we might apply that splendid image of Longinus' : ' Homer in the *Odyssey* may be compared to the setting sun ; the grandeur remains, but not the intensity.'

We have, however, to bear in mind that at about the same time Euripides was going through a similar development. The comparison is interesting. Euripides had his great tragic period (so unlike Sophocles'), culminating in the *Troades*, and then turned to non-tragic, or at least specialist drama. In plays like the *Ion, I.T., Electra*, we have, to speak generally, the sheer interest in plot as our basis, and on top of this, damaging attacks on Delphi, or an interest in character which we may reasonably call pathological. These are clearly descendants of the two chief interests of his tragic

[1] *Milton* (English Men of Letters), p. 197.

period; his pitiful Electra and Orestes are heirs to such as Medea and Hippolytus—all of them abnormal, but the one pair tragically, the other pathologically; the anti-Apolline strain is a natural successor to the strong social element in the war-tragedies. In the *Philoctetes* plot-interest is the most obvious thing; on it is laid a close study of character and mind, allied to interesting (no longer terrifying) turns of circumstance, in clear descent from character and circumstance as presented in the *Tyrannus* and *Electra*, but without the tragedy. In this we see clearly a bias personal to each of the two poets continuing through two stages of a parallel development.

This raises the question whether something else was not at work, the *Zeitgeist* which we have so studiously neglected. It obviously was, particularly in Euripides, who was so much more immediately in contact with social and political life than the more poetic and philosophic Sophocles. It seems clear that in these later plays Sophocles was writing for an audience which no longer demanded to be transfigured in the theatre, only to be seriously interested; had this not been so, he might have stopped writing, like Shakespeare. Nevertheless, Sophocles is always so directly explicable from his own work that the invocation of something external seems unlikely to increase our understanding of it. Disregarding externals is less dangerous than working from them. We may, with Pohlenz,[1] safely relate the *Philoctetes* with the new political morality if we remember that this is treating the play as an historical event, and is social history or biography, not criticism. The danger is that we may interpret drama as politics —imagining for example that political views and not dramatic thinking governed the portraiture of Creon or Oedipus.

The whole question of the relation between an artist's activities and external events is a difficult but important one. On the assumption that the Greek dramatist was the Educator of his people we can set up a close correlation between Greek drama and contemporary history which makes everything clear except the plays themselves. If the poet is a poet, his work can be explained only as poetry, and imaginative poetry

[1] *Gr. Trag.*, p. 355.

is not in direct contact with life. The poet is, but not the
poetry. The relation between poetry—for this argument I
should not count Tennyson's *Ode on the Great Exhibition*
as poetry—and the external event is that the external event
affects the poet's thought or imagination in a certain way, and
this affection produces the poem. That is, the ' reality ' which
concerns the poem, and ought to concern the critic, is not
the external event but the event in the poet's mind ; this it is,
and this alone, which will explain what the critic wishes to
explain in the poem—its content, form and style. This can
be derived only from the poet's own work. The external
event itself will give no explanation that can be relied on, but
will be very likely to lead to a misunderstanding of the work
itself, and the more imaginative the work, the greater the risk
of misunderstanding.[1] Knowledge of the external event is
by no means to be despised ; we may be able to establish an
interesting chain from the political reality through the poetical
reality to the poem—as in fact we allowed ourselves to do with
Euripides and the war ; but to the literary critic, as distinct
perhaps from the historian of literature, the first part of the
chain is of little value ; the second he must have. Let us not
confuse the realities, lest in the fact that Ajax commits suicide

[1] Those who do not believe this should turn again to Pattison,
Milton, p. 196, where they will see Nemesis in her most terrifying
form descending on the critic for confusing his realities. *Samson*
is the agonized cry of the defeated Puritans, here is ' that real basis
of truth which was necessary to inspire him to write '. ' The basis
of reality becomes so complete that the nominal personages of the
drama almost disappear behind the history which we read through
them. ' Exactly ; and the nominal poetry and the nominal drama
disappear too ; so that, although *Samson* is ' the intensest utterance
of the most intense English poet ', ' while as an expression of real
suffering no fictive drama can equal [it], as a composition the
drama is languid, nerveless, occasionally halting, never brilliant '.

We, in our Classical studies, never penetrate nonsense to this
depth ; for one thing, we have much less biographical information.
Still, when we see between a work of Greek literature and a contemporary event such a relation as obviously exists between
Milton's own experience and *Samson*, we should do well to ask ourselves what that relation means, what reality is, and what an artist
does with his experience ; also perhaps what is the difference between ' fictive ' and any other form of drama that we can think of.

while Euripides' Heracles refrains we see not different dramatic characters but ' der Geist einer neuen Zeit '.[1]

Sophocles was so purely a poet of the creative, imaginative type that to take the further and, strictly speaking, unnecessary step backwards from the poetic reality to a reality of fact that may have influenced or even caused it is particularly hazardous. He was an active citizen, he knew everybody ; but between his political and social experiences and his plays there intervenes his mind, and his mind was deep and imaginative. Euripides, more intellectual than Sophocles, preyed more obviously on what was happening around him, but even so we should not forget that his tragic reality was something other than the War : he did not need the Sicilian disaster to suggest the *Troades* to him. Even more clearly the reality from which came the *Persae* was not the Persian War but a religious conception suggested by it. If we neglect this we may say that Aeschylus 'idealized' Salamis and Plataea ; which is not true, and does not explain the play. He simplified Salamis and he falsified Persian history because his dramatic conception had become distinctly out of touch with ' reality '.

It seems safer, therefore, in considering the change which came over Sophocles' work to stick to what seems to be the fact, that a change came over his mind. This enables us to give a rational account of all the differences between the *Philoctetes* and his earlier work. If we knew why this change came over his mind it would be interesting, but it would add nothing to our understanding of the plays.

[1] Pohlenz, *Gr. Trag.*, p. 316.

CHAPTER XI

NEW TRAGEDY : EURIPIDES' TRAGI-COMEDIES

This term, not altogether a satisfactory one, is intended to describe the *Alcestis, Iphigeneia in Tauris, Ion,* and *Helen,* four plays which are essentially akin, even though the *Iphigeneia* ought perhaps to be called romantic melodrama and the *Helen* high comedy. There is indeed ancient precedent for inability to classify these plays convincingly. The second Argument to the *Alcestis,* in a passage which is a perfect example of rule-of-thumb criticism, calls the play *satyrikoteron,* ' in the manner of the satyric play ', and states, simply on the ground of its happy ending, that it is comedy rather than tragedy, like the *Orestes.* Strange reasoning leads to strange results. There is something common to the *Alcestis* and the *Orestes,* but it is hardly comedy, and certainly not to be detected by a comparison of endings.

Needless to say, in the urbane and sophisticated *Alcestis* there is no trace of the satyric ; the slightly tipsy Heracles is at the most a touch of low comedy. The play is pure tragicomedy, like the *Ion.* Twenty years later Euripides could put a non-tragic play in the honourable part of the tetralogy ; in 438, within five years of the *Antigone,* this seems to have been impossible, so that a play more tragic and less comic than the *Helen* (which ranked as tragedy) was put in the position normally occupied by the farcical satyric play.

The differences between these four plays are considerable, but what they have in common is more fundamental. In sharp contrast with Euripides' tragedies these tragi-comedies have plots whose construction is not only free from fault but even deft and elegant to a remarkable degree ; the character-drawing is no longer inconsistent, but is neat and entirely unembarrassed ; and no longer are we puzzled or irritated by untimely rhetoric and sophistry. The dramatist who has been accused of utter helplessness suddenly becomes a model of virtuosity. But for all that there are problems, problems

which again unite the four plays. It is not altogether easy
for us to take up the correct critical attitude to them. We
find, in disturbing proximity, the grave and the gay, or what
is worse the grave and the flippant. Alcestis' death is sand-
wiched between a flippant treatment of the grim figure of
Death and a scene between Admetus and Pheres which is
never far from comedy or satire, and the burlesquing of
Heracles is to follow. Calling the play ' satyric ' may stand
for an explanation of the burlesque, but it does not explain
the tragedy. The *Ion* offers on the one hand the anguish and
the mortal danger of Creusa, and on the other the broad
comedy of Xuthus. The *Helen* is comedy from beginning
to end, yet its messenger-speech costs the death of fifty or so
innocent Egyptians, and its first formal ode (1107 ff.) touches
a purely tragic note when it deals with the Trojan War.

If Euripides is a good and consistent dramatist, one worthy
of his fame, there should be one explanation of these features,
or at least a critical point of view from which they appear
logical and coherent. Or can we, time after time, only shrug
our shoulders and say ' Oh ! Euripides again ' ? Pearson, a
discreet critic, remarks—in the introduction to his *Helen* (p.
22)—' It will be observed how Helen, in referring to the story
of Leda, qualifies her reference by the expressions " if this
story is true " (21), " as they say " (259). No reasonable
excuse has been, or can be, offered for this defect.' In these
points, then, details indeed but obtrusive ones, was Euripides
quite insensitive ? It is possible ; it is possible too that the
critic is looking from the wrong viewpoint. It is a simple
matter to see that these plays are tragi-comedies, but it is
also necessary to draw and apply the correct critical deduc-
tions from this.

Verrall, as often, helps us with one of his illuminating mis-
takes ; he could not bring himself to believe that these plays,
or at least the *Ion,* were not deadly serious : ' If the speech
of Athena is really the Poet's last word . . . then Euripides
cannot be acquitted of trifling and paltering with everything
that deserves respect . . . then indeed, for such a purpose and
to such an end, he had no right to drag us through the wind-
ings of such a labyrinth.' His Introduction to the *Ion* suggests

that tragi-comedy is perhaps one of mankind's intermittent tastes. Certainly this criticism of Verrall's might be aimed with as much effect against Shakespeare. Is it possible that the awful scene of the wicked Jew sharpening his knife against Antonio is contrived only to excite the audience? Portia holds the ace of trumps all the time, and Shylock has committed himself irretrievably; why does she hold it back? Why is Antonio put to the agony of baring his breast, of seeing his vindictive enemy stretch out his hand to him? Surely nothing but the most intense tragic conception can justify this? But the tragic conception is not there. The play proceeds to the comedy of the rings, and ends with a passage which school editions discreetly omit. The agony of Antonio serves only to give the audience its thrill—yet the *Merchant* is a good play, not a monstrosity to be excused by the plea of Elizabethan taste. The reason is that it is composed within the conventions proper to tragi-comedy, which are by no means the same as those of tragedy. One important difference is that the plot of a tragedy must appear real, but the plot of a tragi-comedy may be, and normally is, entirely artificial. The crucial point seems to be that the existence which Antonio enjoys is considerably less real than that of a tragic hero; for, to go no further, the single and improbable fact that on this particular occasion all Antonio's argosies are wrecked demonstrates of itself that we are moving in a world of make-believe different from the more serious make-believe of tragedy. Antonio has his being within the conventions proper to tragi-comedy, and we can accept the momentary agony because we know that these conventions will somehow prevent the knife from cutting.

In considering these four plays of Euripides' we must begin, as always, by asking ourselves what the dramatist was trying to do. We have seen even the admired Sophocles laying himself open to the charge of faulty construction because he was concerned not with making impeccable plays but with expressing a tragic idea; we have seen, from the *Medea* onwards, that Euripides' loyalty to his tragic conceptions led him further and further from academic standards of dramatic form; more than once we have seen our dramatists disdaining a stroke that would have been superficially effective because it was not the stroke that the idea demanded ; we have remarked that the word 'effective' belongs to a late stage of the art.[1] That stage has now arrived. The philosophic historian of Tragedy is wont to say, with some justice, that it now becomes secular ; from our merely literary point of view it does not matter much that tragedy becomes secular ; Sophocles himself is secular in spirit in comparison with Aeschylus ; what has a most important bearing on the form of drama is that it ceases to be informed, and therefore controlled, by some dominant tragic conception, whether that be religious or not. For when all allowance is made for the serious, critical strain in the *Ion* and *Iphigeneia,* it is evident that the first purpose of the dramatist in writing these plays was to create an effective stagepiece ; to exploit the resources of his art for their own sake, not for the sake of something bigger.

Therefore the dramatist, for the first time, is free to attend entirely to his 'form', unhampered by any tragic conception working its imperious will on the play. He can devote himself completely to excellence of workmanship ; in fact he must, for this is now his whole 'meaning'. In this respect only, we may compare these plays with minor poetry ; it is when the poet has nothing in particular to say that he must be most elegant and attractive.[2]

Because these plays have a more limited scope than the tragedies we have entirely to change our critical premisses. Alcestis and Antonio are less real than Oedipus and Macbeth ; theatrical reality takes the place of tragic, that is to say universal, reality. It is to be noticed that all these plays are founded on an impossibility, and that not a 'probable impossibility', like the evocation of Darius, but one which is presented as a fiction. By cheating the Fates Apollo pro-

---

[1] See above, p. 37.

[2] The critic of Euripides has much to complain of, but in one important point he is fortunate. We know the date of two of these well-made plays ; the *Alcestis,* 438, and the *Helen,* 412 ; the ill-made plays come between. The critic is not therefore under the obligation of refuting a theory that at one period of his career Euripides made good plots, at another bad ones. Here at least it is evident that date explains nothing, dramatic purpose everything.

longs Admetus' life—if he can find a substitute ; the *Iphigeneia*
and *Helen* start from a miraculous substitution ; the *Ion* is
based on a divine parentage and miraculous rescue which
—told as they are here—nobody would believe.   But the whole
basis of serious Greek tragedy has been reality.   The supernatural could readily be admitted as a dramatic accessory—
a probable impossibility—but the essence of the whole thing,
from the Suppliants down to the Greeks of the *Troades,* was
that real persons in a real situation act and suffer in a real
way.   Medea's chariot is no exception to this principle ; it is
not a mere accessory, and it is miraculous ; but it is used
symbolically, a pointer to an even higher reality.   Greek
tragedy is always in immediate contact with the conditions
and problems of life.   The whole reason why attention has
always been directed to the improbabilities in the *Tyrannus*
and not to those in the *Philoctetes* is that the *Tyrannus* is
tragic, so that it is vital that its basis should not seem to be
impossible and out of contact with real life.[1]

This basis is now cut away.   From artificial situations like
these there can grow no tragic *mythos,* no action which will
show us, as it develops, what are the terms and conditions of
mortal life.   Instead of the tragic reality which we have been
studying we have what we may call a theatrical reality—for
Reality, like the gods, has many forms.   Euripides expects us
to be moved by Alcestis' death, but not as we are moved by
Antigone's or Polyxena's.   The emotion is limited to the play
and to the moment—like our emotion in the presence of Antonio's peril ; we feel (if we choose to examine our feelings)
that the emotion is temporary because the whole situation is
fictive and unreal ; it is tempered by our assurance that the
outcome must be a happy one—for otherwise there would be
no point at all, since the death of Alcestis cannot prove, illuminate or reveal anything in particular.   The happy ending in
fact takes the place of the tragic catharsis.

Further, although if we are wise we shall make the most
of the delicate sentiment of the scene, what we make of it is
necessarily modified by what we have heard in the prologue
—by Apollo's remark to Death for example : 'What ?   You

[1] See above, p. 318.

among the intelligentsia ? ' [1] Our deepest emotions can be engaged only lightly ; the appeal is by turns to our sentiment, to our intelligence, to our curiosity. In the *Iphigeneia*, Orestes and Pylades stand in deadly peril which they, like Antonio, have done nothing to deserve ; Euripides thrills us with the peril, but obviously only that he may also thrill us by the escape. These emotions have no roots in the eternal order of things ; they are lightly engaged, and can therefore be lightly transferred to something else, to comedy, satire, criticism, burlesque. In fact, they must be, for the dramatic material in these plays is not such as to bear the weight of long concentration on any one point.

In this new world of theatrical convention the scenes of pathos are delicately edged with conventionality. Helen's seventeen years of widowhood are not funny—for tragi-comedy means not that everything is comic, but that nothing is tragic—yet it would be silly of us to grow indignant with the gods about them. We must not play the game by the wrong set of rules. Creusa's suffering and Iphigeneia's grief come nearer to tragedy, but, between ourselves, these things are not real. We must indulge our sentiments only within the convention ; in five minutes we shall be smiling again— the showman will be showing us the amusingly pious cowherd or a ridiculous scene between Ion and Xuthus. How real these scenes of pathos are to be, each spectator must decide for himself. No doubt there were those in Athens who found the death of Alcestis infinitely tragic and beautiful, so much less disturbing than that terrible affair of Antigone ; but for all that the distinction between tragedy and pathos is a clear one.

It appears then that the absence of a tragic theme is the direct explanation both of the regular form and brilliant execution of these plays, and of the blend that they present of the pathetic, the amusing and the melodramatic. But intellectual profundity is as alien to this tragi-comedy as is moral profundity ; we look in vain for any serious purpose beyond the serious purpose of creating such elegant drama. What we do find is flashes of satire and criticism such as we can

[1] Only a slight over-translation of v. 58.

take in our stride ; passages of serious moralizing, common
in the tragedies, are altogether absent. The *Ion* is full of
obvious criticism of Delphi, but it is conveyed easily, never
allowed to stand for long in the foreground. Ion may briefly
expound the doctrine that if the gods are not just they are
not gods, but the interest of the passage lies in the manner
rather than in the matter, in Ion's delightful ' I must speak
to Apollo. What is he thinking of ? ' [1] ; and in his conclusion
that if they do not mend their ways the gods will find their
temples empty. The play indeed contains more ridicule than
criticism ; the key-note is given by the ludicrous behaviour of
Hermes in the prologue—hiding in the laurels in order to see
the play not proceeding according to plan. Nowhere do we
find serious passages like those of Hecuba on education or of
Theseus on democracy. It is true that we have from Menelaus an abundance of solemn adages, and from the messenger
in the *Helen* views about divination,[2] just as in the *Electra*
we have the advantage of hearing Orestes, the honest Peasant,
and the Old Man successively on True Nobility, but in none
of these passages is Euripides saying anything which he considers to have any but a purely dramatic value. The plays
are a constant appeal to our intellect, but in order that we may
appreciate the intrigue, the wit, the irony, not in order that
we may grasp a thesis.

Indeed it is a capital point in the estimation of these plays
that in them Euripides is not a minority poet, as Verrall supposed. Euripides makes fun of legend, exposes divination,
attacks Delphi, ridicules Heracles, the Dioscuri and Hermes—
but how ? Much as Aristophanes did, and certain vase-
painters before him. ' Belief ' is a complex thing. Athenians
who would believe heartily at the Panathenaea were obviously
prepared to laugh just as heartily when a comic poet asked
what would happen to the estate when Zeus died, whether
Athena would be married off as an *epicleros*. The Greeks,
never having had much personal reverence for their anthro-
pomorphic gods, were ready to take them (in Homer as
well as in the fifth century) seriously or comically. Because,

[1] *Ion*, 436–7.

[2] On which see below, p. 334.

for serious political, ceremonial or artistic purposes, they
could take them seriously, we are not to suppose that they
could not also see their funny side—or call them remarkable
people because they did.   They were ready to laugh when
Aristophanes supplied Prometheus with an umbrella, and with
obscene jokes against the upper gods, or when Euripides
makes Hermes hide in the shrubbery.   This does not mean
that the Athenians had ' outgrown ' the serious treatment of
the gods, such as Prometheus and Hermes received in the
Prometheus Vinctus.   Euripides guyed Heracles in the *Alcestis*, but a dozen years later he could treat the same Heracles
with a splendid earnestness in the *Hercules Furens*.

Euripides offends his critic by making Helen cast doubt on
the story of Leda's egg.   But he is not, with a maladroit
solemnity, informing Athens that in his opinion this ancient
story is not true.   Nobody believed that it was true, so that
everybody found it extremely funny that Helen herself should
share their scepticism.   Euripides ' attacks ' divination
(*Helen*, 744 ff.).   And how does this attack compare in tone
with the attack on the war-spirit in the *Suppliant Women* ?
The passage is introduced by the laughable dismay of the
Messenger at finding Helen on the stage after all ; it is delivered after the sententious fellow has been ordered off on
important business by Menelaus ; then, when he has declared
his views, the Chorus emphatically corroborates (being also
among the elect) ; and Helen remarks, upon his exit,

' Very good.—So far then all is well.'

If all this contained the serious publication of an important
view, it would be incredibly inept ; if, however, the poet is
so sure that the audience is with him that it will laugh at
rationalism when it is untimely, then the comedy is exquisite.

Athens had experienced enough in recent years to warrant
mistrust of superstition and divination, and there was Aris-
tophanic precedent for laughing at oracles ; Delphi however,
as a powerful corporation, was a different thing and had to
be taken more seriously.   Yet here too it is evident that Euripides felt himself going with the tide.   In the *Iphigeneia* he
suggests that in sending Orestes to the Tauri ' Apollo ' was
trying to rid himself of an awkward client—having failed to

buy off more than half the Furies. In this, Euripides is serious ; but how serious ? If the suggestion was one which he felt would not be accepted without resistance, one which he would have to maintain strongly, he must have put it in the forefront of his play, free from the distractions of an exciting plot. If on the other hand it was a view which the audience, or a sufficient part of it, would be ready to accept with satisfaction and without advocacy, the treatment of Apollo takes its place naturally as an intellectual stiffening in a play which is essentially one of incident and romantic colour.

In the *Ion* the point seems clear. Creusa was ravished by Apollo, bore her child in secret, laid it where the god had taken her—and nobody was any the wiser. Obviously Euripides does not believe the story ; is he trying to suggest to his audience that it is not true and would be discreditable if it were ? No ; he solemnly pretends that it is true. It is Ion, not his creator, who is the simple-minded rationalist, who points out that the god will not answer questions to his own discredit, who warns Zeus against bankruptcy, who at the end takes his mother aside and says, Look you, Mother ; are you sure you are not doing what so many women do, throwing the blame on to the god ? But Ion's suspicions are wrong. As Athena says (1595 ff.), ' Apollo hath done all things well. First, he brought thee to the birth without sickness, so that none of thy friends knew . . .' This must be accepted as dramatically true, not because a goddess says it, but because it is an assumption necessary for the whole play. Besides, the supernatural machinery must stand or fall together ; if there is no Apolline paternity there can be no Gorgon's blood, no Erichthonius sprung from the soil, no miraculous olive. But the wit of the whole piece lies in the conspiracy which Euripides makes with the audience ; the conviction that these things are false was held so widely in Athens that there is no point in insisting that they are false, but great amusement in pretending that they are true. So with the respectable old legend that Delphi was the centre of the earth :

CHORUS. And there is another thing which perhaps I may
not ask of thee . . .

ION. Speak : what wouldst thou know ?

CHORUS. Doth the house of Phoebus in very truth stand
           upon Earth's navel ?
ION.   Yea, girt with garlands, and around it are Gorgons.
CHORUS. So have I always heard.

It is the perfect picture of the awe-struck tourist.

In the *Ion* Euripides is not earnestly protesting and perpetually uncertain whether it is comedy or tragedy that he is
writing. The actual untruth of the story of Creusa removes
it from the world of tragedy to the world of pathos ; but the
pretence that all is real—and that Hermes is looking on—is an
inexhaustible source of dramatic interest, from delicate in-
sinuation to broad farce, one mood swiftly succeeding another
until, after many thrills, checks, surprises and disappoint-
ments, Athena appears, to build a magnificent structure on
some very shaky foundations, and to assure us that from this
very bewildered Ion will spring the detailed heroes of the
Ionian race, and that for the sake of Greece at large Xuthus
and Creusa also will have their ancestral sons. This, of
course, we receive in reverent silence ; and it all goes to prove
(as the chorus points out) that the good prosper and the
wicked don't.[1]

Such then are the most important of the conditions which
governed tragi-comedy : absence of a tragic theme, avoidance
even of an intellectual theme such as would demand serious
advocacy, the adoption of a new standard of reality which,
by reducing the tragic to the pathetic, made it possible to

---

[1] It is surely a mistake to take this antiquarianism seriously (as
does M. Grégoire, ed. Budé, pp. 168 ff.). The Attic legends are
handled in exactly the same sly way as the Delphian one above.
As soon as Ion hears that Creusa is from Athens he says, with the
eager *naïveté* just shown by the chorus, ' Was your father's grand-
father really born of the soil ? ' ' Did your father really slay your
sisters ? ' Again, Creusa cannot bring herself to mention the
Gorgon's blood without telling the whole tale from a ridiculously
long way back. Is all this the pious commemoration of national
legends ? No ; the manner is all wrong. Even in matters of
patriotism style counts for something. If Attic patriotism is connected with these passages (as may well be the case), it is surely
that other tragedians were patriotically antiquarian, while Euripides
reserved to himself the humbler role of laughing at their efforts in
this good-humoured way.

combine harmoniously into one theatrical whole a wide range
of emotional effects.   It is unnecessary to examine the separate plays as fully as we have done the separate tragedies,
because the form is very similar to that of Middle Tragedy,
and in these plays it undergoes no essential development.
We may, however, consider some points in which the style of
tragi-comedy differs notably from that of Middle Tragedy.

We have seen already that the Euripidean tragi-comedy
reverts to the normal type of plot.   Formally, the *Iphigeneia*
obeys the same Aristotelian canons as the *Tyrannus* ; a fact
which Aristotle duly acknowledges.   But though these plots
obey the laws (a fact that we need not stay to demonstrate)
they obey them in a new spirit, and the new spirit causes
interesting changes in technique.

The impetus and the real unity of the typical Sophoclean
plot come from the purity and force of the original tragic
inspiration.   Now we find the same general plan, the development of a dramatic situation through surprise and disappointment to an unforeseen close ; but since there is no big tragic
theme to absorb the attention of the audience, the dramatist
has to do other things.   No longer do we find scenes like those
between Haemon and Creon, Oedipus and Creon, in which
one unbroken dramatic rhythm sweeps through the whole,
from a level start to an exciting climax ; the intrinsic importance of the dramatic material would not be big enough
to support it.   The events which compose the plot now have
a different status ; they have their dramatic value simply as
events, not as the revelation of a tragic character or as the
significant play of circumstances upon a tragic character.   Accordingly the flow of events must be made as interesting and
varied as possible ; compare with the typical Sophoclean scene
the long stichomythia between Ion and Creusa, which moves
easily and naturally among half-a-dozen topics ; or any scene
in the *Helen*.   Characteristic of the new style is the most
amusing ' recognition scene ' between Ion and Xuthus.   Underlying all the wit and fun is the exciting possibility that
Xuthus may after all turn out to be the father and not Apollo ;
there is the amusing contrast between Xuthus' happy confidence and Ion's puzzled reluctance ; when all this has di-

verted us, Ion gives a sudden check to the plot, and to Xuthus'
cheerfulness, by considering the situation in an analytical
speech which is a new source of interest, and by deciding
that on the whole he prefers to stay where he is. This typical
stroke is repeated at v. 1340, when Ion thinks it better not to
examine the tokens and not to search for his mother. The
dramatist is, as it were, playing cat and mouse with his
audience ; he erects unforeseen obstacles in order to surmount
them with éclat. In the same way, Theoclymenus comes
near to wrecking the plan of escape in the *Helen*. Helen
should stay on shore—lest grief for her dead husband should
cause her to drown herself. The irony is pleasing, and we
are set on the *qui vive* to see how Helen will overcome this
unfortunate considerateness.

The *Iphigeneia* offers a good example of this new necessity
of keeping the plot always on the move. Iphigeneia (578–
96) suggests sparing Orestes and sacrificing Pylades, in order
that the one who knows Argos so well may take her letter.
Orestes objects ; let her save Pylades, who has no cause to
welcome death. She agrees, and the brother and sister discuss the manner of the sacrifice (617–43)—Pylades all this
time remaining silent. Why ? Is he screwing up his courage
to the point of self-sacrifice ? No ; he is silent simply for the
sake of the plot. He does not speak until v. 672—and then
he says the wrong thing ; he insists not on dying instead of
Orestes, but on dying with him. Is this because he is a
romantic and foolish young man ? If such he appears, it is
an added point, but Euripides was not really concerned with
Pylades' character—what indeed is Pylades ? The whole
manœuvre is intended simply to keep the situation moving.
First the sister proposes, on pathetically flimsy grounds, to
save the brother ; then the dreadful substitution is made and
allowed to pass unchallenged ; then Pylades insists on dying
too because if he does Iphigeneia cannot be rescued and the
whole thing is ruined. The situation is screwed up tight, and
our interest in the recognition-scene becomes the more intense.

Above all, now that there is no tragic climax, the dramatist
must see to it that his ending does not fall flat. The *Iphigeneia* has its palpitating story of the contrary winds and the

last-minute reprieve.[1]   The *Helen* cannot be allowed to peter
out in an easy escape followed by the divine summary of
things present and to come ; therefore the messenger-speech
itself is made exciting with its tale of sanguinary combat on
the high seas, and then, in order to make the expected arrival
of the *Deus* opportune, the wicked Theoclymenus must
threaten to murder his sister.   Now the god can step in to
some effect—but no ; Euripides still finds life in his plot, and
gives us yet another thrill by producing a gallant slave who
forbids the murder and cries ' Only across my dead body ! '
So, as in all these plays, the movement is kept up until the
last possible moment—but the last moment too needs attention.
The entirely artificial *Deus* is a happy way of bringing to a
close plots which were artificial too in their inception,[2] but,
unless the god is presented satirically, his winding-up speech
may be a little perfunctory and dull.   This danger Euripides
meets with aetiology and topical allusions.

But the *Alcestis* has the most instructive ending.   The
simple restoration of Alcestis by Heracles, with speeches of
bewildered gratitude from Admetus—Alcestis too saying something suitable to the occasion—would obviously be flat, and
(because out of keeping) uncomfortable too.   Shakespeare
used in similar circumstances to keep up the atmosphere of
tragi-comedy by pretending that his restored heroine was a
statue ; Euripides is cleverer.   Alcestis is veiled, and by a
convenient excuse (1144 ff.) kept silent.   This enables Euripides to present one of his few triangular scenes, one as cleverly
used as any of Sophocles'.   With a very piquant irony Heracles declares her to be the prize he has won in a wrestling-

[1] This is very much like the reprieve at the end of *The Beggar's
Opera.* (The obvious artificiality of it may be intended to suggest to
us the more tragic ending, that ' Apollo ' did in fact trick his client
to his death.)

[2] We may notice that had Euripides felt as apologetic about the
Deus as do some of his critics, he might have ended the *Helen*
with Theonoe, who is already on the premises, and knows things
present and things to come quite as well as the Dioscuri (vv. 13
ff.).   But it is much more interesting to see the deified brothers of
our late heroine, and they also enable Euripides to contrive the
little melodrama mentioned above.

match, and his request that Admetus should look after her
produces the delightful scene in which Admetus deplores
temptation, protests, before the living Alcestis, his complete
devotion to the dead Alcestis, rehabilitates his reputation with
us, and lays the foundation for a future matrimonial happiness
which otherwise must have seemed insecure. Now the happy
disclosure of the truth can be made briefly, in the agreeable
atmosphere of unreality. It is a brilliant scene which avoids
all the dangers and brings the play to a triumphant close
within the conventions.

The enacting of an exciting story makes for unity of plot,
but the need for continuous piquancy of situation appreciably
tempers the logic of that plot. The willing suspension of
reason which we have to make in order to accept the initial
situation is called upon again and again. For example,
Pylades could have ruined the *Iphigeneia* by doing an obvious
and natural thing, turning to the chorus at v. 669 and asking
who the strange Greek woman was. In the *Helen* we are
asked to assume that the fall of Troy was unknown in Egypt
seven years after the event—this in spite of the presence of
Theonoe the omniscient. In tragedy such weak links in the
chain would be ruinous, for the strain on it is great ; the
succession of significant cause and effect must be close, and
improbability in behaviour avoided. Now, since little depends
on it except our own enjoyment, we are content to be bluffed
if the bluff is worth while ; and if the play is a comedy, we
may even relish a *non sequitur* for its own sake. The entirely
' unjustified ' introduction of Teucer is in keeping with the
delicious comedy of the whole of the *Helen* ; such invaders
as the Boeotian or Meton in Aristophanes are not far removed
from him in spirit.

The effect of the new theatrical reality can be traced a little
further. Because the plays are not, as it were, about anything
in particular, material can be used which would have been
intolerable earlier. Because no serious theme is going to fill
the *Ion* the play can start with an extended movement drawing most of its interest from sheer naturalism. Ion busy
about his morning tasks—and dropping remarks like ' Phoebus,
the father who begot me '—is indeed both dramatic and

naturalistic, for we both enjoy the scene for its own sake (saying with Aristotle ' How very lifelike ! '), and absorb the holy atmosphere of the temple, as at the beginning of the *Eumenides,* in order that the breaking of that calm may be the more effective. The chorus, however, wandering tourist-like about the precincts, is pure naturalism ; we are very close now to Herondas and to Gorgo and Praxinoa in Theocritus. Tragedy may offer a touch of realism occasionally as a foil, but only the absence of a tragic theme can permit the complete diversion of our minds to naturalism for its own sake.

The point is even clearer in the messenger-speech. This has to announce that the plot against Ion has failed, that Creusa's guilt is patent, and that the Delphians are hot upon her trail to kill her for the attempted murder. The moment is one of extreme urgency, but this does not prevent the messenger from delivering a speech twice as long as those usual in Sophocles. What is stranger, the first third of this speech is devoted to the pitching and decorating of the marquee—a topic which surely could wait.

Obviously, if our minds were seriously engaged on an important issue this elaborate irrelevance would be unendurable ; but they are not. Creusa's attempt on Ion's life has been treated in a perfectly conventional and non-moral spirit[1] ; we are to be interested in the events simply as facts, and the more remarkable the facts, the greater our interest. Noble simplicity is in abeyance. In the *Septem* the messenger says ' The brothers have slain each other ', and it is enough ; if the messenger here had said ' Ion has escaped ' it would be nothing at all. We must hear the manner of the escape, and it must be an interesting story, and if the poet chooses to elaborate it with a brilliant bit of descriptive introduction, so much the better. It is a new source of interest, and tragi-comedy is very hospitable.[2] Here we are even nearer

[1] See below, p. 343.

[2] Comparison with the messenger-speech in the *Hippolytus* is instructive. That brilliant description sounds a little frigid because it is, to some extent, mere decoration on a tragic theme.

to Alexandrianism, for example to the maker of that cup of ivy-wood and to Theocritus who describes it so vividly in his first idyll. Neither the carver nor the poet is possessed with any intrinsically important idea, so that both can devote themselves to showing the veins swelling in the old fisherman's neck. That Euripides knows perfectly well what he is doing here, and is not merely giving way to a brilliant garrulity, is shown by the fact that he keeps Creusa herself off the stage while the speech is going on.[1]

The opposite of naturalism is sheer theatricality, and this is admitted freely, particularly in the lighter plays. The delightful extreme is surely the appeal to Theonoe in the *Helen* (761 ff.). After the suicide-pact and the ensuing rhetoric from Menelaus comes in the omniscient priestess, to Helen's dismay, announcing that she is the arbiter between Hera and Aphrodite : shall she or shall she not reveal Menelaus' arrival to her brother ? So ridiculous a situation cannot move in us any serious emotion, but we shall be ready to enjoy a neat piece of argumentation or any other intellectual pleasure that can be offered. Accordingly first Helen puts forward the appropriate arguments in an effective speech ; then the chorus, perfectly appreciating the unreality of the occasion, says, ' Piteous words ! Piteous art thou too ! I long to hear what speech Menelaus will make in defence of his life.'

Menelaus is wonderful ; the Rev. Mr. Collins himself could have done no better. He cannot bring himself to weep—a disgrace to Troy—though they do say that it is quite proper to weep in misfortune ; but such propriety, if it be propriety, he will not place before Courage. Theonoe may well think it right to save them ; if not, he will be miserable and she wicked. But, he says, I can best do myself justice and touch your heart by addressing this tomb. Accordingly he invokes Proteus' aid, though ' I know that thou, being dead, canst never give me back Helen, but thy daughter

[1] Similar examples of naturalism are to be found in the *I.T.*, 67–76 and 620–40. Both passages recall the *Philoctetes* ; the reconnaissance of the temple is paralleled by the search for the cave, and both Iphigeneia and Philoctetes spend some time asking about old friends. There is no reason to suspect direct imitation : the effect is natural to this kind of drama.

here will never tolerate a blot on thy name'. Even this is surpassed by the terrific and convincing argument addressed to Hades : ' For her sake thou hast received many dead, slain by my sword ; thou hast thy fee. Now either restore these to life again, or make Theonoe give me back my wife.' Finally to a shivering Theonoe the direful alternative to honour is proclaimed—two corpses slain by this sword lying side by side on this tomb.[1] ' There,' he says, ' action for me, not tears ! '

The *Helen*, as is natural, is full of wit :

MEN.   Gates whence I was driven away, like a beggar.

HEL.   What ? Thou wert not begging, surely ? Woe is *me* !

MEN.   Such 'twas in fact, but 'twas not called so.   (790–2.)

The wit approaches parody as the dramatist, no longer fiercely intent on the matter in hand, can look about him in a critical spirit. Thus Helen begins to outline her plot by saying that she will cut her hair in mourning-fashion :

MEN.   And what help lies there ? For there is a certain antiquity in the suggestion.

In the *Ion* fun and parody are used for a special purpose. Creusa's old servant, who arrives rather mysteriously from nowhere, is funny first in the naturalistic way opened up by Clytemnestra's Watchman. He puffs his way up to the temple with ' Oracles are a bit steep ! ' (referring to their notorious obscurity), and produces a stream of things like ' I can't do the impossible,' ' Slow in the legs but quick in the head '— excellent peasant-wit. But when he goes off on his poisoning errand, he is absurd in another way, for his apostrophe to his ' aged foot ' is a deliberate parody of tragic diction ; and it may legitimately raise doubts about v. 753 :

CHOR.   Ah ! God !

O.M.   The prelude of thy speech is not auspicious.

Was Housman the first to write this kind of thing in fun ? But calculation as well as ebullience lurks here, for all this fun surrounds the laying of the murderous plot by Creusa, and it is there partly to prevent us from taking the plot too

---

[1] ' This sword *here*,' ' this tomb *here*,' clearly suggesting Menelaus' overacting.

seriously. There is none of it in the *Medea*, where also a
murderous plot is laid ; Euripides wants to see to it that we
shall not make the mistake of turning Creusa into a Medea.

This whole scene is a good example of the new ' theatre '.
Indignation and amusement, rage and despair, follow each
other swiftly. Creusa's confession is put in the form of a
monody not because that is the most natural form but because it is the most effective ; in fact Euripides could scarcely
afford sober simple eloquence, for that would at once raise
Creusa from the theatrical to the tragic. Again, the laying of
the plot is steeped in convention—to prevent us from considering it morally. There is the Old Man, the bad adviser, quite
certain what has happened and what is going to happen.
He puts forward the usual string of fantastic suggestions
(' Burn down the temple ! ') which the clever Euripidean
woman [1] disposes of before outlining her own plot. There
is the assumption that to murder Ion is the most natural thing
in the world : ' Come ! do something womanly ! Take to
the sword, or to poison.' It is magnificent—but it is not anti-
femininism. Finally, there is the absurd pedantry by which
Creusa cannot mention her poisons without going back and
back to the ' battle of the earth-born '. The comedy must
not obscure the pathos, but we must not mistake good
' theatre ' for simple tragedy.

One more surface-effect should be mentioned, the new
irony. The *Iphigeneia*, naturally not very rich in wit and fun,
is full of this. At v. 149, just after we have seen Orestes in
the flesh, Iphigeneia appears lamenting his death.[2] This
ironical situation becomes the basis of further ironies ; at v.
344, for example, when she hears that Greeks have come,
Iphigeneia exclaims that before she was always full of pity
when Greeks fell into her hands, but now, made cruel by the
dream, she will have no mercy, whoever they are. The
psychology of this does not seem very clear, but the theatrical
effect is excellent. This is not tragic irony, though in this play
it may make a similar effect, since Iphigeneia is in apparent

---

[1] These two characters already smack of New Comedy.

[2] The use made by Sophocles of Clytemnestra's dream affords an
interesting contrast with this.

danger of fulfilling the dream. Tragic irony assumes security where there is none, in order to emphasize the hero's blindness ; now a state of affairs contrary to the truth is assumed merely to increase the piquancy of the situation. The real purpose of the dream is to make the eventual recognition more striking ; not only does Iphigeneia not know that her brother is present, but she even has reason for thinking that he cannot be. In more strenuous days the gap between the real and the apparent truth was used for quickening our tragic apprehensions ; now, at the most, it quickens our theatrical apprehensions. Very often (as at *I.T.*, 611, 627, 629) it amounts only to a double-entendre ; in at least one passage in the *Electra* it becomes practically a stage-aside [1] ; thus, being addressed only to our intellect it is really a kind of wit, akin to the ironies of comedy—which it soon becomes, in the *Helen*.

Tragi-comedy then may obey certain important canons derived from Middle Tragedy, but its style and its real logic are totally different. As it appeals to our sensations rather than to our apprehensions, it must make its plot continually exciting ; in place of the steady development necessary to tragedy it must present sudden changes of mood and unexpected turns of plot. It can do this the more easily because there is much more room for sheer artificiality of contrivance, and because it can call upon a very wide range of effect—pathos, pure excitement, amusement in all its forms, simple naturalism, exciting even if irrelevant description. Besides plot there are two other elements of drama that we must briefly consider, the use of the Chorus, which we can more conveniently deal with in our next section, and characterization.

Characterization, like plot, becomes in Euripides' tragi-comedies something very different from what it was in his tragedies. We lose altogether the stridency which the tragic theme imposed on some characters and the inconsistency to

---

[1] Eur., *El.*, 224, where Orestes says to the frightened Electra, ' There is no one whom I have a better right to touch '. Since Orestes is not about to reveal himself—quite the contrary—the remark has no dramatic point but it does amuse the audience. The effect is repeated at v. 282.

which it condemned others, but for all that we do not return to Sophoclean standards of variety and conviction. It was of course impossible, for in plays which are essentially plays of incident, characterization cannot be very significant and becomes very largely a mere decoration. The *Alcestis*, inasmuch as one side of it is close to the comedy of manners, has its lifelike characters in Admetus and Pheres ; and Alcestis, who might so easily have been a purely conventional figure in that unreal setting, derives individuality from her evident mistrust of her husband (cf. vv. 371 ff.); but in the *Iphigeneia* and *Helen* nothing depends on character except the contriving of an escape by a clever woman. The two savage kings must be conventionally pious and credulous, but Orestes and Pylades, Menelaus, Teucer and the minor characters can be, one might almost say, what they like (provided that they are interesting when they have a chance), while the fairy-godmother Theonoe can hardly be anything but a vague outline. But if they can be what they like they cannot be anything profound, for profound characterization implies a strict relation to significant action ; they may however be interesting, and Euripides makes them interesting when he can.[1] Character-drawing has become an ' effect ', like the others we have examined. Thoas' character goes a little beyond what his part demands ; he is pleasantly and unexpectedly considerate—like the cannibal king in the parable, he too is a Balliol man. Menelaus' unfailing pomposity and complacency is a continual delight—but what are Orestes and Pylades ? It would perhaps be possible to tabulate qualities for them, but they do not make an individual impression ; the drama in which they move is too strong for playful or decorative character-drawing, and as it is not a drama of their own making (except for Iphigeneia's scheme) it does not vividly illuminate what they are. In the *Ion* we have, besides the hero, a pleasantly silly Xuthus, and a Creusa about whose characterization we must be careful, lest we turn her into a tragic, Medea-like person whom Euripides did not want. Ion himself is a brilliant sketch—as brilliant as Plato's Ion or his

---

[1] The qualification is added because Pylades and Orestes, for example, can have little chance to display character.

Euthyphro—and he has his *Aufklärung*, which is neatly done ; but the contrast with the *Philoctetes* is interesting. Sophocles' play is a psychological adventure with a brilliant plot as the subsidiary interest ; Euripides' a brilliant plot with the character-interest as a subsidiary.

CHAPTER XII

NEW TRAGEDY : EURIPIDES' MELODRAMAS

1. THE ELECTRA   The *Electra* and the *Orestes* are of the
same kind of drama as the tragi-comedies, though perhaps of
a different species.   That they are grim and not gay, and
are based on character-drawing rather than on the excitements
of an intricate plot, are important differences ; but what is
common to them is much more fundamental, and that is the
new attitude towards the dramatic art.   These two plays are
melodramatic, not tragic ; like the four plays we have just considered (and the two that we shall consider next) they aim
first and foremost at being theatrically effective, and it is this
that gives them their character and explains their form.

The first question that should suggest itself is what impelled
Euripides to turn to this part of the Atreid legend—twice ?
On the moral aspect of the vengeance he had nothing new
to say, and that little was not enough to make drama from.
There was no point whatever in writing a play to show that
vengeance by matricide was horrible, for who had ever, or
could ever, say anything else ?   Certainly not Aeschylus ; he
makes it quite clear that though Apollo's command recognized
a necessary principle, it was entirely unsuccessful as a solution
of the problem, it was an outrage, and outraged the Erinnyes.
Not Sophocles, although he had made it an act of *dikê*.   As
we have seen, this does not make it glorious ; it is an awful
deed brought about inevitably by a monstrous crime.   To
Euripides, Apollo was neither the defender of some principle
in society nor the embodiment of a universal law ; he was
simply the god of Delphi, an immoral and reactionary institution.   Therefore he brings the god out of the enigmatic
background in which Sophocles had placed him, makes him
command the act of vengeance, and makes that as repulsive
as he can.   Then, in the second place, though the situation
precipitated by Clytemnestra's act, properly treated, can be
intensely dramatic, the actual problem of what to do with

her is not dramatic at all. There is only one answer—public justice. Euripides gives that answer, but it was not a new one, for Aeschylus had given it too, and we cannot suppose that it was a desire to say so obvious a thing that led him to write these plays. Even in the *Choephori* and *Eumenides* the real drama is not the solution of a problem on which there is only one thing to say; the real drama is something very much wider of which this question and its answer become only symbols.

What is interesting in the comparison of the three dramatists is not their moral attitude to a very simple problem, but their dramatic attitude to the situation and to the actors in it. Aeschylus assumes that no system of public justice exists, because his real drama is the development of the moral order which results in its establishment. Sophocles assumes the same in order that his tragic heroine may be placed in a really tragic situation from which her temperament allows her no escape; the attitude of Chrysothemis indicates what the normal woman would do in these circumstances, but Electra is not normal. In this play there must be no public justice, or Electra would be simply flying in the face of society and would cease to be tragic. Euripides adopts different methods in the two plays before us; in the *Orestes* Argos has its judicial assembly, and Tyndareus can make the obvious point (493 ff.) that Orestes should have appealed to the law; but in the *Electra*, though the Dioscuri condemn Apollo and Orestes (1244, 1302), nothing whatever is said about the possibility of bringing Clytemnestra to judgement. The explanation of this difference is, naturally, purely dramatic. The point of the *Orestes* is the picture of three aristocratic degenerates who, completely lost to reason and devoid of any moral responsibility, do fly in the face of an ordered society; therefore the existence of public justice is emphasized. In the *Electra* Euripides is doing something rather different. He is drawing a certain extreme type of character (reminiscent of Medea) and therefore wishes to place her in circumstances which push her to the extreme. The existence of public justice would have blurred the sharpness of the situation, as in the *Medea* it would have weakened and dissipated the drama to suggest that Medea could have sought legal redress for her wrongs. In each play the conception demands a terrifying character in an absolute situation.

But why does Euripides allow the Dioscuri to condemn the vengeance without stating the alternative? It seems hardly logical, and if Euripides had really been writing social drama this alternative would have been his triumphant conclusion; but he is writing melodrama. First, no alternative, in order to preserve the purity of the situation; then a hint, but no statement, of the alternative, to prevent us from taking the melodramatic Electra tragically—from thinking that she was a bedevilled creature who had to do something of this sort. For we may note another significant point. When the Dioscuri aetiologize about the trial on the Areopagus, they avoid saying 'And henceforth private vengeance shall be superseded by law'. That would have been natural, and it would have advertised Euripides' views if he had thought them worth advertising, but it would have implied that Electra and Orestes really had been in a tragic situation in which they could hardly have escaped murdering their mother. Therefore the trial is made to institute nothing more important than that henceforth equal votes shall bring acquittal.

It was not then a desire to say something new about the problem (as distinct from the situation) that attracted Euripides to this legend. Nor was it a simple desire to set Sophocles right. The vexed question of the priority between the two *Electras* need not detain us here. It has too often been attacked with arguments that work either way,[1] and on the assumption that the later play is full of implied criticisms of the earlier. Thus in Euripides' play, v. 94, 'I do not set foot within the walls', and v. 615, 'Thou couldst not, even if thou wouldst, enter the palace', are a criticism of the im-

---

[1] The general tendency is to make the Sophoclean play the earlier. This I believe to be correct, though the belief has more faith than reason in it. One argument may be added to an already long list; would Sophocles have invited an unnecessary and unsatisfactory comparison by writing (v. 190) 'In this mean garb' if Euripides' realistic play were already before the public? It is a small point but at least it does not work both ways, like many of the comparisons adduced.

probable facility with which Orestes does this in Aeschylus and Sophocles. Was then Euripides so stupid a critic as not to know that a highly poetic drama can make assumptions impossible to a realistic one ? In fact his play needs both of these remarks ; the former emphasizes that this Orestes, unlike his predecessors, is hanging about the back-doors of Argos ready to run if recognized ; the latter makes necessary the two separate plots for entrapping Aegisthus and Clytemnestra. Therefore the assumption that Euripides is indulging in petti-fogging and mistaken criticism is gratuitous.[1]

But even if we could determine the order of the two *Electras,* and even if we were right in assuming that it was dissatisfaction with the earlier work that prompted the later,[2] we should be no better off, for it would remain that since neither is a still-born, academic play, neither is in any way based on such a negative. Each embodies a very positive attitude to a very dramatic situation. Let us first determine what that was ; then we may guess—if we must guess—what it was that directed the later poet's thoughts to this extremely out-of-the-way legend of Agamemnon and Clytemnestra.

The key lies in the different conception of Electra. The difference is not merely that Euripides took Sophocles' heroine and with his customary moroseness and hard realism turned her into a middle-aged virago. Euripides may have taken a gloomy delight in blackening the characters of respectable heroes of legend ; certainly had he disliked doing this he

---

[1] The skit on the *Choephori* is clearly in a different position. This may be mistaken, but it is not pettifogging.

[2] Why should we not, for a change, begin to assume that Euripides and Sophocles, being very great and sincere artists, though entirely different in temperament, were, as artists, sympathetically interested in and appreciative of each other's works and methods ? There is no evidence for such a view, but neither, I think, is there real evidence for the impression one is given that they were self-conscious, self-righteous and censorious rivals.—A good theme for an imaginary conversation : the two poets in a group of Athenian notables, from Pericles downwards ; the others try desperately to start a philosophic or moral discussion between the poets, but the poets will talk of nothing but dramatic technique—how to use the chorus, and whether a resolved is more effective than an unresolved dochmiac.

could never have written the *Electra* and the *Orestes* ; bu
the important point to us is that the different conception
belong to different types of drama and are therefore boun
up with all the other differences between the plays.[1]

Both plays are plays of character, but different kinds of plays
Sophocles approached the subject tragically.   His Electra i
a creation who, as it were, means something more than he
stage-self ; she is typical of one aspect of the human tragedy
in that circumstances combine with one element in her char
acter to ruin what is conspicuously admirable in the rest of it
The Aristotelian conception implies the Sophoclean method
The characterization is complex—heroic dedication to duty
and pure affection for father and brother set against a dread
ful error of judgement inevitable in such a character, and a
pitiless hatred for the guilty ones.   This produces the com
plex unity of action in which the constant variety of mood and
dramatic rhythm are subordinated to the long sweep tha
embraces everything essential and excludes everything merely
decorative and sensational.

The other Electra is not Aristotelian, nor is the play
Aristotelian tragedy.   This Electra is a woman in whom it i
hardly possible to find a virtue ; she is implacable, self
centered, fantastic in hatred,[2] callous to the verge of insanity
Why does Euripides invent this woman ?   What does she
prove ?   What is the point of a dramatic hero who is al
black ?   We must distinguish.   In Xerxes and Agamemnon
we had heroes whose characters, as presented, were nothing
but error, yet they were tragic.[3]   Electra is not one of these
Euripides does not limit himself to the catastrophic side
of her nature and exclude the rest as irrelevant to her tragedy

---

[1] It is this that makes point-by-point comparison of the *Electra*
so useless.   We can say that Sophocles is more natural here, Eurip
ides more pathetic there, and the remarks may be true ; but unti
they are related to the different dramatic purposes that the poets
had they remain only the raw material of criticism.   (Cf. p. 117.)

[2] Sophocles' Electra was wrong about Aegisthus, but this one is
wild.   Contrast the foolish monster she describes (326 ff.) with
the courteous Aegisthus whom we meet later in the play.

[3] See above, p. 122.

he draws her in detail—and then omits the tragedy. She is not tragic in the Sophoclean way because she is not representative, 'like ourselves', and therefore cannot illuminate. She resembles Medea in not being representative, but no further ; the whole meaning of Medea is that the hamartia which comprises practically the whole of her character is a universal one, so that Medea, though not Aristotelian, is symbolic of the human tragedy ; but Electra, equally nothing but faults, is an entirely private and personal assemblage of faults with no universal significance. She is a Medea without the tragedy—but with all Medea's *Grand Guignol* effects ; in other words, a heroine of melodrama.

Accordingly we find the whole play cast on melodramatic lines. The *Electra* and the *Orestes* are as pure melodrama as the *Iphigeneia* ; they may contain incidental themes of wider interest, but their first purpose is to attract and sustain our interest by the sheer force of theatrical effect. The difference is that the *Iphigeneia* and the *Ion* do this through an exciting plot with characterization as an accessory, while the *Electra* and *Orestes* rely on exciting characterization with the interest of plot as an accessory. In discussing tragicomedy we saw that plot had none of the ethical or spiritual significance that it has possessed in Middle Tragedy, no longer the illuminating interaction of a typical character and typical circumstances, but only an exciting series of events ; now we see that character, even in a 'play of character', loses that deeper significance and becomes only something to move and hold our palpitating interest.

We must show that the melodramatic conception explains the general methods used in both plays ; we may perhaps excuse ourselves from pursuing this into the details, since to point out how the frequent touches of realism, irony, piquancy in situation and satire are addressed to the audience rather than to the furtherance of a fundamental theme would be only to duplicate what was said in the last section.[1]

---

[1] Typical points are : Realism—*Electra,* the invitation to the festival (167 ff.), Electra's nagging of her husband (404 ff.), and the general atmosphere of domesticity ; in the *Orestes,* the keeping guard upon the stage (67 and 1246 ff.), the sick-bed scene, the

We may begin with the character of the heroine. Sophocles' Electra, because she is to be tragic, must remain in close
touch with ordinary humanity, even though she is of necessity
an unusual woman ; we must be made to feel the tragedy that
a loyal and affectionate woman should have been brought to
hate her mother like this. Therefore her love for her father
and brother is stressed everywhere, particularly at the end
of the recognition-scene. But Euripides has no interest in
modifying Electra's character by strong natural affections,[1]
therefore, although for the sake of verisimilitude affection for
Orestes is mentioned in the monody (130 ff.), when we come
to business and to the actual recognition no transports of joy
are allowed to come between us and the grim story that
Euripides is working out for us. Desire for vengeance is, in
this Electra, stronger than affection for a brother. This is
the reason why the recognition-scene is finished off as
brusquely as possible—though no doubt we must be prepared
to hear that the real explanation was a desire to criticize
Sophocles' undramatic prolixity at this point.

For this same reason, that the tragic Electra, however extreme, must remain broadly *homoios,* representative, Sophocles
must palliate the horrors of the actual crime, or at least abstain
from emphasizing its crudities, for we must not lose sympathy
with Electra. It is not merely a matter of taste or literary
judgement that Euripides emphasizes the crude details and
Sophocles does not. It may be a matter of taste to write
melodrama at all, but having chosen so to treat the subject,
Euripides had to underline the hideousness of Electra and
Orestes, and he does it with remarkable virtuosity. The plot
to kill Aegisthus is based on a confidence in his courtesy ;

---

escape of the Phrygian (1371 ff.). Irony—passim, especially in
the symposium on the True Gentleman in the *Orestes.* Piquancy
in situation—*Electra,* the recognition (552 ff.), the prolongation of
suspense at 747 ff. ; *Orestes,* Helen's secret return, her hair-
offering (128 ff.), Orestes' sudden attack of madness and his delusion about Electra (255 ff.), Menelaus' failure to recognize Orestes
(768 ff.), Diomedes addressing an Assembly (893). The sudden
check to the plot common in tragi-comedy is hardly found here, as
the plot-interest counts for much less.

[1] In the *Orestes* he has ; see below, p. 367.

he is a very different person from the tyrant whom Sophocles presents. The plot sounds a little discreditable, but it is surpassed by Electra's heaven-inspired trap for her mother—again a trap based on confidence in her humanity. Orestes and Pylades kill Aegisthus with every circumstance of dishonour—he is their host, at a sacrifice, and the conspirators recognize the situation by refusing the lustral water that he offers; finally, after a delay (contrived for its theatrical value) Orestes hits him in the back, with a chopper. Sophocles' dramatic plan, if nothing else, excludes this kind of effect; his Aegisthus must be slain with that grim reticence, not described as lying on the ground with his back split, screaming and dying in convulsions.[1] Sophocles cannot pretend that the death of Clytemnestra is anything but a necessary horror, but he must not go further; he must show that his heroine rejoices at the deed, but he may not allow her to share in the physical act. Such extreme treatment would have ruined his tragedy by depriving it of any semblance of universality; Sophocles' reticence would have ruined Euripides' melodrama by robbing it of half its effectiveness. Far from making his chief actors as broadly human as the scene admits he must make them as striking as he can, true to the theatre rather than to life.

Between the murders comes the scene in which the melodramatic intention is most apparent and perhaps most surely achieved, the grisly passage with Aegisthus' head. Euripides makes it a practice to introduce these purely rhetorical speeches deliberately,[2] and the deliberateness is extremely effective here. There is no unreal pretense that Electra's emotions relieve themselves in a torrent of abuse. A certain stylization, the imitation of reticence, sets off the horror excellently; in particular, Electra, like her brother in the matter of the lustral water, has moral scruples whose light violation is an added indecency. In a speech conceived in this spirit we shall hardly expect the accents of simple tragedy, but shall look rather for point. Euripides, because he is using the situation only as a situation rich in dramatic thrills, is careful to satisfy our aroused interest by throwing new light on the

[1] Eur., *El.*, 842–3.

[2] See p. 342 on *Helen*, 943–5, and p. 358 on *Electra*, 297–300.

old situation—not because the new light is something vital to
his mind, but because the old light is useless to him. Accordingly we are given not Electra's joy at the death of one
of her father's murderers, but a highly interesting analysis of
Aegisthus' position as the husband of Clytemnestra.

The same sort of calculation underlies the treatment of
Clytemnestra. The pomp of her arrival contrasts most
effectively with Electra's poverty, and this is now an effect
quite as important as any of the moral questions involved. In
Sophocles' play, Clytemnestra is a harsh character who argues
with Electra solely on the grounds of justice—because false
ideas of justice are the heart of the tragedy. In this play
the debate is given a more personal tone because that is more
immediately interesting. Clytemnestra uses a bold rhetorical
argument for our pleasure, supposing the case that Menelaus,
not Helen, had been stolen away ; she brings in Cassandra,
whom Sophocles had omitted because she was not the main
issue ; she explains (as if answering Electra from the other
play) why she took Aegisthus : she had to. In reply Electra
makes the point that Sophocles did not want[1]—and a very
interesting point—that as soon as Agamemnon was gone
Clytemnestra showed herself a wanton, wishing only for his
death. Euripides is not so anxious to raise the question of
justice as to treat the situation in a naturalistic and interesting way.

But the finest stroke here is Clytemnestra's dissatisfaction
with herself. Sophocles' murderess must have no regrets,
that the revenge, from Electra's point of view, may be an unqualified act of justice. Therefore he makes her say :
' I then have no misgivings at what has passed ' (vv. 549–50).
But Euripides contrives a splendid effect when, with Aegisthus' head hidden in the cottage, he produces that gleam of
a possible reconciliation now impossible. His Clytemnestra
says :

' I will pardon thee. For, my child, I am not so very glad at
what I have done ' (1105–6). Note the clever change from
the impersonal ' what has passed ' to the personal ' what I
have done '.

[1] P. 139.

The dialogue continues :

EL.   Why dost thou then whet thy husband's wrath against
        us ?
C.   He is like that. Besides, thou wert always headstrong.
EL.   Because of my grief. But my wrath will cease.
C.   Then his anger too will cease.
EL.   He is haughty ; he dwells in my house.

But not, as Clytemnestra thinks, in the Palace.

It is splendid theatre, and it completes the utterly unqualified picture of the heroine—except that we have still to
learn that she actually assists at her mother's murder.

And what of Orestes ?   It is evident that in determining his
character Euripides had a wider choice than Sophocles.   The
tragic nature of Sophocles' play dictated that Orestes should
be neither the simple servant of Apollo whom Aeschylus
needed, nor a complex character, overshadowing Electra, nor
a conventional or overdrawn figure, out of keeping with
Electra.   The fact that one of his chief motives is the recovery
of his rightful heritage prevents him from standing in Electra's
light, and materially helps to keep him plausible and human.
But Euripides was much less restricted ; his Orestes might with
equal logic be an infatuated bigot, a cruel avenger, a pathetic,
misguided lad, a mere schemer—anything that would allow
him to perform the murders effectively.   Euripides chooses
to make him irresolute, and it is interesting to see why.

That Orestes is no bold hero is at once made clear in the
prologue ; he has come to spy out the land, ready to run if
necessary.   He has made the offerings at Agamemnon's tomb
by night, to escape the notice of the authorities.   This, to be
sure, is mere prudence ; still, there was no reason for Euripides
to mention the reason unless he had wanted to reinforce the
idea of Orestes' caution.   But there is more than this in the
detail.   M. Parmentier remarks, 'Euripide affecte de faire
prendre à son heros des précautions meilleures que celles
imaginées par ses devanciers' ; but Euripides was much
more intent on his own play than on mistakenly criticizing his
predecessors.[1]   The point is that when Electra appears

[1] If Euripides, not having found out that there are different kinds
of drama and therefore of dramatic methods and conventions, were

Orestes is not whisked away to perform his ritual duties as he is in Sophocles' play; these are already done, so that he can sit in hiding and listen to Electra's monody (109-111).[1] Therefore when he and Pylades jump out at v. 215 he knows who Electra is, and there is no reason why he should not in turn say who he is. But he pretends—for quite a long time. Then at v. 270, we suddenly see why :

'Are these friends of thine that hearken to our words ?'

Of course : Orestes does not realize that these fifteen women are the Chorus, and therefore trustworthy. Electra reassures him, and Orestes' expected declaration—does not come. He still pretends, changing the subject. Electra makes her speech, the Peasant returns, they accept his hospitality, and still there is no disclosure. Can there be any reason but pure lack of resolution ?

But if this is Orestes' reason, what is Euripides' ? It is very interesting to see an Orestes so different from the hero of the *Choephori*, but there were other possibilities—for example, the criminal blunderer of the *Orestes*—which would have been no less interesting. There must have been something that made Euripides choose between equally possible alternatives, and that something was evidently the theatrical value of this Orestes in this situation. His nervous excess of caution makes possible this long scene, full of an obvious but effective kind of irony, Electra's tirade against Clytemnestra and Aegisthus,[2]

_____

showing Sophocles and Athens how 'a Greek Play' should be made, we can be sure that he would have avoided the major improbability here which gives his critics such cynical pleasure, namely that the patient Pylades must already know all that this prologue contains. Melodrama, like Tragedy, has its conventions—and Euripides was neither a pedant nor a fool.

[1] This seems to me a strong argument for the priority of Sophocles' play. The 'overlap' is common to both, and it seems almost certain that the satirical use of it is the later. The recollection of tragedy is spice to satire, but the recollection of satire inconvenient to tragedy.

[2] This speech is less 'naturally' introduced than the corresponding speech in Sophocles (354 ff.). But then, Sophocles is presenting a heroine in whose complete reality we must never cease to believe ; an obviously 'made-up' speech would be a bad mistake. Euripides' Electra is much more a figure on the stage ; she is there

and above all the skit on the recognition in Aeschylus, followed by the detection of Orestes by the Old Man. That is to say, characterization is close, vivid and consistent, but it is subordinated to stage-effect, as it was in the tragi-comedies.

Every dramatist must study stage-effect, but in the severer forms of drama this should be only a means to a further end ; that this principle is no longer effective we can demonstrate further. We do not admit that Euripides was covertly criticizing Sophocles in the manipulation of his plot, but there is no question that he explicitly parodies Aeschylus in the scene between Electra and the Old Man. Whether this is a piece of impertinence or only an entertainment we need hardly discuss here [1] ; from our point of view the significant thing is that it should have been possible for Euripides to turn aside from his theme to write such a passage at all [2] ; the more significant since he does something not very dissimilar with the chorus.

For of the three odes in the play, two turn aside completely from the context in order to describe remote marvels, the Shield of Achilles and certain miraculous events in the history of Atreus and Thyestes.[3] The latter have indeed a mechani-

---

for effect, and this speech is here for effect. There is more room for artifice, and Euripides does in fact introduce the speech artificially ; he even makes the chorus invite it, as at *Helen*, 945 ; a point which, whatever we think of it, at least shows that he was thinking theatrically and rhetorically, and was not anxious to pretend that this was tragedy.

[1] Euripides makes things so easy for himself—as for example by giving Orestes ' boots ', which make nonsense of the ' footprints ' —that we cannot suppose him to have mistaken this for criticism. M. Parmentier, who writes temperately and sensibly about it, calls it ' une improvisation burlesque ' (ed. Budé, p. 184). It is perhaps worth while to point out that the stupid Old Man proves to be right and the clever Electra wrong.

[2] This recalls the stray bit of dramatic criticism in the *Suppliant Women* (846–56). The play is a tragedy, but the report of the battle, which the dramatic criticism immediately precedes, contains very little of its essence. It is a necessary stage in the story, and Euripides, with disconcerting frankness, treats it as such. As there is nothing really tragic going on, but merely a dramatic narrative, he allows his attention to wander from the tragic theme to the criticism of dramatic narratives.

[3] The last, and very short, ode, sung during the killing, sticks

cal kind of connexion with the plot, but the Shield has none at
all—a fact which is emphasized by the rather awkward return
to Clytemnestra at the end. Yet in Sophocles' *Electra*
Euripides had (probably) an excellent model in the dramatic
use of the chorus ; and this play, unlike several of Euripides'
tragedies, has an organic plot which might be supposed to
invite and to benefit from a consistently dramatic chorus.
There was material much nearer to hand than Thyestes : why
did Euripides not use it ? Why does he refrain from imitating Sophocles—and why is it that he made a better play by
following his own judgement than he would have done by
following Sophocles' example ?

In both these odes, and in the parody, Euripides is evidently doing something to interest his audience, but presenting this directly and not through the drama ; not as an interesting turn given to the plot or colour to the treatment, but as
a separate decoration. This is worth a moment's consideration, especially as in all the non-tragic plays (except the
Alcestis and the *Ion*) the chorus is given more or less decorative and ' undramatic ' odes like these two in the *Electra*.

2. THE CHORUS IN NEW TRAGEDY There seem to be two
separate points. The new drama deals with matters of
purely private interest ; even the subject of the *Electra,* which
Aeschylus made so vast, is treated as only a personal matter.
The chorus therefore can have no independent status in the
play, as representing humanity or the City, but becomes either
a useful Confidante or a nuisance. It is a small matter that
the dramatist is put to the necessity of having to explain away
the chorus when confidential affairs are being discussed on the
stage ; this is a convention that we can accept without de-

---

closely enough to the drama ; at such a moment even Euripides can
refrain from writing a brilliant account of the chariot-race between
Pelops and Oenomaus or the story of Tantalus. We may, however,
notice what this ode does not do : it does not speak of justice,
nor, on the other hand, does it question what Electra and Orestes
are doing. It is objective : Clytemnestra killed Agamemnon ; now
she is being killed.

mur.[1] More important is it that the old Parodos, the en-
trance-hymn, had to disappear. No longer could the chorus
enter magnificently, as in the *Antigone* and the *Tyrannus*,
with a song of communal importance ; it now comes in pretending, on various excuses, that it is not a Chorus, but a
group of individuals. In the *Iphigeneia* indeed it enters singing a solemn hymn to Artemis, but alas ! the religion is only a
Wagnerian effect—not even that, for the purpose of their coming, we soon learn, is nothing but to hear of Iphigeneia's bad
dream. This entrance no doubt was an impressive spectacle
—that was what it was meant to be ; but it is only the counterpart, suggested by the circumstances, of the realism of the
Parodos in the *Ion*. It is now logical, and usually necessary,
to bring on the Chorus realistically ; the successor to the
Parodos is the lyrical conversation. As for the other odes,
what was the richest source of material is now dried up. The
chorus used commonly to illuminate the action from a different point of view—from a specifically dramatic one—as when
the chorus of the *Tyrannus* defends Oedipus in its capacity
of citizens of Thebes, or from the point of view of the ' ideal
spectator '—but now, since the action raises no question of
morality, religion, public policy, or even private philosophy,
not even in the *Electra*, but only the question whether so-and-
so will escape, and how, it becomes a little difficult for the
Chorus to remain both dramatic and interesting. Certainly
in the *Iphigeneia* (392 ff.) the chorus can participate in the
curiosity that we also feel, and ask ' Who are the Greek
strangers and how have they come ? ' but such speculations
are in general an unpromising theme for lyric utterance, and
Euripides does not use them often, nor without a good deal
of adventitious ornament.

But even in Sophocles' *Electra* the dramatic action is
treated as a private rather than a public matter—we saw that
for this very reason the new style of Parodos is used—yet

[1] We may observe that the chorus never became a conventional
lyrical appendage which could be simply ignored, one which the
audience would never expect to be noticed from the stage. It
remained an integral part of the play, and if it was in the way, the
dramatist had to explain that it wasn't. (Cf. the chorus at Medea's
murders, p. 200.)

Sophocles can still manage to make his chorus not only relevant but actually one of the most eloquent of his dramatic
instruments.[1] Was then Euripides not so clever, or did he
care less for these things? We cannot escape so easily.
Although Sophocles' theme was private and did not give the
old scope to the chorus, the implications of the theme were
more than personal, and these gave new opportunities. This
is our second point. Events on the stage are in melodrama
only events ; there are no wider implications—or none that
matter seriously. In the older drama a necessary intermission
in the stage-action was an opportunity for the chorus to express, through the lyrical medium which was so well fitted for
the task, some aspect of the inner spiritual drama ; in Sophocles' *Electra* the chorus could accentuate some aspect of the
tragic personality of the heroine. Now, when the stage-
action stops, what we most want is that it should begin again,
for we are really interested in nothing else. It would have
been idle for Euripides to imitate Sophocles and to write an
ode which should carry over the spirit and personality of
Electra from one scene to the next, or one which, going back
to Agamemnon, should accentuate one of her motives or one
of her tragic difficulties. This Electra stands out at once,
complete, as a hard, vindictive woman ; she is there only for
our astonishment. When Orestes goes off to encounter Aegisthus the chorus can in honesty neither speculate anxiously
what the outcome will be—the pretence would be too hollow
—nor talk of justice and vengeance. We know that Aegisthus
will be killed ; we await only the exciting details. The question whether the vengeance is just or not forms no part of the
play ; it was settled long before the play began. An Electra
like this the chorus cannot praise without being revolting, nor
blame without wasting our time. As for the plays of intrigue,
it is even clearer that the gap between scene and scene is
really empty space. Drama has become sensational, and
when the actors leave off there is an intermission in the sensa-
tion. What can the chorus do to enhance the intrinsic excitement of the *Iphigeneia* or the comedy of the *Helen* ? As far
as it can, it keeps out of the way.

[1] Above, p. 174.

But it cannot keep out of the way for long (though Euripides writes eleven hundred lines of the *Helen* before introducing a stasimon), and, seeing that it can so well produce what the plays themselves are aiming at, namely theatrical effect, it is not desirable that it should. The chorus can very seldom contribute in the old way to the drama, but it can please or astonish us lyrically, as the messenger in the *Ion* did verbally. What the chorus sings about in these plays depends, naturally, on the dramatic context; if there is suitable material lying to hand they use it, if not they fill the gap with something else. In either case the ode does not profess to be anything but an effective diversion filling the gap which the actors have left. So in the *Electra*, Euripides prefers arresting narrative and vivid description, though of something quite remote, to an insincere imitation of tragedy; in the *Helen* (1301 ff.) he writes about Demeter—an intolerable irrelevance if our minds were to be seriously engaged on Demeter, but they are not; the ode is only a picturesque and brilliant piece of decoration.[1] Closer to the context are the three odes of the *Iphigeneia* and the remaining two of the *Helen*. Iphigeneia's servants ask who the strangers can be, they lament their own position, they tell how Apollo secured for himself the oracle at Delphi; but the curiosity and the pathos are little but an excuse for a graceful operatic movement, full of birds, festivals, mythological prettiness and pathetic verbal repetitions,[2] and the story of Apollo is quite Alexandrine in feeling. There is not a trace of reverence in the poem, nor of irreverence; it is simply a charming tale, told with due attention to the piquant details, and leading cleverly to the high light, the appearance of the precocious infant before Zeus, the request for the prerogatives of the golden shrine, and Zeus' indulgent smile. Again it is but a short step to Theocritus and his friendly Epyllia. The chorus of the *Helen*

---

[1] Characteristic of the composition is the obvious imitative effect in the words, rhythm, and therefore probably music too in 1346–7.

[2] Some of these odes sound quite as empty and nearly as silly as some of Mozart's libretti; if we had Euripides' music, and Greek ears to hear it with, would it all perhaps sound as marvellous as Mozart's operas?

makes a very pretty song (1451 ff.) out of Helen's return;
but the first stasimon is a little surprising. It begins conventionally enough by describing the inevitable bird, but in
the second stanza it gets serious. The dramatic situation is
that we are awaiting the King and the springing of Helen's
plot. Of this the chorus can obviously take no lyrical notice,
because there is nothing to say and nothing to do but wait;
instead it occupies our minds and gives us a change from the
prevalent flippancy of tone by singing seriously, consequently
without verbal tricks, of war, chance and folly.

It is natural that the *Alcestis*, which, for all its burlesque, is
very much closer to tragedy in manner than the later tragi-
comedies and melodramas, should approach tragedy also in its
use of the chorus. What is perhaps a little remarkable is that
the *Ion* should have so much more dramatic a chorus than its
fellows, though based no less than they on a private theme
and an exciting plot. The first stasimon indeed relies on long
invocations and commonplaces about having children, and can
be called dramatic only because it is not obviously undramatic, but the second (676 ff.), foreshadowing Creusa's rage,
and the third, praying for Ion's death and complaining of
Apollo, attend strictly to the business of the play and do in
fact contribute something to it. The reason for the difference
between the *Ion* and the other tragi-comedies in this regard is
not difficult to see. It is something that this chorus, as
servants of Creusa and Athenian women, have a definite interest and a definite point of view of their own, but the important
point is that the character of Creusa happens to count for
much more in the action of this play than the characters of
Iphigeneia and Helen do in theirs. These heroines have simply to be ingenious at the right moment, and our chief interest
is to see what will happen next; in the *Ion* we also want to
know what will happen next, but that depends very much on
what Creusa will think about it all. The play in fact is to
some extent animated by that active personal will which was
the unifying element in Middle Tragedy. The chorus therefore, because it stands in close relation to Creusa and shares
her sentiments, can contribute more to this play than it usually can in New Tragedy.

Thus we see that the chorus, like characterization, takes a new and a logical position in the new drama. Its odes are now never more than three, for speed and continuity in plot are the dramatist's chief object, and whether their subject-matter is taken from the context or not their function is no longer to help, still less to illuminate the drama, but in an appropriate manner to fill the gaps in the action with lyrical ornament that will be acceptable for its own sake.

One point more may be mentioned. The dramatist may find it expedient to cut down the number of stasima, but music has charms, and he has no intention of foregoing more of them than he must, so that what the chorus loses the actors gain, now encroaching upon the chorus in its own field. In the quasi-parodi of the *Iphigeneia*, the *Helen* and the *Electra* the heroine is the *prima donna* and the chorus subordinate— this perhaps inevitably arising from the uncertain or sub-dramatic status of the chorus in these plays—while elsewhere we find an actor singing a solo aria when we might have expected a stasimon.

For example, the Messenger has informed Electra (*Or.* 957) that she and her brother are to die at once. For comparable moments in tragedy we may turn to the report of Orestes' death in Sophocles' *Electra* or to Tecmessa's discovery of Ajax' body. Electra, in Sophocles' play, says very little, and what she does say is provoked by her anger at Clytemnestra ; then her grief begins to find its natural outlet in the exchange of brief ejaculations with the chorus. Tecmessa cries inarticulately, then masters herself sufficiently to tell the chorus what she has found, then laments to herself in a very natural way as she attends to the body. It is left to the chorus to express the emotion of the moment lyrically. Iocasta and Deianeira receive their death-warrants in silence, and Oedipus meets his discovery with a brief cry of despair ; the Trachinian maidens can sing about Deianeira, and the Corinthians can express something of the tragedy of Oedipus, but the actor is more convincing and eloquent if he remains silent. Imitating such eminently successful passages Euripides could have given to Electra wild cries of terror, and to the chorus an appropriate ode on the end of the royal house or some other suitable topic ; but Euripides is not an imitator. Without a moment's hesitation his Electra sets to work and produces a long, elaborate aria which leaves the chorus nothing to say but 'Lo ! here comes thy brother, with the faithful Pylades.'

This is perfectly correct, and the tragic imitation would be dull, even if not ridiculous. The whole drama, like the aria, is addressed to our nerves and sensations rather than to our minds ; and at this stage of the play we are not going to accept Electra as a tragic heroine. Once more, it is the tragic poet who must be realistic in these matters. The melodramatist must attend to the conventions and demands of his own art, and use a moment like this operatically.

It is the same with Creusa's monody. We know how Sophocles would have made her tell her story ; if we do not, we can see how dramatically Oedipus tells a tale that is filling him with terror.[1] Would the terror have been more obvious or dramatic if he had stopped his speech at v. 813 and gone off into lyrics ? The difference obviously is that we do not want to see how Creusa's character and mind work under the strain ; to us it is simply a sensational story. A speech of Sophoclean force and passion followed by a choral ode would have been insincere and far less to the purpose than Creusa's dramatic aria.

But the *Orestes* contains a much more remarkable extension of stage-lyricism—a messenger-speech cast in the form of wild, incoherent arias ; and this, far from being a sign of increasing laxity of form, is a fine and logical stroke in the making of a fine play.

3. THE ORESTES   The *Orestes*, like the *Electra*, is a melodrama based on character-drawing and character imagined sensationally, not tragically ; and its contrivance displays a control of dramatic rhythm more marked even than that of the *Electra*, for while the *Electra* proceeds steadily from hard unpleasantness to the limit of unnatural hatred, the *Orestes*, proceeding from folly to reckless criminality and from delusion to mania, advances from the usual dry prologue and com-

[1] *Tyrannus*, 771 ff.

mon Euripidean realism to nightmare ; and in the engineering of this splendid spectacle the Phrygian's lyrics are an important structural feature, as we shall presently see.

Only in the most obvious sense is the play a continuation of the *Electra* ; in conception and feeling it is very different. The earlier play has a grim concentration, the later a spectacular, almost frenzied, sweep of melodramatic action ; but in spite of this we are nearer tragedy in the *Orestes*. The Electra and Orestes of this play are not the simple characters that they were in the *Electra*. The unaffected tenderness for each other that they display in the sick-bed scene stands in stark contrast with the utter folly shown by Orestes in all practical matters and the criminal recklessness that infects both. In itself such a contrast might be no more than a theatrical stroke, but it derives a tragic quality from one suggestion in the play, that these two are the last tainted offspring of a tainted house. It is natural, or at least conventional, that in the prologue Electra should proclaim her ancestry, but it is not inevitable that in doing this she should emphasize the crimes of which it has been guilty ; and throughout the play Orestes and Electra, and Pylades too, are represented as degenerates, except for this streak of ordinary humanity; possessed, like the traditional Cleopatra, of a certain unhealthy brilliance, a menace to the society which has to endure them. We are to see how they send up the house of Tantalus in flames. The prologue prepares the way ; the Chorus (vv. 345–7) continues the idea ; Tyndareus declares that Electra, by her criminal suggestions to Orestes,

' She set her house on (metaphorical) fire.' (V. 621).

Menelaus, in the last scene, cries

' What ! Wilt thou destroy this, thy ancestral house ? ' (V. 1595.)

and in obvious fulfilment of Tyndareus' accusation, Orestes calls out, in an access of frenzy,

' Come, Electra ; set this house on fire ! ' (V. 1618).

Certainly the play is the spectacular portrayal of insane behaviour much more than the tragic working-out of this idea, yet the contrast between natural affection and inherited criminality does give a tragic colour to the spectacle, though it may be a colour more like that of romantic than of Aristotelian tragedy.

Euripides' firm control of dramatic rhythm is the making of the play. Every scene is brilliantly constructed, but over and above the individual strokes of dramatic surprise and pungency there is a gradual crescendo in dramatic excitement keeping step with the growing frenzy of Orestes and his accomplices. The stages are clearly defined. The exposition is given in a dry prologue. The early realistic scenes show first the hopeless position of Electra and Orestes, and then the extreme folly of Orestes which makes it worse. The arrival of the foolish Pylades quickens the tempo, and with the announcement of the Assembly's verdict begins a wilder passage in which criminal recklessness is added to folly and insane vengeance to extreme danger. The third stage is one of fantastic horror culminating in the wild scene in which Orestes is on the point of murdering Hermione and setting fire to the palace ; and the finale, a brilliant return to the formality of the prologue, is the *tableau vivant* in which Apollo, like a Shakespearian magician, dissolves the mounting nightmare into familiar fact.

As for the details of the dramatic technique, we must restrict ourselves to a few points. The difficulty of the chorus is met most successfully. Not only does the general situation not readily accommodate a chorus, but as Orestes is asleep on the stage, its arrival is actually a nuisance. Euripides boldly makes capital out of this by allowing Electra to treat the chorus as a nuisance ; it becomes fifteen sympathetic but untimely visitors who are earnestly implored to stop singing and to go home again—a new experience for this ancient institution. We may notice too how cleverly Euripides conveys the blindness of Electra and Orestes to realities, practical and then moral. During the prologue Electra is anxiously scanning all the roads for signs of Menelaus, their one hope ; yet this same Menelaus has had to smuggle Helen up from Nauplia by night, for fear of the people. When Menelaus does arrive he clearly cuts no very regal figure—though he contrasts effectively enough with the ghastly Orestes—and Orestes' appeal to him is sentimentally argued and obviously useless.

At this point, most dramatically, Tyndareus is announced. The unhappy father of Clytemnestra and Helen was not a frequent visitor to the Athenian stage, and his arrival excites the liveliest interest.[1] This is increased by the ecstasy of shame and dismay into which Orestes falls—natural feelings which, if only he could sustain them, might have earned him at least Tyndareus' pitying contempt; this would have been less injurious than the active hostility which he succeeds in provoking by his foolish speech. The speech is not sophistry but plain lunacy; the sophist pretends to answer his adversary's argument, but Orestes is so lost to all sense of reality that he does not see what the argument is.

Tyndareus departs, and now Menelaus, whose embarrassment has been doubled by the interruption, has to listen to Orestes' elaborately silly appeal; his reply to which, the only possible reply, is received with a volley of insults, and is later to be the excuse for the murder of his wife and daughter. The climax to this insane behaviour is the appearance of the death-like matricide and his exiled friend at the trial, and the speech which destroys his chance of escaping with a penalty lighter than death.

The mere folly of these young aristocrats is followed in the next scene by their natural facility in giving fair names to shameful deeds; and the dramatic skill which has led Orestes from his sick-bed to the climax in the Assembly repeats itself in the piling of crime on crime. They are as lost to moral as to practical realities. First the drama inherent in an enforced suicide is exhausted, and the self-deception of which Orestes is capable is crystallized in this outburst:

'Come! let us die nobly, accomplishing a deed worthy of Agamemnon. I will prove to the city my nobility by piercing myself to the heart with my sword; and thou must follow my courageous lead.'[2]

Then Pylades (who in the Argument attributed to Aristophanes of Byzantium is said to be the only character in the play who is 'not wicked') suggests that they may at least involve

---

[1] The juxtaposition of persons here recalls the scene in the *Troades* between Hecuba, Helen, and Menelaus.

[2] Vv. 1060–5.

Menelaus in their ruin by murdering Helen. The scheme is taken up with a horrible enthusiasm, and Pylades, worthy companion to Orestes, translates it into moral terms as follows:

' If we unsheathed our swords against a better woman, the killing would be inglorious ; but as it is, she will be making amends to all Greece—those whose fathers she slew, those whose sons she destroyed, the brides whom she widowed of their husbands. A shout of joy will arise, fires they will light to the gods, vowing blessings to thee and to me, that we encompassed the death of an evil woman. Slaying her thou wilt not have the name Matricide, but casting this behind thee thou wilt mend thy fortune, acclaimed the Slayer of bloody Helen.'

Pylades can yet continue:

' Never, never must Menelaus prosper while thy father, and thou, and Electra are dead ' ;

and he ends this fine oration by proclaiming that if they cannot slay Helen they will burn down the palace and themselves in it, thus either saving themselves like heroes, or like heroes dying.[1]

The only difficulty that this creates for Orestes is that of keeping within bounds his eulogy of Pylades' faithfulness ; but when Electra adds the refinement that they should seize Hermione to be either a security for Menelaus' good behaviour or an easy victim to avenge his bad, his brotherly pride is stirred to the depths :

' In beauty thou dost excel other women, but thy heart is a man's. How much more thou dost merit life than death ! Such, Pylades, is the wife of whom, alas, Death will deprive thee—unless thou live to have her as thy wonderful bride.'

It is fitting that the scene should end with an imitation of the triple invocation in the *Choephori*, which, shocking enough in the *Electra*,[2] sounds positively blasphemous here. As the two men proceed to the pointless murder of Helen, Pylades invokes ' ancestral Zeus and thee, Majesty of Justice '.

This Elizabethan excess of wickedness can hardly be carried through with a Periclean sobriety of dramatic method, espe-

[1] Vv. 1132–52.

[2] Vv. 671 ff.

cially as the miraculous escape of Helen is to take the action
still further into the fantastic. For the contemplation of
tragedy we need a certain repose of mind ; quick and sensational action is the proper vehicle for this febrile melodrama.
Accordingly we have at this point not a stasimon but an
excited dialogue in lyrics while Electra and the two halves
of the chorus anxiously watch the approaches, then as Helen's
shrieks are heard, Electra bursts into wild triumph ; there is a
sudden change to stealthy irony as Hermione arrives ; she is
seized by Orestes, Electra triumphs again, the chorus wonders
what has happened within ; and then comes a most unexpected diversion—a slave, terrified for his life, drops perilously
from under the roof. He, though we hardly suspect it, is the
Exangelos, the Messenger-from-within ; but what messenger-
speech could sustain the savage frenzy of the scene ? He
tells his frenetic story of treachery, slaughter and miracle in a
series of wild lyrics, in which Euripides takes full advantage
of the fact that the fellow is an excitable barbarian. As well
as his terror will allow him he pours out his story. Then
there is another swift change as Orestes comes out, sword in
hand and now obviously a maniac, to play horribly with the
slave, drive him back, and make all ready for the last frantic
and bloodthirsty scene on the roof, Orestes still believing that
Menelaus could ' persuade the city ' if only he would.

The *Orestes* is an outstanding illustration of the freedom
and strength of the Greek genius. Almost at one bound we
have passed from a drama which is at least called statuesque
to drama whose imaginative tumult rivals anything on the
romantic stage ; yet this is done with the minimum of interference with the traditional forms and with a firmness of control hardly surpassed by Sophocles himself.

4. THE PHOENISSAE When Voltaire complained of the pau-
city of material in a Greek play he was not thinking of the
Phoenissae, which contains enough to keep any modern dramatist going at full stretch for his five acts. Drama, as was
suggested above, consumes material at this rate when the
dramatic interest lies in the incidents themselves and not in
what the actors think and feel and do in relation to them.

The *Phoenissae* is a remarkable play, and it illustrates, with the *I.A.*, yet another type of the late drama. It entirely excludes the comic, and makes no use of complication of plot; novelty in plot, so important in the *Ion* and presumably in Agathon's *Antheus,* is one element in the *Phoenissae,* but not the most important; characterization, whether complex as in the *Philoctetes* or melodramatic as in the *Electra,* plays a very small part; and although both of these plays contain the material of tragedy, neither is, or was intended to be tragedy. On the assumption that they were designed as tragedies it is impossible to explain either their material or their style and method, unless we abandon the hypothesis that Euripides was an artist and a good craftsman. We will abandon it if it fails, but until then it must obviously hold the field. We will set forth the structural and stylistic features in the *Phoenissae* that most attract notice, and we shall expect to find that one simple explanation covers all, and that we need not postulate shortcomings in the poet.

Some important facts are noted in the Argument. The play is *polyprosopon,* ' contains many characters '; there being in fact no less than eleven, without counting the chorus. The ancient critic has his misgivings about the Unity of Action; ' Antigone watching from the walls is no part of the action, Polyneices enters under safe-conduct to no purpose, and the scene of Oedipus being driven into exile, with its diffuse lyrics, is an idle addition.' Of modern critics, some have excised the Teichoskopia as an interpolation, others have drastically cut down the Exodos. From the Aristotelian point of view the criticisms implied are just, but what in fact is gained by these surgical operations ? What is left is still nothing like a normal play, for it remains true that Polyneices' visit achieves nothing and is not even ethically or psychologically valuable ; and what have the sacrifice of Menoeceus, Creon's attempt to save him, and the discussion on tactics, to do with the rest of the play or with each other ?

Still dealing with structure, we may enquire why Euripides, having already so much material, arranged the catastrophe—if indeed the death of the brothers and Iocasta is the catastrophe—in such a way that it takes four messenger-speeches to cope with it? Why does Iocasta take Antigone to the battle-field? Why is the chorus elaborately made to consist of Phoenician women, not Thebans? Why has Oedipus been kept a prisoner in Thebes, and Iocasta been made to survive the disclosure of her tragedy?

As to style, why is the single-combat, far from being treated with Aeschylean reticence, described as if it were a gladiatorial fight? Is this an error of taste, brilliant drama, or both? Why does Euripides in almost every detail arrange the course of the battle differently from Aeschylus? Why is Antigone led to and from the roof with such ostentatious circumspection? Why does Teiresias go out of his way, twice, to inform us that being a prophet is not all jam?

As to characterization, why is Antigone represented first as simply a nice girl—curious, eager, naïve, but with no particular distinction—then as a devoted daughter and sister capable of driving Creon off the stage? What is the point? Is there any reason why in Eteocles melodramatic wickedness should be combined with puerility in military science? Or why Creon, who can teach Eteocles how to manage a campaign, cannot manage Antigone? Such combinations in a character are no doubt possible, but in a play possibility is not enough; we demand significance.

To ask all these questions is to see the answer at once. Euripides is not developing a tragic theme, or he would need neither this amount nor this variety of material; not even a non-tragic but dramatic theme, or the material would have more cohesion (as it has for example in the *Ion*). Out of the Theban legend he is creating what we may call a dramatic pageant, presenting scene after scene for the sake of their immediate and cumulative effect, but not for the sake of an inner drama; therefore he needs a lot of material, and need not be particular about its cohesion. He is bringing before us the whole lively history of the line of Cadmus, presenting on the stage the incidents attending its actual downfall, but bringing in, as opportunity offers, both earlier and later events. This explains the chorus, why it is composed of Phoenicians, and why it is both more active and more consistent than the chorus usually is nowadays. The picturesque

origin of the house of Cadmus is dwelt on in the Parodos and
in the first stasimon.   Any chorus could have recounted these
Phoenician legends, but it is infinitely more effective to have
them recounted by a company of Phoenician maidens whose
presence is a proof of the traditions they celebrate.[1]   When
it has discharged this task the chorus proceeds to such recent
events as lie just out of the reach of the actors—the history of
Oedipus (801–17) and the terror of the Sphinx.   Oedipus is,
of course, one of the actors himself, but he is being kept back
to make the climax.   If he covers this same ground himself—
we must say ' if ' as vv. 1595–1614 are spurious—the thrill of
hearing the story from the lips of the chief actor in it will
prevent us from feeling that it is an idle repetition.   The
Sphinx-ode (1018 ff.) is especially noteworthy.   It is written
in the operatic style,[2] and like all the references to the incident (indeed, like the whole play itself) it is quite devoid of
tragic colouring.   We are not made to feel the tragic irony
that Oedipus could be so brilliantly intelligent here yet so
blind elsewhere.   It is only a story of terrible danger, deliverance, and an astonishing sequel.   The short stabbing
phrases create an atmosphere of excitement and unrest, swiftly
taking us through the startling series of events.   The ode, in
fact, is a chorus of the kind that a Covent Garden audience
would insist on having repeated, accurately judging, in its
unsophisticated way, its dramatic purpose and value.

The two scenes which separate Polyneices' exit from the
messenger-speeches are interesting.   There has to be an
Eteocles-Creon scene in which Eteocles may provisionally
hand over the sovereignty and so carry on the narrative
smoothly, but no very intense dramatic interest develops inevitably from this.   We may infer that it was to supply the
deficiency that the passage on strategy was introduced.   The
end of the scene calls upon another source of interest that we
meet more than once in the play, literary reminiscence ; for
the posting of the chieftains at the gates justifies itself dramatically (like the story of Polyneices' espousals, and like a

---

[1] The chorus has also the advantage of being more picturesque
than a Theban chorus would have been.   Cf. vv. 293 ff., 1301.

[2] For example, vv. 1034–37.

great deal of Tennyson) as an echo from the great past. It
is possible that there is a cheap sneer at Aeschylus in this
passage when Eteocles says 'To give the name of each would
be a great waste of time, when the enemy is before the gates'
(751 f.). It is equally possible that there is nothing of the
sort. Giving the names was not a waste of time in the *Septem,* and it would have been a waste of time in the *Phoenissae,* facts of which Euripides must have been aware ; and
Aeschylus had safeguarded himself against the criticisms of
smart people by seeing to it that unfavorable omens should
hold up the attack. Here we can be charitable without
discredit, and suppose that Euripides is explaining to his audience why he omits a passage that they would certainly look
for.

The Menoeceus scene is a bit unexpected, for it lies beside
the main stream of the play, but if Euripides can justify it we
shall not object. This time there is no doubt why the scene
is there. In the first place it contains pathos of a dramatic
kind, and an interesting and characteristic novelty,[1] for Creon
refuses to be a tragic character and orders Menoeceus to run
for his life. Euripides does in fact make the best of both
worlds—deadly sin in a would-be tragic poet, but good business for the melodramatist—for he has his 'realistic' Creon
and can extract the heroics from Menoeceus. In the second
place, the scene has the advantage of showing us Teiresias
once more. After all, a Theban play without Teiresias would
hardly do now. But Teiresias is not the man he was. Gone
are the days when his supernatural machinery could crush a
much stronger Creon than this one is, or when he could successfully measure himself in strength and majesty against
Oedipus himself. Had not Eteocles tactfully excused himself
at the end of the previous scene we might have had from
Teiresias denunciation of a man hardly worthy of it ; as it is,
only Creon is there, and the demand that he makes of Creon
smacks more of irrational magic than of the just anger of
offended Heaven. The demand, however, links us again with

---

[1] Cf. the speech in which Iphigeneia, seeking to avoid the
sacrifice, declares 'Ignoble life is better than noble death' (*I.A.,*
1252).

the legendary past, and Teiresias does his best. To compensate for his loss of tragic dignity he introduces a pathetic note which he had disdained in earlier plays. His part, he feels, is in danger of being only a *succès d'estime*, so that he plays on his blindness and weariness. To be the more interesting he brings with him his ' lots ', carried carefully by the daughter who has succeeded to the boy-guide in the *Antigone*. He lets fall that he has just had a distinguished success in Athens, and he gives us glimpses of the man behind the prophet. It is very interesting to see a great figure at closer quarters, and on the whole Teiresias carries off a difficult situation with dignity, but there may have been those who thought his coming a mistake.

When at the end of the Sphinx-ode the first of the two messengers bursts in we are for the moment made to feel that the late Greek dramatist is as close to the neo-classic as the late Greek scientist is to his sixteenth-century successor. If we are unwary, we shall naturally assume that the messenger has come to announce Menoeceus' death—but no ; it is the fortunes of Eteocles and Polyneices that he has on his lips. Menoeceus receives a tribute as parenthetic as that accorded to Macaria in the *Heracleidae*, and he passes completely from our minds until Creon opens the scene following with a lament for his death ; and then again Menoeceus is superseded by Eteocles and Polyneices and is heard of no more. He is in fact very like the hero of a by-plot, anticipating in his alternate appearances ' the happy loves of Theseus and Dirce '. In tragedy, where thought is superior to incident, it was unnecessary and would have been intolerable so to combine stories ; now this is an agreeable source of relief. Complication is succeeding to complexity.

Because incident is now superior to thought we are treated to four messenger-speeches, and of these the first alone is the longest we have yet heard. Not since the *Persae* has there been such a flood of narrative. The reason why we have here five times as much messenger as in the *Antigone* is plain enough. The usual function of the messenger-speech was to make some decisive contribution to the tragedy growing on the stage or in the orchestra ; narrative-detail was subject therefore to the chastening effect of the tragic burden. But what tragedy is growing here, either on the stage or in the orchestra ? All that these speeches do is to follow and report scenes of the pageant which escape the limits of the stage.[1]

The resemblance to the *Persae* is quite superficial. Aeschylus is contriving a tragic theme, not reeling off a story ; therefore he makes the Queen direct things. She, naturally, so directs them that the merely personal affairs—the safety of Xerxes, the names of the slain—are cleared out of the way first ; this being not only what probability suggests but also what the interests of the tragedy demand, for in this way Aeschylus can develop unhampered his tragic theme, the descent of Heaven's wrath upon the Persians. It is because the speeches present a tragic action in the first place and a narrative only in the second that they have such weight and poise. Incident is subordinated to thought, and it is the thought that makes the form. But Euripides is presenting narrative, and it is the events themselves that must create the form, the presentation obediently following them. He does not want weight and poise, but speed and vividness. Aeschylus, because he was using the dramatic form for a dramatic purpose, found that the arrangement which was tragically necessary was also natural ; Euripides, because he is using the dramatic form (or at any rate the Greek dramatic form) for a purpose which is strictly speaking alien to it, namely narrative, finds that what is dramatically necessary is not natural. The actual situation demands that the Messenger should at once tell Iocasta the news which so urgently calls for her intervention, and that the story of the assault on the walls should be told afterwards to whoever cared to listen ; the dramatic necessity, however, is that we should hear the whole thing from the beginning, and should realize gradually that there is to be no traditional meeting of the brothers at the seventh

[1] This was one of the functions of the Teichoskopia. The brilliance and the extent of the Argive host are used neither to emphasize the peril in which Thebes stands nor to throw into relief the courage or wickedness of a hero. It is decoration, in the Epic manner ; that is why it can be set in a decorative frame—the careful emergence of Antigone on to the roof and her careful descent are as much part of the total effect as the Argive army itself.

gate; and the dramatic necessity must prevail. Since we are ourselves all agog to hear the whole story in due order, and since our interest in Iocasta is sensational, not tragic and therefore paramount, the difficulty is not grave, and the pretence that the Messenger has a childish aversion from telling bad news is quite enough to lull our conscience. This is not a play in which we scrutinize motives and characters very closely. Indeed, the knowledge that the Messenger has something up his sleeve lends an extra thrill to his first story. Atossa directed the Persian, but Iocasta is led by the Theban.

Euripides' manipulation of the events invites comparison with Aeschylus' in the *Septem*. As he is using the same story as Aeschylus but omitting the thought, we must expect him to make good the loss in other ways, not only by covering more ground, but also in making that ground more superficially attractive. He must introduce novelty. To the tragic poet novelty of incident is a trifle; to the romantic or melodramatic playwright it is everything; so that either he invents an original plot, as Agathon did (and Euripides, virtually, in the *Ion* and the *Helen*), or, using a traditional plot, he gives it unexpected turns. Euripides completely refashions the story of the attack, partly for the sake of doing something new, but always in the interests of fuller and more exciting narrative.

The brothers do not meet at the seventh gate. As the *Phoenissae* has no moral basis worth mentioning, such an event could hardly be made significant of anything but chance—perhaps not a bad effect; but how much more melodrama there is in avoiding this classic dénouement and inventing a direct challenge and a single-combat. We have our assault on the walls notwithstanding, we have the dreadful thrill of seeing the brothers deliberately seeking each other out, we have the brilliant account of the fight (so studiously avoided by tragedy), the suicide of Iocasta, and a general battle to finish with. The vividness of the whole is increased by the serialist's device of breaking off at critical moments (1263, 1424). Euripides is not writing tragically, and the effect of immediacy given by this device actively prevents us from thinking tragically ourselves.

In the first speech Euripides retains the description of the Argive champions, but it is a purely physical description. Mottoes, boasts and taunts are left out ; in this non-moral play they would have been so much lumber. In the interests of speed the Theban defenders are passed over ; they were essential to Aeschylus, but would not have justified their presence here. Of Amphiaraus, so tragic a figure in the *Septem*, Euripides can make nothing ; on the other hand Zeus' destruction of Capaneus becomes the sensational climax of the whole story, and when an enthusiastic interpolator added that Capaneus' limbs cartwheeled in all directions, like Ixion's, his hair reaching Olympus and his blood the earth, he was but going too far along a road upon which Euripides himself had discreetly entered.

Iocasta's visit to the battle-field is a good stroke ; even more picturesque is her summoning of Antigone—still fearful of the conventions. When she gets there Antigone does not do much, for all our attention in the fourth speech is concentrated upon the dying brother and Iocasta, but she had to be there in order to lead the procession home and so to be in position for the Exodos. In every conceivable way the old tragic material is rejuvenated—and ' rejuvenated ' is the right word. Euripides will have no nonsense about tragic restraint, for he knows perfectly well that tragic restraint is for tragedy.

Some competent versifier, thinking more of the story than of the tragedy, added a scene to the *Septem* ; but nevertheless the *Septem* ends where Aeschylus ended it, and the lean-to shed is a plain disfigurement.[1] Aeschylus' play is complete when his tragic thought is complete. But the death of Eteocles and Polyneices is not obviously the end of this pageant, and there is no train of thought here to reach its fulfilment. Without doing Euripides any injustice we can imagine him asking himself how and where he could best wind up his play. The succession of incidents goes on—there is for example the burial of Polyneices. There cannot be a tragic full-close, for there is no tragedy, but there can be a scene

---

[1] As that very simple-minded metrician Hephaestion says of his ' hyper-catalectic syllable ', it is something added ' to the completed verse '.

more impressive and pathetic than any that has gone before. After the ten other characters, after sacrifice, fratricide, suicide and battle, Oedipus himself is sent in to bat. It was then for this that he has been kept in Thebes, hidden in the palace. The old King can make a grand finale, telling his astonishing story and then departing into hopeless exile. This must be the end.

It involves one difficulty. If Antigone is to defy Creon and bury Polyneices, she must suddenly grow into heroic stature. But the audience has not been seriously interested in her and her character, and Euripides can take the bold, and logical, course; he puts side by side Antigone the nice girl and Antigone the heroine. In an ethical drama this would be impossible; it is possible here because our interest in her has been purely sensational and momentary. If she helps to round off a grand story in a grand way, we shall not examine too ungratefully the means by which the dénouement is brought about.[1]

It seems certain that the last scene, as we have it, is not what Euripides wrote. It is most unlikely that he struggled into the confusion whereby Antigone both buries Polyneices and accompanies Oedipus.[2] It is likely that it was an interpolator, not Euripides, who provided Oedipus with his refuge at Colonus (a *contaminatio* with the *Coloneus*), and that Euripides ended with Antigone remaining in Thebes to bury Polyneices, and watching Oedipus as he groped his sightless way into the unknown. This would be a spectacular

[1] Some critics, naturally, have seen an interesting psychological development in her character. This is impossible. Between the Teichoskopia and v. 1264 Antigone has been in her dressing-room, neither seen nor mentioned; for us therefore she has not existed—certainly not vividly enough to ' develop '. All that has happened to her since v. 1265 is that she has been carried off (still fearful of the conventions) to a battlefield and has witnessed the violent deaths of most of her family. If then development was intended it is quite unexplained and is therefore totally uninteresting. (See below, p. 387, on Iphigeneia.)

[2] H. O. Meredith, in an attractive and ingenious paper (*C.R.*, LI, 97 ff.), has tried to defend everything, but by using so many special assumptions that the result is unconvincing. The view adopted here I have argued further in *C.R.*, 1939, pp. 104 ff.

finish to a spectacular play, an interesting contrast with the end of the *Coloneus*. Both are fine endings, but Sophocles' means more.

In the examination-paper with which we began we might have asked this question : Explain why in the prologue these details are mentioned, that Laius gave way to pleasure in the heat of wine, that Merope persuaded Polybus that the child was her own, that Oedipus gave Polybus Laius' chariot, that Oedipus named Antigone, Iocasta Ismene. None of these details comes to anything in the play ; all might be omitted without loss—except, significantly, loss of brightness. The purely spectacular course that the play takes might be prophesied from the prologue. It is more than the conventional rehearsal of events which we have seen to be its usual and reasonable task in Euripides, for throughout it takes pains to be lively. We have distinguished three ways in which Greek drama has regarded past events : they have (as in the *Agamemnon*) been used as a living element in the present ; they have been something affecting the present and therefore mentioned as required (as in the *Tyrannus*), and they have been only the casual prelude to the present, stowed away therefore in the conventional prologue. Now, in so far as the prelude is not conventional but bright and interesting, they are once more a real part of the play. Iocasta's intimate details, like Oedipus' narrative, are part of the pageant. They enable the dramatist to overstep the narrow limits of the stage in his search for the picturesque and dramatic ; the chorus enables him to go still further back and to colour the present scene much more effectively. This is what it did in the *Agamemnon*—but now the colours are only pretty. The chorus in this play has a more assured position than it has enjoyed for some time, but its position so clearly depends on the accident of the dramatic setting that it must feel its end drawing near.

The *Phoenissae* then, because it is not tragic, but aims simply at creating a certain theatrical effect, falls into the same broad category as the tragi-comedies and the melodramas, but it differs from them in choosing for special development a different element of the complete dramatic form. Complication of plot, comedy and satire play no part in it,

character-drawing hardly more ; *mythos*, in the form of extended narrative, and *pathos* predominate, with naturalism,
operatics and a certain autumnal literary reminiscence to lend
variety.   A legend in which tragedy has found some of the
noblest of its material is, for this new age, passed in review,
with every attention paid to the possibilities of dramatic situation and narrative, but with no trace of tragic thought.   Greek
Tragedy in fact is ending where Wilamowitz said it began, in
the presentation of Saga.   Early tragedy (meaning, of course,
the best of it) developed, as in a vertical plane, the tragic implications inherent in a situation that did not need to move
at all.   Now we are at the opposite pole ; the situation must
always be moving, and the inner drama, the vertical development, which had been everything, has ceased to exist.

Therefore we ought again to reconsider the meaning of
Unity of Action.   The criticisms made in the Argument to our
play are true and irrelevant ; if the scenes were as strictly
related to each other here as they are in the *Ion*, we should
have not a better play but a different sort of play.   Aristotle's insistence on intellectual unity of plot must not be
applied blindly to a play which is sensational and not intellectual.

Greek drama, Greek art in general, is conspicuously intellectual ; what distinguishes the Greek dramatists from
Shakespeare more perhaps than anything else is the point at
which they begin to apply pure intellect to their work.   In
neither case is there the faintest doubt but that the drama
originated where all living art must originate, in the intuitive,
non-intellectual part of the mind ; but with the Greeks it is
impossible for criticism to penetrate to a point at which the
poet's intellect is not already active, while in the finished work
of Shakespeare there are whole tracts of which his intellect
seems never to have had cognizance at all.   At times nothing
intervenes between his imagination and his pen ; hence the
silliness of some of his plots, the mere break-down of others,
the not infrequent irrationality of his characterization, the
fact that the incomparable quintessence of the man is to be
found often in his parentheses.   In the Greeks, however far
back we go, we find the pure tragic feeling already pre-

cipitated as a tragic thesis, already embodied in a plot ; so
that a Greek Tragedy without Words, if the thing were possible, would still be tragic ; the ' meaning ' is woven into the
structure itself.

This suited Aristotle admirably. It was inevitable that he
should insist on the intellectual virtues of Greek drama—not
knowing that Shakespeare was going to exhibit some of the
most marvellous of his pictures in makeshift buildings. But
when we come to the *Phoenissae*, whose origin is not a tragic
apprehension such as set the dramatist's intellect greedily at
work, we must question the validity of Aristotle's intellectualism. His canons make for elegance of form, but elegance
of form is a minor virtue ; the Greek dramatists never made
it their aim, but attained it, usually, as a by-product of the
effort to present their idea as clearly as possible. In the
Phoenissae the dramatic idea is to obtain a certain dramatic
effect by presenting certain scenes from a certain legend ;
everything therefore which does in fact contribute to that
effect is a logical part of the scheme, and a criticism which
says that this scene or that is not ' logically ' connected with
the rest shows only that it has not realized what that scheme
was. The self-sacrifice of Menoeceus has a connexion with
the rest of the play which may be found but is not very close,
yet since it gives depth to the story no objection can be taken
to it. We are entitled to say that we think this a relatively
poor form of drama, but we must not apply to it canons which
have no validity. When the Athenians heard the fight between the brothers described with such relish, when they
saw material which Aeschylus had charged with such tragic
significance being used up for the sake of a romantic scene on
the roof, some irreconcilable conservatives may have grumbled
that Euripides was turning a church into a cinema. So he
was, but it is very good cinema.

5. THE IPHIGENEIA IN AULIS   The *I.A.* has its merits, but
Greek Tragedy has its standards. Judged by these it is a
thoroughly second-rate play ; but it has considerable interest
in literary history. It is important to realize that the play is
relatively feeble not because Euripides missed his aim for

once, being incompetent, tired or uninterested ; he did what
he set out to do, and did it with his accustomed sureness of
touch.   The play is second-rate because the whole idea was
second-rate.

It might be interesting to speculate on the influences which
led Euripides to write this West-end half-tragedy at a time
when he had the elemental stuff of the *Bacchae* in him.   Did
he begin and nearly finish it in Athens, for and under the influence of an audience which no longer wanted tragedy pure
and strong ; then, going into the fresher air of Macedonia,
drop this pretty but tired play unfinished in order to rise, like
Samson, and shake the world with his *Bacchae* ?   In rescuing
the *I.A.* from his father's literary remains Euripides the
Younger did little to increase his father's fame, but he helped
us to understand why the Alexandrian scholars thought nothing later in Greek Tragedy worth preserving.

Our affair, however, is not with speculation but with literary
fact.   What is the play about, and will its general conception explain its features without sending us for refuge to *ad
hoc* assumptions of old age, political references, or ineptitude ?

In order that the Expedition may proceed, Agamemnon has
bidden his daughter to come to Aulis, nominally to be married
to Achilles, really to be sacrificed.   He is not a man of firm
character (332), and in the romantic scene which follows the
original plain prologue he is seen countermanding that order.
The second letter is intercepted by Menelaus, a brutal ruffian
who can see only that Agamemnon is breaking his word and
letting a brother down.   His scornful speech draws a picture
of Agamemnon—one which passes unchallenged—as a mean
careerist ; Agamemnon in reply throws just as disillusioning a
light upon Helen and upon the famous Oath of the Suitors.
Suddenly Menelaus changes what we have to call his mind—
but it is too late, for a messenger has announced the arrival
of Iphigeneia and of her mother too.   This is extremely
awkward, but for a moment we may wonder how it justifies
the tragic to-do that Agamemnon makes about it.   The reason
is that although apparently he could safely have refused to
send for his daughter at all, now that she is here the army will
insist on her being killed.   Odysseus, a very wicked man in-

deed, who exercises a complete ascendancy over the Greeks, will stampede them, even to the sacking of Argos, and nothing can be done about it. Nor is this a private nightmare of Agamemnon's, for in the event the enraged army pursues Achilles—his own Myrmidons in the van—thirsting for Iphigeneia's blood and for the attack on Troy. Agamemnon has no choice but to go through with the miserable business, deceiving his wife and daughter as long as he can.

He does not deceive them for long. Achilles appears, demanding reasons for the delay in sailing ; his men insist on going forward or going home.[1] But he meets Clytemnestra instead of Agamemnon, and the secret is soon out. He gallantly undertakes the defence of Iphigeneia, but this comes to nothing. Iphigeneia, who has at first tearfully protested, changes her mind as suddenly as Menelaus did, and goes willingly to the altar, where Artemis makes the miraculous substitution of a kid.

Now this is not a bad story, but it is not really tragic, and Euripides knows it. That is the reason why he does not trust to the story alone for his dramatic effect. There is tragedy in the story : Aeschylus showed us that when he made it part of the tragedy of Agamemnon, of the blind sinner who, sacrificing his daughter to his ambition, lays up retribution for himself. Agamemnon has his torments in this play, but he has no tragic choice, and as the play proceeds the emphasis is laid not on what the guilty man will have to suffer but simply on the fate of the innocent Iphigeneia. Indeed we can hardly call Agamemnon a guilty sinner as he is here presented. The chorus in its only reference to the situation (1080–97) says something to this effect, but he is in fact drawn as a man who has levered himself into importance by unworthy means, a crafty, indecisive character, undeserving of our serious interest. His indecision at a critical moment lands him in a situation in which he has no choice but to com-

[1] Why does Euripides so carefully avoid the strong contrary winds of Aeschylus ? The Greeks are suffering from *aploia* ('the holding up of the ships') (88), they lack favouring winds (352), and Achilles complains of waiting in the light breezes of the Euripus (813). The Myrmidons see no reason for waiting except the irresolution of the commanders.

mit an atrocious crime ; but in order to apply the squeeze to
him Euripides has to pretend that the Greek army is composed entirely of ogres.   We see Agamemnon squirm ; it may
be a dramatic but it is not a tragic spectacle.   Aristotle rightly
said that the downfall of a bad man is *philanthropos* but is not
tragic [1] ; here even *to philanthropos* is wanting, as the play
moves right away from Agamemnon.   Tragic illumination
ought to be the justification of this cruel story, but we have
only the story.[2]

There is no tragedy of Agamemnon, nor is there a tragedy
of Iphigeneia.   From her point of view the incident is nothing but a cruel blow of fate.   As such it may perhaps be
compared superficially with the blow that fell on Pelasgus,
but the comparison is valueless.   An incident is tragic or not
tragic according to the treatment.   We cannot in fact isolate
an incident in literature from its treatment.   What happened
to Pelasgus is filled with significance ; what happened to
Iphigeneia remains what happened to Iphigeneia.   We are
no wiser ; this combination of an unexplained demand from
a goddess, an incompetent father and a frenzied army is a
particular and not a universal.

These remarks would not surprise Euripides.   He knew
that he was not, like Aeschylus, writing a tragedy of Agamemnon ; that is the reason why he abandons him.   He
knew that the story, as he tells it, was melodramatic, with no
illumination, no catharsis, to relieve and justify its cruelty ;
that is the reason why Iphigeneia is not after all slain.   Once
more the happy ending replaces tragic catharsis.[3]   Above all,

---

[1] Poetics, 1453a, 2 ff. *Philanthropos* means, roughly, satisfactory
to our sense of justice.

[2] Emerging once from a performance of a gloomy modern play
which took itself to be tragedy, I met a stupid acquaintance who
said to me ' I don't like these tragedies.   What I always say is that
there is enough tragedy in real life. '   Now to be a critic no doubt
one has to be clever, but a stupid man can tell one end of a stick
from the other.   My friend was not clever enough to see that the
play was not a tragedy, but he had the sense to feel that it was a
cruel story which meant nothing and was therefore an unnecessary
infliction.

[3] P. 331.

this explains why the theme is subjected to such picturesque and diverse ornament. After reading the *Electra* and the *Orestes* we can imagine Euripides turning this incident into a morbid psychological study, and a very different play it would have been. After reading the *Hecuba* and the *Troades* we can imagine him turning it into social tragedy ; that too would have made a very different play. The structure of this play is consistent with neither of these dramatic aims, but it is consistent with the dramatic aim that made the *Phoenissae*. Let us look at it a little more closely, beginning with the sacrifice.

Iphigeneia is first quite natural ; recalling Creon in the *Phoenissae* she declares that it is better to live ingloriously than to die gloriously. Then she sings an elaborate and wild song against Paris, Helen, her father, the whole expedition. Finally, when it becomes clear that there is no defence and that Achilles is in serious danger, she readily offers herself for sacrifice ; not as one still thinking the whole thing monstrous yet preferring to face the inevitable before it involves others, but as one who is going to die gloriously, save Greece and ' set it free ', teach barbarians a lesson—all sorts of nonsense. Shakespeare at his most patriotic never wrote like this, and we are justified in calling it nonsense because even Menelaus has seen that Helen is not worth fetching back and that Iphigeneia has nothing to do with the affair.

Either Iphigeneia has changed her attitude fundamentally for reasons which are not divulged and for a dramatic purpose which remains obscure, or her characterization is, as Aristotle said, inconsistent. It is idle to defend the change of attitude by saying that it is possible ; what indeed is not ? Those who make this brave apology should look again at the *Poetics* : ' if a character is inconsistent . . . let it be consistently inconsistent.' Inconsistency, to be permissible, must be significant of something, since a play, or any other work of art, exists not to record the possible but to create something of meaning. In the street we do not expect to see the meaning of everything ; in a play we certainly do.

But why did Euripides do so extraordinary a thing ? He was no novice, and if he were he would surely have avoided

this error, and that too without much trouble. We have
therefore to see if there is an explanation a little less improbable than that when he wrote the end of the scene he had
forgotten the beginning. It may help if we recall Polyxena.
Her sacrifice was a part of an undoubted tragedy, and it admitted of no miraculous substitution. She met death willingly, explaining that she had no reason to prefer life ; the
reason for this being that there was no need to add horror to
tragedy. The tragedy would not have gained in significance
had she had, like Antigone, every reason for clinging to life.
Iphigeneia also goes willingly—because nothing else is dramatically decent. Why then does she first speak and sing so
passionately on the other side ? Because nothing else would
have been interesting. That is to say, her character, like
that of Antigone in the *Phoenissae,* is controlled entirely by
what the situation of the moment requires ; but since the
two Antigones are separated by the length of the play while
the two Iphigeneias could shake hands, the inconsistency is
much more glaring here. Whether Euripides has justified his
neglect of consistency here no one can say who has not seen
the play acted, and acted properly ; the real test is whether
it comes off or not. To the reader it certainly appears that
he has gone too far.

But if Iphigeneia's character is notoriously obscure, what of
Menelaus' ? When he first appears he is the simple melodramatic ruffian, outraged that Agamemnon has recanted ; for
entrapping and killing a daughter is, to him, a trifle compared
with the crime of letting a brother down. But within a hundred verses he has veered round completely. Grasping
Agamemnon's hand he is all repentance, magnanimity, clear-
sightedness ; he can even declare that Helen is better where
she is—a point which Euripides has already suggested to him
in several plays. He enjoys his repentance (502 f.)—but
what has brought it about ? The sight of Agamemnon's distress : really, until this very minute it had never occurred to
him that killing a daughter might be unpleasant.

This too is no doubt possible, but it is a little thin. One
would in fact easily suspect him of playing some deep game
were it not that a moment later the reformed villain makes

the constructive suggestion of murdering Calchas : dead men tell no tales. But, possible or not, where is the point ? Euripides could easily have kept his Menelaus consistently brutal and yet dramatically interesting by not allowing Odysseus to have cognizance of the prophecy and making Menelaus tell him of it. The point is simply the sudden reversal of situation, Menelaus saying ' No, don't kill her ', and Agamemnon ' Yes, I must '. We may look for deeper significance, but we shall not find it.

Because Euripides knows that his theme is not serious enough to sustain the play unaided, he does not rely on it. The play, like a modern biography, must at all costs be bright and interesting, but there is a brightness of truth, and there is a brightness that is preferred to truth. With a sort of satisfaction we have been learning lately that our heroes were not heroic ; Athens at this time was experiencing similar delights. The wicked Menelaus of the *Andromache*, the cunning Odysseus of the *Philoctetes* were dramatically true, because their badness was a logical part of a serious dramatic plan ; it is difficult to say as much for the meanness of Agamemnon here. Agamemnon is being ' debunked '. The picture of the King of Men ' on the make ' is entirely consistent with the pictures of Iphigeneia unheroically natural and unreally heroic, and with this artificial reversal of situation of which at least the one half, Menelaus', can have no real significance.

In default of a real theme, Euripides taps every other source of interest. He plays for all he is worth on the sentimental appeal of the infant Orestes ; he makes a very good and romantic scene out of Agamemnon's writing of the second letter.[1] But Clytemnestra and Achilles are more revealing. Clytemnestra gets out of her chariot with unrivalled impressiveness, and presently, when she is confronting Agamemnon with his wickedness, she speaks of her past relations with him

---

[1] It seems that Euripides the Younger still further brightened up his father's play by dropping the plain conventional prologue and starting off with the anapaestic passage between the King and the Slave. The scene in fact is extremely good, and sounds oddly Elizabethan.

and tells us something that Aeschylus never knew (1148 ff.). It is nothing to the point, but it is a vastly exciting piece of gossip. In this speech she does everything except what the situation, if it were a real one, would demand, namely that she should destroy Agamemnon in about ten verses. But then, the truth would have been a little too plain and unsophisticated ; how much more elegant and interesting it is for us to see Clytemnestra getting into her stride and threatening Agamemnon with the *Agamemnon*.

The search for brightness magnifies Achilles' part beyond all recognition. His intervention alters nothing and affects nobody, except that its complete failure is used as an excuse for Iphigeneia's heroics. Achilles does nothing which, if this were tragedy, could not have been done through a reasonably competent Messenger—except one or two things which, if this were tragedy, would not have been done at all. Only Achilles in person could complete that intriguing scene of cross-purposes in which Clytemnestra, so very much the lady, greets Achilles, so very much the gentleman, as her imminent son-in-law. Only Achilles in person could provide us with that delicate character-sketch, so cleverly beginning with the word *hypselophron* ('high-minded'), so full of ironical humour, so reminiscent of Plato's young men ; or the sketch of the young aristocrat who has graduated in Chiron's cave and can therefore write himself a glowing testimonial—which includes parenthetically the fact that ten thousand girls are pining for his love. This has nothing to do with Iphigeneia, but it all helps to pass the time pleasantly and intelligently.[1]

The chorus, naturally, has to be very discreet. It may feel disposed to make the orchestra re-echo with gloomy prophetic thunders, but it has to be careful lest it blow the play to pieces. The long parodos is couched in the same style as the odes of the *Phoenissae*—non-moral, non-intellectual, a piece of pure description. The first stasimon philosophizes mildly about Love, with special reference to Paris ; the second describes by anticipation scenes from the war ; the third sings prettily about the marriage of Achilles' parents. Not until

[1] Is it simply in order not to raise our tragic expectations that the winds are not allowed to howl against the waiting ships ?

we reach the final stanza of this last stasimon is there any serious reference to the matter in hand.

We see then that neither in the choral odes nor in the general lay-out of the play is there anything to persuade us that Euripides was thinking tragically about Agamemnon or Iphigeneia. The sacrifice is a dramatic and pathetic incident; but from the romantic night-scene with which we start to the miracle with which we end everything demonstrates that Euripides was less concerned with what he could put into the story than with what he could get out of it. In comparison with the *Phoenissae* the *I.A.* is weak, and the weakness seems to lie in this, that although the *Phoenissae* no less than the *I.A.* uses in a relatively superficial manner material which we might expect it to use tragically, the Theban pageant has a sweep and a movement which lends itself to this objective treatment. The *I.A.* lacks this sweep, and it insistently raises but evades issues which we feel ought to be faced. It was very unconventional but clever of Agathon to invent a new plot for himself which he could treat as romantically as he chose without encountering at every turn the disconcerting ghost of Tragedy.

CHAPTER XIII

TWO LAST PLAYS

The *Bacchae* and the *Oedipus Coloneus* may seem an oddly
assorted pair of plays, but they have an historical nexus which
an historical study of Greek Tragedy may recognize with advantage : for both were produced posthumously. We may
go further, for both plays are markedly different in form and
in manner from their immediate predecessors. As if the
thunder from Heaven that so impressively warns Oedipus of
his approaching end had been audible in Macedonia as well
as in Sophocles' native Colonus, Sophocles and Euripides alike
seem to gather their forces for one last effort, to embody, as
in a testament, his final vision of the tragedy of man. Each
develops a theme which is recognizably a continuation of
earlier work, and the result is surprising ; for Euripides writes
a drama which, for all its wild movement and romantic colouring, is much more regular in form than most of his earlier
tragedies, while Sophocles, the master of structure, approaches
an almost Euripidean looseness of form.

1. THE BACCHAE   The freshness and beauty of its poetry puts
the *Bacchae* almost in a class of its own among the tragedies
of Euripides ; so does its dramatic style, which is our immediate concern.

This posthumous tragedy offers the remarkable spectacle
of a dramatist returning to the methods and style—of his youth
we cannot say, as he was nearly 50 when he wrote the *Medea*,
but of a period of twenty or twenty-five years earlier. The
Bacchae is the best constructed of all his tragedies. Many
would claim this honour for the *Hippolytus*, perhaps rightly ;
yet the *Bacchae* has more unity, and it has a dramatic impetus
not felt in every corner of the *Hippolytus*. With the tragedies
that followed the *Hippolytus*, from the *Heracleidae* to the
Troades, the *Bacchae* has very little in common—a fact which
of itself shows the absurdity of trying to treat dramatic style

as something that develops and can be studied separately, independently of dramatic content. Nor can we attribute to
any one external cause, whether old age or contemporary
taste, both the relative looseness of the *Coloneus* and the
unusual tautness of the *Bacchae*.

A very rapid survey of the *Bacchae* will establish the contrast that we are considering. The theme is begun, the
impetus started, at the very beginning of the prologue. Already in the first ten verses we hear of a miracle, the still-
burning fire that had consumed Semele—a miracle which
ought to have been enough to silence the sophisms of Cadmus
and to instil some doubts into the dogmatic mind of Pentheus.
Another miracle follows ; the god has caused the vine to grow
over his mother's tomb. Next the prologue asserts the universality of the new religion (13–22), and continues by
presenting the situation of the moment. Leaving Asia for
Greece, Dionysus has come first to Thebes ; his kinsmen, misled by Cadmus' sophisms, reject him, and, since his own city
must be brought to accept him, he has driven the women out
upon the mountains, mad ; Pentheus, his particular opponent,
must be made to recognize the new godhead.

Here, in fifty verses, not only is the scope of the play defined
with perfect clarity, but also the dramatic rhythm is already
started. Not often are these introductory monologues so
incisive in style.

This incisiveness remains with the whole play. The first
scene goes with an admirable vigour, and it has variety beyond
what is usual in the tragedies. The old prophet, who
sincerely accepts the new religion,[1] the old King, who accepts
it, but not sincerely, and the young King, who rejects it
utterly—these make a scene of a vividness which we can
parallel from the tragi-comedies, but hardly from the tragedies.
After the stasimon there is the terse Servant who brings in
the disguised god with a warning story of fresh miracles ;
then a vigorous and natural stichomythia leads to the im-

---

[1] Perhaps, as Mr. Grube thinks, only with the sincerity of the
professional ecclesiastic. (My references to Mr. Grube are to
his interesting article on the play in *Trans. American Philolog.
Assocn.*, LXVI, 37 ff.)

prisonment of Dionysus by the infatuated Pentheus. There
is his miraculous escape, the first Messenger's speech, so well
placed—a final warning to Pentheus, which however serves
only to provoke him to his last act of hybris, the calling out of
the army, as foreshadowed in the prologue. Now comes a
very dramatic surprise. At v. 810 Dionysus, realizing that
Pentheus is inaccessible to both persuasion and warning,
changes his tactics ; instead of overwhelming Pentheus and
his Theban army as he had proposed (vv. 50–2), he decides
to take a more terrible revenge on Pentheus alone, the revenge
that we are soon to see.[1]

We need hardly continue. The whole plot moves with
unwonted speed and directness, and is so well constructed
and balanced that it is made to turn visibly at this one point.
It is an organic unity, a complete contrast to the plots of all
the surviving tragedies later than the *Hippolytus*. There is
indeed one difficulty, the famous Palace-miracle,[2] but its
solution is simple, and in any case it is a difficulty of a different order from the intrusive scenes and ill-made plots of the
earlier plays.

To the schematic tragedies the *Medea* and *Hippolytus* also
stood in sharp contrast, yet the *Bacchae* does not very closely
resemble these either. The *Medea* has its formal inconveniences in the Aegeus-scene and the 'irrational' ending,
while the *Hippolytus* falls dramatically (though not tragically)
into two parts, and cannot make its chorus an integral part of
its structure. No criticisms of this kind can be urged against
the *Bacchae* ; it has formal unity and it has a dramatic impulse
which drives the action forward without deviation or slacken-
ing. The last scene is no exception. Critics who, in spite of
the prologue, fix their attention exclusively on Pentheus have
to make the familiar excuses. Tyrrell for example says[3]
that a modern dramatist would have ended, with applause, at
v. 1372. No doubt he would, but the reason why Euripides
does not is not that he had no curtain, that he wanted to

---

[1] This point I owe to Mr. Grube.

[2] Of this Norwood and Verrall had one explanation ; a different
one will be adopted below.

[3] Introduction to his edition of the play, p. 39.

connect his story with the whole cycle of surrounding myths,
that he wished at the end to raise the god above these
mundane adventures. Such considerations have, sometimes,
their place, but here the first point, which makes others unnecessary, is that Dionysus is not avenging himself on Pentheus only but on all those—Cadmus and his dupes—who have
rejected him. The theme is stated in the prologue and would
be incomplete without the epilogue.[1]

It is perhaps in plot that the special position of the *Bacchae*
among the tragedies is most evident, but in other respects it
differs noticeably from at least the tragedies of the second
group. For example, we cannot fail to be struck with the
much more normal treatment of character. To assert that the
characterization here is more convincing (in the ordinary
dramatic sense) than that of the *Meda* and the *Hippolytus*
might needlessly provoke dissent ; certainly it is to those plays
that we must turn for a parallel, and some would perhaps
agree that in Medea, Jason and Hippolytus there is an exaggeration completely absent from Pentheus.[2] His honest
narrowness makes him a round, not a flat character. Moreover, we see his defiance of the new religion growing ; each
successive event that ought to make him pause serves only to
drive him to still more uncompromising opposition. Not since
we saw Phaedra have we been so strongly reminded of Sophocles' methods. To make Pentheus even more Aristotelian
Cadmus praises him (1308–12) for his filial respect and piety ;
he is a normally well-meaning man, but his complete lack of
imagination ruins him.[3] We may notice too how the novelty
of the Dionysiac religion is emphasized (e.g. 219, 467) ;
this, as it is some excuse for Pentheus, plays its part in making
him so much of a Middle Tragedy hero.

Situation as well as plot is handled more after the fashion

[1] As Wilamowitz impatiently asked, ' Kann man denn nicht
lesen ? '

[2] I do not wish to suggest that therefore the *Bacchae* is a better
play. We are not awarding certificates but comparing methods.

[3] I cannot agree with Mr. Grube's view of this passage, ' white-
washing of the villain '. It oversimplifies both Pentheus and the
play to make him ' the villain '.

of Middle Tragedy. We should look long in the Euripidean
tragedy before we found another triangular scene as natural
and significant as that between the two old men and Pentheus.
The Helen-Hecuba-Menelaus scene is at least as successful
—success is not in question—but it is rhetorical rather than
natural; throughout the *Bacchae* there is real interplay between the characters. We have seen from the tragi-comedies
that Euripides can manage these effects; we have seen why
the earlier tragedies did not use them; now we are inquiring
why the *Bacchae* does. Reminiscent too of Middle Tragedy
is the unforced contrast between the Servant, who arrests
Dionysus, and Pentheus. The Servant feels shame at his
treatment of the unresisting captive, fear too; Pentheus cannot
feel either. It is a simple enough point, and would hardly
deserve comment except that its naturalness is uncommon in
the Euripidean tragedy. Characters like Medea's Paedagogus
are natural, and effectively so, but their naturalistic touches
do not illuminate the tragedy of the central figure in this intimate, Sophoclean way.

With this more normal treatment of character and situation
there goes an actuality or imaginativeness in the treatment
which has for some time been lacking. Not often does Euripides remind us of Aeschylus, but there is assuredly an Aeschylean flavour in the first of the scenes between Pentheus and
Dionysus : Pentheus is so confident, so unconscious of his
hybris and the rationalistic infatuation that possesses him; he
marches so blindly towards the doom that awaits him. His
presumption is symbolized terribly in his actions. He cuts the
lock ('the sacred lock') from the unresisting god's brow; he
wrests the thyrsus from his hand. It is the method of
Clytemnestra's carpet over again.

Nor is it accidental that this same scene recalls Cassandra's
'To what house have I come?'[1] The chorus prosaically
answered 'To Atreus's'. So here Dionysus says 'Thou know-
est not . . . what thou art doing nor who thou art' (506),
and Pentheus answers 'Pentheus, son of Agave and Echion'.
Aeschylean too is the recklessness with which Pentheus orders

[1] P. 81.

the destruction of Teiresias' seat of augury. Sophocles'
Oedipus may insult the prophet, or his Creon defy him :

' Him shall ye never bury in the tomb ;
    No, not though Heaven's own eagles were to snatch
    And bear him in their talons to the throne.
    Not even so, for dread of that defilement
    Will I permit his burial.'

It is shocking, but it is hyperbole :

' For well I know
There is no mortal can defile the gods.' [1]

Sophocles' characters remain in touch with the instinctive
scruples of mankind [2] ; this Pentheus is an Aeschylean infatuate, he is another Agamemnon burning the temples of
Troy.

But Euripides at his most Aeschylean does not cease to be
Euripidean. Typical of his wry and rather disconcerting
manner is the apparent comedy of the two old men dressed up
for the dance. Since Euripides was not English, we must
not hastily credit him with the doctrine that any joke is
better than no joke ; nevertheless the apparent comedy was
avoidable. To Pentheus the two old men are a revolting
sight, but it is part of the lesson which he must learn that the
claims of Dionysus are absolute. The comedy is purposeful,
and the clue has been given in the prologue. We have heard
of the universality of the new religion, and that Dionysus
has driven the women mad ; it would be poor acting that
allowed us to guffaw at Cadmus and Teiresias. Dionysus
has nothing to do with Pentheus' respectability ; the old men
are to own his sway, as Pentheus himself will do, so much
more terribly, in his last scene.[3]

Before we leave the topic of the general dramatic style of
the *Bacchae* there is one further point to notice. It was suggested in an earlier chapter that some of the prominent
features in Euripides' tragic style—the prevalence of rhetoric
and dialectic, excursions into political, ethical or literary

[1] *Antig.*, 1039 ff. Trans. Harrower.

[2] See above, p. 352 (the comparison between the two Electras).

[3] ' The god has made no distinction, whether young or old are to
dance to him. He will be honoured equally by all ' (206-8).

theory—were to be explained directly, though perhaps not wholly, by the general nature of those plays. If so, we should expect the *Bacchae*, a play much more akin in structure and feeling to Middle Tragedy, to be free from these things. In fact, it is. Reflections are made about 'wisdom', but they all arise directly out of the conflict of Pentheus with Dionysus ; there is no discussion whatever of extraneous topics. Now at last the tragedy that Euripides is presenting on the stage fills his mind to the exclusion of everything else. There is nothing of the tragic idea left over.

Such is the real 'problem of the *Bacchae*', that suddenly Euripides returns to tragedy (Macedonia helps to explain this), and what he writes a tragedy in which plot, characterization, and general dramatic style are not only entirely different from anything that we have seen in his tragedy since the *Hippolytus*, but even more normal than the *Hippolytus* and *Medea* themselves. It is not difficult to see the explanation of this, but before we discuss it, we may conveniently deal with the one special difficulty of the plot, namely, the Palace-miracle.

The bleak rationalism of the last generation could not allow that in the *Bacchae* Euripides was doing anything but attacking, exposing and ridiculing the Dionysiac religion. Norwood and Verrall, sceptics more fortunate than Pentheus, seized on the Palace-miracle with delight ; it was the refinement of wit that though in the middle of the play the palace should be shaken and burned to the ground, during the rest of it nobody should notice the fact and Pentheus himself should go in and out as if nothing had happened. There is a real difficulty here, not lessened by the silence of commentators.

But what does the Palace-miracle amount to ? Mr. Grube (to whom it occurred to read the text) points out that the chorus feels an earth-tremor, sees pillars and entablatures parting asunder, and predicts that the palace will fall to the ground—but does it ? The chorus calls upon Dionysus to burn down the palace, and indeed a fire-miracle does take place (one that could be easily contrived on the stage), for the fire smouldering around Semele's tomb suddenly flares up. Dionysus escapes unquestionably, and that by wrecking or partly wrecking the building in which he was confined, namely the stables. There is no reason at all to suppose that these were visible to the audience.

But though a calm study of the text reduces the miracle to these dimensions a difficulty remains, namely, to explain why the difficulty arises. Why did Euripides so contrive matters that we have to look into the text so carefully before we can decide whether it is sense or raving nonsense ?

We should remember that the back-scene was the usual palace-front and that the last thing the audience would look for would be an elaborate display by the stage-carpenter whereby pillars would be thrown to the ground and the orchestra filled with stage-rubble. The chorus could safely say that the palace-front was rocking and likely to fall ; their excitement would be communicated to the audience through the dance and not by the contrivances of the stage-mechanician. Then this miracle, however great or small, is to be essentially an event in the minds of the actors and audience ; its whole meaning is that Dionysus is a god with divine power. It is one of a series of miracles which is already begun in the prologue and continues up to the destruction of Pentheus ; all serve the same purpose, though with increasing force. Euripides does not want this one to be given a significance different from that of the others ; it may be more striking than the new flames at the tomb, but it is not different in kind. Therefore when it has made its effect Euripides passes on. Pentheus emerging frantic, completely under the god's control, might indeed have assisted us, who read these plays in our studies, by shouting ' What has brought my Palace (or Stables) to the ground ? ', but would this have assisted the audience, whose minds are now being filled with something else and whose eyes saw the pillars still standing intact at the back of the stage ? Would it add to the poetic fact if every new arrival (who was not in fact picking his way among rubble) exclaimed ' Gods ! What has happened to the Palace (or Stables) ? ' Each new arrival has new miracles to announce, fresh proofs of Dionysus' power ; the palace-miracle, like the miracle of the fire, is superseded.

We may now turn to our chief question, why the *Bacchae* is so different in composition and style from most of the earlier tragedies. The answer lies, as so many answers do, in the nature of the theme. In this last tragedy we pick up a thread which we found in the first two, Euripides' feeling for the strength of certain natural and non-moral forces. Love and vengeance are the basis of the *Medea* ; Aphrodite and Artemis in the *Hippolytus* are instinctive, non-moral forces, jealous of each other, beneficent to man only when each receives her due honour. The war brought a new tragic theme to the fore, and the tragedy of rational man preyed on by irrational but necessary passions is pushed into the background. The war continued and the spirit of Athens flagged. Athens, and Euripides with her, turned from high tragic issues to a lighter or a more intellectual drama. At last Euripides escaped from the agony and weariness of Athens, and in Macedonia, where spirits were fresher and the tragic implications of political life were out of sight, he returns to his sources.

The *Bacchae* does not present a conflict between rationalism and belief, for Pentheus is too pitiably weak to fight. It presents the overwhelming power of the god whom the narrow-minded Pentheus presumed to deny and the politically-minded Cadmus to patronize. Did Euripides approve or disapprove of Dionysus ? The question is silly, as silly as to ask whether he approved or disapproved of Aphrodite. Dionysus, or what he typifies—for we need not tie Euripides to a literal belief in his mythology—exists, and that is enough.[1] We are not to suppose that Euripides believed in the miracles, and we cannot suppose that he believed the primitive story he presents of the birth of Dionysus ; we must, if we want poetry and drama, allow the poet his symbols. That done, we can see in this Dionysus the symbol of an ecstasy that is above, or beside, reason, one which the plodding rationalist or moralist rejects at his peril.

For Dionysus is more than the god of wine ; in this play

---

[1] In Euripidean criticism it is important to distinguish between gods. Euripides does not ' attack ' Aphrodite or Dionysus, but he does ' attack ' Apollo, who represents only Delphi, and such as Hermes, who represents nothing at all.

e is the god of ecstasy in religion (and the sender of panic),
y in nature, natural purity, happiness, beauty.   He is not
ndeed the only source of these good things, but he is a very
mportant one.   It is interesting to note that the only other
leities mentioned in the play, besides the Hesiodic, functional
eus, are Aphrodite herself and Demeter the earth-goddess
274).   Two deities, Teiresias says, are first among men,
Demeter who gives food, Dionysus who gives wine, sleep, rest
-a picture to which the chorus adds a great deal.

But we must mark that Dionysus, like Aphrodite, was non-
moral and non-rational ; not indifferent to morality, but it is
ot his province.   This was more than Verrall could endure.
The chorus (404 ff.) longs to be in Cyprus, in Paphos, haunts
f Aphrodite ; it longs too, in the same stanza, for the
oly slopes of Olympus, Pierian home of the Muses.   That
s to say, this chorus, unlike Hippolytus, Pentheus and other
ectaries, can reconcile apparent contraries—but our modern
ationalist will not let them do it ; Cyprus and Paphos, painted
n their blackest colours, are, by a fantasy of punctuation,
nade the object of the Bacchants' strongest reprobation.[1]
But the conjunction of Paphos, the revels on Cithaeron, and
he arduous slopes of Olympus is the very kernel of Euripides'
hought.

This religion Pentheus cannot understand ; to him it is a
closed world.   He is rooted in intellectualism and a narrow
morality ; characteristic of the man is his question ' What is
he use of these rites ? ' (473)   What indeed is the use of
ecstasy ?   No answer is possible except what Dionysus says :
They are worth knowing—but I may not tell thee.'   Pentheus
hinks that the revels are only an excuse for unchastity (225,
54, 686, 957–8), but the Messenger informs him (686–8)
hat he is wrong in fact, Teiresias and Dionysus that he is
wrong in theory.   Dionysus says (487) that daytime lends
tself to evil no less than night, and Teiresias (314 ff.) that
t is no concern of Dionysus' to make women chaste ; that
ies with themselves.   The chorus indeed shows us that Diony-
us is not indifferent to morality, but this does not happen to
e his province, and within his province his claims are

[1] C.R., viii, pp. 85–9 ; Tyrrell, Preface to 2nd edn. of the play.

absolute. As the chorus reconciles Paphos with Pieria, as we
have to reconcile in ourselves Aphrodite and Artemis, so we
must reconcile the claims of Dionysus with those of reason
and morality. To deny either is to deny life itself. The
confident dogmas of the ' wise ' and the moral are not enough.

Dionysus then is non-moral and especially non-rational. It
is not his business to inculcate chastity and sobriety, nor will
he obey the laws of our reason—resembling in this the deities
in the *Hippolytus*. Aphrodite gains her ends ruthlessly,
sacrificing Phaedra without a thought, and just as recklessly
Artemis promises to avenge Hippolytus. Hippolytus' servant
thinks vainly that the gods should be wiser than men ; in the
same way Agave protests that her punishment has been too
heavy. It has been severe indeed, but these gods do not
share our aspirations to mercy ; natural forces are ruthless and
insensitive. Dionysus therefore answers only ' Zeus my father
consented to it long ago ' (1349).

Now we can see why the *Bacchae* is so complete a contrast
with plays like the *Troades* ; it is because once more the tragic
theme can be entirely projected into the action ; there is real
symbolism, not a diagram. No longer do we see collective
or impersonal oppressors wronging collective victims whose
characters can be of very little significance. The theme of
the *Bacchae* is neither abstract nor passive ; we have said
good-bye to women crouching at altars. The theme is not
public wrong-doing or folly, but a sharp opposition between
one mind and another [1] ; one that can not only be completely
expressed in dramatic imagery, but also expressed in a single
situation brought to a sharp focus and developed ' inevitably '.
All the dramatic inconveniences of the earlier method have
disappeared.

---

[1] Really between two minds (Cadmus' and Pentheus') and another. Each ' mind ' can be projected into a life-like character,
and the dramatic genius of Euripides appears in the skilful way
in which these two persons avoid obscuring each other. The
sophistical, political attitude is given to Cadmus, and through him
to his daughters, the moralism to Pentheus ; and instead of making
Dionysus (in a duplex plot) destroy these separately, he makes
the one destroy the other.

But we have suggested too that the composition of the Bacchae is superior even to that of the Medea and Hippolytus. For this also an explanation lies to hand. In the Medea the 'irrational' is the character of the heroine, and in order to give this full scope, to suggest that it symbolized a cosmic force, Euripides had to incur the censure of Aristotle, for Medea is subject to the limitations of being human. In the Hippolytus the 'irrational' is symbolized by the goddesses. These have to work behind the scenes, so that the drama exists on two planes at once. But in the Bacchae, thanks to the brilliant stroke whereby the god takes the form of a votary, the symbol of the 'irrational' is in the thick of the fight all the time, yet without the human limitations of Medea.

This stroke made possible another, the chorus of Bacchants. In the Medea and the Hippolytus the chorus is, at one time or another, of little dramatic use, if not even a positive inconvenience; certainly it is not in a position to keep before our minds, as this chorus does, the necessity and the power of that against which the victim is pitting himself: with this chorus Euripides returns to the great tradition. It is no ideal spectator but an actor; not in the obvious sense that it engages with the actors on the stage—though when it is involved with them, in Pentheus' threats which provoke it to call upon Dionysus, the result is highly dramatic—but that it presents always one of the spiritual forces at work in the play. It presents the mystery, the holiness, the joy of the Dionysiac religion, and (as Mr. Grube acutely observes) it reflects the dramatic attitude of the god himself, for when he abandons all attempt to make Pentheus see the light and resolves to destroy him, the chorus sings of the thrill of triumph, the danger of being 'wiser than the laws', and prays that the 'Hounds of Frenzy' may destroy the blasphemer. These odes, most of them couched in the exciting Ionic rhythms, are full of that spirit of natural religion which Dionysus so terribly vindicates.

The Euripidean chorus often fails to remain continuously in touch with the action; this one succeeds. And not only that; no less than the chorus in the Hecuba and the Troades does it maintain the undertone of the tragic action, but it does this, not as they do by remaining aloof from the action; it is as

much part of the action as any chorus in the whole of Greek
Tragedy.[1]

For the first time therefore, certainly for the first time since
the *Hippolytus*, we see Euripides dealing with a tragic theme
which lends itself to orthodox dramatic methods—once the
transformation of Dionysus and the chorus of Bacchants
had been thought of. The result corroborates what we inferred in comparing the tragedies with the tragi-comedies, that
the structural and stylistic shortcomings of the former cannot
be put down to carelessness or incapacity in the dramatist, but
are the natural result of the nature of his tragic inspiration.
The war-tragedies presented passion rather than action;
therefore characterization was restricted, sometimes downright inconsistent, and plot was disconnected and inert. The
Bacchae presents action and conflict again, therefore style
changes completely. The tragi-comedies assure us that Euripides could make masterly plots when he had nothing more important to do ; now for the first time he is able to put this skill
unreservedly at the service of a tragic theme. The play as a
whole is admirably planned. Of the god's opponents, the
women misled by Cadmus are sent off to Cithaeron to serve
the action as a sort of unseen chorus, leaving the stage free
for Pentheus, an opponent of a different kind—all being at
last united in the common woe of the epilogue. Equally
admirable are the details. The character-drawing is firm and
natural, because the theme allows it ; and there are neither
rhetorical or dialectical diversions nor merely decorative lyrics.
When we add the disconcerting comedy of the two ' comic '
scenes and the sustained brilliance of the messenger-speeches
we can say that in the *Bacchae* we find all the qualities of
Euripides.

---

[1] It is the doubly dramatic position of this chorus that renders so
idle the conventional attempts to extract from its utterances Euripides' own views. The Bacchants reprobate intellectualism and
praise a natural, untaught virtue : if they did not they would
not be Bacchants. We need not suppose that Euripides in his old
age renounced the free use of the intellect, only that he saw that
it has its limitations—and this we knew already, from the *Medea* and
Hippolytus.

. THE OEDIPUS COLONEUS This singularly impressive play
: not easy to criticize. Its plot is composed of two distinct
hemes, the reception and death of Oedipus in Attica, and
he attempts made by Creon and Polyneices to claim him for
ome Theban interest. Even if we say of the Creon-scenes
hat they are closely connected with the Attica-motif (which
s substantially true), we can hardly say it of the Polyneices-
icident. Looked at formerly, the *Coloneus* is episodic,
nanifestly lacking the unity and dramatic sweep of the
yrannus and the *Electra*.[1] We can see the same fact re-
lected in the choral odes. The Colonus ode, however wonderful a poem, and the ode on old-age, however poignant, do
ot link scene to scene as do the odes of the earlier tragedies,
vhile the second stasimon is a mere ' curtain ' of the Euripi-
lean kind, relevant but not illuminating. It even begins
vith the formula *eith' eien*.

This relative looseness of form we cannot ascribe to the
nexperience of youth, for the play implies the *Tyrannus*, nor
o the weakness of age, for no play shows more strength ;
o say that Sophocles was simply following the legend to its
onclusion is to offer the artist in him an affront which he has
iot yet been shown to deserve, and to fall back on an abstrac-
ion, such as that Greek Tragedy had by now relaxed the taut
tructure of an earlier time would be neither true nor explanatory. The fact that the play feels like a unity warns
is that the real explanation lies deeper than this.

Before we inquire where it does lie, we may consider for a
noment this question of the dramatic style and Sophocles'
old age. The statement made in the second Argument that
he *Coloneus* was produced four years after Sophocles' death [2]

---

[1] If dramatic style were as separable a part of drama and as
obedient to the calendar as is sometimes assumed, odd things might
be said of the *Coloneus*. For example, that since it resembles the
earlier plays (*Ajax, Trachiniae, Antigone*) in its duplicity of interest
but shows an advance in technique (the Theban interest being
cleverly embodied in the Attic, A—B—A and not a mere A—B), it
must have been composed after these early plays but before the
perfectly constructed *Tyrannus*.

[2] 406 or 405 B.C. It is thought that this may have been a revival, not the first performance.

is perhaps a mistake, but there seems to be no good reason
for doubting the tradition that it was composed at the very
end of the poet's long life. Signs of extreme age have
been seen in the excessive length of the concluding lyrics and
in the garrulity with which Polyneices gives the names of his
companions-in-arms (1313 ff.).[1] Only those can safely call
the lyrical ending tedious who have heard it sung in performance ; to the reader the lyrical ending of the *Antigone*
approaches tedium ; in the theatre it is not a moment too long
Sophocles' judgement may for once have erred ; on the other
hand, the death of Oedipus does leave a big gap ; this, and
the scale of the whole play, may well be able to carry the long
lament.   Nor is it necessary to see only garrulity in Polyneices'
list ; an actor, we may suspect, would make much more of it
Polyneices is nervously playing for Oedipus' support ; that terrible old man says not a word.   Polyneices gives the names of
his companions—whom, we must remember, he is going to
deceive (1427–30).   Is he trying to impress Oedipus ? or to
encourage himself ? or is he talking because Oedipus will not ?
Sophocles' stage-directions might have enlightened us, but we
need not hastily assume that the passage is only a conventional
fill-up.

On the other hand, the dramatic style and the poetry are
finer than ever.   No scene in Greek Tragedy is grander or
more imaginative than the end of Oedipus.   On that overwhelming apostrophe to Polyneices (1354) a scholiast cries
out in just admiration.   Hardly less impressive is the sudden
prayer to the Eumenides in the prologue : 'Is the stranger
gone ?' 'Gone,' Antigone replies ; 'you may say what you
will at your ease.   Only I am here.'   We expect conversation ; what we get is the sublime appeal

    'Stern-visaged queens . . .'

Such power is found everywhere.   There is no longer scope
for the frightening irony and tragic juxtapositions of the earlier
plays ; the dramatic power which invented these is directed to
a new purpose, to suggest the almost supernatural stature of
this Oedipus.   The villagers are seen coming towards that
sacred grove which they are afraid to look at ; into that same

[1] See Masqueray, ed. Budé, pp. 152–3.

grove Oedipus retires for safety. How simple the means, how great the effect! Or we may consider the strength of the contrast between the quiet prologue (into which the casual Stranger fits so exquisitely) and the succeeding passage with the chorus. The revulsion that they feel makes a splendid foundation for a play which is to end, so to speak, in the apotheosis of Oedipus.

Nor do the details show any sign of tiredness. There is the old vividness of minds in action :

THESEUS :   Foolish man! Hot temper is no help to mis-
            fortune.
OEDIPUS :   Censure me when you have heard. Till then,
            forbear.
THESEUS :   Continue ; I ought not to speak so hastily.

There is the old economy of dramatic effect, as when Creon anounces 'Of thy two daughters the one I have seized already, the other I shall take now'. Very effective are the scenes between Oedipus and Creon. Creon, it has been observed,[1] is the Creon neither of the *Antigone* nor of the *Tyrannus*, but a smooth hypocrite. But why? One reason lies in Oedipus' first speech to him : he is made false in order that the prophetic knowledge which is now accorded to Oedipus may be the more triumphantly displayed. After some twenty verses of fierce denunciation Oedipus tells him the truth which he supposes to be his own secret, ending with the prophetic curse launched against his own sons. He con- tinues, in the very accents of the blind prophet of the earlier play :

' Do not I know better than thou what passes in Thebes ? '

It is magnificent ; magnificent too is the later scene in which for the last time Oedipus proclaims his innocence (939– 1013). Again the hypocritical Creon is the perfect foil. We can imagine how effectively Euripides would have argued this theme ; Sophocles is still plastic, and fuses together Oedipus' passionate self-defence and his indignant spurning of Creon.

Even more marked is the beauty and increased authority of the verse. That is a noble speech in which Ajax proclaims

[1] Jebb, *Introd.*, xxv ; Masqueray, *Introd.*, p. 147.

the Greek, and especially the Sophoclean doctrine of the
instability of things :

> ' All things doth long, innumerable time
> Bring forth from darkness and then hide from light . . .
> The snow-clad winter yields to fruitful summer,
> And night's dark orb makes room for shining day
> Whose horses blaze with light . . .'

But Oedipus' speech [1] is stronger, and less ornate :

> ' Dear son of Aegeus, to the gods alone
> Do age and death not come.   All other things
> Doth Time, all-mastering Time confound.   Earth's strength
> Decays, the body's strength decays ; faith dies
> And faithlessness increases ; never the same
> The spirit of friendship blows, nor man's to man
> Nor among cities . . .'

If the *Coloneus* was first produced posthumously, it must have
been with a shiver of emotion that the Athenians heard, later
in this noble speech, the dead poet's words :

> ' And then my body, hidden in earth and sleeping,
> And cold, shall sometime of their warm blood drink,
> If Zeus be still Zeus, and Apollo true.'

The comparison of two couplets illustrates the difference,
both in power and in spirit, between the *Coloneus* and the
Tyrannus.   Oedipus taunted Teiresias with the verses

> *All' esti, plen soi : soi de tout' ouk est', epei*
> *tuphlos ta t' ota ton te noun ta t' ommat' ei.*

Twenty years later Oedipus can still speak like this ; there is
the same rush of monosyllables, the same harsh alliteration of
s and *t*, the same string of elisions, and the same ' light ending' in his words to Creon :

> *Ouk esti soi taut', alla tad' est', ekei . . .*

And the second verse ?   Weighty, smooth and awful, re-echoing like Cithaeron itself :

> *choras alastor houmos ennaion aei.*[2]

There is no sign of relaxing grip here.

[1] 607 ff.

[2] *O.T.*, 370–1, *O.C.*, 787–8.   Translation, naturally, means little.
' There is (sc. power of Truth) except to thee.   Thou hast it not,

We have argued before that the special dramatic virtues of the middle plays of Sophocles were not sought independently, for their own sake, but were born of the effort to express a certain dramatic ' idea '. We have applied the same doctrine to Euripides ; now we must apply it anew to Sophocles. The difference in form between the *Tyrannus* and the *Coloneus* is not a matter of age or circumstance, unless it was age or circumstance that made Sophocles in 430 or thereabouts dramatize a tragic action and in 406 a tragic passion. Age evidently had a real connexion with the play, but let us be clear about it. The form is relatively loose, not because the old man's hand is shaking, but because, his hand being still firm, his mind moves into a new region which demands, and finds, a new dramatic style.

The *Coloneus*, like other late works of genius, is more imaginative than the earlier works of that same genius. The late quartets of Beethoven—and if this particular parallel means nothing to the reader he will be able to find his own illustration in Rembrandt or some other artist—are less definite in statement, more fluid in form, deeper and more remote in feeling, than the great works of his middle period. The difference between the *Coloneus* and the *Tyrannus* is similar ; so too is that between the *Tyrannus* and the *Ajax* or *Antigone*. We have here a gradation which it is not ridiculous to compare with that in Beethoven ; first a relative simplicity of outlook and positiveness in statement, then a period of greater complexity and depth (for the tragic philosophy of the *Tyrannus* and *Electra* is subtler and more penetrating than the comparatively simple, or at least clear-cut, moral contrasts of the earlier plays), and finally a purely poetic and almost apocalyptic vision which cannot be confined to the hard-won perfection of form of an earlier period. As Beethoven needed a much more fluid form for his last utterances than that which he had forged for the dramatic and intense utterances of his middle period, so Sophocles now transcends the bounds of his own Aristotelian perfection. This most poetic of plays con-

---

for | thou art blind in ears and mind and eyes.' 'That (sc. possession of Oedipus' body) is not for thee, but this is, there | on thy land my avenging curse dwelling in it for ever.'

vinces us of its unity, but as to where that unity lies, there
is room for difference of opinion.

For since the play does not, in the old manner, display the
inevitable march of a course of tragic action, such that the
action or plot is itself the tragic idea, the meaning and therefore the unity of the play does not necessarily reside in that
action. For example, Polyneices' request is not in itself a
development of the plot as the statements of Teiresias were.
Polyneices' coming is indeed part of the story, but that is not
why it is here : the *Coloneus* is no *Phoenissae*. The real
meaning must be looked for through the event, not in it ; it
lies, as we shall see, in the contribution it makes to the presentation of Oedipus.

There is, in fact, between the real unity of the play and
the bones of the plot a slight but definite gap which distantly
recalls Euripides' tragic technique. We must not exaggerate
this, for Sophocles goes to no Euripidean extremes, but we
must not overlook it, or we shall fail to explain the play. The
real unity is impressionistic rather than factual. ' Pourquoi ',
asks Masqueray in his excellent introduction to the play,[1]
' dans sa longue vie, Oedipe a-t-il été si malheureux ? Etait-il
coupable ? C'est la question qui est annoncée, discutée, ré-
solue dans la première partie de la tragédie, avant qu'Athènes
donne asile au vieillard. Et quand le jugement est prononcé,
il reste acquis ; on n'y revient plus.' ' Il est, en effet, fort
remarquable qu'après le plaidoyer final d'Oedipe (960–1013)
il ne soit plus dit dans la pièce un seul mot de cette cul-
pabilité.' The play would be easier to understand if it had
been built to this pattern—the self-defence of Oedipus, its
acceptance by Athens, the protection actually afforded by
Athens, and the passing of Oedipus ; but at least in one
respect it is not so neatly arranged, for Oedipus is definitely
accepted by Athens, indeed offered asylum in his palace by
the King, long before ' le plaidoyer final '. That the first part
of the play disposes of Oedipus' guilt, even that it is mainly
concerned therewith, is an illusion.

What in fact does happen during the play ? There is a
certain gradation. First the Stranger allows Oedipus provi-

[1] P. 141.

sionally to remain on sacred ground ; then the chorus, which
is so profoundly shocked first by the mere voice and aspect of
Oedipus, then by his name and story, is with difficulty persuaded to allow him to remain, provisionally, in Colonus
until the King shall decide. In this scene the motif of Oedipus' essential innocence is prominent. Now, if Sophocles'
scheme were simply to dramatize the story, we should surely
have an ode followed by the arrival of Theseus, then a grand
vindication of Oedipus and his final acceptance by Theseus.
There are no dramatic difficulties, and if the threat of Creon's
interference were wanted to make Theseus' decision a more
serious one, that could easily be introduced by Oedipus himself, or by a dramatic entry on the part of Ismene. We cannot suppose that a smooth progression like this could not have
been engineered by Sophocles if he had wanted it. But instead of the expected Theseus we get Ismene with new
oracles ; and when Theseus does come the question of Oedipus' guilt or innocence is not raised at all, nor even is the
benefit that Oedipus can confer on Athens made very prominent : Theseus is not one who needs bribing. The enlightened generosity of his first speech virtually assures Oedipus
of protection before he has said a word, and in the question
of Oedipus' innocence Theseus seems hardly to be interested.[1]

A plain presentation of the story was not Sophocles' idea—
and we need not be sorry for it. In the separate themes of
the play—the local interest, the innocence of Oedipus, the
working-out of the legend, the character of Oedipus—we shall
find only variety, not unity ; but if we stand back and look
at the play from a distance, we see that there exists in the
whole piece a certain governing movement or rhythm. We
can see that Oedipus enters the play a disregarded outcast and
leaves it—followed by the King of Attica—to keep a strange

---

[1] Sophocles was no doubt as religious as everyone says he was,
but his great characters noticeably act out of purely intellectual
motives, except Antigone, who acts out of instinct. Theseus thinks
like Odysseus in the *Ajax* ; he is calm, unafraid, generous because
he himself has experienced or may need generosity, and because
' I well know that I am a man, and have no greater share in to-
morrow than you have ' (*O.C.*, 567 f. Cf. *Ajax*, 1346 ff., and above,
p. 153).

appointment with Heaven. This rhythm controls the play,
and will explain it.

It is complex. We may notice, from our present point of
vantage, that Oedipus enters as one who has learned resignation from suffering.[1] Perhaps he has ; but gradually, through
successive references to his sons, then through his resistance
to Creon, finally in the tremendous scene with Polyneices, he
passes from resignation to the full height of the wrath that is
in him. We may notice that in the opening scene Oedipus is
at everyone's mercy, a blind old man, dependent on the decency of a casual passer-by ; at the end he towers above
everybody.

This complex rhythm pervades everything in the play.
There is no sudden revelation of a new Oedipus ; Sophocles
leads us step by step, almost insensibly, with the same skill
that made the *Electra*. The important difference is that it is
rhythm which cannot incorporate itself in one sweeping,
heroic action, but must be created from the outside, out of
separate actions or interests on which it draws as need arises.
We may trace this rhythm in some of its aspects. Let us
take our sense of Oedipus' power, not the power of his personality, which culminates in the scene with Polyneices, but
that mysterious reflection of this, the power which is entrusted
to him by the gods—or found in him by the gods, as there is
no suggestion that a special gift or honour has been accorded
him.

We must begin with the impression which the blind old
man makes when first we see him. To the Stranger he is
'noble except in fortune' (76) ; the Chorus on the other
hand, seeing him rise within the sacred grove, is terrified at
the mere sight of him and the sound of his voice. Such is
the figure whom we see, led in by his daughter. We hear
that rest has been promised him at the grove which he has
now reached, but of his strange power, that of benefiting
Athens, we have only two bare hints (vv. 72 and 92–3).

The revulsion which the chorus feels towards Oedipus
brings this rhythm, if we can yet call it begun, back to its
starting-point. Oedipus has to fight to maintain his position,

[1] Vv. 7–8.

but it is maintained, and at v. 285 there is a slightly more explicit reference to his power. Then Ismene comes, with new oracles. We feel perhaps a little hazy about them all [1]; what exactly is the difference between these new ones and those that Oedipus had received before? As the earlier ones are not quoted we cannot possibly say. But why was the Ismene-scene wanted? Why cannot Oedipus have all the oracles at the beginning? Because our sense of his new power must be made to grow. As far as the action of the play is concerned Ismene's part could be considerably reduced; she might well, as we suggested above, enter after Theseus, and announce nothing but the coming of Creon. The rhythm of the play however needs the reinforcement that her fresh oracles give, and to emphasize the reinforcement Oedipus is twice made to refer to his present lowly position, both times before the oracles are declared.[2] Afterwards (455 ff.) Oedipus speaks with a new confidence, as one whom Athens may be glad to welcome and Thebes may vainly hope to capture.

The next stage is the Theseus-scene. What Oedipus can do for Athens is fully set forth; it is such as to outweigh even the chance of embroilment with Thebes. The stature to which Oedipus has now attained can be seen in the speech from which we have already quoted, 'Dear son of Aegeus,' vv. 667 ff. This is a very different Oedipus from the one who had to ask favours of the Stranger and of the old men of Colonus. Next, Creon and the violence which he is prepared to use emphasize Oedipus' importance even more; finally in the two scenes which concern Polyneices he is presented as the arbiter of destiny.

Here we have one aspect only of the dramatic rhythm of the play. We can in the same way follow the course of the growth of his wrath, from the resignation professed at the

---

[1] As about other details on the outskirts of the play. See below, p. 414.

[2] Vv. 299 f. (to the Chorus) 'And do ye really think that Theseus will have care or thought for a blind man, and come to see him?' Vv. 385 f. (to Ismene) 'And didst thou come to hope that the gods would ever have regard for me and my deliverance?'

beginning to its climax just before the end. In vv. 339 f.
Eteocles and Polyneices are the men who 'sit at home weaving', like Egyptians. During the tense dialogue in vv. 385–
420 it becomes apparent to Oedipus that his sons have betrayed him ; this moves him to the terrible denunciation in the
speech 421 ff. Nothing, we may perhaps think, can be more
awful than this, except the actual meeting with Polyneices.
But Sophocles' hand has lost neither its cunning nor its daring.

There are two points to observe. This first denunciation is
couched in optatives, the wish-mood : 'May the gods not
quench their fated strife ; may it become mine to decide the
issue, for in that case neither would he who now holds the
crown keep it, nor would the exile return home again.'
When next the topic occurs it is treated in more definite
language : 'There remains to my own sons an inheritance of
my soil, enough—to die in' (789–90). Finally, when the unhappy Polyneices stands before us, there are no longer optatives and conditionals, but confident futures. The crescendo
is maintained ; the gods have, it appears, given to Oedipus
the decision he hoped would be his. When ? Where ?
We do not know ; nothing overt has happened. It is part of
the general rhythm, a very imaginative way of increasing our
sense of Oedipus' power.

This delicate piece of manipulation is the first point ; the
second is very interesting. Sophocles seems to be very hazy
about the relative position of the two brothers and the Theban
crown. It is true that the Greek (and other) dramatists often
leave out of focus matters just outside the play, and that in
such matters, which no sensible audience would try to bring
into focus, there may be latent contradictions. But here, as
the facts do come into the play, the haze is noticeable, and
Masqueray, penetrating it, points out that there are four distinct situations assumed at successive moments of the play :
(1) that Eteocles and Polyneices have never enjoyed royal
authority at all (367 ff.), (2) that they might have prevented
Oedipus' exile (427 ff.), (3) that they jointly decreed this
exile (599 ff.), (4) that Polyneices was solely responsible for
it (1354 ff.). This, as Masqueray says, is too regular to be

accidental—but what is the explanation of it all ? Sophocles had complete liberty, in spite of what Aeschylus or Euripides may have done, to assume what situation suited him best [1] ; why has he assumed four ? Because it helps this dramatic movement. We thought that in this matter of the sons there could be no climax after the denunciation of 420 ff. We were wrong. Not only does the curse increase in definition and certainty, but also, thanks to these delicate shifts, what was a curse launched impartially at two absent men becomes one launched with particular violence at the one who is present.[2]

We have now considered two aspects of the complex rhythm of the *Coloneus,* the way in which we are made to feel more and more the power of Oedipus, and the gradual

---

[1] As he has done in making Polyneices the older. (See Jebb's note on v. 375.)—For other such deliberate confusions, see T. von Wilamowitz, *Dram. Technik.*, 20 ff.

[2] This affects the word *prosthe* in v. 1375. Oedipus says to Polyneices ' I have let fly such curses at you before (*prosthe*) and I repeat them now '. Does ' before ' refer to the two earlier passages in the play, or to an undisclosed occasion in Thebes ? Most commentators prefer the former (though not the Scholiast, who had the advantage of knowing from the Thebais what that undisclosed earlier incident was) ; but why should Oedipus impede the torrent of his wrath by putting in a reference to vv. 420 and 789—a reference unnecessary for us and unintelligible to Polyneices ? The plain dramatic sense of the passage would be that Oedipus, as Polyneices well knows, uttered some kind of a curse before. This is inconsistent with the colourless reference to the brothers ' sitting at home weaving '—but so is the whole of this present speech. We are in the fourth situation ; the sudden production of an earlier curse, of which we have heard nothing, is consistent with it and dramatically intensifies the present position. Jebb objected to this view (*Introd.*, xxiv) that it makes of Polyneices a helpless victim of fate—a serious objection if true. But here Sophocles misses a theatrical opportunity in order to demonstrate that Polyneices is no victim of fate. Polyneices is not allowed, like Iocasta and several other characters, to stumble off the stage in an effective silence, though such an exit would be at least as dramatic as the farewell-scene that we have. Evidently Sophocles did this not for the sake of the pathetic farewell (he did not deal in such things), but in order to make it quite clear that Polyneices can nullify the curse by doing as Antigone suggests, by not being a fool and a traitor to his companions. As in the *Tyrannus,* curses and oracles do not compel ; they only predict.

revelation of his full personality. There remain two important points—the question of Oedipus' innocence, and the winning of his final rest. We may consider the latter first.

This theme is woven as one strand in the complex web of the play, largely by the use of the chorus. It is the chorus that insists that Oedipus shall leave the grove and comes near to driving him away forthwith. His peace is in jeopardy, but his demeanour, and the oracles that Ismene brings, alter the attitude of the chorus—how much, we can see by comparing vv. 139–236 with 510 ff. ; in the latter passage the chorus can hear the worst without flinching. Oedipus, already accepted by the gods, is beginning to impose himself on men. The climax of this, the first part of the movement, is near when Theseus offers to the outcast the shelter of his palace. As to this Oedipus is quite clear ; his real defence is spiritual, not temporal power, and he must remain at Colonus.

The climax is the ode. The point now reached, the culmination of a long development, is by the architectonic imagination of the poet marked and emphasized with the first stasimon. The Colonus-ode, renowned for its beauty, famous as one of the few nature-poems in Greek, is no less notable for its dramatic qualities. It does not connect act with act, but it is no mere curtain. It marks an important point in the structure of the play, and it emphasizes a decision which is soon to be put to the test. To the blind man, who knows the inward peace and beauty of this appointed spot, the chorus describes its outward peace and beauty ; on the sanctity of the grove it says nothing ; Oedipus knows that already. It does, however, reinforce this sanctity with others in Colonus of which Oedipus knows nothing. ' The place ', said Oedipus, ' is here ' ; and the ode is here, outdoing in its supra-dramatic effect the dramatic ' timing ' of the odes in the *Electra*.

As for the Creon-scenes, from our present point of view they do but reaffirm the position reached already ; the wanderer is safely anchored at last. The second stasimon, which divides these scenes, does little more than fill a gap suitably. It describes, by anticipation, an event which the actors have neither time nor cause to describe. The third is very differ-

ent. A mechanical dramatist might have placed here an ode
that had particular reference to Polyneices ; Sophocles does
something else. Just before 'the god' summons Oedipus
Sophocles places this harsh, frightful incident of Polyneices,
and across it, between the two scenes, he lets fall the even
darker shadow of his bitterest ode. Like the earlier hyporchemata it prepares for the catastrophe, but by representing
Oedipus' old age as a misery from which death will be welcome release.[1] The fine image of the storm-beaten cliff raises
its head above the immediate surroundings. Even now a last
storm is raging around its base, but the cliff, and the ode too,
look beyond that over the whole of Oedipus' past life, and,
forward, to the end that is so near.

In this way the motif of Oedipus' release is finely kept
moving until, with Polyneices' departure, the thunder from
heaven is heard. Now all these separate threads are drawn
together. He who was impotent and disregarded has come to
wield, first tentatively and then with confidence, superhuman
powers ; he who was a homeless wanderer has been received,
and defended, by the Athenian state, and is now summoned
by the gods themselves ; he who was resigned has been
brought, gradually, to that last display of majestic wrath.

In a scene whose imaginative power only the end of the
Eumenides can rival, the blind hero, like the blind prophet of
an earlier play,[2] becomes guide to those who can see, and
leads them with a sure step to the spot fixed for his end.

In this complex but always mounting rhythm one thing
remains stationary, Oedipus' insistence that what he did was
no sin. It remains stationary because it was no part of Sophocles' plan to develop it ; it is an axiom, implicit in the assurance with which he first addressed the Eumenides. To the
horrified chorus he develops his argument at length (285

---

[1] It is surely not necessary to suppose that Sophocles was drawing
upon his own experience of old age. What we know of his personality makes the description 'Impotent, lonely and friendless' a
little surprising ; what we know of his dramatic resources assures
us that had a serene picture of old age been called for Sophocles
could have written it.

[2] *Antig.*, 1014, 'He leads me, I lead others.'

ff.) ; later (510 ff.) this chorus is made to drag the most
repulsive details from him in order that his innocence may be
set in the strongest possible light. Yet, we must observe,
there is neither discussion nor judgement. The chorus professes neither belief nor disbelief. Theseus comes, and before
him no claim to purity is necessary ; his large humanity can
accept Oedipus as he is. When next the chorus speaks in the
Colonus-ode, there is no reference to this question ; Oedipus
is simply accepted.

Nevertheless we have one last passionate assertion before
Creon—and how dramatically it is managed. Again, men
and not arguments are at grips, for the speech is as much an
onslaught on Creon as it is Oedipus' own apologia. In the
mechanics of the play the apologia is nothing, for Theseus
does not need it nor Creon merit it, and the substance has
been given before. The argument is repeated because it has
become part of Oedipus' very soul, and because it is the very
core of Sophocles' philosophy, that virtue alone cannot assure
happiness nor wickedness alone explain disaster. Oedipus
has suffered *anthropinon ti*, one of those things which may
happen to us whatever we are. His innocence is not a question that Sophocles cares to have discussed and judged ; it is
accepted instinctively by the fine intelligence of Theseus, and
his acceptance of it is enough for the chorus.

Now we may try to answer the last and most fundamental
question : what made Sophocles write, or at any rate complete, this play at the extreme verge of old age ? We can
well imagine that Oedipus, Sophocles' most splendid symbol
of humanity, must have been a close companion of his
thoughts ever since he had finished his *Tyrannus*. Now,
some twenty years later, no longer an oldish man but an
extremely old man, he finds himself impelled to undertake
the labour of composing the *Coloneus*. What has he to say
now ?

It is easy to see what the *Coloneus* is not. It is not, in the
first place, a mere sequel, deriving its charm from its more
mellow echoes of earlier work. Here there is no charm, no
autumnal browns and gold. Nor is it a work of pious duty,
the finishing of a great legend, for the play is as vital as the

Tyrannus itself. It is not a study in the effects which years of suffering have had on Oedipus; in the *Philoctetes* Sophocles had used such a theme, but the *Coloneus* is no neat dramatic exercise. Nor is the play in this sense religious that it portrays resignation, wiser counsels, submission to the mysterious will of heaven. Oedipus is indeed too great a man to be querulous. He does say ' So the gods willed it, wroth perchance with my race from of old ' (964), but it is no part of the dramatic idea that the sufferer, by learning to kiss the rod, wins peace—or why, when Oedipus has been established in Attica, when he might pass straight to his final peace, does Sophocles throw the dark shadow of the Polyneices-scene across the path? Oedipus does indeed end in peace, but it is a peace that is accorded him, not one that he wins for himself.

Further, ' On the part of the gods there is nothing that can properly be called tenderness for Oedipus '.[1] There is no friendly deity, like the Athena who cares for Odysseus in the *Ajax*. Apollo issues oracles—c'est son métier—but he is not in close relation with Oedipus as in the *Oresteia* he is with Orestes. The god who summons him is most impressively impersonal, like ' the god ' who laid him low. Oedipus is remote from the gods. He is still the Oedipus of the earlier play—even more so: hot-tempered,[2] wrathful, with no trace of submissiveness. Nor are we told that the gods have repented for what they have done or forgiven him for what was no sin. What has happened is that adversity has not crushed Oedipus, and that strange new oracles gather round him.

In the *Coloneus* we have the same Oedipus, but now he can look back on his ruined life. He has nothing with which he can reproach himself; repentance is not in the picture at all: ' Pure before the law, unwitting I have come to this ' (558). He thinks of some wrath of Heaven, but this is his explanation, not Sophocles'. To say that he could not have escaped is indeed neither true nor tragic; he could have escaped, but only if his towering intelligence had towered as high as the

[1] Jebb, *Introd.*, xxiii.

[2] As Ismene (420), Creon (804, 852), and Antigone (1195) all point out.

peculiarly malignant circumstances arrayed against him. It did not; if it had he would have been more than a man, he would have been a god. There was no sin, only the necessary frailty of being human.

Such was Oedipus, such he remains, and we may doubt if it was ever in Sophocles' mind to leave him crushed, hidden from sight in the Theban palace. Pessimist Sophocles may have been, with little faith in future bliss, with no confidence in present prosperity, but no Greek believed more firmly in the dignity of being a man, and it was because of this belief that he had to write the *Coloneus* before he died. Oedipus could not be left there. So, with even more sufferings and indignities heaped upon him, with his one fault, hastiness, defiantly unmodified, he is driven forth. To the gods he has made no concessions; just before his last summons he is at his most violent. But this play, though it presents the same Oedipus, reverses the movement of the *Tyrannus*, for Oedipus goes not from greatness to misery but from misery to greatness; and it reverses it in a higher plane, in the dark, not in the light. The kingly power that shines from him in the *Tyrannus* is still in him, but now, on the edge of death, it is transmuted into a superhuman power, and we see it growing. It is not a recompense given him by the gods; why should it be? Apollo in the *Tyrannus* was no enemy of Oedipus'; he merely saw what was coming and answered questions. So now, Apollo is no friend and champion of his; he sees the greatness that is in him and states facts. In taking Oedipus to themselves as a Hero the gods are but recognizing facts. By his stature as a man Oedipus imposes himself on the gods; it is not forgiveness, for there was no sin. The *Coloneus* is Sophocles' answer to the tragedy of life. He knows that he cannot justify God to man, but he can justify man to man.

We have said nothing about the imaginative use of topography in this play, how the sacred grove is gradually charged with as much significance as the Atreid Palace in the *Agamemnon*. At the end, the contrast between the familiarity of the spots which Sophocles so minutely describes and the remote majesty of Oedipus' passing must have given the scene strange and thrilling colour which we can only faintly recapure.

This the *Coloneus* has now lost ; in compensation it has ained something. A fate of which we have probably little eason to complain—none at all if the miserable *Rhesus* is a air specimen of later tragedy—has decreed that for us Greek Tragedy shall end here ; and where more suitably than at Colonus, with ' the towers that guard the city ' in sight ? No pot could be more appropriate ; Tragedy comes home to die.

For Greek Drama is peculiarly the creation and glory of Athens. Athens and the Theatre of Dionysus are, in a very eal sense, its Unity of Place. Not only were the plays perormed in this theatre, not only was nearly every dramatic poet of eminence an Athenian, not only does the art as a vhole bear indelibly the mark of Athenian intelligence and plastic imagination ; beyond all this, Greek Drama is in a pecial degree the work of the Athenian people. All Attic drama, tragic and comic, was composed for one of the Festivals of Dionysus ; this fact is capital. It was therefore eligious in origin and for two or three generations remained eligious in outlook ; so was that tumultuous, hilarious and requently obscene thing, Old Comedy—a contradiction which s disabling to the understanding until it is remembered how lifferent are the Greek and the modern connotations of the vord ' religion '. The difference is so wide that we may well void the word here and use the reality instead ; for the essenial point, the only one which a literary study of the subject can profit by, is that in practice the Festival was a solemn national celebration ; not the celebration of an event, but of the City herself. It was serious and it was important, it had ts origin in a religion and a ritual, but it did not compel the dramatist to be religious, still less Dionysiac ; Aeschylus was a religious poet not because of the Festival but because of Aeschylus. To the dramatist the significance of the Festival was that it gave him as his audience nothing less than the Athenian people. That same people which, in a practical and political mood, met a few hundred yards away to discuss and determine high matters of state, met in the Theatre, in a more exalted mood, to watch plays ; and the dramatists them-

selves appeared almost as their chosen laureates. Thus the
dramatist, tragic or comic, was always writing for a big occasion, one which demanded and made natural big ideas and
serious utterance, one which made impossible, in comedy as in
tragedy, private themes and clever, coterie-literature. The
modern world began in Alexandria ; there for the first time in
the history of Greek literature a homogeneous audience was
lacking.[1]

To this public drama our nearest modern parallel is perhaps
Church-music ; in one sense the *Mass in B minor* is the modern *Oresteia*. But Attic tragedy was not restricted by creed
or convention (the dramatist could take a political and contemporary subject if he chose), nor was it in any way an official art, an adjunct to politics. It was necessarily in close
touch with its audience, as any living art must be, and its
audience had come not as individuals looking for entertainment but as the City ; an audience accustomed to handle the
biggest issues in another place, not afraid of them therefore
in the theatre. The Athenian drama necessarily reflects in its
varied course the general aspect of contemporary thought and
outlook ; in Athens a dramatist who was not in touch with at
least a substantial part of his audience would have been
dumb, for there was no ' Little Theatre '. Nevertheless this
art, as I hope we have seen, remained highly individual ;
remained, that is, an art. Greek myth provided the dramatist, as Pentelicus did the architect and sculptor, with as noble
a quarry as a race of artists could hope for ; the people, lively,
sensitive, and educated in affairs, came to see plays, not
merely to attend a ritual ; and the occasion challenged the
dramatist to clothe in this noble material his profoundest apprehensions about the life of man. Nothing less could live
in this atmosphere.

The Festival conferred one other priceless advantage : it
imposed external restrictions to which the poet had to conform ; not cramping restrictions like those of a censorship, but
liberating ones like the number of verses in a sonnet or of
instruments in a string-quartet. His theatre was fixed ; he

---

[1] Hence the public and topical themes of Old Comedy, the public
and universal themes of Old and Middle (and some New) Tragedy.

could not choose between a big and a small one, nor could he
elaborate beyond an elementary point the mechanical resources of the big one. He was restricted in the number of
his actors,[1] and above all he had to make terms with the
Chorus—which however was but the technical reflection of his
major restriction, the audience. Thus he was protected from
the easy subterfuges of more prodigal days, thrown more
upon his own intellect and artistic integrity, trained, like the
Argive sculptors, on nothing softer than bronze. We have
seen how the greatest of the Athenian dramatists responded.
Within these restrictions they found a range of expression
and a variety of form equal to their most exacting demands.
There is no such thing as a typical Greek play ; the form was
something created anew, and differently, year by year, play
by play, by dramatic poets of genius.

But dramatic poets of genius were not enough. Athens
was necessary, and her spirit, and her spirit during this remarkable century, in which she gathered from the world
around her what she wanted and could assimilate, until she
became sufficient for herself and ' an education to Greece '.
When Athenian Tragedy comes into our ken it ranges from
Egypt to Argos, from Argos to the remote Caucasus, from the
Caucasus to Egypt ; if accidents can be inspired it is by an
inspired accident that it passes from our ken in Attica itself,
and with Oedipus ; at Colonus the birthplace of Sophocles,
not two miles from the Theatre of Dionysus. Here is the
Unity of Place. ' And the place is holy.'

[1] This is not undisputed, but it still seems the better view.

GLOSSARY

Choriambic metre : $\underline{}\,\cup\,\cup\,\underline{}$. Since this metre was regularly used to express perturbation, it was presumably not a steady triple rhythm, but a duple rhythm with a cross-accent, as here indicated.

Commos : Literally, 'beating of the breast.' A lament. It was a regular feature in Tragedy; a *duo* for actor and chorus, both singing.

Dochmiac : A strongly emotional rhythm peculiar to Tragedy, except when comic poets parodied it. In its simplest form it was $\cup$ — — $\cup$ —. Essentially, it was eight short syllables, or their equivalents, divided unevenly : 3 + 5.

Glyconic : A flexible rhythm of which the following are typical forms :

— $\cup$ — $\cup\cup$ — $\cup$ —

— $\cup$ — $\cup$ — $\cup\cup$ —

— $\cup\cup$ — $\cup$ — $\cup$ —

Hyporchema : A short and cheerful dance.

Parodos : The ode sung by the chorus at its entrance.

Periacti : Devices, apparently, for indicating the scene of the action. They were introduced by Sophocles.

Stasimon : Any ode subsequent to the parodos.

Stichomythia : Formal line-by-line dialogue.

$\cup\cup\cup$ *Tribrach* : ; representing either $\cup$ —, an iambus, or — $\cup$, a trochee.

INDEX

Actor, single, 24, 30, 31 ff., 47
  second, 2, 24, 27, 31, 33, 36,
  47 f., 54, 55, 105 f.
  third, 24, 33 n., 49, 58, 60 f.,
  68, 123, 156–63; Aeschylus'
  use of, 60 f., 71 f., 78 ff., 88,
  94, 111, 156

Aeschylus
  compared with Sophocles: in
  outlook, 49, 55, 74, 100, 110
  f., 153, 330; in method, 25,
  43, 48, 69, 71, 111–15, 157,
  164
  compared with Euripides: in
  outlook, 212 f., 315, 396; in
  method, 94, 198 n., 221, 261
  dramatic (tragic) outlook: 23,
  107 ff., 212, 326, *et supra*
  and the gods: 5, 21 ff., 42
  ff., 48, 59, 67 n., 96–7, 107
  ff.
  style: 4, 7 f., 28 f., 33 n.
  (See also *Characterization,
  Chorus, Plot, Tragic hero*)

Agamemnon, 40, 56, 97, 111–16,
  384–5

Agamemnon, The, 65–81; 40 f.,
  82, 83, 86, 87, 89, 92, 97–
  113 *passim*, 141, 156, 164,
  221 f., 296, 390, 396. (See
  also *Cassandra*)

Agathon (the *Antheus*), 194,
  372, 378, 391

Ἀγών, 33

Aition, 302 f., 339

Ajax, 69, 111, 150 ff., 155, 157

Ajax, The, 124–9; 112 n., 131,
  150 ff., 157, 158 f., 165, 167,
  408, 409

Alcestis, The, 327–47 *passim*,
  364

Alexandrine poetry, 106, 363 f.

Amphiaraus, 53, 80, 379

Andromache, The, 241–7; 178
  n., 266–72 *passim*, 276–8,
  281, 289–91 *passim*, 299,
  300 f.

Antigone, 70, 92, 110, 117 f.,
  152, 267, 284

Antigone, The, 129–35; 4, 25,
  64 n., 86, 148 ff., 156 f., 157,
  165, 167, 168, 178 n., 200,
  203, 216, 273, 283, 289, 406,
  409 (See also *Creon*)

Aphrodite and Artemis, 15, 17,
  21 f., 209, 211 ff., 259, 400

Aristophanes, 81, 196, 333, 340

Aristotle, 24, 25, 39, 43, 100,
  101, 103, 110–20, 123, 194,
  196, 263, 280, 288, 292, 315,
  337, 341, 352–3, 387
  and ἁμαρτία (hamartia) 28,
  116 f., 133, 156, 197 f., 202,
  204 f., 217, 236, 262, 306,
  353, (395)
  'beginning, middle, and end,'
  16, 81, 303
  and the Chorus, 115, 165,
  167, 200. Also 26 n.
  pity and fear, 118
  and plot (probability, τὸ εἰκὸς
  ἢ ἀναγκαῖον), 61 f., 197,
  200, 206–9, 221, 224, 253,
  288, 295, 340 f., 381
  poetic universal (οἷα ἂν
  γένοιτο), 203–4, (313), 319,
  386
  the 'revolting' (τὸ μιαρόν),
  196, 199, 203, 209, 267,
  286 (bis), 301, 354–5
  the tragic hero, 112 f., 155 f.,
  197 f., 243, 352, 386, 395
  the transit (μεταβαίνειν), 113,
  114, 276. (See also *Happy
  ending*)